COMBAT IN AN AGE OF TERROR

COMBAT IN AN AGE OF TERROR

The 7th Infantry Regiment In America's Modern Wars
Korea through Iraq

JOHN C. McMANUS

UNIVERSITY OF MISSOURI PRESS
COLUMBIA

First published 2008 by Tom Doherty Associates, LLC

The Curators of the University of Missouri
University of Missouri Press, Columbia, Missouri edition published 2025
Printed and bound in the United States of America

ISBN 978-0-8262-2344-9 (paperback : alk. paper)

∞™ This paper meets the requirements of the
American National Standard for Permanence of Paper
for Printed Library Materials, Z39.48, 1984.

Typefaces: Anton and Minion

To a dozen generations of 7th Infantrymen,

especially the generation that is now serving

under the proud colors of the regiment.

Throughout the decades you have fought,

and sometimes died,

so that others might be free.

To Nancy, love of my life.

I am the Infantry—Queen of Battle!

For two centuries I have kept our Nation safe,

purchasing freedom with my blood.

To tyrants, I am the day of reckoning;

to the oppressed, the hope for the future.

Where the fighting is thick, there am I . . .

I am the Infantry!

FOLLOW ME!

FROM THE CREDO

OF THE INFANTRY BRANCH,

UNITED STATE ARMY INFANTRY CENTER,

FORT BENNING, GEORGIA

Contents

Maps

MAP KEY

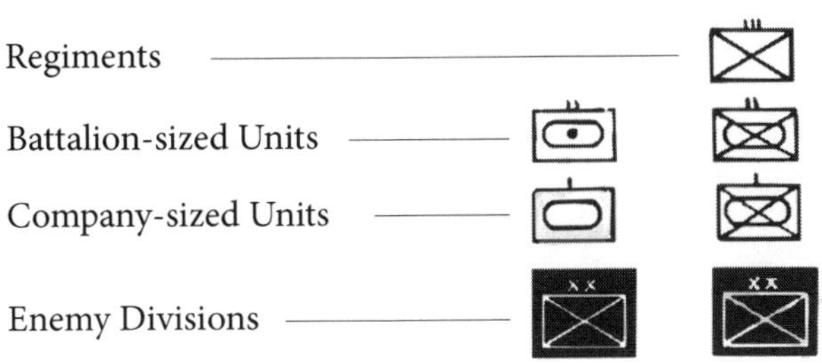

Regiments
Battalion-sized Units
Company-sized Units
Enemy Divisions

Preface

THIS BOOK IS THE SECOND in a two-volume series on the history of the 7th Infantry Regiment. The series was born over dinner at an Italian restaurant in St. Louis. In the midst of a discussion about the history of the U.S. Army, my wife, Nancy, wondered if there was any infantry unit that had fought in all of America's wars dating back to the Revolution. I admitted I did not know, but I was greatly intrigued by the possibility that one organization might enjoy that kind of tradition. That night I stayed up until the wee hours—much to Nancy's chagrin— surfing the Internet, researching the lineage and history of the Army's oldest infantry regiments. I found that none of them could claim existence since the Revolution, but that several trace their history back to the early national period, specifically the years leading up to the War of 1812.

As I sifted through the various synopses of each regiment's past, one unit's story clearly stood out. This unit was one of only a handful that had been in continuous service since that second war with the British. More than that, this outfit always seemed to be in the middle of the action when America went to war. Not that the others were derelict in any way, but this particular regiment was especially busy and active. For example, among the oldest regiments in the U.S. Army, the 1st through the 10th Infantries, only one served in every nineteenth- and twentieth-century war. It is called the 7th U.S. Infantry Regiment, and its story, I quickly came to realize, is a remarkable journey through the history of America's conflicts. The regiment even has a colorful nickname, Cottonbalers, for reasons I'll explain in the Introduction.

I knew right then and there that the story of this regiment must be told. But how best to tell it? I eventually came to the conclusion, after much research and writing, that the history of the 7th is so extensive it cannot be told in one book. This volume covers the modern period, from Korea through the initial stages of the War in Iraq. The previous volume tells the regiment's story from its inception during the War of 1812 through World War II.

Acknowledgments

FOR THIS BOOK, I CONDUCTED research at many archives and would like to thank the archival staffs and select individuals who proved particularly helpful to this volume. Mitch Yockelson and many others at the National Archives in College Park, Maryland, helped guide me to a treasure trove of sources on the regiment's history in Korea and Vietnam. Lewis Bernstein at the U.S. Army's Combined Arms Center at Fort Leavenworth, Kansas, promptly provided me with valuable information on the activities of one 7th Infantry rifle company in the Gulf War. Rich Baker and David Keough at the U.S. Army Heritage and Education Center in Carlisle, Pennsylvania, were two of the best military archivists in the business, and they proved it by shepherding me through a tangled web of sources in the extensive holdings of the USAMHI. Bob Wright, Jim Knight, and their colleagues at the U.S. Army Center of Military History in Washington dispensed much needed advice and alerted me to many excellent sources in their holdings. My friend Kevin Hymel, an erudite military historian and all-around good guy, opened his D. C. area home to me and helped make the pictures of this book much better than they otherwise would be.

Closer to home, the library staff at Missouri University of Science and Technology, especially Jean Eisenman and Scott Peterson, did terrific work in obtaining books and other materials for me through interlibrary loan. The College of Arts and Sciences and the Department of History at Missouri S&T provided me with much appreciated travel funds for my research. I would like to thank all of my colleagues in the history department for their advice, wisdom, and forbearance, especially (the late) Wayne Bledsoe, Michael Meagher, Tseggai Isaac, Harry Eisenman, Jack Ridley, Jeff Schramm, Shannon Fogg, Diana Ahmad, Patrick Huber, Michael Bruening, Chris Ketcherside, Alanna Krolikowski, Justin Pope, Andrew Behrendt, Petra DeWitt, and Larry Gragg. Special thanks go to two of the most profound influences on my work and life: the late Russ Buhite, for being a great mentor, historian, and friend (and a pretty fair first baseman too), and the late Tom Fleming, one of the most accomplished historians and novelists of our time. He was, over the many years I had the pleasure to know him, so generous and forthright with his considerable expertise and wisdom. If I accomplish one quarter of what Russ and Tom achieved in their respective careers, I would count myself lucky.

Thanks go to my original editors at Tor-Forge, Eric Raab and Bob Gleason, for their patience and insight. Thank you, Melissa Frain, for taking care of the details. I also want to thank my first agent, Ted Chichak, for his expertise, his guidance, and his belief in me. The same holds true for Michael Congdon, my good friend and current agent. Andrew Davidson, the brilliant editor in chief at University of Missouri Press, has sprinkled his considerable wisdom over so many of the pages in this and the other volume of this series. I can't thank him enough. Thank you, Rick Britton, master cartographer, for an outstanding set of maps. They add much to our story.

I wish to single out several other key individuals whose help has been instrumental in the writing of this book. Without their generous input, *Combat in an Age of Terror: The 7th Infantry Regiment in America's Modern Wars, Korea through Iraq* would never have gotten off the ground.

David Jones and Fred Long of the 7th Regiment Association were both quite receptive to the idea of this book. They pointed me in the right direction, introduced me to many people, and gave me a great many sources. Ed Dojutrek and Jim Drury of the 3rd Infantry Division Association provided help in finding back issues of their association newsletters. Sherman Pratt holds a special place in my heart. He was a historian himself and, in that capacity, guided me to many key sources on the regiment's history, including Korea. A distinguished veteran of the regiment, Sherm kindly trusted me with his back issues of *The Cottonbaler*, the veterans' association newsletter for those who have served in the 7th's modern wars. Sherm also gave me plenty of moral support and bequeathed his position of regimental historian to me. I will be forever thankful to him.

I want to thank several Korean War Cottonbalers for their time and memories: Paul Mentis, Oliver Green, Lou Schindler, Hiroshi Miyamura, Stan Cahill, Bob Barfield, and Louis Hotelling. Joan Blair assisted me in finding transcripts of several revealing interviews that she and her late husband, Clay, conducted with 7th Infantry officers who fought in Korea. By far, my biggest thank-you goes to the late Bill Strobridge. Bill gave me a tremendous amount of material about the regiment's experiences in Korea. In the course of an interview and several phone conversations, he related so many important recollections of his combat service. In addition, he put me in touch with several other veterans and even interviewed a couple on his own.

Records at the National Archives told me the basic story of the 7th Infantry's combat service in Vietnam, but those "big picture" facts were considerably fleshed out into a cohesive narrative by many unit vets who generously, and forthrightly, related their experiences: Gary Masuda, Mike Braun, Andy Krasnican, Paul Hindelang, Jim Norris, Larry Compton, George Sheehan, Al Watson, Reverend James Edwards, and Father Phil Salois. Roland Merson proved to be particularly helpful. He sat for two interviews, filled in many details over the course of numerous e-mail conversations, put me in touch with many veterans, and passed on copies of relevant information on the 7th in Vietnam. One time he even referred to me as an "honorary member" of his Alpha Company, something that made my chest swell with pride (even though I felt I was not at all worthy of that designation).

Gulf War Cottonbalers also proved to be just as generous with their time and recollections as previous generations of 7th infantrymen. Kirk Allen, Bryan Crochet, Jamie Narramore, Craig McClure, and Kurt Dabb graciously explained the answers to all of my prodding questions. In so doing, they agreed to be featured in this book, even though they wanted no special accolades. Rick Averna gave me many hours of his time in an interview. He sent me a tremendous amount of information on his Charlie Company and even opened up his private life to me by giving me copies of the letters he and his wife, Elaine, exchanged during the Gulf War. From the first, Alan Huffines demonstrated enthusiasm for this book and made himself very accessible to me, in terms of e-mails and phone conversations. He also sent me a complete copy of his diary/memoir/letters from the war. I am very thankful for his expertise and openness. Captain David Gardner kindly and promptly answered numerous questions during the regiment's Kosovo tour in the fall of 2001.

As for the Iraq War, literally hundreds of Cottonbalers shared information or helped me in some way. I cannot hope to thank these men individually, but a few must be singled out. Lieutenant Tim Garland sent me a copy of 2-7's after-action report and an excellent DVD with photographs, maps, and a useful PowerPoint presentation. Captain Mark Schenk collected and sent me many soldier questionnaires that I had dispensed among the troops. Lieutenant Colonels Todd Wood and Dave Funk made sure that their soldiers helped me as much as possible. Major Rod Coffey, a thoughtful military historian himself, went out of his way to share his own experiences and put me in touch with many other soldiers in the unit. Chris Carter welcomed me into the world of his Attack Company soldiers and provided me with much useful information. My greatest debt is to Lieutenant Colonel Kevin Cooney. Without Kevin's considerable assistance, the Iraq War chapters would not be as comprehensive or vivid. Kevin arranged the many group interviews I conducted, sat for an interview himself, answered several questions, and dealt with a great many logistical issues that must have taken valuable time from his real job as XO of 2-7. Thank you, my friend!

In a blanket sense, I wish to thank all Cottonbalers, living and dead, for their service in this remarkable organization. Their story is, I believe, the very story of America's combat experience. A nation can never really repay its combat veterans for risking their lives in the line of duty; it can only recognize such sacrifice and express gratitude for it.

My biggest debt of gratitude, of course, goes to my friends and family. I want to thank Mike Chopp, Mark Williams, Joe Carcagno, Dave Cohen, Ron Kurtz, the Vincent brothers, John Villier, Ed Laughlin, Steve Kutheis, Chris Anderson, and Sean Roarty (to name but a few) for being true friends and for helping make the world a better place in every way. The whole Woody family, including Doug, David, Ruth, and Nelson, has never ceased to welcome me into their family like one of their own. They will probably never really understand how much I appreciate that. I could not ask for better in-laws. I wish to thank my sister, Nancy, and my brother, Mike, for tolerating a brother who is pretty much obsessed with his work. My parents, Michael and Mary Jane, have my undying gratitude for all their sacrifices to give me a good life. I cannot really repay them for that, but maybe this book might, in some measure, eat away at that debt. I often wonder why I was so fortunate to be blessed with such great parents. My biggest thank you, of course, goes to my wife, Nancy, the love of my life. This history of the 7th was, of course, her idea in the first place. She assisted with many research details but, more than that, served as a sounding board for every last detail of the project. It is no exaggeration to say that the research and writing of this series completely absorbed my life for several years. Nancy cheerfully put up with this intrusion in our lives (even if it was of her creation) and showed what a special person she is in every way. The word *thanks* does not convey the gratitude I feel.

COMBAT IN AN AGE OF TERROR

Introduction

April 3, 2003

Iraq

SOMEWHERE UP AHEAD, THROUGH SHIMMERING, languid waves of Euphrates heat, battle waited—palpably, inexorably, perhaps even inevitably. Like a living being, yet with no passion and no emotion, no love or hate, no pleasure or pain. It simply waited, just as it always had before in so many other places: the muddy embankments of the Chalmette Plantation; the confusing swamps of the Florida backcountry; the freezing ditches of Fredericksburg; the fiery knolls of Big Hole; the sweaty, grassy slopes of El Caney; the anonymous, desperate wheat fields of the Marne; the grainy sand of beaches named Fedala, Licata, Anzio, and Cape Cavalaire; the frozen hell of Chosin; the hopeless rice paddies of Binh Chanh', and now here in Iraq, on the humid banks of the Euphrates, the cradle of civilization. No matter the place and no matter the time, battle was, in so many respects, the same—a dangerous, sometimes deadly, animal with no pity for those who must endure it and no remorse for those who do not prevail.

It had always been this way for the soldiers of the 7th US. Infantry Regiment, but, at the moment, Sergeant Raul "Rudy" Belloc couldn't have cared less about history. Far away from home, stuck in an alien, inhospitable land, the only thing that really mattered to Belloc, the twenty-seven-year-old infantry fire team leader in Bravo Company, 3rd Battalion of the 7th Infantry Regiment, was the fact that his life was in mortal danger. Nevertheless, he kept his cool, concentrating on the three feet in front of him, thinking and acting as all infantrymen must in combat.

He was a good-natured, diminutive man with kind eyes and a quiet presence. He hailed from Arizona but spoke with a vaguely northeastern accent. Less than three years before, he had left college and joined the Army in search of some adventure. In the three years that followed, he had proven himself a natural soldier—an excellent shooter, a reliable individual, a calm person whom others looked to in difficult times. He was totally dedicated to his wife and children as well as the three young soldiers in his fire team.

Now, on this anonymous Iraqi road, Sergeant Belloc huddled alongside a Bradley Fighting Vehicle armored personnel carrier, listening to the sound of enemy bullets zipping by in angry clusters. Nearby, the three men he led did the same, all of them sweated profusely in the sweltering heat and humidity of the marshy river land. Even though it was more dangerous here outside their Bradley, they were grateful to have left the crowded, claustrophobic compartment in which they had been riding only a few minutes earlier. At least they were breathing fresh air, albeit even moist, thick air.

Beyond Belloc, a staggered line of Bradleys and tanks stood in stationary clumps along the road. Tracer rounds bounced crazily along the road. Here and there, they clanked off the armored skin of the tanks. Inside the vehicles, crewmen busily searched for the source of the enemy fire, quickly realizing that their Iraqi Republican Guard antagonists lay in deep fighting holes alongside the road, too close and too low for the armored monsters to shoot them. Only dismounted infantrymen, like Sergeant Belloc and his team, could get them.

Now realizing this, too, the sergeant looked around at his anxious men, his comrades, those for whom he was about to lay his life on the line. Each man clutched his weapon, eyes on Sergeant Belloc, waiting for whatever might come. Their youthful faces were typical; whether white men, black men, Hispanic or Asian men, right now the ethnicity of these American soldiers did not matter. Theirs were simply a collection of faces that one would see in the halls of most any public high school or any McDonald's restaurant on a Friday night most anywhere in the United States. Like some of their forebears, they were here and serving in the U.S. Army because they had chosen to do so. Their motivations for making that choice varied—money for college, adventure, career, self-sacrifice, economics, a better alternative to a life of crime and drugs—but none of that mattered now. They were here because they believed in something bigger than themselves, something bigger even than love of country. They believed in one another. Like generations of 7th infantrymen before them, when battle called, they would fight for one another.

Belloc's eyes wandered from his men to the roadside. He was now dimly aware of the existence of a long line of enemy holes, cleverly dug into the underside of an embankment that gradually sloped up to the road. He knew that each of those holes had to be cleared, and that only he and his guys were in a position to do that. That would mean killing other men. The awful time had come to perform the classic role of the infantry—to close with and destroy the enemy. He checked his M4 Carbine rifle to make sure it was ready to fire. He made sure he had plenty of grenades. He glanced at his squad automatic weapon (SAW) gunner and told him to lay down some covering fire. Then Belloc went forward.[1]

He did not know it but, at that moment Sergeant Belloc spiritually joined a long line of infantrymen, spanning many generations, who experienced the exact same emotions and the same sort of mortal danger. These unseen men, many of whom lived and died decades or even hundreds of years before Belloc was born, would have been very familiar with his situation that day, for they had dealt with similar experiences in their own lifetimes. They dressed differently, spoke differently, looked at the world differently, and fought with different weapons. But if they could have huddled against that Bradley with Belloc on that humid day in 2003, they would have had at least one thing in common with him: service with the 7th Infantry Regiment in combat.

For it had always been this way and very probably always will be. The 7th U.S. Infantry Regiment has existed since before the War of 1812, and it continues to serve today. It has fought in every major war after the American Revolution, ranking as one of the oldest combat organizations in the U.S. Army. It possesses more battle streamers and campaign citations than any other infantry regiment, and its ranks include more Medal of Honor recipient than all but one outfit. The history of the 7th Infantry Regiment is *the* great unwritten story in American military history, every bit as fascinating and illustrious as the exploits of the 1st

Marine Division, the 2nd Rangers, the Big Red One, the 101st Airborne Division, the 7th Cavalry Regiment, the Stonewall Brigade, or the Iron Brigade, to name a few famous units.

The soldiers of the 7th Infantry are known as Cottonbalers. This is because regimental lore says that 7th infantrymen, in the unit's infancy, fought from behind cotton bales at the Battle of New Orleans in 1815. Although this is probably not true, the nickname has stuck. The 7th Infantry's motto, "Willing and Able" (*Volens et Potens*), speaks volumes about its past. Throughout America's history, the soldiers of this regiment have proven, through their sacrifice, their bloodshed, and their sweat, that they were willing and able to fight their nation's wars. It is fair to say that the history of the 7th Infantry Regiment encompasses much of the span of U.S. military history. Their history, then, also is a guide through the changing face of America over decades and centuries. What kind of people served in this unit and why? What motivated them to fight? Above all, what was combat experience like for them and how did it change through time? At practically every crucial moment in America's wars, the 7th has been there, shaping the future of the country and, by extension, the world. What's more, this legacy will continue for the foreseeable future because the regiment remains on active duty in the twenty-first century. Organizationally it functions differently from before, and while the soldier's weapons, uniforms, and the slang terms they use to refer to their weapons and each other are different than in the past, all who serve in the storied regiment still exude the same sense of discipline, courage, and sacrifice of their predecessors.

Great and famous men have served with the unit, including future U.S. presidents such as Zachary Taylor and Ulysses S. Grant, along with Texas president Sam Houston. The 7th has also been home to many outstanding soldiers, such as John Gibbon, George Marshall, John Heintges, William Rosson, James Gavin, and Fred Weyand.

But more than that, the 7th Regiment's story is really that of the ordinary infantryman, the guy who does the toughest, dirtiest, and most dangerous fighting in almost all wars. The infantryman's job is to close with the enemy, destroy him, and then control ground taken: simple in conception and yet so complicated in execution. Those who have carried out this grisly task on behalf of all the American people have typically been unremarkable, ordinary individuals, but all of them have been, and probably always will be, the heart and soul of the U.S. Army. Theirs is a story of so many things: struggle, alienation, anguish, fear, heartbreak, privation, sacrifice, triumph, and pride; and perhaps this is fitting, because these are the ingredients that typically encompass the infantry experience.

I want to stress that neither this volume nor the first one is a standard unit history. Most such histories have been written by someone serving with the unit whose main agenda is to memorialize (and perhaps glamorize) the unit's past. As understandable as this kind of unit pride may be, it is not always conducive to good history. Often these unit histories are packed with a mind-numbing depth of de. tail on the comings and goings of a particular regiment, division, company, or battalion. This series is not like that. I have never served in the 7th. I am merely its historian. My aim here is to write an objective, compelling, combat history of the 7th, not to chronicle the regiment's every move or establish its exact lineage to the complete satisfaction of army researchers.

Some battles will inevitably be emphasized over others, and some individuals will figure more prominently in the narrative than others. For every man I mention, there are dozens or even hundreds of others who will forever remain anonymous. Regrettably, many took their stories to the grave with them. For those living veterans who feel that their experiences or those of their comrades deserve a more prominent role, I can only apologize sincerely and plead space limitations or editorial license. Needless to say, any errors are my responsibility and mine alone.

What, then, is the scope of this series? My goal is to take you, the reader, on a trek through the past by describing, as accurately as possible, what combat was like for the generations of men who served in this unit. After-action battle reports and other firsthand accounts make this possible. Ultimately, my hope is that the story will come to life for you, almost as if you were there, so that you can envision these men as flesh. and-blood human beings, people who loved, fought, cried, prayed, and bled. In addition, I hope to paint a vivid and accurate picture of the world of battle these soldiers faced: what it looked like, smelled like, sounded like, felt like; what was at stake and why; along with a sense of the human cost of the battles they fought.

I have chosen to divide this story into two major parts, and this choice requires some explanation. The first volume in this two-book series covers the regiment from its inception sometime during the War of 1812 through its vital contribution to the winning of World War II. Picking up where the first volume leaves off, this second volume covers the modern period, from the Korean War through the War in Iraq when the 7th Infantry fought a variety of enemies in what one can only term a post-World War II Age of Terror, when the world faced—and still faces—nuclear catastrophe and unconventional high-tech weapons and tactics. The nature of this terror varied, from cold war tension, to a desperate struggle with fundamentalist Islamic jihadists.

But, for now, our story begins in the immediate aftermath of World War II, in the early days of the cold war.

CHAPTER 1

Hot and Cold War

Korea

THE PROBLEMS BEGAN ALMOST IMMEDIATELY. The Cottonbalers, from the vantage point of their post-World War II occupation zone in rural southeastern Germany, quickly realized that all was not well. The Soviets, wartime allies, were going to be very difficult to get along with in this new atomic era. Truthfully, only mutual fear of a powerful Germany brought the communist Soviet Union and the capitalist United States together during World War II. With the common enemy vanquished and their lands occupied, the inevitable, bitter differences between the antithetical ideologies of communism and capitalist republicanism soon arose. Eventually these differences became so pronounced that the two nations locked horns in a fierce forty-five-year diplomatic, economic, cultural, political, propagandistic, and military struggle generally known as the Cold War.

Thus began a new age of terror that would extend well beyond the Cold War. The existence of nuclear weapons threatened death on an unprecedented scale, essentially terrorizing human beings into new patterns of limited, but vicious, warfare. In the new era, world opinion was often the ultimate prize, not territory. The Cottonbalers who had fought World War II deeply hoped that their terrible war would be the last. They prayed that the forces of modernity would make war obsolete. Sadly, those forces did just the opposite. For the 7th Infantry, modern combat was just beginning.

WORLD WAR II IN EUROPE had no sooner ended than, in the summer of 1945, the occupation troops of the 7th Infantry started to experience difficulties with the Russians—mind games, border incursions, and looting mostly. The Cottonbalers were responsible for patrolling seventy-two miles of border, and they had nowhere near enough manpower to do so effectively. Knowing this, the Soviets often descended on undefended German towns, engaging in various forms of mayhem, from serious violence to relatively harmless looting and drunkenness. "It was really bad," Colonel John Heintges, the commander of the 7th, recalled. "I would say we had five or six incidents every night, and in some cases [a] whole village of 300 people would be burned down to the ground. They raped the women; didn't make any difference what ages they were."

Soon German mayors came to Heintges begging for protection from the avenging Russians. The German-born colonel, who sympathized with his kinsmen, took the drastic, and controversial, step of arming the Germans. He kept his new policy as secret as he could, but it was a harbinger of the future.[1] Soon western Europe and the entire "free world" would join together out of mutual fear of communism, not just Soviet communism but Asian as well.

This new conflict between East and West affected nearly every corner of the world, including Korea, a small peninsula nation sandwiched between China and Japan. The Koreans survived half a century of Japanese occupation, which ended with the Japanese defeat in World War II. The Soviet Union and the United States jointly occupied Korea after World War II, disarming the Japanese and generally making the transition from the old imperial Korea to the new independent Korea. When relations between the two superpowers deteriorated, the same thing occurred between the northern (Soviet) and southern (American) portions of Korea. By the late 1940s a communist regime was in place in the north, above the 38th parallel, and a staunchly anticommunist government in the south. These two glared at each other and itched for the opportunity to unite the peninsula under their total control.

The communists were better prepared to do so. Before heading home, the Soviets had armed the North Koreans with their latest weaponry and had helped train their army into a formidable force. Also, the triumph of the communists in China, partially with the help of North Koreans, further strengthened the North Korean People's Army (NKPA). By contrast, the Americans went home and left South Korea with nothing but a few antiquated weapons and a poorly trained, militia-style army. This power imbalance proved to be an irresistible temptation for the communists, who attacked their southern countrymen with an all-out invasion on June 25, 1950.

The U.S. government, committed to a worldwide policy of containing communism, decided to send American troops to aid the South Koreans, who, without such outside help, faced imminent defeat. Thus, in the summer of 1950, the 7th Regiment received orders to deploy to the theater of war, as part of the 3rd Infantry Division, a unit the 7th had belonged to in both World Wars.

The 7th had come home from occupation duty in 1946 and set up shop at Fort Devens, Massachusetts. The unit was now a shadow of its World War II self. Postwar demobilization of conventional armed forces (along with an obsessive, misguided belief among policy makers in the talisman-like powers of "push button" nuclear weapons) led to drastic cuts in the size and readiness of the regiment. In truth, the unit was little more than an ill-armed battalion by 1950. To make matters worse, the 7th Regiment saw most of its 3rd Battalion cannibalized to outfit the 8th Cavalry Regiment, which was closer to deploying to Korea than the 7th. The crisis situation in Korea left the Cottonbalers with little time for refurbishing. The regiment went to Japan in September 1950 and began feverish preparations for war.

In the words of one regimental officer, "The 7th was a skeleton regiment—but it was a healthy skeleton" when it arrived in Beppu, Japan.[2] In other words, it was understrength, underarmed, and not ready yet for war, but the small number of men who made up the unit were good soldiers. Most of the officers were solid professionals, and the same went for the noncommissioned officers. Many had seen combat in World War II. Most were imbued with the kind of educated, committed professionalism that so marked the American military in the post-World War II era. The vast majority of the enlisted soldiers were reservists and volunteers. Like many of their sergeants and officers, some of them had served in World War II as well.

In anatomical terms, the unit had a strong "skeletal system" that badly needed to be augmented with blood, muscle, and flesh. To that end, American and Korean authorities literally swept two thousand young Korean men from the streets of Pusan, shipped them to Japan, and put them under the charge of the 7th Regiment's sergeants and officers, who were told that they had four weeks to ready these men for battle. These Koreans were not the first foreign-born Cottonbalers in the unit's history, but they were the first foreigners to serve in the regiment without ever setting foot in America. "They were rounded up, their heads shaved and bodies sprayed with delousing powder, and shipped to Japan," Captain Fred Long, a regimental officer, later wrote. "They had no warning, no training, spoke a different language and had a different culture."[3]

Not surprisingly, their performance in battle was not the best. They fell asleep on guard duty, panicked too easily, and shot at anything and anyone with trigger-happy abandon. Probably about one in five turned out to be worth something in combat.[4] The others were merely filler until the ranks of the rifle companies could be filled with U.S. reservists, a process that steadily took place in the closing months of 1950 and early months of 1951. After that, the number of Koreans in the unit rapidly diminished. Generally these Korean holdovers belonged to one of two categories: scouts or laborers. The former consisted of properly trained, well-motivated troops who performed valuable combat service as guides, interpreters, and scouts. The latter were, plain and simple, cheap labor to haul supplies and wounded.

So the typical American Cottonbaler for the war's first year was a volunteer of some sort, either a professional or a reservist, almost always white, and often under the age of twenty-five. As the war dragged on into a long stalemate, the composition of the unit changed somewhat. Reservists went home because of the newly implemented rotation system in which a soldier earned points for time served in Korea and especially for time on the front line. A man needed thirty-six points to rotate home, and he earned four points for every month on the front line. Draftees, in ever-increasing numbers, replaced the reservists.

As this happened, the 7th Regiment experienced a landmark change in its composition. For over 130 years, the regiment had been almost exclusively white. The Korean War changed that forever. In 1948, President Harry Truman signed Executive Order 9981, committing the U.S. military to integration. In practice, not much had changed by 1950, but within a year after the start of the war the U.S. Army began to disband its all-black units and integrate white and black soldiers in combat formations.

This had occurred in experimental instances in World War II, but Korea led to the wholesale implementation of the integration policy. By 1952, the typical Cottonbaler rifle squad of twelve men included one, perhaps two, African Americans. Within this typical squad, about half of the men were draftees, from working-class backgrounds and with little education, probably tenth grade or less. The average age of each squad member was twenty-two, and almost all were native born. Thus the composition of the regiment slowly changed from a core of committed professionals to younger, uneducated men, most of whom wanted little more than to do their jobs and go home.[5]

Naturally, there was some degree of tension between black and white soldiers, but, by and large, the integration policy worked well. Instances of overt racism were quite rare; if soldiers had prejudices they generally suppressed them in combat, when men could ill afford such mindless hatred. Like infantry soldiers from time immemorial, the GIs in Korea needed one another and grew close under the strain of battle. Race mattered little when death lurked around every corner; only reliability and courage mattered. The sentiments of one white Cottonbaler rifleman were typical: "They were just as brave as the white men. I have no grievance against the black men. They were soldiers and they were doing their job. I would call them first-rate. We had a young fellow named Broussard in our squad. He did everything the white guys did and the white guys didn't complain and the black guys didn't complain. I think we were all trying to do the same job and get ourselves back home. I did not see any falloff in morale or ability to perform when we integrated."[6]

The Korean War was the first war in the history of the 7th Regiment that began with a climax. Most of the Cottonbalers' toughest, bloodiest fighting in this war took place in the first nine months, the mobile phase, when both sides saw a chance to win the war outright. The North Koreans came very close to doing just that in the summer of 1950 when they pushed the Americans and South Koreans, fighting under the auspices of the new United Nations, into a crook of territory known as the Pusan perimeter. Somehow, these embattled forces held out, and, in mid-September, even as the Cottonbalers trained in Japan, the theater commander, General Douglas MacArthur, turned the tables on the North Koreans. He pulled off a risky amphibious invasion at Inchon, near Seoul, the South Korean capital. The success of this invasion reversed the entire course of the war. Retreating North Korean forces could not prevent the UN troops from crossing the 38th parallel. Truman and MacArthur decided to go for total victory; this meant overrunning North Korea and uniting the peninsula under the Seoul government. There was just one problem with this otherwise desirable course of action—the reaction of the Chinese communists. Would they stand aside and allow an American-led army to overrun North Korea, their southern neighbor, without some kind of response?

MacArthur naïvely thought they would do exactly that, but he was wrong. In fact, the Chinese had been planning to get into this war all along. They had merely been biding their time. Now, in late October and early November 1950, as American and South Korean forces pushed north, the Chinese sent troops into North Korea and shadowboxed with the UN forces. The weather grew colder by the day. American troops on the scene sent reports of Chinese resistance to MacArthur's notoriously foolish, arrogant intelligence chief, Major General Charles Willoughby, in Tokyo. Willoughby and his boss, from their comfortable Tokyo enclaves, imperiously rejected these reports from those on the scene. MacArthur kept issuing orders to go north as quickly as possible. Worse, he split his forces on either side of North Korea's rough spine of mountain ranges; in so doing, he provided the numerically superior Chinese with a geographic opening to surround and cut off UN troops.

On November 17, 1950, the Cottonbalers disembarked from LSTs at Wonsan, North Korea, and joined this emerging theater of the absurd. In spite of recent bloody fighting against undeniably large groups of Chinese, MacArthur and his generals still ordered UN forces north, into the unknown. For about a week, the Cottonbalers, along with the rest of the 3rd Division, patrolled and covered the flanks of the 1st Marine Division and the Army's 7th Infantry Division. The Marines were advancing due north in the direction of Chosin Reservoir, and the 7th Division was advancing northeast.

Thanksgiving came and went. The regimental cooks did the best they could to provide each soldier with a turkey dinner. The weather presented them with quite a challenge. Cold, steady rain poured down all day. The cooks set up their wares in the backs of trucks, under the shelter

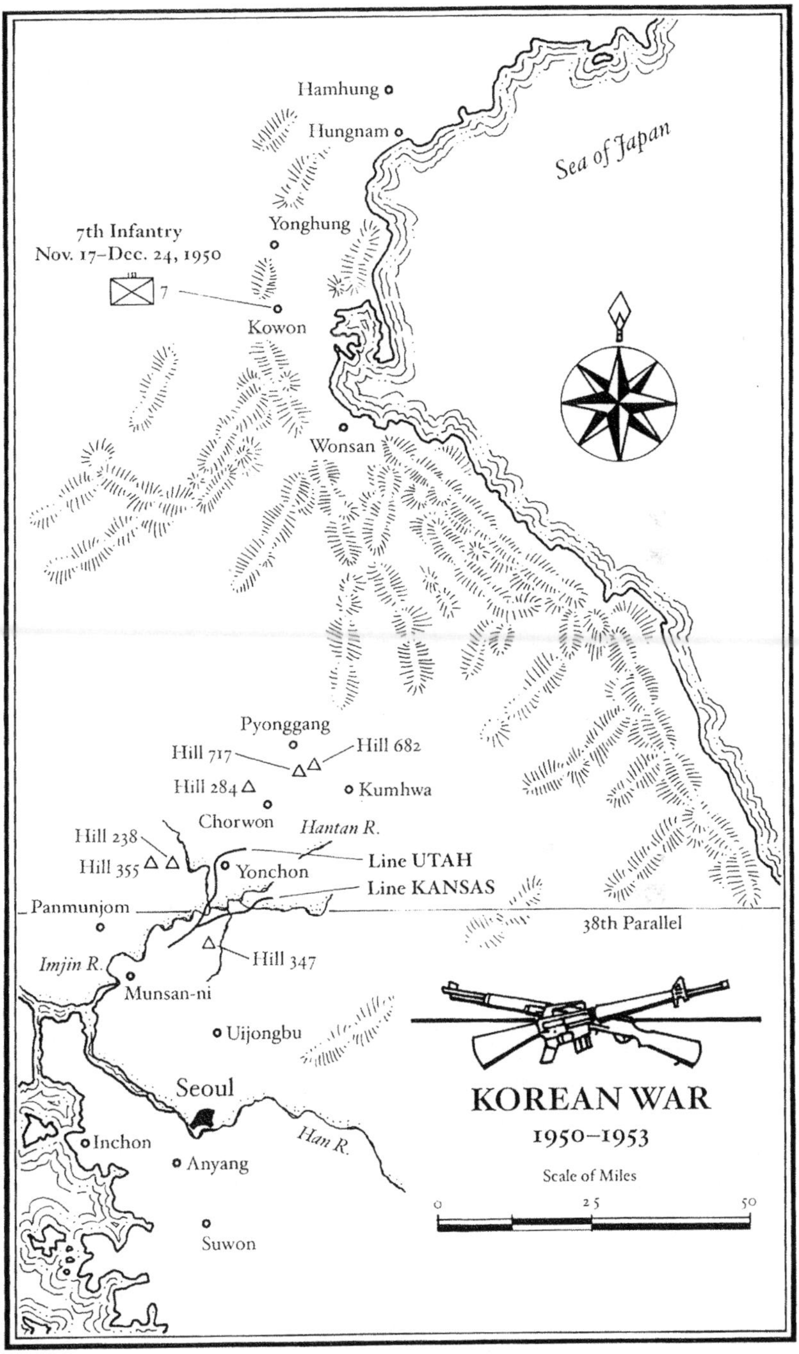
Hamhung
Hungnam
Sea of Japan
Yonghung
7th Infantry
Nov. 17–Dec. 24, 1950
7
Kowon
Wonsan
Pyonggang
Hill 717
Hill 682
Hill 284
Kumhwa
Chorwon
Hantan R.
Hill 238
Hill 355
Yonchon
Line UTAH
Line KANSAS
Panmunjom
38th Parallel
Hill 347
Imjin R.
Munsan-ni
Uijongbu
Seoul
Inchon
Anyang
Han R.
Suwon
KOREAN WAR
1950–1953
Scale of Miles
0
25
50

of canvas covers, and dispensed the food to sopping-wet lines of soldiers. Terry Tennant, a mortar squad leader, patiently waited his turn. "Everything was soaked and the wind was blowing. When our turn to get served came . . . I picked up a clean mess kit and went through the chow line." His food—turkey with all the trimmings—started out hot, but the driving rain soon changed that. "So I stood along with most everyone else in the . . . rain, eating as fast as I could before the food got too cold and soupy. Of course, it only took a matter of minutes before everything was cold and swimming in the water."[7]

The weather got much worse. Soon temperatures dipped below freezing, then into the teens, then below zero. The cold was mind-numbing, awful, and painful. The soldiers wrapped themselves in blankets and made do the best they could. Some of them wore summer uniforms beneath their blankets, yet another symbol of the hurried unpreparedness so typical of the early stages of the Korean War.

The regimental commander now was Colonel John Guthrie, a forty-two-year-old West Pointer and grandson of a Civil War general. Guthrie was army through and through: born, bred, and programmed for a life in the service. He had spent World War II as a training and staff officer. The 7th Infantry was his first combat command. He basically had two battalions to work with (the gutted 3rd was still being rebuilt). Guthrie's commanding officer, Major General Robert "Shorty" Soule, ordered him to push into the northwest mountains to a place called Sachang. Once there, his troops were supposed to protect the left flank of the Marines who were moving north toward Hagaru.

In late November, Guthrie sent the 1st Battalion on the difficult trek to Sachang. Mountainous terrain, winding roads, and bitter weather posed most of the hazards for the soldiers. A few North Korean guerrillas sniped at them, but that was about it. The Americans set up perimeters, circular positions with interlocking fields of fire. Frozen earth prevented any effort to dig in, so the men used rocks for cover or blasted shallow ridges with TNT. They spent their time trying to keep warm, patrolling, watching, and waiting.

Meanwhile, the Chinese unleashed a massive offensive aimed at sweeping UN forces from North Korea. Hundreds of thousands of Chinese soldiers crossed the Yalu River, infiltrated into the mountains of North Korea, and attacked. Much of the brunt of this offensive hit the Marines at Hagaru and the 7th Division farther east, but powerful forces also attacked the 1st Battalion at Sachang. Very simply, if they punched through the 1st Battalion and captured the road from Chosin Reservoir to the main Allied supply port at Hungnam, then the entire X Corps (3rd Division, 1st Marine, 7th Division, ROK forces) would be in deep trouble.

JUST AFTER DARK ON NOVEMBER 27, the Chinese struck. They blew bugles, screamed an odd mixture of war cries (most notably "GI!"), and ran at the U.S. positions. The Cottonbalers could hardly believe what they were seeing—mass waves of soldiers, bearing straight for them. On the far end of the perimeter, Master Sergeant George Zonge, a World War II vet and professional soldier, studied them for a fascinated split second. Then he sprang into action. He was in command of a weapons platoon made up of 60mm mortars and recoilless rifles (an anti-tank and bunker-busting weapon). Just three months earlier, Zonge had been at Fort Lee, Virginia, overseeing a photo lab. Now he found himself fighting for his life, commanding a platoon of ill-trained Koreans and American reservists.

Zonge, along with every other platoon leader, gave the order to open fire. "It was the damnedest thing I ever saw—they came swarming over the hills making all kinds of noise, blowing bugles and rattling cans and shooting off flares and yelling their heads off in these high-pitched singsong voices. They had no armor. No vehicles of any kind. It was like one of those old-time infantry charges you read about in the Civil War."

American fire laced into the Chinese, tearing them into shreds. Their battered, bleeding soldiers fell in clumps, but still the enemy attack did not lose momentum. "They were shooting burp guns and rifles but . . . they were lousy shots. What caused us the most trouble was grenades. And the fact that there was so goddamn many of [the Chinese]. Just wave after wave. You'd shoot down a whole line of Chinamen and another line would be right behind. They'd stop to pick up the weapons of the ones that had been shot, and then they'd come on like the first ones. We'd shoot them down, and there would be another line right behind them."[8]

On and on into the night, the Chinese launched these kinds of sporadic attacks, but with no success. By 0330 on the twenty-eighth their flares burned out, and the Chinese, bloody and stunned, retreated into the shadows.* The Cottonbalers stayed in their perimeter and kept watch in the freezing darkness, exchanging sporadic shots with isolated enemy troops. Mortar and artillery rounds began dropping in the perimeter. As they exploded, they kicked up frozen chunks of earth and scattered them like chunks of gravel behind the wheels of a truck. The men could do nothing but crouch against the earth and hope no fragments (manmade or natural) hit them. Most of the soldiers could not even feel their faces or extremities in the subzero cold. Any movement brought discomfort as the cold infiltrated trousers and blankets and penetrated to the bones. In haphazard circles of gore, twenty-five Chinese bodies lay just outside the edges of the perimeter. One American had been killed in the night fight and three others wounded.[9]

On the evening of the twenty-eighth, the Chinese attacked in even greater force. About eight hundred of them massed together and hit positions held by A and C Companies. Located on a series of low hills just behind the lead riflemen, Master Sergeant Zonge's men spotted plenty of targets. "Three or four times the Chinese broke our forward defenses, but we always beat them back. We learned to listen for their attack whistles. We'd pile all our grenades in the empty ammo boxes and hold our fire until we heard the whistles, and then we'd shift positions so that all our firepower was concentrated in the direction of the whistles. They'd try spot after spot, and we'd beat the hallelujah out of them."[10]

Chinese mortar rounds scored direct hits on the battalion command post, causing casualties and knocking out communications between the commanding officer, Lieutenant Colonel Charles Heinrich, and his company commanders. The isolated rifle companies fought all night, fending off strong enemy probes. As Zonge indicated, the enemy kept regrouping and searching around, looking for a weak spot in the perimeter, a place they could exploit, pour through, and annihilate the Americans.

At one point, they infiltrated D Company's spot on the line and inched toward the command post. Many of the D Company soldiers fled to the low hills, no doubt seeking the firepower comfort of Zonge's weapons.

But two men found cover in a shallow foxhole and defended the remnants of the CP. One of the men, Private First Class Oliver Green, was the eighteen-year-old son of a career noncommissioned officer from Alabama. Green noticed a group of Chinese soldiers steadily crawling toward his position and the CP. "Bullets were popping inches over our heads. Five Chinese came running up to the CP, about 15 yards from us. I cut them all down at once with my M-1. . . . I wounded one, and I could hear him moaning and crawling over the frozen ground. I was afraid he was going to throw a grenade, so I raised up and put two more bullets in his back. Then the sixth one ran up, and I cut him down. It wasn't a very pretty sight the next morning." Almost single-handedly, Green fended off a Chinese attempt to overrun D Company. He earned the Silver Star for his actions that night.[11]

As Green's reference to the Mi Garand indicated, American infantry soldiers in Korea mostly fought with the same weapons used in World War II. The only exceptions were the prevalence of recoilless rifles (basically an improved bazooka) and the M2 Carbine, an improved version of the M1 Carbine. The M2 fired a thirty-round banana clip whose bullets packed a bit more of a wallop than those of the fifteen-round clip of the M1 Carbine.

Using these weapons and many more, the Cottonbalers fended off the Chinese attacks all night and in the early-morning hours of the twenty-ninth. Try as they might, the Chinese could not circumvent 1st Battalion and cut the Hagaru-Hungnam road. By daylight, the enemy had faded away. The Chinese then contented themselves with lobbing mortar and artillery rounds at the Americans.

The biggest problem now for Guthrie was how to resupply his beleaguered 1st Battalion. True, they were holding off the Chinese, but they were essentially cut off at Sachang, high up in the mountains at the end of a winding, treacherous road. The colonel arranged for an airdrop of ammunition and medical supplies. To do this, he employed a new piece of technology, the helicopter, to evacuate the 1st Battalion's most seriously wounded men. The battalion by now had lost thirteen men killed and thirty-nine wounded. The supply and helicopter evacuation proceeded well, but Guthrie knew they were only stopgap measures. The 1st Battalion needed relief, the kind that could only come from linking up with other ground troops. So, Guthrie sent soldiers from the 2nd Battalion on an expedition to Sachang.

All day long on November 29, this relief expedition, named Task Force Kail after the 2nd Battalion's executive officer (and eventual commander), Lieutenant Colonel Sam Kail, negotiated the icy roads leading to Sachang. The main column reached Huksuri, about ten miles east of Sachang. At this point, G Company under Captain Ed Bruger drove straight into the 1st Battalion perimeter in the hills around Sachang. Lieutenant Colonel Heinrich plugged G Company right into his defenses, and they helped repel a small Chinese attack that night.

The next morning, even as American aircraft and artillery raked suspected enemy positions around the perimeter, Kail and much of his force made it to Sachang, fighting each step of the way against scattered groups of Chinese, and dispensed badly needed food, ammunition, and medicine.

Some of Kail's relief column, including Sergeant Tennant and his mortarmen, did not make it as far as Sachang. "About a mile or so before we arrived at our destination, we came to a bridge that crossed a small river down below. The bridge had been badly damaged . . . and some quick, temporary repairs had been made. As each truck crossed the repaired section, it became weaker, and pieces started collapsing and breaking away." His squad's truck was at the end of the convoy. Everyone except the truck driver jumped out of the truck to reduce weight. When the driver reached the rickety section of the bridge, he felt it collapsing. Completely spooked, he jumped out of the truck. The vehicle rolled off the bridge and crashed into the river below.

They hastily conferred and decided to stay put. No more vehicles could get across the bridge while it was in this state. So they were stranded, at least for the night. After hours of backbreaking toil, they retrieved most of their mortars, ammunition, food, and blankets from the truck, which lay wrecked on the frozen river. Tennant's squad and men from the other stranded trucks formed a little perimeter consisting of two trucks, one half-track, one antiaircraft vehicle, and twenty-five nervous soldiers.

Luckily for them, no Chinese spotted them, but the cold proved to be just as dangerous an adversary. "All of our Koreans and some GIs got into the rear of the trucks and slept together, packed like sardines in a can. I just kept walking around . . . sometimes running in place for a few minutes trying to generate some heat. The top of my head ached from my steel helmet being so cold. My hands and feet felt numb, and the blowing wind was like a knife cutting my flesh. I can't remember . . . ever being so cold and miserable as I was that night."

In the morning they exchanged a few shots with a Chinese patrol and then headed back east for the main 2nd Battalion perimeter at Huksuri. "We didn't have any water and had to eat snow until we got back." They made it at midday, just after the soldiers there had eaten lunch. "They had just finished their meal and had some chow left, but no clean mess kits to eat with." Tennant and his men were so hungry that they ate the leftover chow off dirty mess kits.[12]

Even as Tennant and his men shivered that miserable night away, a significant change had taken place in the battle situation. In the face of this massive Chinese intervention (even Willoughby and MacArthur had to face reality now), the objective for UN forces now had to change from the Yalu to the Sea of Japan. Clearly, the idea of advancing any farther north toward the Yalu was not only crazy but completely unrealistic. Worse, the UN forces faced the very real prospect of annihilation if they did not retreat south and evacuate through Hungnam on the Sea of Japan. So the focus now changed from offensive to defensive. The Americans and South Koreans began a desperate retreat to the sea, fighting every step of the way against throngs of Chinese soldiers hell-bent on preventing them from escaping.

Understanding this radical shift in the fortunes of the Allied army, Guthrie ordered 1st Battalion to leave Sachang and retreat east, covered by the 2nd Battalion, to Huksuri and then, ultimately, the coast. In bitter cold weather on the morning of December 2, the frostbitten, red-faced men of the 1st Battalion began moving along the Sachang road east. "When we got the word to pull out we still didn't know much about what was going on, except that we were now retreating, and we still had to fight all the time," Zonge recalled. "The marines were flying support for us, strafing and bombing, trying to keep the road open. They'd fly their Corsairs so low, the spent cartridges from their wing guns would bounce off our helmets."[13]

Company B served as rear guard, covering this withdrawal against the inevitable enemy response. Soon a force of three hundred enemy started shooting at the B Company soldiers from a distance of five hundred yards. The Americans steadily returned fire and retreated east, in a continuous effort not to lose contact with the main column of 1st Battalion soldiers. If they lost contact, the Chinese could surround them and kill them all. The same aircraft Master Sergeant Zonge mentioned now swooped down on the Chinese and kept them at bay. Periodically, the soldiers of B Company had to slow down while engineers fixed bomb craters that marred the roads at various points. These same engineers had fixed the bridge that stranded Tennant and his group.

The soldiers from B Company kept moving in this fashion, making agonizingly slow progress in their quest to reach Huksuri, even as the rest of their battalion reached the town and boarded trucks that took them to Pungsong to the southeast. In the wintry distance, the B Company soldiers could see large groups of Chinese forming up to attack them. The Americans had to keep moving if they wanted any chance of making it out of there alive. Thanks to air support and sheer determination, they made it to Huksuri by late afternoon, with a swelling force of sixteen hundred Chinese uncomfortably close behind.[14]

The commander of the 2nd Battalion, Lieutenant Colonel Robert Besson, had spent much of December 2 organizing a defensive perimeter outside of Huksuri. His executive officer Kail explained: "We had moved up on the high ground overlooking the town (only a few huts really) and the road junction."[15] This high ground was a series of mountains on the tops of which the riflemen, machine gunners, and recoilless rifle gunners of the battalion set up positions. From this hastily prepared defensive line, the Cottonbalers of the 2nd Battalion now had to delay the Chinese as long as possible.

The brunt of the enemy attack, which came at dusk, fell on G Company and two platoons from F Company. These unfortunate men occupied positions on either side of the road, in the westernmost portion of the 2nd Battalion sector. Sergeant Rick Cardenas, one of the F Company rifle squad leaders, was part of this group. Cardenas was born in El Paso, Texas, in 1923 but grew up in the Mojave Desert in California. As a kid he had wanted to be a cattle rancher, but World War II changed those plans. Cardenas joined the Army and served as a rifleman in the Pacific with the 41st Infantry Division. Like many other World War II veterans, he joined the reserves after the war and got called up for Korea.

Cardenas commanded a mixed squad of Koreans and Americans at Huksuri. He and his men prepared the best positions they could to face the onslaught of Chinese. "It was cold, real cold. The ground was not only rock hard, it was frozen solid. The entrenching tool was useless. I could only get sparks as I struck the ground! Nobody could dig. Impossible. We were defending fingers that were separated by very deep ravines. The finger we occupied dropped fifty or more feet, then continued toward the base of the valley. It . . . snowed hard that night."[16]

All throughout the night, in driving snow, the Chinese pressed forward into the deep ravines and valleys and up the "fingers" or mountaintops. The fighting was as desperate as any ever experienced by men wearing the emblem of the 7th Infantry. The Cottonbalers blazed away at groups of Chinese who suddenly appeared through shrouds of darkness, like some kind of malevolent homicidal ghosts. At times, the soldiers fought hand to hand as Chinese stumbled into their positions. The Americans did the best they could, but they were heavily outnumbered (about two hundred men versus close to two thousand).

By 0500, the Chinese had overrun several platoons, most of whose men escaped, but the enemy occupied their positions. Quite often platoons could not see one another because of the mountainous terrain. They could hear shooting but had no idea what was going on around them. Fortunately, they maintained communication with the mortar sections a few hundred yards closer to the town. Tennant later wrote about their frantic calls for help: "The troops . . . were requesting us to drop rounds almost on top of them. In order to do this we disconnected the standards that held up the barrels of our mortars, and held them up with our hands and eyeballed the angle of the barrels. We were firing almost straight up, and the troops were calling back, 'Yes, send more!' It was a hell of a night with heavy losses on both sides, and no one had time to think how bitterly cold it was. We did hear those bugles blow, and their eerie echoes through the valley."[17]

The sun rose and still the attack did not abate. Chinese buglers sounded their battle calls, and the enemy soldiers pressed forward, waving weapons, screaming, and shooting. Bruger moved among his men directing fire. Chinese troops closed to within twenty yards of his position. A Chinese soldier opened up on him with a Thompson submachine gun. Bruger felt two slugs rip into his legs, knocking him over. Stunned but conscious, he sat up, drew a bead on his assailant, and shot him dead. For a few frightening moments, Bruger considered ordering his men to fix bayonets and fight to the last man, but he soon realized that this order would be futile. The Chinese were attacking in such overwhelming numbers that such an Alamo-like course of action would be foolhardy. "I checked the positions, and found that the Chinese had overrun nearly all of them," Bruger wrote. "We were forced to withdraw." Bruger and his men had already accomplished their mission. They had delayed the enemy significantly and inflicted horrendous casualties on them (probably between five and seven hundred in total).

Bruger ordered his men to get back to the rest of the battalion any way they could. In tiny groups they attempted to do so. He and his first sergeant wandered for a day, evading capture, and finally linked up with the battalion. "We managed to walk out and found some friendly units two days later. My 1st Sgt. went snow blind. I . . . spent five months in hospital."[18] A couple of his medics were killed by friendly tank fire. Others were captured or never heard from again. The majority made it back, though. Kail later wrote of Bruger: "He did a marvelous job . . . against vastly superior odds. The fact that he and G Company stayed there as long as they did, helped the rest of the battalion escape from the spot they were in."[19]

On the morning of the third, the rest of the 2nd Battalion boarded trucks and got out of Huksuri as quickly as they could. Artillery and air strikes blasted the pursuing Chinese, keeping them at bay. American engineers blew up bridges as the convoy retreated. They only had one route out of this disaster, a crude, unpaved mountain road that had to be kept open for survival. As usual, the extreme conditions made the retreat of the column even more difficult. Sergeant Tennant sat in a freezing truck, hoping that the vehicle would not slip off the road and crash. "[The road] was icy and snow-covered. It would have been a treacherous trip down out of those mountains even if we hadn't had to fight our way out. The road was clogged with vehicles and the progress was very slow.

If a truck stalled and caused a backup, it was shoved over the side where it would roll down the embankment." He even saw a tank slide over a cliff. The crew barely escaped from their stricken steel monster. Small numbers of Chinese infiltrators materialized and attacked the column at various times. "I shot a Chinese soldier with my M-1, and saw him fall next to the road. The one and only time I took aim, pulled the trigger, actually saw my target fall." One of Tennant's Korean soldiers got hit in this same attack. "He . . . caught a bullet in the middle of his back. He pitched forward, landing on top of me." The medics evacuated him, and Tennant never saw him again.[20]

The battalion finally made its way to prepared positions about a mile southeast of Huksuri. From there, American artillery kept the Chinese at a safe distance. Their patrols sometimes clashed with American patrols, but, for the most part, the situation had stabilized.[21] Clay Blair, author of one of the best histories of the Korean War, later wrote that the efforts of the Cottonbalers at Sachang and Huksuri drew off substantial Chinese forces that might have been used to crush the Marines and the 7th Division to the northeast. In addition, the 7th Infantry prevented the enemy from cutting the vital Hamhung-Hagaru road to the sea. Without that road, the Americans had no hope of escape.[22]

Meanwhile, Guthrie made use of his newly arrived 3rd Battalion, which, like the other two battalions in the regiment, had been hastily thrown together with a mix of Americans and Koreans. The 3rd Battalion served with a force of 3rd Division troops known as Task Force Dog. Task Force Dog pushed north on the Hamhung road to Chinhung. Their mission was to relieve the Marines at Chinhung and keep the road open while the leathernecks withdrew south from Chosin all the way to Hamhung. They began their trek up the road on December 6 and quickly reached Chinhung. The battalion fought off a substantial enemy attack on the evening of December 10 and kept the road open. "We knew that the Chinese were dug in on both sides of the road," Sergeant Harry Cooke later wrote, "high up in the cliffs that overlooked the road. We knew that it was certain that we would be hit." He was right. The Chinese soon opened fire with "small arms fire from both sides of the hills around us, mortar rounds were being lobed [*sic*] in. We were scared and thought that we would never make it out of that death trap.

However our C.O. called for air support, what a sight it was to see the Navy planes, firing into the hills and letting go with napalm, to watch it splash and roll over the hillside. Soon the small arms fire ceased and we picked ourselves out of the ditch."[23]

Soon the Marines started filtering in. They had been through quite an ordeal. For many days, they had fought their way south against swarms of Chinese who harassed them at every turn with roadblocks, blown bridges, and human-wave attacks. The Cottonbalers of Task Force Dog watched the battered Marines limp into their perimeter. One of the Cottonbalers, Sergeant Ben Winser, never forgot the sight of these brave, long-suffering men. Winser was another World War II veteran pressed into service. A talented artist, he spent most of his previous army service as a cartoonist. But when the war in Korea broke out, the Army did not need cartoonists; it needed infantry soldiers, so Winser found himself leading the security squad of the regiment's Headquarters Company. Four of his men were South Koreans. He mostly used them as scouts.

On this morning of the eleventh, Winser and his men did what they could to help the Marines. "Members of my security squad stood around on guard as our medics checked out their feet for frost-bite and wounds. As the inspection was taking place, one young, bearded and bewildered Marine glanced around and, looking at us with a half smile on his face, said, 'Boy, am I glad to see the Army today!' It was quite evident that this young Marine was on his way to a state-side hospital, suffering with a severe case of frost-bite."[24]

Winser's young Marine probably never forgot the role that army soldiers played in his deliverance, but the same cannot be said for posterity. The Marines have dominated the story of the "great escape" from Chosin and its environs, but the Army, particularly the 3rd Division, also played a notable part in the campaign, and helped save the Marines. "Everybody says the marines saved themselves, especially the marines," Master Sergeant Zonge deadpanned, "and after all this time you can't argue with people because they won't believe you. But I know. I was there. It's been my little secret."[25]

Now that the Marines had escaped from the Chosin area, the withdrawal to the sea could begin in earnest. When Task Force Dog successfully shepherded the Marines out of Chinhung and then south to Hamhung, the 1st and 2nd Battalions of the 7th Infantry retreated steadily to a new perimeter surrounding the port of Hungnam. The 3rd Division, anchored by the 7th Infantry, received the job of holding that perimeter while the rest of X Corps evacuated from Hungnam.

The Cottonbalers occupied static positions just outside the city. They patrolled daily and nightly. They skirmished with the Chinese. They dealt with the dreadful weather. In case of an enemy attack, they could call on a devastating selection of fire support—mortars, artillery, and air strikes.

David Cliffton, a twenty-one-year-old mortarman and reservist, wrote years later about the pace of life on the lines at this time: "At night, we had guard 2 hours on and 2 hours off in foxholes around the perimeter. The night was cold, very clear." For warmth he had "two wool blankets, summer sleeping bag and field jacket, combat boots. I . . . had leather gloves but the liner had worn down when the gloves got wet. I sat in the hole with my legs inside the bag and blanket around me." One night, Cliffton began to feel very warm, strangely so. He was suffering from hypothermia and lost consciousness. His buddy figured this out, pulled Cliffton out of his hole, and, according to Cliffton, "slapped me for 15 minutes before he could get me awake. He put my arm over his neck and walked me until daylight. My legs were numb and had no feeling; my hands were the same way."[26]

Between December 13 and 15 the Chinese launched three separate attacks on the 7th Infantry. On the thirteenth they hit E Company. They swarmed out of the hills in front of the company. Many of the enemy troops wore American clothing (probably for warmth) and shouted, "GI!!" as they attacked. The Americans mowed them down in waves—enormous swaths of snow were literally drenched red with their blood—but they kept coming. Some of them infiltrated the line of outposts held by E Company and surrounded a few of the American soldiers. American counterattacks rescued the surrounded men, and the Chinese retreated back into the hills.

Two days later, they sent twenty-five hundred screaming troops at B and F Companies. Again, the fighting took place at close range, with the Americans using every possible source of firepower to kill the enemy, but the Chinese infiltrated. Their numbers made such penetrations inevitable. The question was whether they could exploit these little breaches in the American security zone and push through to the beach at Hungnam. They couldn't. The Cottonbalers called in a withering succession of mortars, artillery, tanks, and air strikes. Napalm roasted the Chinese. White phosphorous rounds sent angry, searing fragments burning through their padded uniforms and straight into their bones and muscles. Fragmentation rounds shredded them and wounded them in every way imaginable. Machine guns, rifles, and grenades punched big holes through these hapless men, who were little more than pawns in the fingers of unsavory leaders who cared little for the lives of their soldiers (or, for that matter, practically anyone else).

In the face of these furious attacks, the Cottonbalers fought back and slowly withdrew to more defensible lines. The men dragged the frozen bodies of their fallen with them as they went. Litter teams did everything they could to evacuate the wounded. Artillery and air strikes kept the Chinese at a safe distance. By December 16, the Cottonbalers had withdrawn into the Hamhung area, where the UN forces had set up a continuous, defensible line, as opposed to the series of strongpoints and outposts the Cottonbalers had manned only a few days before. "It was comforting . . . to finally be in a situation where we actually had a closed line of troops, all joined together," Sergeant Tennant commented, "without any breaks such as we had up in the mountains. We knew if we were on our side of the line, we could be pretty certain no enemy would be behind us."[27]

As it turned out, the 7th Infantry defended the Hungnam perimeter for over a week while the Marines, the South Koreans, and the 7th Division evacuated. Day by day, the perimeter shrank. As it did so, the Cottonbalers worried that the Chinese would, at any moment, mass their hordes for one last all-out attack and overrun the 7th Regiment. The Cottonbalers need not have fretted. The perimeter featured such a lethal blend of firepower that the enemy could not get close to Hungnam. Any time the Chinese probed or attacked, death rained down on them from the skies in the form of airplane ordnance and artillery.

The trump card for the Americans was naval gunfire. Once the UN soldiers retreated to Hungnam they were now within range of supporting naval gunfire, including that of the great battleship USS *Missouri*. The Chinese had no answer for the sixteen-inch shells of this behemoth.

Each shell weighed a ton. The *Missouri* and other ships fired countless shells in support of the Cottonbalers. One night the gun crews aboard the *Missouri* worked especially hard. The battleship's forward observer took up station at the 1st Battalion's headquarters. He sat down at the switchboard and called in fire. "I could read the Artillery, it was huge and whispered as it entered the enemy's territory," one 1st Battalion officer remembered. After several minutes of this, the naval officer decided to take a nap at 2200. Everyone forgot about him. The shells shrieking overhead became part of the night, a sound that seemed almost as natural as the wind. In the morning the shells were still flying. The naval officer had overslept. He woke with a start and said, "Hell, those guys must be lying all over the decks, I forgot to cease fire." Needless to say, the soldiers did not mind the overkill one bit.[28]

The enemy prudently kept his distance, and the evacuation continued more or less unabated. On Christmas Eve, the perimeter had shrunk so much that it included only Hungnam and its beaches. The Marines, 7th Division, South Koreans, and much of the 3rd Division were all long gone. Now it was finally the Cottonbalers' turn to leave. Engineers demolished anything of value. Ships cluttered the harbor. Just after noon, the soldiers lined up and prepared to leave. Marine amtracs churned through the water and picked them up on the beach. Sergeant Tennant and his men, along with hundreds of others, jumped aboard their assigned craft. "We threw all of our equipment on board, jumped in . . . did a quick one-eighty, and were back in the water on our way to the waiting ships in the harbor."[29]

As the Cottonbalers sailed away, a terrific explosion rocked the harbor. A demolition party of mortarmen had inadvertently ignited their powder bags and, with them, a slew of ordnance that had been stacked on the beach. The explosion killed and wounded several men, including some Cottonbalers. One of the wounded men was a friend of Corporal Cliffton's. "The blast blew my friend off the beach out into the water and concussion smashed his mess kit on his back; he was bleeding when he got on the ship." Colonel Guthrie restored order and supervised the evacuation of the demolition party.[30]

The Cottonbalers crowded aboard ships and enjoyed their first warmth and decent food in weeks. On Christmas Day the Navy fed them a turkey dinner. They made it to Pusan in a day and waited several days before debarking, resting, eating, and sleeping. Sergeant Winser, like so many others, contemplated what had just transpired. He decided that the men of his security squad, and the rest of the regiment, had performed very well. "Realizing that their lives depended on team-work, they did their job, no matter what, and did it well. I thought we did a good job of fighting the bitter-cold weather, 30 below zero in North Korea, and the enemy."[31]

The Chosin ordeal was over.

THE CAMPAIGN HAD NEARLY BEEN a diaster of unprecedented proportions (the Cottonbalers have never in their history been in more imminent danger of complete elimination). Instead, it emerged as a halfhearted "victory" in a Dunkirk kind of way. The Navy did brilliant work at Hungnam, successfully evacuating 105,000 troops, 17,500 vehicles, 350,000 tons of cargo, and 91,000 Korean refugees. The Army and Marines inflicted terrible damage on the Chinese attackers, probably as many as 45,000 casualties. Roughly 90 percent of the enemy soldiers had frostbite. Their padded uniforms and "sneaker"-style footgear proved wholly inadequate for protection in the fierce Korean cold. The twelve Communist Chinese Force (CCF) divisions that had opposed X Corps succeeded in ejecting the Allies from North Korea but were shattered as any kind of combat-effective force.[32]

Even so, wars are not won by evacuations. The Chinese intervention had turned the tide of this war. In mid-November, UN forces had been poised for a total victory. Weeks later, they were fighting for their lives, hoping only to escape to South Korea to fight again another day. The Chinese pushed American and South Korean forces out of North Korea, recaptured Seoul, and then paused to lick their considerable wounds. The communists had enough strength to force the United Nations out of North Korea, but could they overrun the entire south and push the vaunted Americans into the sea? For that matter, could they even hold on to the territory they had recently won at such great cost? The answer to both of these questions was no. The Chinese had absorbed such terrific losses in November and December that they lost the initiative in January. Slowly and steadily, UN forces began moving north toward Seoul and the 38th parallel.

The Cottonbalers spent most of the month in reserve, training, re-equipping, and replenishing their ranks with newly arrived Americans. Soon Americans constituted two-thirds of the unit's strength. The men ate and slept well, but the freezing, hellish retreat from North Korea had taken a toll on their collective psyche. "There was no morale worth talking about," Master Sergeant Zonge asserted. "Most of the men wanted to leave Korea to the Koreans. They didn't think it was worth it, what they were going through. The Chinese coming in like that had really affected everybody. It was a terrific shock."[33]

The only thing that could salvage that morale was to go back on the offensive. Some of the soldiers may have doubted Korea's worth, but they certainly preferred a proactive, aggressive approach to combat, not to the fighting retreat they had just endured. Like Cottonbalers in all of America's wars, they wanted to finish the job and go home.

The 7th Infantry and 3rd Division were now assigned to I Corps in western Korea near the town of Ch'ŏnan and given the assignment of steadily pushing to the Han River, which flowed through Seoul. In late January the 7th Infantry began a steady, deliberate advance north, reconnoitering carefully and cautiously to ascertain CCF strength and intention. The Chinese did not have many units in the area, but sometimes the enemy stood and fought for small pieces of high ground.

Sergeant Glenn Hubenette, a squad leader in F Company, remembered one such encounter: "This mountain formed a natural defensive position for the Chinese, and they didn't want to give it up. After two days we finally climbed to the top but were still fired on by snipers and well-dug-in machine guns. Every time we left our holes we were shot at." On the third day of this small battle, Hubenette's platoon sergeant, a Greek-American and World War II veteran by the name of Sergeant Ted Turkos, got hit. "I ran over to him and, after pulling him behind some rocks, yelled for the medics. I could see the back left side of his head was gone. Our medic . . . put two large field dressings over the hole." They waited helplessly for Turkos to die, but he hung on.

Half an hour later, they decided to carry him off the mountain. They improvised a litter out of pine branches and a shelter half and began the laborious process of hauling him down the mountain. "We had to work hard because . . . the trail was slippery. When blood and saliva blocked

Ted's breathing we'd stop and clear the passages." They reached a road and finally found a jeep to evacuate Turkos. The jeep took Turkos to a hospital in Pusan where doctors fitted him with a steel plate, but he died later at a hospital in San Francisco.[34]

As in North Korea, harsh winter weather continued to be a problem. "Snow was more than plentiful," the division historian wrote. "Temperatures dipped below freezing. Vehicles had to be started and warmed at intervals through the long nights in order to prevent congealed lubricants from immobilizing engines. Feet had to be inspected and massaged frequently to prevent the black, swelling disfiguration of trench foot."

For about ten days in late January and early February, the regiment functioned in a reserve role, trailing behind the other two regiments of the 3rd Division sweeping up bypassed resistance (Chinese regulars or sometimes Korean guerrillas). On February 4 the Cottonbalers took the lead. The unit attacked by day, capturing key hills or road junctions, and defended by night. Enemy resistance was uneven—sometimes strong, sometimes not. American firepower chewed up Chinese divisions south of the Han, and by the middle of February General Soule foresaw the possibility of reaching the Han and cutting off the enemy. Allied ground forces in Korea, lumped together under the umbrella of the 8th Army, had a new commander, General Matthew Ridgway of World War II fame, and Ridgway imbued his troops with a new offensive spirit.

Ridgway's command presence was a positive development, but much hard fighting still remained to be done before the Allies could claim the Han and Seoul, and the Cottonbalers found that out firsthand. On the twelfth of February, K Company fought a fierce battle with determined Chinese troops. Captain Harry Williams, the company commander, led a platoon-sized patrol somewhere in the vicinity of Chomchon. The Americans cautiously advanced over rugged, ridge-ridden terrain. The men were spread out in the standard patrol formation: point men at the front, automatic weapons in the middle, along with the command group, and riflemen walking Tail End Charlie, craning their necks at various intervals, eyeballing the terrain behind them to make sure they were not being followed.

All of a sudden, just as the patrol came to a slight hill, the enemy opened fire. The Chinese were dug in on the hill. Their machine-gun, rifle, and submachine gun fire swept the area. The Americans immediately hit the dirt and scrambled for whatever concealment they could find. Bullets kicked up little chunks of frozen, frosty earth. Everyone hugged the ground and hoped for deliverance. Williams, like any good commander, knew he had to get his men in motion as quickly as possible. The longer they were pinned down, the more vulnerable they were.

Williams screamed orders at his men. He told one squad to flank to the left and the other to the right. The one on the right, led by First Sergeant William Wong, a professional soldier of Chinese descent, ran into withering machine-gun fire. The gun was no more than thirty or forty yards ahead of them. Wong's men could almost feel the horrifying presence of the bullets as they whipped past them. Some could hear the supersonic snapping of near misses—like quick cracks of a whip—as they whizzed past their eyes. The snapping noise meant the bullets were perilously close. Wong did not seem to care. He charged the machine gun. One bullet hit him, then another, and another. Weak and bleeding, he collapsed into a heap about five yards in front of the enemy machine gun.

Captain Williams saw the whole thing. His men on the left flank were keeping up a steady stream of fire, but they were pinned down behind Wong. Williams crawled over to the right flank and assessed the situation. Seconds later, he charged the machine-gun position himself, tossed grenades into it, and shot up the crew. A hail of enemy small-arms fire tore up the ground around him. He flopped back to Wong and tried to get him to move but couldn't. Williams picked up the sergeant and carried him, under fire, fifty yards to the medics. Having found out everything he needed to know about the enemy's disposition and strength, Captain Williams gathered his men and got them out of danger.[35]

The 2nd Battalion also ran into tough resistance during this advance over terrain that was vintage Korea—hilly, dotted with ridges, deep ravines, tree-covered peaks, and rocky outcroppings, eventually leveling off into choppy, muddy, incredibly noxious rice paddies and swampy, sticky river flats. Sergeant Hubenette and his F Company squad were climbing a series of hills when they ran into enemy machine guns. He and another man dropped into a shallow ditch. "Uphill of us the machine gun opened up. I lay face down while that Chink tried to get me. Slugs slammed into the hard dirt. This was the first time I knew—really knew—what gut fear was. Pure, unadulterated fear ran up and down my spine."

He and the other man maneuvered themselves, extremely cautiously, into good escape positions. They waited for the machine gun to fire elsewhere. Hubenette worried that his posterior was sticking up too high. He thought, "That Chink is gonna nail me . . . right in the middle [of it]." Before long, he and the other man heard the machine gun firing at another target and took off. Somehow, they made it back to their platoon near the bottom of the hill. "For the rest of the day we stayed where we were, shooting and taking cover, pumping clip after clip into the Chinese positions."

Several Americans were killed and wounded during this running battle. "A young soldier named Cox was hit and died before our eyes. The week before, he'd been notified his wife had just had a baby." The Chinese tried an attack, but the Americans opened fire on them and easily warded them off. Then Hubenette got hit. In the days leading up to this action, he had experienced a premonition of this. His buddies laughed at him, but unfortunately he was right. "A shell exploded behind me. The blast killed Lieutenant Chris, Sergeant Coffee, and Corporal Meyers. It blew me down the hill." It also wounded several other men, all of whom were evacuated before Hubenette. "I was the last wounded man taken off that cursed hill. On the way down we were ambushed. The medics dropped my stretcher and hid behind some rocks. When the Chinese were finally driven off, they came back and carried me to the road."

He rode in an ambulance to a MASH unit. After treatment there, he went back to a field hospital that had been set up in an old schoolhouse. "One young lad sitting next to me in the hallway was hysterical. He'd shot himself through the foot. A doctor/major began working on the young GI. Told the kid if he had his way, he'd let him bleed to death, and that the guy didn't belong in the same army with men who'd been legitimately wounded. The GI didn't hear a word he'd said. Who knew what the kid had gone through before he shot his foot?" Like many other combat infantrymen, Hubenette had at least a bare minimum of sympathy for those with self-inflicted wounds, even if he did not necessarily approve of what they had done: "I told him, 'Take it easy, kid.' "[36]

On the thirteenth and fourteenth of February the communists attempted to forestall the 3rd Division's advance with a series of confused night counterattacks. The most notable of these attacks was carried out by a newly organized Chinese-equipped regiment of North Koreans—the 81st North Korean People's Army Regiment. For about a day they infiltrated and clashed with the 3rd Division's other two regiments before ending up in the 7th Infantry's sector.

Some of their heaviest attacks hit the 1st Battalion near Chungung. They hit the men of B and C Companies on their hilly outposts, forcing them to fall back a short distance. The men of B Company got pushed off their positions on Hill 151 during an overwhelming attack. Screaming enemy soldiers were everywhere, firing at anything that moved. Master Sergeant Joseph Dick rescued his wounded platoon leader and led a counterattack back up the hill. Dick fired his rifle until it ran out of ammunition, threw it aside, and picked up an enemy weapon. He emptied it and then picked up another. He kept fighting in spite of a nasty-looking bullet wound. His men swarmed into their old positions.

Some of the enemy soldiers stumbled into the regimental intelligence and reconnaissance (I & R) platoon late in the evening of the fourteenth and early in the morning of the fifteenth. Sergeant Bill Strobridge, a reconnaissance squad leader, was busy trying to keep warm during the frigid night when he noticed shooting in the distance. "Tracers and WP [white phosphorous] were seen flying wildly around the valley . . . some two thousand yards away." He and his men learned from division headquarters about the North Korean marauders. They were even attacking headquarters. "In the growing light the tracers became amber streaks as they again began arching into the hill across the road." Strobridge and his men stayed very alert. Their job was to protect regimental headquarters, a task they often carried out, but it took on a greater sense of urgency and immediacy on this night.

Strobridge did not feel the least sense of panic at the close proximity of enemy troops, somewhere out there in the darkness, among the ridges and hills. He had already been through the Chosin ordeal and had led many perilous reconnaissance patrols during this drive to the Han

River. In truth, he thrived on this. From the earliest age, all he ever wanted to be was a soldier. Strobridge came from a farm in New Hampshire. His family had deep roots in New England, tracing back to the seventeenth century. In 1947, when he turned eighteen, he joined the Army, and he served for three years as a recon trooper with the 25th Infantry Division. He reenlisted in 1950 and was transferred to the 7th Infantry, this time as a recon squad leader, a perfect assignment since Strobridge was a born scout.

On this freezing Korean night, Strobridge kept a keen watch and made sure his men did too. As dawn approached, he saw something. "Eight or nine figures appeared on the skyline across the road and halted about halfway down the slope." At first he thought these men were from a friendly patrol. Strobridge and the others watched them until they were out of sight. After sunrise his platoon leader, finding out about the strange patrol, ordered Strobridge's squad to investigate. They searched the area, at first found nothing, but then spotted two mysterious figures sleeping in a field just beyond a grave. Just as they moved closer for a better look, an enemy soldier appeared almost out of nowhere. "The enemy raised his hands and another pair of raised hands appeared from behind the grave." Strobridge leveled his rifle at them. "A third Communist lay moaning on the ground with a bleeding wound in the jaw. The weapons of the group, a Russian telephone, and a reel of wire lay on the ground."

A South Korean squad member questioned the prisoners and identified them as part of the 81st Regiment. Strobridge's squad found two other North Korean soldiers and turned them over to regimental headquarters. Those enemy troops who tried to evade surrender had little other recourse but to die. Trapped in small pockets within the 7th Infantry's area of operations, they ran into the killing firepower of American machine guns, tanks, and riflemen. Having suffered 1,000 killed and 418 captured, the 81st Regiment effectively ceased to exist. At most only 400 North Korean soldiers escaped to the north side of the Han.[37]

On the fifteenth, the final push to eliminate the enemy from the south side of the Han began. The Cottonbalers made good progress, but sometimes the American infantrymen ran into tough, stubborn groups of enemy troops, bound and determined to hang on to high ground. Sometimes the enemy cut off small numbers of American troops. This happened to Corporal Elmer Eugene Owen's platoon of L Company near the walled town of Kwangju. Owen was a twenty-year-old army reservist from Nebraska who had been called to the colors after the start of the war. He joined the 7th Regiment in February 1951 as an assistant machine gunner. He hated the extra burden of carrying the .30-caliber machine gun, in addition to his pack.

In the early-morning hours of the fifteenth his platoon overextended itself and was cut off. The men had no choice but to fight their way back to the rest of L Company. They mustered as much firepower as they could and shot their way out of the town. Then they had to cross a small open area "while being fired upon by small arms and machine gun fire. I had the machine gun, still on its tripod and with the belt of ammo in place, on my right shoulder with the can of ammo under my left arm. When it came my turn to dash across the open area, I got about three-fourths of the way across and I stepped on a rock under the snow and turned my ankle." He went down "like a hundred pound sack of potatoes!! Falling down probably saved my life, because a burst from their machine gun went just over my head as I fell." He made it to safety and hitched a ride from a tank to an aid station. His platoon ended up with one man wounded—a South Korean shot in the arm.[38]

The going was tougher for K Company the next clay. The Chinese still held a few small hills south of the Han, and they needed to be cleaned out as soon as possible so that supply columns could move along key roads leading to the river. The company received orders to take one such hill despite terrible conditions. Subzero temperatures had set in, and 40-mile-an-hour winds drove sheets of snow all over the place. The men had a tough time seeing anything beyond the range of three feet. Trucks dropped them off at the jump-off point, and the soldiers dutifully trooped up the hill, each trying to limit movement in an effort to stay warm.

The ominous tearing sounds of Chinese machine guns pierced the air. Enemy bullets stitched several men. Their blood spurted in random directions, smearing the snow and their uniforms alike. The Americans burrowed into the snow. Some of the drifts ran three feet deep. The cold moisture seeped deep into every nook and cranny of the soldiers' clothing and froze exposed skin, but it beat getting shot. As usual in this kind of deadly situation, no one wanted to move for fear of drawing enemy fire.

The commander of the lead platoon, Second Lieutenant Darwin Kyle, knew that such inactivity was not an option. His men had to move forward and take the hill or die. Kyle was a thirty-two-year-old World War II combat veteran from Charleston, West Virginia. He left the Army after that war but decided to reenlist two years later. He made sergeant and joined the 7th Regiment before it shipped out for Korea. He performed so well at Chosin that he earned a battlefield commission.

Now, as he watched bullets from Chinese machine guns punch odd-looking holes through the snow around his men, he knew what he had to do. He got up, walked up and down the line of prone soldiers, and slapped them on the back, urging them to get up and attack. Six more men were hit, quelling the spirit for any such attack, so Kyle took matters into his own hands. "[He] personally charged the emplacement," one of Kyle's squad leaders, Sergeant James Yeomans, recalled. "Why he wasn't hit I'll never know. The enemy was firing everything he had and it all seemed to be directed at Lieutenant Kyle. He threw a grenade into the position and then killed the occupants, three Chinese, when they came out of the hole. He then waved us forward and we killed six Chinese who were defending the gun. We began to move toward the objective but only had fifteen men left. The Chinese allowed us to pass through and then opened up on us from the rear. Lieutenant Kyle closed in among the enemy and led us in a savage bayonet attack. He killed four more Chinese in hand-to-hand combat. It was after this that a Chinese killed Lieutenant Kyle with point-blank submachine-gun fire from about ten yards." The fire ripped open Kyle's face and he dropped backward, dead before he hit the ground. Steam rose from his dead body. Yeomans and the other man killed the enemy submachine gunner and took the hill. The last vestiges of enemy resistance south of the Han collapsed. Kyle was later awarded the Medal of Honor.[39]

THE UN ADVANCE SLOWED DOWN a bit as American and South Korean soldiers neared the Han. The Allies needed time to prepare for what they thought would be a major river crossing and a bloody battle to retake Seoul. American soldiers set up outposts and strongpoints on the hills overlooking the river area. Most of the hills were about a mile or two from the river. Flat rice paddies bordered the Han. The 7th Infantry rotated on and off the line for most of the rest of February.

The hills afforded the men a panoramic view of the area. Corporal Owen quickly recovered from his sprained ankle and returned to L Company. He was promoted to first gunner when the old one transferred out of the unit. One day in late February, Owen watched a tank-reinforced American patrol duel with the Chinese and wrote to his parents about it: "We are on a hill and the hill levels out to rice paddies at the bottom. We can see the tanks in the patrol shooting up a storm now. The small arms fire, mostly automatic can be heard clearly. I just heard a Chinese 'burp gun' [submachine gun] open up an—explosion of a tank's 76mm cannon—and no more 'burp gun.' Chinese mortars are coming in around the tanks now. The tanks are safe from them because they won't penetrate the armor." Soon a flight of American planes swooped in: "The planes are strafing now. Boy do they get down there!! They all but go into the holes after the Chinese. They will run out of 50 cal. ammo in a minute and then start with their rockets. Pretty soon they will Napalm when their rockets are gone. Well, it is over now. Nothing but silent, smoking terrain."[40]

For several weeks the regiment remained in these positions. Patrols crossed the Han every night. Most did not run into the enemy, but some did, provoking little skirmishes. Ridgway was busy planning Operation Ripper, the Han crossing and liberation of Seoul. In early March he set this offensive in motion. The 7th Regiment had mostly a supporting role in this phase of the operation. They "feinted" toward the Han River in a deception exercise to distract the enemy from the real crossing being made by the 25th Infantry Division a few miles downriver.

In the middle of March the regiment began to take a more active role in Operation Ripper. The I & R Platoon crossed the Han River at 0630 on the morning of the fifteenth. As they boarded boats and paddled across the water, they did not know what kind of reception they would get. Their job was to move northwest as fast as they could and assess enemy strength on Hill 348, a key piece of high ground that dominated Seoul. If the Americans could control this strategic hill, they could probably control Seoul.

Because of this tactical fact, the 7th Regiment's new commander, Colonel James Boswell, expected a tough fight for Hill 348. Boswell had assumed command after the Chasin campaign when Guthrie was promoted to brigadier general and transferred to a job at X Corps. Boswell was a forty-year-old army brat and West Pointer who had found time, before World War II, to earn a degree in Russian from Harvard. When war broke out, his language proficiency slotted him for a liaison job in the Soviet Union. In 1944 he wangled a transfer to the 90th Infantry Division, where he served as division intelligence officer. When the Korean War started, he was serving as Guthrie's executive officer, so he moved up to the top job when Guthrie left. Boswell was a fiery, profane commander who enjoyed immense popularity with the men.[41]

On the morning of March 15 he briefed the I & R Platoon leader, Lieutenant Malcolm Sussel (Sergeant Strobridge's boss): "I told [him] . . . to go over and, if he could, get on that mountain over there on the other side and stay there and let us know what the hell was coming off and I'd tell him when to come back. Well, they got over there and they didn't hit anything at all. They got on top of the goddamned mountain." Sussel radioed Boswell and asked if he and his men should come back. "I said, 'Hell, no. You stay there.' He says, 'Overnight?' and I said, 'You're goddamned right, overnight.' We made a river crossing practically unopposed the next day."[42] Recon Sergeant Strobridge wrote later about the giddy experience of capturing the hill so easily: "Startled enemy soldiers left their warm food and scurried away at the approach of confident-looking Cottonbalers."[43]

The communists had decided not to fight for Seoul. They retreated north toward the 38th parallel. The Americans and South Koreans liberated the capital, never to relinquish it again. The 7th Regiment trucked to an assembly area northeast of Seoul and spent the next ten days in reserve. Using Uijongbu as a jump-off point, the Cottonbalers left their reserve positions and continued the advance north in late March.

Generals and policy makers were debating whether to cross the 38th parallel again. MacArthur wanted to do it. He wanted to unleash an all-out invasion of North Korea, and of China too if necessary, and crush communism in Asia. Truman disagreed. He did not want to risk another disaster in North Korea, or World War III for that matter. He wanted to wind this war down, achieve the limited goal of maintaining South Korea's sovereignty, and rebuild America's conventional forces for renewed commitments around the globe.

This dramatic disagreement between America's leading general and its president was playing out in Tokyo and Washington as the Cottonbalers fought their way north with the goal of reaching the Imjin and Hantan rivers some thirty miles north of Seoul. Once again, the terrain was rugged, honeycombed with steep hills and ridges from which the enemy could pick and choose where to defend in strength.

On March 30, the enemy held up the Cottonbalers at a couple of such hills. One of them was Hill 347 in the 3rd Battalion's area of responsibility on the left (west) flank. Corporal Owen set up his machine gun and covered his L Company riflemen as they approached the hill. "About the time they reached the ridge Chinese mortars dropped in on the squads and badly wounded one man. The squads pulled out but the platoon medic stayed out with the wounded man while mortars kept coming in. He was being fired upon by snipers also. He would carry the wounded man a ways then put him down and run up to a Chink hole, shoot the hell out of it, then go back and pick up the wounded man again." Later the company tried again to take the hill. "We got fired on before we even reached the spot where we were to stay. We opened up with the machine-gun and covered the withdrawal of the rifle squads. We got tank and half-track mounted 40mm and 50 cal. support and assaulted the hill. We made it to the top, but didn't have the ammo to stay so we withdrew. No one [was] injured. We estimated about a dozen Chinese were killed."

That night the Chinese counterattacked. "We went around and around for close to an hour. They had a BAR which really raised hell with us. If he had fired six inches higher he might have done some good. As it was he just gave his position away by his muzzle blast. I cut loose on him and I guess I got him. We didn't find his body but there was plenty of blood all over. We only had two men slightly wounded in the action. Two Chinks were hit in their grenade pouches which they carry on their hip. The grenades exploded and blew half of their hip off. The next day we took [the] mountain." Once again, the Chinese had bugged out.[44]

For the first ten days of April the Cottonbalers pushed north against almost no resistance to the Imjin River and dug defensive lines that became known as Phase Line Utah and Phase Line Kansas. The outfit received replacements. "[They] started flowing in from reserve officers and NCOs and individual drafted soldiers—many from Hawaii," Captain Long later wrote. "These were welcome assets and they caught the spirit of the 7th and soon were professionals along with the veterans. The Korean fillers, who were an apparent rather than a real strength, were reassigned to Korean units." Most of the Americans were happy to see them go. Under Boswell's able leadership the 7th Regiment had once again become one of the best units in the U.S. Army. Indeed, Clay Blair later wrote that the 7th "became the workhorse regiment of the 3d Division, standing above the others in aggressiveness and dependability."[45]

TRUMAN SHOCKED THE COUNTRY ON the eleventh of April. He relieved MacArthur for insubordination because the general had publicly spoken out against the administration's containment and limited-war policy and, worse, had defied the commander in chief by sending troops across the 38th parallel. Ridgway now took overall command. The Cottonbalers heard this news as they left frontline positions and trucked to the rear for a stint in divisional reserve. The war now entered a new phase. In essence, Truman's firing of MacArthur meant a halt in place while the president waited for the communists to make the next move.

They did so in late April. For more than two weeks the Americans had been expecting an enemy offensive. They could feel it, sense it, perhaps even smell it. The drive to the 38th parallel, like the invasion of North Korea the previous year, had been just a little too easy. The UN commanders understood this. They knew full well that the communists still had plenty of fighting power and plenty of manpower husbanded in the hills and valleys above the 38th parallel. They would come out to fight again, and, according to intelligence reports, that would happen soon.

On April 22 the Chinese and North Koreans finally set their soldiers in motion. Their strategy, as usual, was to overwhelm the Allies with mass manpower, force a retreat, maybe annihilate an American unit here and there, before pushing on Seoul, which they hoped to capture in time for May 1, the great communist holiday. At 2200 hours on the twenty-second they unleashed a massive artillery barrage on UN positions. Two hours later the mass waves of enemy soldiers moved forward under the light of a favorable moon.

They put tremendous pressure on the outposts and forward positions of the 3rd Division and its Allied components—British, Belgians, Turks, and Filipinos. The UN soldiers grudgingly gave ground (roughly about ten miles over the course of the night), but many of them, including the British and Belgians, were in serious danger of being cut off and destroyed.

As this crisis took shape, the Cottonbalers were in reserve, preparing to go into the lines. Colonel Boswell ordered the 2nd and 3rd Battalions to occupy hilltop positions overlooking the approaches to the Hantan River and also the main supply road south to Uijongbu and Seoul. He gave the 1st Battalion, under the command of a rising star, thirty-four-year-old Lieutenant Colonel Frederick Weyand, the perilous mission of extracting the Belgians and British from their terrible predicament. Weyand's vigorous combat leadership had made the 1st into the kind of formidable fighting force that could pull off such a mission. The future army chief of staff trucked his battalion to an assembly area and attacked immediately northwest, into the teeth of two Chinese regiments, late in the morning on April 23.

At the suggestion of Captain Long, his operations officer, Weyand geared his attack for the capture of Hill 257, a piece of high ground overlooking the Imjin River at one of its northward bends. The Belgians were on the other side of the river, trapped unless the Cottonbalers could rescue them by drawing off enough Chinese soldiers.

Supported by British tanks, the Americans attacked. "From early morning the 1st Battalion . . . engaged in seeking out and destroying pockets of the enemy which had broken through friendly lines," First Lieutenant John Middlemas, the weapons platoon leader of A Company, remembered. "It [was] a long hard day of fierce combat." The Allied soldiers systematically leapfrogged forward from knoll to knoll, ridge to ridge, crossroads to crossroads. If the enemy opened fire, the tanks swung their barrels in their direction and blasted them. Then the infantry closed in and shot up anyone who moved. The bloody, smoking carcasses of Chinese soldiers bore mute testimony to the effectiveness of Weyand's attack.

With Hill 257 secured, the UN troops now sought to hold out long enough for the Belgians to escape. They succeeded, but even Middlemas and the others could not see the Belgians filtering back across the river. "The distraction allowed our Belgian friends to side slip, and an orderly withdrawal with full equipment, vehicles and supplies took place."[46]

Most British units south of the Imjin were hard-pressed but not in imminent danger of extinction. The same could not be said for one of their battalions, the Gloucesters ("Glosters"), on the western flank. The men of this unit were surrounded and in seriously bad shape by the afternoon of the twenty-third. They fought off attack after attack, but their demise was only a matter of time. A task force of 3rd Division and Filipino soldiers failed to save them, essentially guaranteeing the Gloucesters' annihilation. But a few of the Gloucesters did escape, thanks to the efforts of Sergeant Strobridge's I & R Platoon.

As was customary, the I & R Platoon was screening the movement of the 1st Battalion. The recon men acted as a kind of early-warning system for the battalion. They gathered information on enemy whereabouts and intentions. In doing so, they hoped to avoid an out-and-out fight, because they would almost certainly be outgunned and outnumbered. But if need be, they all knew that they would have to act as sacrificial lambs to protect the larger body of men who made up the battalion.

In the early afternoon of the twenty-third, Strobridge's men were riding west in their jeeps when the Chinese spotted them and opened up with mortars and artillery. The Americans jumped out of their vehicles and took cover. The enemy troops were under cover on a series of nearby hills. Strobridge told his men to get back in their vehicles and spread out into fighting formations. In a flurry of motion, he was all over the place—kicking butts, directing fire, straining his eyes for any sign of the British. Chinese mortar rounds exploded everywhere. Enemy machine-gun and rifle fire echoed all around the area. Strobridge took control of a .30-caliber machine gun mounted on the back of a jeep and opened fire. He and the other men could actually see a small group of desperate British soldiers attempting to escape the Chinese.

The Americans poured as much fire into the Chinese-held positions as they could. Corporal Don Grant, Strobridge's radio operator, shook his head in disbelief at the bravado of his sergeant. It seemed impossible that he had not been hit. "I can still see you . . . directing fire on the hill as the Glouchesters [sic] were trying to come down with the Chinese right on their heels," Grant later wrote to Strobridge. "I also remember somebody hollering at you to get your ass down, and you replied that the Chinese were the worst marksmen in the world and couldn't hit the broad side of a barn and you continued to stand totally exposed and ordered us to open fire at that hill." An entire platoon of Gloucesters made it out, and the tiny force of escaped British troops and American recon soldiers quickly vacated the area.[47]

The rest of the battalion followed suit, initiating the frightening maneuver of withdrawing in the face of an attacking enemy who possessed a huge edge in numbers. "At some point around midnight the 1st Battalion began its disengagement, with Chinese on three sides," First Lieutenant Middlemas later wrote: "It was a most interesting period. Total darkness made it almost impossible to tell whether the fellow next to you was an American or a Chinese. At one point a squad of Chinese almost joined Company 'A'; however after a short firefight they faded into the darkness."[48]

The 1st Battalion made it back to the Kansas Line, where the rest of the regiment had occupied their hilltop positions north of Uijongbu. Weyand's men quickly hunkered down on the right of the regimental line between the 3rd Battalion on the left and the 2nd Battalion on the right. The Cottonbalers had now assumed the role of holding off the Chinese onslaught (probably about ninety thousand strong) while the rest of the division retreated south to prepared positions just north of Seoul.

Like coastal residents boarding up for a fast-approaching hurricane, they spent the daylight hours of the twenty-fourth preparing for the imminent Chinese attack. The Cottonbalers dug deeper and better positions along their improvised line of hills. Officers and sergeants set up effective fields of fire for their machine guns. The spring air crackled with tension. Most of the men dreaded what they knew was coming and wished they were somewhere else, but they knew they had no choice but to hold fast.

On the night of April 24-25, the entire brunt of the CCF offensive hit the 7th Infantry. The attacks began at 2000 hours. All along the line they came in droves. On the left (west) flank they hit the 2nd Battalion with incredible ferocity and determination. Out of the shadows of the night thousands of Chinese soldiers resolutely strode forward, to the accompaniment of shouts and bugle calls. In the weird half-light of flares, the scraggly, barren hills seemed to be moving, literally crawling with enemy soldiers. Many of the 2nd Battalion men had been fighting hard for over two days, repelling such human-wave attacks. They were tired, hungry, dirty, and terrified at the sight before them, but they had no choice but to stay put and fight. "About an hour after dark we heard a burp gun fire," Sergeant Edward Bunn of I Company later wrote, "followed by the detonation of several large hand grenades, we called potato mashers. [An] ROK soldier with me drew up in a knot and I couldn't even get him to look up. It was as if he was dead."[49]

The Americans opened fire. Red tracers from their machine guns streaked through the night. Explosions, rifle shots, and the rhythmic cadence of machine guns filled the air with a wall of sound. Chinese soldiers went down in mass groups, almost like bloody rag dolls, their bodies full of holes or torn apart by machine-gun bullets. The Americans chucked grenades in huge numbers, creating the effect of a wall of shrapnel in front of them. Then artillery started coming in, landing immediately ahead of the American hilltop positions, so close the American soldiers nearly found themselves blinded by the flashes and explosions of "friendly" shells.

Somewhere out in front of the main positions, Private Louis Gaybrant of Newark, New Jersey, lay in a foxhole, braving those shells and enemy soldiers too. Gaybrant was spotting targets for a machine gun one hundred yards behind him, along the main line of resistance. Gaybrant's eyes darted from side to side. The Chinese were all around him, but they seemed to have no idea of his presence. He bellowed instructions into his radio: "Shoot three yards to my right! There's fifteen Reds there." The machine gun dutifully responded, killing and wounding most of the enemy troops.

Gaybrant peeked out of his hole and saw a company-sized group of Chinese heading straight for his position. He knew he was dead if he did not take drastic action. He stood up and yelled, "As soon as I shut up, shoot over my head. It looks like the whole Chinese Army is coming." The Chinese company was walking right into the deadliest part of the American machine gun's kill zone. Thirty-caliber bullets caught them flush in the face, the chest, the hands, and the throat. They fell backward and screamed in agony. Others turned and ran away. A few dived to the dirt and tried to crawl forward, but the machine gun's fire soon hit them too. The attack was repulsed.[50]

But the enemy came back, in even greater numbers, screaming, "Kill Americans! Damn GI!," firing their burp guns from the hip, throwing their stick grenades. They pressed along the left flank of the battalion, but American firepower made mincemeat out of them. Plenty of Americans were getting killed and wounded, though. In distressingly large numbers, GIs fell with shrapnel and bullet wounds. Some of them died instantly, their eyes wide open, with surprised looks on their faces. Others wailed in pain. The cry of "Medic!" rose above the din of battle. Somehow the line held. The Chinese seemed to have a terrifying lack of concern for American firepower. They just kept coming. The Americans would shoot down one squad of enemy troops, only to see two or three more take its place. The enemy seemed to have an inexhaustible number of soldiers. At some point they had to run out, didn't they? The whole scene did not seem real; it seemed like something out of a nightmare.

All night long they kept attacking, weakening the 2nd Battalion front-line positions. Heavy machine-gun crews were down to two or three men; the same went for mortar crews. Rifle squads were operating at half strength. The Americans had fought hard, but they could not hold out much longer.

At 0050 hours, after a brief lull in the fighting, the enemy massed fifteen hundred soldiers and charged at the Americans again. This time, the Chinese found a gap in the line between E and G Companies. The battle became a free-for-all. The closer the Chinese could get to the American positions, the more they could negate the advantage of American firepower. They knew it, and the Cottonbalers knew it too.

At one section of the line an H Company machine-gun squad leader named Corporal Hiroshi Miyamura watched as the enemy inexorably moved closer, almost by the second. Born in 1925, Miyamura was the son of Japanese immigrants who settled in Gallup, New Mexico, and became restaurateurs. He graduated from high school in 1943 and learned from his brother how to become an auto mechanic. Miyamura's family was fortunate. They escaped the infamous U.S. government relocation policy for Japanese-Americans because the town of Gallup simply refused to comply with the government edict.

In 1944 he was drafted and ended up serving in the famous Japanese-American 442nd Infantry Regiment, the most decorated army regiment in World War II. He saw no combat, though, because he joined the unit in the spring of 1945 after the fighting was over. After the war he signed up for the reserves but eventually returned to his auto mechanic job in Gallup. Then he grew bored with the job and the town. Part of him was glad he had not seen combat in World War II, and part of him regretted it. He decided that he had not gotten the Army out of his system. He still hankered to serve. So in June 1949 he reenlisted in the reserves, over the strenuous objections of his parents, with the understanding that he would eventually be called to active duty. That call came in August 1950. He was assigned to the 7th Infantry Regiment and served as a heavy machine gunner with the unit in the battles of 1950–51.

Now, in the early-morning hours of April 25, here he was sitting in a gun pit on a barren Korean hill, overlooking a small road, watching in horror, along with his gun crew, as hundreds of enemy soldiers approached the hill. "After I heard the bugles and saw a flare or two going off, that's when the firing commenced. I was positioned between two other machine gunners, I had two cases of grenades, an M-1, a Carbine and a pistol." He directed fire, pitched grenades, and fired his rifle at the slew of targets. "I don't recall how long the guns were firing, but pretty soon, the first gunner came by and said it was getting 'too hot.'"

The Chinese were swarming up the hill and behind Miyamura's position. His squad members wanted to get out before they were killed or captured. Everyone, except Miyamura, was in a state of panic and wild-eyed terror. He wondered why the squad's air-cooled machine gun (a "light" .30-caliber machine designed to be carried and fired by two men) had fallen silent. Miyamura made his way over there. Along the way he shot and bayoneted several enemy soldiers who had infiltrated the American positions. Inevitably, their blood splattered on his uniform and rifle. When Miyamura reached the machine-gun position, the crew was gone. They must have bugged out or gotten word from a runner to withdraw. Miyamura decided to go back to his one remaining machine gun, the heavy on the right.

In a low crawl, almost half-squat position, he hurried to the heavy machine gun. Suddenly he stumbled over something and fell on his face. Stunned, he looked to see what had tripped him; it was the body of the runner. The runner had told the light-machine-gun crew to withdraw but had been killed on his way to give Miyamura and the heavy crew the same message.

A few minutes later, Miyamura reached the heavy machine gun and found two of his men bleeding badly from shrapnel wounds. He bandaged their wounds while the two remaining able-bodied men kept the enemy at bay with a steady stream of fire. When Miyamura finished attending to his wounded men, he glanced down the hill in the direction of the enemy. He noticed a small group of Chinese silently moving up the slope of the hill, obviously hoping to surprise and kill the stranded group of Americans.

Miyamura grabbed his bayonet-mounted Carbine and slid down the hill, right at the approaching enemy! The young Nisei achieved complete surprise. He shot and slashed at the enemy troops. At close range, his bullets blasted huge holes in them and even left powder burns. He stabbed at anything that moved, opening huge gashes in their throats, their stomachs, and their sides. Some of them tried to duck away, but he found them and killed them. Their screams gurgled in the night. The whole scene was primal, like something out of ancient warfare.

When Miyamura's grisly job was done, he clambered back up the slope. In spite of his recent victory in hand-to-hand combat, he could tell that it hardly had any effect on the tactical situation. The Chinese were everywhere—on the flanks, in front of them, even behind them. He knew that his men could not stay there much longer and hope to survive. He turned to them and said, "Take off. I'll cover you." They stared at him in disbelief. The man had just single-handedly killed ten Chinese soldiers in hand-to-hand combat. Now he proposed to take on the full weight of their attack, all alone. Even he could not expect to survive in such a hopeless situation. He repeated his order. They didn't have to be told twice.

Reflecting fifty years later on the magnitude of what he did, Miyamura still could not explain what motivated him to sacrifice his life for his men. "I still don't know why I did that." Most likely he had already written off any chance of personal survival. An excellent and courageous leader, he probably worried at that moment more about the welfare of his men than his own. He manned the heavy machine gun alone and kept firing until he exhausted its ammo. Then he fought with small arms. "I just fired and threw [grenades] all that I could. Our mortars started dropping phosphorous shells on our position. That woke me up to the thought I've got to get out of here."

He had spent the whole night fighting for the lives of his men. Now he was finally fighting for his own life. He destroyed the machine gun with a grenade and made his way down the crude trench position. All of a sudden, he collided with an enemy soldier. Both of them were shocked. For a split second each tried to regain his senses and kill the other. Miyamura was quicker. He shot the Chinese soldier. The man recoiled and fell against the wall of the trench. He was still alive, though, and threw a grenade at Miyamura. The corporal kicked the grenade back, soccer style. It exploded, killing the Chinese soldier and wounding Miyamura in the shin.

Miyamura painfully negotiated his way down the south side of the hill and spotted an American tank in the distance. Fixated on the tank, waving and screaming for help, he ran straight into a long strand of US. barbed wire. "Once I got to the base of the hill, I got caught up in our own barbed wire entanglement. I didn't know it was set up down there. I wanted to get on the other side of the wire so I could get his attention and get out of there, but he didn't see me."

By the time he made it under the wire, the tank was long gone. Exhausted and bleeding now from the shrapnel and many barbed-wire puncture wounds, he collapsed into slumber in a ditch and lay there until after dawn. "I heard troops going by my position. I was lying face down, but I didn't move because I didn't know if they were the enemy or ours. I heard the noise die down, and then thought I was safe but before I even moved I heard a voice in English saying, 'Get up, you're my prisoner. Don't worry, we have a lenient policy. We won't harm you.'" It was a Chinese soldier brandishing an American .45-caliber pistol.

Thus began a two-and-a-half-year ordeal as a prisoner of the Chinese. Miyamura lost over fifty pounds and endured all sorts of propaganda and "brainwashing" mind games before being repatriated in August 1953. "I didn't want to think about what was happening. I wanted to concentrate on raising a family once I got home. I think that's what kept me going." Upon repatriation, Miyamura received the Medal of Honor for his actions on April 24–25. The citation was prepared in secret and only awarded when Miyamura's freedom was guaranteed. The Army feared that if the Chinese had found out how many of their soldiers Miyamura had killed (probably anywhere between sixty and one hundred), they would exact terrible revenge. Returning home to Gallup, Miyamura made good on his dream of raising a family. He had three children, parlayed his mechanic's expertise into ownership of a service station, and retired to pursue his true passion—fishing.[51]

As Miyamura's experiences indicated, the 2nd Battalion front was collapsing under the sheer weight of enemy numbers. Another H Company man, Private First Class James Cart, was serving as a mortar gunner a couple hundred yards behind Miyamura's forward positions. "We could hear all the gunfire to our front, but nobody called in the mortars. One of the men from a line company ran into our perimeter. He told us the Chinks had overrun his position and that they were heading in our direction. My platoon sergeant told me to pick up the mortar base plate and head back for the hills to our rear. It would only be a matter of minutes before the Chinks had us surrounded." He lugged the baseplate and his personal gear, including a rifle, canteen belt, bandoliers, and mess kit. "I . . . ran as best I could into the night and headed for the hills." He and the others simply kept walking, mile after mile, almost all the way to the northern outskirts of Seoul.[52]

Like seeds in the wind, the 2nd Battalion had been scattered in every direction by the Chinese onslaught. Colonel Boswell spent much of April 25 putting the pieces of the battalion back together. The unit had not been annihilated, but it certainly was disorganized and combat ineffective.

In the meantime, several hundred yards to the east, the other two battalions of the 7th were also fighting ferociously, strung out on a succession of hills and outposts. The Chinese sent human-wave attacks against these Cottonbalers all night as well. The 1st Battalion's B Company anchored the extreme eastern side of the line. The men of this rifle company, augmented by machine gunners, dug into a wooded ridge and fought like demons during the early-morning hours of the twenty-fifth. The Chinese threw an entire regiment at the battalion, and the brunt of their attack hit B Company.

The fighting here was similar to what Miyamura and his buddies experienced. The Americans opened fire with every weapon at their disposal and killed or wounded untold numbers of Chinese troops, but still the enemy kept coming. Their screams and bugle calls echoed through the night, and the muzzle flashes of their burp guns flickered like overgrown fireflies.

Somewhere near the left flank of B Company's positions, a twenty-one-year-old machine gunner, Corporal Clair Goodblood, fired his weapon in short, accurate bursts. Born and raised in Fort Kent, Maine, Goodblood came from a New England farm family with deep roots in that region. The oldest of eleven children, Goodblood enlisted in the Army upon graduation from high school in 1947. He was looking for adventure, and he more than found it on a Korean hillside in the spring of 1951.

Corporal Goodblood and his loader fired belt after belt at the approaching enemy. In the brief glimpses afforded by the muzzle flashes of his gun, Goodblood could see the Chinese staggering under the weight of his bullets. But he couldn't hit all of them. There were just too many. In a matter of a few minutes they enveloped his position. Enemy fire swept into several Americans on either side of Goodblood. The corporal and his assistant were confronted with the most frightening choice a soldier could make—leave or die. Goodblood chose to stay. He and his assistant poured cover fire while the other Americans retreated.

Out of the darkness a Chinese stick grenade flew, end over end, right at them. Goodblood shoved his assistant down to the ground and draped himself over the man in an effort to shield him. The grenade exploded, wounding both of them. The corporal grabbed an ammo bearer and told him to evacuate his assistant gunner. When the two were gone, Goodblood remained behind. He manned the gun himself and shot down several more rows of Chinese. Finally, they overwhelmed him.

Lieutenant Middlemas was only yards away when this happened. "Our 57mm rifle was in action until it ran out of ammunition, and then [we] used [it] as a club."

The desperate courage of Middlemas, Goodblood, and several others whose names are not known broke the momentum of the enemy attack, allowing B Company commander Captain Ray Blandin to organize a successful counterattack. Just after daylight the Americans came back to Goodblood's position and found his lifeless body lying beside the machine gun. He had fired eleven boxes of ammunition (2,750 rounds); the Chinese were only able to kill him when he ran out of ammo. More than one hundred enemy bodies were strewn in grotesque positions within the gun's field of fire. Goodblood was posthumously awarded the Medal of Honor.[53]

By daylight, the Chinese were still pressing, but more gingerly than before. The 7th Infantry, at great cost, had fulfilled the mission of slowing them down while Allied units set up new positions north of Seoul. Now it was time for the remnants of those who had fought all night to escape. Boswell ordered Weyand to cover the withdrawal of the 3rd Battalion and then retreat with his own battalion. Over the course of several tortuous hours during the late morning and early afternoon of the twenty-fifth, Weyand skillfully extricated the two battered battalions with the help of fine junior officers such as Middlemas and First Lieutenant Harley Mooney.

The biggest scare came around noon when the Chinese attacked a small outpost on Hill 283, a position that cemented A and B Companies together. If the Chinese broke through, they could infiltrate between the two companies and menace the 3rd Battalion, which was in the process of slowly shuffling its way south on a trail. A series of hills and ridges, protected by 283, overlooked the trail. Any Chinese on that high ground could shoot down on the 3rd Battalion soldiers like the proverbial "fish in a barrel."

Lieutenant Middlemas was in the middle of a phone conversation with Lieutenant Mooney when he heard scattered shooting coming from 283. A couple minutes later, the sergeant in charge of the outpost materialized with a panicked look on his face. "They're coming! They're coming! Millions of them!" Knowing the corrosive effect such panic could have on the men, Middlemas sprinted at the sergeant and knocked him down with a perfect football tackle. The lieutenant noticed that the other four men from the outpost were following the sergeant like "goslings follow after a mother goose." Middlemas knew that if he did not take strong action, the entire company front could collapse. He screamed and pounded men on their helmets. "Get the hell back in your positions! Get up on that damned hill!"

The rallying worked. As if snapped out of a trance, the panicky soldiers changed direction and followed Middlemas up the hill. Others laid down cover fire for them. Middlemas led a ragtag band of about fifteen men back up the hill and fought with a similar-sized group of Chinese at close range. They blasted at the enemy with their rifles. Other Americans soon converged on the hill. The combined firepower of all these Cottonbalers—men from A, B, and D Companies—forced the Chinese away from the hill. The mood of the men had changed entirely from panic a few minutes before to bravado now. Many of them were screaming at the Chinese, "Come and get it!"

While Middlemas held off the Chinese on Hill 283, Mooney hurried the 3rd Battalion men along the trail. Many of them had taken cover at the sound of the firefight on 283. Mooney made his way along the trail until he found one of their officers squatting alongside his men. "For Christ's sake, get up and get these men moving." As quickly as their weary legs permitted, the 3rd Battalion soldiers got off their butts and moved back down the trail to safety.

The 3rd Battalion successfully escaped, and now it was the 1st Battalion's turn. To do so, they needed something to keep the Chinese at bay. That something was artillery. Lieutenant Colonel Weyand had taken the time to study practically every inch of the terrain. He called in astonishingly accurate artillery support, while the men under Mooney and Middlemas slowly withdrew. Then, when the artillerymen began running out of shells, Weyand called in an accurate air strike.[54]

The fire support did the job of extricating the 1st Battalion. By early afternoon the two hard-pressed battalions of the 7th Infantry were retreating steadily south, in orderly fashion, toward prepared positions north of Seoul. The same could not be said for the 2nd Battalion, which was still little more than a disorganized mob. Perhaps the junior officer leadership in this battalion was not quite as strong as the other two. The Chinese ambushed Sergeant Hubenette's F Company as its remnants retreated down the Uijongbu-Seoul road. "An officer yelled, 'Pull out! Get out! Every man for himself!' We panicked and bugged out. The new kids just ran, and we older guys couldn't get a hold of anything to slow it down." Hubenette ran along a rice paddy dike and nearly fell into the paddy when another soldier cut in front of him. He yelled at the man just as an enemy mortar shell exploded between them. "The concussion knocked me down and over. I heard [him] scream, then I blacked out. When I came to, someone was kneeling by me yelling that I should get up and follow him. I recognized the voice of Sergeant Davidson. I was blind and couldn't stand. My sight came back."

He saw a lieutenant helping men along a trail. "My head spun like a top, and the trail went from color to black-and-white to color, then faded in and out. There was a buzzing inside my head. I staggered down a slope and ran into a truck convoy." A machine gun opened up and someone picked him up and threw him in a truck. "A great inner rage began to consume me. If I could ever find that officer who'd yelled, 'Every man for himself,' I'd kill him. I knew enough not to get men running like a crazed mob. That man had screwed up and gotten good men killed." Hubenette's concussion led to battle fatigue. He never returned to combat.[55]

The 8th Army was able to stabilize its front five miles north of Seoul along a series of positions known as the Lincoln Line. The communists had succeeded in recapturing thirty-five miles of western Korean territory, but they did not get into Seoul. The 7th Infantry went into reserve, acting as a kind of fire brigade in case the enemy unleashed another offensive in the area. The fighting between April 22 and 25 proved to be some of the fiercest of the war for the Cottonbalers. Their discipline and determination held off, at the very least, twenty thousand Chinese attackers. A lesser formation might have been engulfed and annihilated, but the 7th managed to escape, bloodied but intact. Weyand's 1st Battalion alone was credited with killing three thousand enemy troops and wounding fifty-five hundred others. He and his men earned a Presidential Unit Citation for their part in the battle.[56]

FOR ROUGHLY THREE WEEKS IN May the Cottonbalers busied themselves patrolling a sector adjacent to the 25th Infantry Division, in addition to serving as the mobile reserve force for the entire 8th Army. The generals were worried that the Chinese would redouble their efforts to take Seoul, and they needed plenty of "fire brigades" in case of such a crisis. Losing the South Korean capital again was out of the question. However, the new attack came not in the west near Seoul but in the eastern half of the peninsula. In the middle of May a total of twenty enemy divisions crashed into the X Corps, consisting of four ROK divisions, the U.S. 2nd Infantry Division, and the 1st Marine Division. The corps gave way, and the UN forces were soon in full retreat through this especially hilly section of Korea.

Ridgway needed to reinforce the hard-pressed X Corps. Once he determined that no attack on Seoul was imminent, he ordered the 3rd Division to board trucks and ride east. On the morning of May 19 the Cottonbalers rode all day. By evening the Cottonbalers had de-trucked, stretched their weary legs, and taken up positions in the hills just south of Soksa-ri. All around them they saw the trappings of defeat and retreat. "Along the roads and out of the hills emerged the remnants of the ROK division fleeing the Chinese," Captain Long recalled. The South Koreans looked haggard, wild-eyed, and dispirited. The roads were clogged with retreating soldiers and refugees. As always, the Americans had to worry about North Korean guerrillas infiltrating Allied lines by disguising themselves as refugees. The Americans searched many of the refugees, making sure to check for weapons beneath the ubiquitous white robes worn by most Koreans.

At 0600 hours on May 20 the regiment began a series of attacks that lasted for one week. The presence of the Cottonbalers stunned the advancing enemy troops. The 7th Infantry, usually supported by tanks, advanced from hill to hill, deep into the mountains, traveling on narrow trails, fighting platoon-and company-sized groups of communist troops. The Cottonbalers steadily pushed the enemy north, where paratroopers from the 187th Airborne Brigade waited to destroy them. On May 25, the 7th captured a key mountain pass northwest of Soksa-ri, effectively dooming the enemy forces in the area; the pass served as their supply artery.[57]

Hence, the maneuver worked very well, although it was not easy. More than anything, supply was a problem, not surprising considering that the 7th was fighting far away from its logistical base and in remote terrain. At one point Sergeant Owen's 3rd Battalion had to be resupplied by air. "The country in Eastern Korea is nothing but hills!" he wrote to his family. "Big Ones!! Not many roads in those hills either. They had to supply us by air while we were on the attack over there. Early one morning the transports came over and dropped ammo, water and rations for us. Quite a sight!"[58]

Owen and the other hungry Cottonbalers enthusiastically dug into their C rations. These prepackaged rations significantly improved from the greasy, mealy versions, prevalent in World War II. The variety of meals had been greatly enhanced to include plenty of entrees. Soldiers could choose from beef stew, beans and weenies, pork and beans, chicken and vegetables, ham and lima beans (always referred to as "ham and motherfuckers"), corned beef hash, meat and noodles, spaghetti and meatballs, and sausage patties. The rations could be heated easily, giving at least the pretense of a nourishing hot meal. Plus, they came with cans of fruit, jam, and candy.[59]

By the end of May the enemy offensive in the east had been crushed. The communists had been cleared out of eastern Korea. They lost thousands of men, including many prisoners of war. Now the United Nations was preparing to launch a counteroffensive of its own. By then the Cottonbalers and the rest of the 3rd Division had trucked 190 miles west to their old sector and taken up positions northwest of Seoul.

The complexion of the war was changing. The Truman administration was now publicly committed to the possibility of armistice negotiations aimed at ending the war on the basis of the preservation of the status quo. This, of course, solidified what the relief of MacArthur had indicated, namely, that the Korean War was now a limited conflict being fought for limited objectives. That being the case, the Army now began to flirt with a rotation policy. Men who had served in Korea for at least six months could now look forward to the possibility of going home, provided new men replaced them. In reality, most men had to serve more than six months; most waited anywhere between two and three months for the word that they were going home. Not surprisingly, combat infantrymen grew obsessed with their prospects for rotation. The topic dominated Sergeant Owen's letters for weeks and ate away at his morale. "Rotation is going as slow as ever. There are still 54 old men left to be rotated before our group is to be rotated. Everyone is hoping that the next couple of shipments [of replacements] are big ones. Seems like all the men being rotated are coming from the rear areas while us guys up on line are getting the old purple shaft!"[60]

In spite of the limited nature of the war, 8th Army commander General James Van Fleet ordered an offensive, Operation Piledriver, to be launched on June 3. The plan called for UN forces, including the 3rd Division, to push north and capture a portion of North Korea called the Iron Triangle. Three cities formed the parameters of this triangle. Chorwon to the southwest, Kumhwa to the southeast, and, at the point in the north, Pyonggang (not to be confused with the North Korean capital of Pyongyang). Van Fleet thought that the costly Chinese offensive of April and May had weakened them so much that Piledriver would be nothing more than a veritable occupation of territory.

The attack proved to be tougher than that. On May 31 the 7th Infantry led the way for the 3rd Division by crossing the rain-swollen Hantan River and establishing a bridgehead on its north side. The infantrymen crossed on bridges built by the 10th Engineers. On the north side, heavy rains proved to be an even greater impediment than the enemy. This was the monsoon season; torrential rains swamped the entire area, turning roads and paddies into complete mud holes. The men found it impossible to stay clean and dry. Mud got into everything from food to throats.

The regiment established springboard positions. The men settled into the mud and waited for the word to attack. Some of them wondered if the offensive was necessary. Why fight for territory that would be given up at the peace table? Their opinions did not matter, though. They would follow orders, just as they always had before, regardless of their personal feelings.

On the evening of June 2 the word filtered down among the men: Piledriver was scheduled to begin the next morning at 0600. Sergeant Jack Sebzda was a mortar squad leader in G Company of the 2nd Battalion. That night he made his rounds, talking to his men, making sure they had enough of everything—equipment, ammo, weapons, food, and the like. He noticed that one of his eighteen-year-old replacements seemed extremely apprehensive.

Sebzda's conversation with the man, Private Tom Reed from Phoenix, Arizona, shed light on the changing composition of the regiment and the culture of mid-twentieth-century America. "He asked me if anyone would think he was 'chicken' if he went on sick call the next morning. I answered by explaining that if he was too sick to do his job, he would be of no use to the squad. Tom was nervous, so I sat and talked to him awhile. I asked him what was wrong, and he told me he suffered from asthma, and in times of stress he had great difficulty breathing. Of course, my next question was 'How did you ever get drafted into the Army?' He explained that where he came from, your skin color, rather than your physical condition, had a lot to do with whether you were drafted or not. Tom was . . . a black man."

In spite of his breathing troubles, Private Reed elected to stay with his squad. The soldiers moved out just after dawn. Rumors swirled about a "cakewalk." After all, their objective had been pummeled during the night with artillery and .50-caliber machine guns. For a time, the going was smooth. The men slushed their way through the muddy, mucky, foul-smelling paddies against no opposition.

Then, in an instant, everything changed. "A machine gun opened fire, catching us in a deadly ambush. Before we could move, Dave Rivers, a close friend who was standing near me, died with a bullet to the head. We scattered for cover and I heard several frantic calls for the medic. I . . . saw that Tom had been hit." The rest of the soldiers returned fire from behind the paddy dikes. The mortar squad ran, under cover fire, to firing positions. "In the meantime, Tom had been attended to and litter bearers, clearly marked with red crosses, attempted to carry him away. The enemy gunner, however, opened fire on them and Tom was killed. The enemy machine gun was quickly silenced but, sad to say, not fast enough to save Tom's life."

The Americans killed off the other enemy gunners and resumed their advance, but Sergeant Sebzda never quite forgot Tom Reed. One day, after the war, Sebzda was leafing through a magazine in his dentist's office when he saw a picture that stunned him. The photo showed the burial of Private Reed. Incredibly, the local veterans' cemetery (Greenwood Memorial Park) had initially refused to bury him because of a "no Negro" policy. The dead soldier's body rotted in a mortuary for six weeks until more intelligent heads prevailed and he was buried, with full military honors, in the cemetery. Sebzda tore the photo out of the magazine and kept it for fifty years. "I look at it once in awhile and remember Tom, the young soldier who never got a break from his local draft board, the merciless Chinese machinegunner, and the Greenwood Memorial Park—even after paying the supreme sacrifice."[61]

FOR OVER A WEEK THE Cottonbalers advanced inexorably northeast, in driving rain (eleven inches in eleven days), through paddies, up and over ridges, through thick woods, and straight up steep hills. As had been the case six months before, the Chinese resisted mightily in some places and not so mightily in others. The experiences of Sergeant First Class John Southern, a veteran professional soldier and platoon leader in the Battle Patrol, were fairly typical. Day and night his platoon advanced until it hit resistance, usually on good-sized hills.

One night they dug foxholes in front of one such hill and watched U.S. artillery bombard it for much of the night. In the morning, Southern received orders to capture the hill. "There was a heavy fog over the hill and surrounding terrain. We advanced up the steep slope to a point about 200 yards from the top when we received fire from two enemy machine guns and other small-arms. I had two men wounded. The rest of the platoon hit the ground." He tried to work men around the flanks, but all they did was slip and slide along the slopes of the hill. Then he called for mortar support. "The gunners tried it, but we were so close to the target area, they couldn't get in on it effectively." There was only one option left—a frontal assault. "We tried with two squads with a LMG in direct support. It was no good. I had more casualties and we fell back."

Southern radioed his captain and asked for artillery fire on the enemy machine-gun bunkers. The captain refused the request and told him to attack again. The sergeant ran around and tried to prod his men up the hill. Most of them would not budge. In the end, he only got six of them to go back up the hill. "We fixed bayonets and charged the hill screaming 'shaw-nee' (Chinese for 'kill with sharp knife'). The Chinks did a little shooting and abandoned their positions. The rest of the platoon came on up and we continued the assault. We took two more hill masses with only light resistance."

In this manner, the 7th Infantry fought its way to Chorwon, capturing it on June 12. By that time, the regiment had killed 692 Chinese, captured 134 others, and taken the division's major objective of Chorwon. The filthy, tired, wet Cottonbalers spent two weeks off the line, cleaning up, eating decent meals, and training for future operations.[62]

In late June the Cottonbalers went back to the front line, relieving the 15th Infantry at a line of fortifications known as Phase Line Wyoming. The two lower points of the triangle had been captured, and now the third, Pyonggang, needed to be taken. Two hills, 682 and 717, dominated access to the Pyonggang plain. For several days the 15th Infantry had fought and bled to take these hills, but without success. Now it was the Cottonbalers' turn.

The regiment's officers studied the terrain intently. Boswell arranged for as much artillery support as he could possibly access. He also coordinated with the Air Force for close air support. Some of the planes were supposed to drop bunker-busting two-thousand-pound bombs on Chinese positions along the reverse slope of each hill. Against the backdrop of these preparations, rumors circulated around headquarters and in the ranks about imminent armistice talks. There was a sense that this could be the last battle of the war. The commanders gave this attack a festive name—Operation Doughnut.

But for the infantrymen who did the fighting, the attack was anything but festive. Boswell assigned 682 to the 1st Battalion and 717 to the 3rd. They moved forward on the morning of July 1. Once the sun rose, shimmering waves of heat hung in hazy clumps just above the paddies. American artillery rounds pounded into the hills. Overhead, planes strafed and bombed. This support was terrific, but, as always, the operation's success depended on the infantry to gain and control ground.

When the Cottonbalers, spread out in cautious advancing formations, began to ascend Hills 682 and 717, the enemy let them have it. The Chinese had fortified the hills in such a way that their well-camouflaged bunkers enjoyed interlocking fields of fire. Enemy machine guns poured out an incredible volume of firepower. The Chinese rounds slapped into many of the attacking soldiers, producing an awful "thunk" sound as they broke bones or tore nerve and muscle tissue apart. The Cottonbalers took cover among the numerous dips, crags, and trees on the hill. These terrain features afforded decent protection for them, but the larger problem was that they had a difficult time spotting the location of Chinese bunkers. They were just too well dug-in and too well-hidden.

For hours the men of both battalions ponderously fought their way up portions of their hills. An advance of forty yards in one hour was good. The Americans operated with the usual fire and maneuver tactics. If anyone spotted a bunker, the soldiers put an enormous volume of machine-gun and rifle fire on it. Then someone would crawl up close and pitch grenades into the aperture. The Chinese fired back with everything they had. When the Americans closed in on them, they threw their stick grenades at the attackers. The experience was grueling and frightening. The men sweated like crazy. Most had emptied their canteens by noon.

Sergeant Owen's L Company was right in the thick of the fight for Hill 717. He and his machine-gun crew were struggling with exhaustion, trying to climb the hill and support the riflemen at the same time. He and the others ran into a hail of grenades and machine-gun fire. "I really think that if they had armed our platoon with ball bats, we would have been more successful. All we would have had to do would be knock the grenades back over the top of the hill to the Chinks that were throwing them. As it was, it was about like every big league pitcher in the business throwing strikes at you.

"I went up to the rifle squads with my machine gun section while my gun kept some other Chinks pinned down on a finger to our left." Chinese grenades flew everywhere. "Dorsey, 1st Squad Leader, got hit in the leg and hand by a grenade . . . but he got back up, grabbed his rifle and went back up the hill to his squad. He could hardly walk, but he was so damn mad he was going to do something! He personally cleaned the Chinks out of two holes before we were ordered to pull back." With an ominous thud an enemy grenade landed near Owen and exploded. A piece of shrapnel tore into his chest. "It didn't penetrate my chest cavity. Must have hit a rib and stopped."

Owen was quickly evacuated and taken to a hospital behind the lines. He recovered nicely. In fact, the doctors did not even see any need to remove the shrapnel. "I will be carrying the fragment, about the size of a quarter, around with me for the rest of my days. It lodged in my ribs, and would be more trouble to take . . . out than it would to leave it as it is."[63]

By 1700, after the rifle companies had spent the entire day fighting at close quarters with no major advances, Boswell knew he had to withdraw. He ordered his battalion commanders to consolidate their people into perimeters at the base of each hill. The Americans dug in, occupied old bunkers, and waited for the Chinese to counterattack.

That night they did so. They wanted to drive the Americans completely off the hills, and in pursuit of that goal, they unleashed their usual human-wave attacks. The fighting was harrowing, even desperate. American firepower chewed up the Chinese. Mortars, artillery, machine guns, recoilless rifles, grenades, BARs, rifles, and even pistols blazed through the night.

In a small foxhole at the base of Hill 682, a twenty-year-old rifleman, Private Paul Mentis, manned his position. To him, the Chinese looked like shadows in the night. He fired at whatever targets he could make out in between the flashes of explosions. Mentis was the son of a Greek immigrant who had left that country in 1916 in pursuit of a new life in Mount Vernon, Ohio. He met Mentis's mother, got married, and opened a Greek restaurant.

Young Paul was an excellent athlete, a quick, undersize fullback with toughness to burn. After high school he spent a year playing college ball at Southwest Missouri State College (now called Missouri State University) but dropped out to go home and work. He learned the draft board was about to snag him, so he enlisted in the Army in hopes of securing a noncombat job. The strategy failed. He ended up in the infantry and joined A Company, 1st Battalion, of the 7th Infantry as a replacement in April 1951.

Now, on a hot Korean summer night, he crouched in his hole and fought for his life. He could not believe how bold the enemy was in charging the American positions. "I really think they thought they were still attacking the 15th [Regiment] which had taken heavy casualties and was thin. The Chinese made three attacks, the first being very forceful, the second maybe achieving halfway up the hill, and the third they didn't have their heart in at all. They fired flares and bugles and so forth. You could see them coming across the valley. As soon as we recognized that they were coming, the field artillery began to unload on them right away. When they reached three or four hundred yards . . . that's when we started firing. Our automatic weapons were burning out a barrel every ten or fifteen minutes. You could see the tracers . . . start tumbling."

The Chinese could not make headway in such a firestorm. Their attacks lost momentum as so many of their troops died; the bugle calls went away, the screaming stopped, and those enemy soldiers who could still move retreated. In the flickering light of fires, Private Mentis gazed at the remnants of the enemy force. "They had tremendous casualties. There had to be four or five hundred down in front of our positions." In the sultry summer air their bodies began decomposing quickly, swelling to two and three times their normal size, bursting out of their clothes, emitting a pervasive, nostril-singeing odor of death and decay. Lieutenant Colonel Weyand saw this terrible scene so emblematic of the waste and tragedy of war, later recalling how "the enemy dead covered the entire hill. Many of them had been killed by our soldiers in our own foxholes. It had been one of the most vicious fights imaginable. It sounds almost routine when I tell it, but it was the longest night of my life."

For three days and nights, the fighting raged this way, along the slopes, peaks, and valleys of these two major hills. The Americans, supported by artillery, mortars, and aircraft, would fight their way up the hills during the day. At night they set up perimeters and absorbed human-wave counterattacks. Finally, on July 4, the Chinese fled Hills 682 and 717. The Cottonbalers, wearied terribly by the previous three days of bitter fighting, settled into the enemy bunkers and stared vacantly at the dreary landscape of war, half expecting the Chinese to come back for another try at the hill. They didn't. The regimental operations officer estimated that the Cottonbalers had destroyed the equivalent of four enemy battalions.[64]

FROM THIS POINT FORWARD, THE WAR settled into a stalemate. Both sides understood that total victory was probably unattainable and certainly too costly. The long-awaited armistice talks began on July 10 and raged, on and off, for the next two years. Every military operation and activity, no matter how small-scale, was now subordinate to political considerations. The Korean War changed from an all-out struggle between communism and anticommunism for the soul of this Asian nation to a limited war of bluff, counterbluff, and rhetoric between the two hostile sides of the cold war.

From the Cottonbalers' point of view, the war now became static, similar to World War I. The two sides entrenched themselves, west to east, along the hills and mountains of Korea, in bunkers, behind minefields and barbed wire, along a series of strong positions known on the American side as the "Main Line of Resistance." Sometimes battles raged over possession of key hills; the rest of the time soldiers from both sides harassed each other with artillery, mortars, snipers, or patrols.

After its victory in capturing Hills 682 and 717, the 7th Infantry Regiment moved to another area in the Iron Triangle near Chorwon. Here they occupied bunkers and observation posts along the main line of resistance. They lived an austere, dirty, molelike existence, constantly on the lookout for enemy activity. Sergeant Owen wrote to his family several times over the course of the summer of 1951, describing the static lifestyle. "Every other night I take out an ambush party in hopes of getting a few Chinks. Last night was the night for our platoon to [lead] the ambush out, so we went out and spent a long sleepless night. Not a trace of Joe Chink! Maybe we will get lucky one of these nights."

A month later, in late August, Owen wrote that "things are rather uneventful right now. Every once in a while, we have an alert, like last night. Someone thought they heard movement in the river bed on our right flank, between us and the Turks. We called for some artillery illumination but couldn't see anything, so we gave up on that exercise. We are loaded for bear in this platoon. We have two machine-guns and six BAR's plus all of our rifles. Plenty of firepower! There are six super-sensitive microphones located out front. They all run into a central switchboard here in our CP where one man sits with a headset on. He can hear anything that walks within 150 feet of a microphone. We got an unexpected treat this morning. COKES!! Really!! Four per man. Wow. Are they ever tasty!!"[65]

Not far away from Owen, life was pretty similar along the 1st Battalion's stretch of the MLR. "It was rather drab," Private Mentis said. "There's not much going on in a combat unit if there's no attack or anything. Our platoon leaders and sergeants were most insistent on . . . making sure your equipment was constantly ready, so you did a lot of cleaning of your rifle and taking care of your equipment and getting your mess gear in order. When we got hot meals, they'd bring them up in canisters. They . . . kept your food warm. We had our breakfast, and then usually you'd get your rations, a candy bar or cigarettes, whatever it might be. Then sometime in the late morning or early afternoon they'd come around with mail. Usually the squad leaders would check and make sure the sound-powered telephones were all working. Early evening, one or two of each squad, maybe three or four even, would catch some really good sleep. Then, when it got dark you started watch, two hours on and two hours off usually. That was a basic day. There was nothing exciting about it." Every now and again they would improve their positions. "We relaid our telephone lines and made sure our communications were in and sometimes our company commander would say, 'We'd better get another bunker over here,' or 'I'd like to have a machine gun there.' So we had some digging to do, and where they found . . . railroad ties and things to put on our bunker, I don't know but supply would get them up there somehow."

On most days the men ate hot meals prepared behind the lines. At mealtimes Mentis and the Cottonbalers would filter down off the MLR in small groups, at planned intervals. "They'd have . . . steak and they'd have macaroni. They used to have a lot of hamburgers. Sometimes I didn't know what exactly the food was, but it was usually pretty good. It would be in some kind of sauce and potatoes and some greens and, if possible, maybe a little shortcake . . . to make your meal complete. Army chow to me wasn't that bad. I grew up in the depression. It tasted pretty good to me."[66]

The toughest duty was serving on an observation post, or forward patrol base, in front of the lines. Sometimes this meant going out and hunkering down as far as two to three miles ahead of the MLR. These lonely groups of men, usually oversize squads, platoons, or companies, conducted patrols or simply sat in modified bunkers and observed enemy activity. The unspoken reality was that they were sacrificial lambs. If the enemy decided to launch a big offensive, the men in each observation post would probably be killed.

In early September the Chinese carried out a limited attack in the I Corps sector and retook 717 and 682 from the 25th Division. In the

7th Regiment sector, most of the attacking Chinese hit an L Company outpost one mile in front of the MLR on Hill 284. The top of this hill was shaped like a crescent with the round part facing north toward the Chinese. A minefield dotted all the approaches to the crest of the hill. The entire complement of L Company occupied this remote hill on the night of September 6 when the Chinese attacked in great strength.

Shortly before midnight they snuck up on the hill and showered the Americans with grenades. The enemy grenades exploded and popped but did minimal damage. The Americans responded with grenades of their own. They did not want to fire their weapons and give away their positions. For three hours nothing happened, but then the Chinese attacked, under cover of a smoke screen. In their usual human waves they charged through minefields, up the hill, through an outer line of barbed wire, and right at the Cottonbalers.

In a matter of seconds the night came alive with shooting. Machine-gun tracers—red, green, white—streaked in haphazard directions. Flares shot up, bathing the area in a ghostly half-light. The enemy blew whistles and bugles. They screamed and roared. As they ran up the hill, they hurled grenades at the Americans and fired burp-gun volleys from the hip. The Americans responded with deadly machine-gun and rifle fire. Dozens of Chinese were hit. Their silhouetted torsos careened in a crazy death dance as they were hit. Some of them lost heads, throats, or jaws. Others saw their stomachs ripped open. American rifle bullets peppered them with small entry wounds. Somewhere inside each enemy body, the bullets tore through vital organs and nerves.

The men of L Company called back to battalion headquarters and pleaded for help. A relief force was organized, and a searchlight battalion provided artificial moonlight, so that the L Company Cottonbalers could better see their attackers. American artillery exploded along the forward slope of the hill, far enough in front of the infantrymen in their foxholes but close enough to kill and maim many Chinese reinforcements.

For two hours the fight raged inconclusively. The Chinese could not infiltrate the American positions, and the Cottonbalers could not persuade the enemy to retreat. Then, just before dawn, the enemy regrouped and, after probing around in the darkness, found a weak spot in the American lines. A battalion-sized force poured through a breach in the barbed wire, up the hill, straight into the foxholes. The fighting was basic, elemental, violent. Men killed one another face-to-face, with rifles, bayonets, and grenades. Blood splashed and splattered everywhere, most of it Chinese.

One NCO, Master Sergeant Richard Bowman, saw that the Chinese had breached the American forward positions on the left flank. The enemy killed a couple of GIs in their holes and wounded several others. To Bowman, the enemy soldiers looked like a screaming, howling mob of fanatical humanity. He could see them in the artificial moonlight, and he knew they had to be stopped or else the entire company could be wiped out. Bowman grabbed anybody he could and pointed them in the direction of the Chinese. "Go get 'em!" he bellowed. Bowman and his group charged into the surprised Chinese, shooting, cutting, and hacking at them. Again, the killing was personal, a real rarity in modern war.

After a few minutes of this awful fighting, the enemy troops broke up and dispersed, but soon Bowman noticed another group of enemy soldiers massing for an attack. He charged into them shooting his M2 Carbine as fast as it could fire. He was a lone American in a sea of Chinese. Inevitably the lopsided odds caught up with him. A Chinese soldier aimed his burp gun at Bowman and shot him. The sergeant, ripped open from throat to pelvis, fell mortally wounded and died quickly. But his men poured withering fire into the enemy, breaking up their attack.

Several yards away, a teenage rifleman from North Carolina, Corporal Jerry Crump, shot clip after clip at an endless silhouette of Chinese soldiers. Still, they got closer; so close, in fact, that Crump left his bunker two separate times to bayonet Chinese. He was a high school dropout from Forest City who had, with his parents' permission, joined the Army at age seventeen. He was a veteran of Chosin and every other Cottonbaler battle since that time, and he was about to pull off one of the greatest feats of selfless courage in the history of the regiment.

Whenever the enemy fire slackened, Crump cautiously left his bunker and dragged wounded buddies to safety He did this four separate times; each time he drew enemy fire. They noticed any movement, no matter how slight. Crump safely moved each of the four men into his bunker and bandaged their wounds. When the Chinese got to within ten or twenty yards of the bunker, he warded them off with well-aimed rifle shots. The situation seemed to have stabilized when, all of a sudden, a Chinese soldier snuck up, unseen, and dropped a grenade into the bunker. The wounded men saw the grenade and screamed in mortal terror. Crump turned, saw the grenade, and hollered, "I got it!"

He curled his body around the grenade. It exploded, sending Crump three feet in the air. The wounded men thought he was dead, but they were wrong. He was alive but seriously wounded. His abdomen was torn open, and fragments were lodged all over his arms and torso. Within minutes of Crump's valorous act, the Chinese withdrew. They knew that daylight would bring every American weapon to bear on them, including air strikes. They left behind nearly 250 dead soldiers. "We fought until daybreak, about 6:00 AM before they finally pulled out," Sergeant Owen later wrote. Strangely, his section of the perimeter was fairly quiet. "Action on Hill 284 was such that I never fired a shot that night. All of the fighting was around the hill to my right. I had no targets. I reloaded BAR magazines for the BAR position 25 feet to my right, who had a very effective field of fire on attacking Chinese to his right."[67]

Four Americans had been killed and another fourteen wounded, including Corporal Crump, who lay bleeding and broken in his shell hole. When medics got to him in the morning, he insisted that they treat the other wounded men first. But Crump was in bad shape and needed to be evacuated very quickly. The usual process of sending litter teams to the hill to laboriously carry him back to the MLR and from there to an ambulance and a MASH unit would not work. Only a medical evacuation helicopter could save him.

The regimental surgeon, Dr. Robert Jensen, knew this all too well. He had spent the night listening to radio accounts of the desperate battle on Hill 284. With the onset of morning, he knew he had to find a way to get to the remote hill if the seriously wounded were to have any chance of survival. An overland hike to the hill was out of the question. The only way to the hill was over a small trail that skirted the edge of minefields for about two and a half miles. Walking that trail would take too much time. Moreover, the territory around it was teeming with isolated groups of Chinese who had tried to outflank the hill. In addition, Jensen had to transport a large container of blood and IV fluids.

Only one mode of transportation would suffice—a helicopter. Jensen spied one at the MLR aid station. He ran over to it and was pleased to see it was flown by a pilot he knew. "However . . . he informed me that his orders barred him from flying out to Hill 284." The pilot's superiors considered a flight to the hill far too dangerous. Helicopters were valuable and they didn't want this one needlessly sacrificed. Jensen argued with the pilot for several minutes and finally persuaded him to disobey his orders. "If we get shot down and killed we won't have to worry about higher headquarters, and if you are injured I can always give you blood and morphine. If you get back safely with the casualties you'll be a hero, and if someone asks you if you were in front of the MLR you can always tell them that you never went beyond the position of the Regimental Surgeon since I'll be with you."

The two men safely flew in ground-hugging fog to Hill 284. Jensen hopped off the helicopter and immediately began treating the wounded, including Crump, who was near death. "I positioned Crump on the ground and started blood running into veins in each arm. Crump was the color of ashes. I could find no pulse. When I examined the large wound in the left side of his abdomen I realized that he was still pumping blood weakly from the lacerated and exposed abdominal organs. There were multiple fragmentation holes in his intestines, stomach, colon, liver, spleen and lungs. All I could do for the many wounds was apply pressure dressings and give blood." The helicopter evacuated Crump and another man directly to a MASH unit. "As the pilot took off Colonel Jim Boswell . . . arrived with food, water, ammunition and replacements. He talked with the officers and men to congratulate and encourage them."

Boswell and Jensen spoke for a while. The colonel wondered sadly if Crump would live. Jensen said that Crump was as close to death as one could possibly be, but that his condition had improved. "It is now up to the MASH hospital to put him back together, and up to the Lord to heal his body and soul," Dr. Jensen said.

Amazingly, Crump did live. He recovered fully enough to go back on active duty and serve over twenty more years in the Army as a master sergeant. In 1952, President Truman personally decorated him with the Medal of Honor.[68]

THE DREARY WAR OF RAIDS, patrols and sniping continued, even as the armistice talks went nowhere. The soldiers on the front line felt a sense of isolation from society and the rest of the world. Their war, which had once dominated the front pages, was now, in a sense, "forgotten" as it dragged on interminably and both sides postured for negotiating advantages. The Cottonbalers' combat experience was now simply a matter of daily survival in a stalemate war no one seemed to care about all that much.

In October, I Corps, commanded now by none other than General "Iron Mike" O'Daniel of World War II fame, launched a limited offensive designed to secure a few miles of key ground. Control of this ground would prevent the Chinese from shelling the Seoul-Chorwon-Kumhwa railroad, a key supply vein for UN forces. In roughly two weeks of fighting, the UN forces took several miles, but at a bloody cost, especially for the 1st Cavalry Division, which encountered the toughest resistance. The Cottonbalers fought in this offensive, but mainly in a support role.

Basically, there was little point to such offensives. They were too costly to be of any value. The war had come down to a deadly game of bluff-counterbluff between the two sides. How many lives would each side spend for control of worthless hills in Korea? That became the overarching question.

Around this time Bill Strobridge got wounded. He had earned a battlefield commission and was now leading a platoon of heavy machine gunners. To say the least, his wounding came about in strange fashion. He was scouting ground during an advance and set off a trip flare that shot into his leg, breaking his tibia and burning his leg quite seriously. His recuperation took twenty-three months and required numerous painful skin graft operations. Even so, he remained in the Army, enjoyed a long career, and retired as a colonel.[69]

In November, the Chinese decided they wanted Hill 355, a strategically placed piece of high ground along the MLR, at Line Jamestown. UN forces had captured this ground during the I Corps offensive in October. Now the enemy wanted it back and, most likely, also wished to test the Allies' resolve in holding it. For most of November the enemy attacked the British soldiers who held 355. The British repelled attack after attack.

On November 22 the Cottonbalers of the 2nd and 3rd Battalions, along with a battalion of Belgians attached to the 7th Infantry, began relieving the British on and around Hill 355. The whole area was constantly under enemy artillery fire. Private First Class Leigh Sullivan was a radio operator for a forward observer attached to G Company. Sullivan remembered the sight of British soldiers happily coming off the hill: "We rode up to the dismount point in trucks, then walked the rest of the way up the hill. On the way up, we passed the British troops we were relieving. You didn't need a crystal ball to tell they were happy to be getting out of there. We moved into our new positions, and the first thing we noticed was that there were only bunkers enough for about half of us." British infantry companies were considerably smaller than American companies.

During their tough fight, the British had strewn a lot of debris around the area, including hundreds of little tea bags. The Americans immediately set about the task of cleaning up and trying to dig new positions, a real challenge on the rocky hill. "My buddy and I dug like hell trying to get our foxhole dug," Private Robert Crepeau, an ammo bearer in F Company, recalled. "It took the rest of the day to dig out 4". That night we sat . . . back to back in that little hole and froze our butts off." Those without bunkers or foxholes simply stacked rocks around themselves.

Most of the positions were located on the forward slope of the hill, directly facing the enemy. Their shells whistled and exploded all through the night, and the wind howled mercilessly from the north, straight into the faces of the Americans. Soldiers huddled together as best they could and willed themselves to keep warm.

In the morning, Sullivan recalled, the front quieted down a bit. "About nine o'clock . . . one of the boys from the company came over to our hole and told us the kitchen crew was going to bring up Thanksgiving dinner at one o'clock. We said, 'Good deal!' and rolled over to sleep until one. But at one o'clock, the Chinese started pouring artillery in and what happens but a shell blows our Thanksgiving chow all over that hill. It was getting bad. The bunkers were caving in with the pounding they were getting, and we were losing men." Mostly the Chinese shells were wounding men with flying rocks and fragments; the afflicted were more than happy to vacate the hill for medical treatment.

One of the officers tried to salvage the soiled food. The Marmite containers with the Thanksgiving feast had been blown "on their sides, lids off, their contents half submerged in the glop made by giblet gravy and mud." Carrying parties salvaged what they could out of this mess and distributed the results to the men in the forward positions, including Private Crepeau. "I was brought a small piece of turkey dipped in dirt. I took one bite and had to spit it out. And that bite of turkey was all I had to eat for three days."[70]

All afternoon on the twenty-third the Chinese shelling increased in intensity. In a matter of minutes, E Company lost twenty men to the shelling, most from direct hits on bunkers, including the one occupied by the company commander. More than four hundred rounds hit the hill in less than half an hour. Clearly, another attack was in the offing. At 1600 it came. The Chinese infiltrated and charged in their typical massive numbers. They charged through their own artillery fire. Some of them tried to use bangalore torpedoes to blow the barbed wire in front of the American positions. The sheer weight of the attack pushed the battalion back to the top of the hill.

The enemy was pushing along the entire line of 7th Infantry positions. Similar attacks hit the 3rd Battalion and the Belgians. For a couple days the fighting raged with the kind of close-quarter desperation so standard for the Korean War. Forward observers called down artillery on their own positions, as well as suspected assembly areas for enemy reinforcements. Men fought for their lives in rocky holes and bunkers. In spite of the deadly circumstances, the men found time for a bit of wry humor. They had taken to calling their hilly home Dagmar—two prominent knolls on the hill mass reminded them of the anatomy of a voluptuous popular television actress.

Private First Class Sullivan described the agony of fighting so hard and so frantically: "All the time the Chinese were pounding us, an aid man . . . worked until I thought he would cave in. With all that stuff flying around that hill, he moved wherever he was needed just like he was takin' a walk in the park. He saved a lot of lives up there. A sergeant I knew . . . was due to go home on rotation. Well, our artillery was just barely clearing the top of the hill so they could get down into the Chinese below us. One of the rounds didn't quite clear the hill. It killed the sergeant and another guy, wounded five others. We weren't pushed off the hill even though we lost a lot of men." They were not pushed completely off the hill, but they were forced from their forward positions. They held fast along the crest and reverse slope of Dagmar.

In the early-morning hours of November 25, the new regimental commander, Colonel Edwin Walker (known later for his extreme right-wing politics), decided to reinforce the hard-pressed 2nd Battalion with C Company. These men were supposed to win back the portions of Dagmar that had been lost in the last couple days. They started at 0330, and as the division historian noted, their experience could not have been much more miserable. "It began to snow. Through the remainder of the night, C Co. struggled upward, slipping and sliding, stumbling and falling, but gaining ground."[71]

Leroy Keeney, a sixteen-year-old C Company mortarman from California, who had lied about his age in order to enlist, never forgot that terrible evening. "We moved up to the base of the hill. We could hear the battle going on on the hill above. I tried everything I could think of to keep warm. We couldn't have any fires or lights. I ran in place most of the night. I only had one light jacket. It wouldn't even keep my shoulders warm but I would take it off and wrap it around my feet. We lost several men that night from frostbite."

At daylight the temperature warmed up a bit and the fight swung decisively in the direction of the Americans. Keeney's company mopped up the remnants of enemy resistance on Dagmar. "I could see the action ahead. The advance troops were crawling, climbing and hiding the best they could. Then when they got to about one hundred yards to the top they all stood up and swept the hill side by side firing if they saw something. Most of the Chinese had pulled out during the night. But they left some of their wounded and some who didn't hear the orders to pull back." With the hill taken, Keeney and his crew sought a position for their mortar. "I found a hole two Belgian soldiers were trying to dig. They were both dead. We rolled both of them out of the hole and were trying to dig it deeper."

Soon Chinese artillery shells began exploding all over the place, further upsetting what was already a ghastly scene of death. "Bodies were stacked on top of each other. They were blown to pieces. Body parts were missing. In one place I saw several American soldiers stacked on top of each other with body parts missing. One sergeant had both legs gone and part of the rest of his body missing, laying on top of several other soldiers. But his face was still there, it wasn't attached to the rest of his body, but I can still see his face, it was kind of peaceful. You would hear a shell hit and people start hollering 'medic.' The medics had their hands full, and I really respect them. The shelling . . . increased. They would hit above us and throw rocks and dirt hard against us. Every shell you're sure is going to come right in the hole with you. I will challenge anyone to name anything . . . more terrifying than that. Every shell drew my stomach into a knot. I knew mortal terror that day. I lost all thought of life and death. Dead people were just things to me."[72]

Eventually, the shelling ended and the front settled down again. The Battle of Dagmar was over. It lasted over four days, and during that time the two sides chewed each other up, over a hill that really had no tactical value. As usual, the Chinese paid a sharply heavier price than the Americans; the 7th Regiment killed a staggering 2,134 enemy soldiers in the battle and lost 25 killed, 149 wounded, and 8 missing. In spite of the agony, strife, and cost of the fighting, Dagmar would only be remembered by those who were there. The fighting quickly faded into the obscurity and anonymity so typical of the latter stages of the Korean War.[73]

FOR THE NEXT YEAR AND a half very little of tactical consequence happened. The communist and UN sides bickered in an infuriating and frustrating series of armistice talks, the main sticking point of which was the disposition of prisoners. The Cottonbalers fought a stalemate war that saw them occupy positions on the MLR. The soldiers patrolled, conducted raids, kept watch, fended off minor enemy attacks, dodged enemy shells and mortars, and periodically enjoyed rest periods off the line. It was almost a routine, workaday war. Men thought of little else besides doing their job, surviving, and rotating home. Their front-line lives were stressful and difficult, but the combat endemic in such a stalemate was not as costly or devastating as the fluid campaigns of the war's first year. Men went to Korea amid no fanfare and came home the same way.

In June 1953 the regiment engaged in one more big fight. After months of negotiations, the end of the war was near. Both sides wanted to finish the war on their terms, and, once again, the communists decided to test UN resolve. Starting in the spring, the enemy began a series of major attacks for various hills along the MLR, the most famous of which was Pork Chop Hill in the 7th Infantry Division's area.

In the middle of June the Chinese decided to focus on UN positions in the vicinity of the Cottonbalers. On the evening of June 14 the enemy unleashed a massive artillery and mortar barrage on the MLR bunkers of the 2nd Battalion. Two rifle companies of the battalion, G and F, manned hillside positions (the men called their position Boomerang) in between Belgians on the left and South Koreans on the right.

The barrage was one of the heaviest the enemy unleashed over the entire course of the war. By one estimate, they lobbed more than forty-five thousand shells at Boomerang that night. The Americans could do nothing except pray that their sandbagged, log-reinforced bunkers and trenches held. For three hours the shelling went on with no respite. Words could not describe the feelings of terror and helplessness in enduring this barrage. Sergeant Bob Barfield, a rifle squad leader in F Company, watched in horror as the bunker in which he sought cover threatened to collapse. "We took several direct hits on the roof thinking any minute a round would come through. We could feel the ground sliding down the hill as rounds would hit in front of the bunker. Unreal! It was like being in a bass drum. Thank God we had such good bunkers and thank God for the help the engineers gave us."[74]

The artillery petered out, and quiet returned to the front, but the reprieve was short-lived. The Americans, stunned and concussed by the thunderous bombardment, waited in their bunkers and watched by the light of flares for any sign of a Chinese attack. Half an hour before midnight they came, in overwhelming strength. Private Ernest Clifford's bunker had taken two direct hits by artillery shells and several other near misses. He and a buddy gazed down the hill, at the no-man's-land valley where they expected the Chinese to approach. "Some flares were fired and someone . . . yelled over the sound power phone, 'There are Chinks all over out there.' Almost instantly the air was filled with the loud 'buzz' of incoming artillery rounds. It reminded me of [a] nest of giant bees swarming. The phone went dead immediately." His buddy opened fire with a machine gun while Clifford covered the bunker entrance.

All along the MLR the Americans opened up with every weapon they had—mortars, machine guns, rifles, grenades, recoilless rifles, and artillery. Dozens of enemy soldiers fell dead and wounded in the valley, but many more kept pressing on, through minefields, barbed wire, straight uphill and into the trenches and bunkers of the 7th Infantry. Clifford's bunker came under attack. "Grenades started exploding in the entrance and knocked me back two or three times and I was hit with fragments in the left foot but no serious injury. We decided to take care of those people throwing grenades. I went out of the bunker first to draw any fire so that Miles [his buddy] could come out and get a good shot. The grenade thrower or throwers must have been killed by artillery. Outside we found no Chinese or U.S. You could see for some distance because of flares but could hear nothing due to intense artillery fire [U.S. and Chinese]."

The enemy soldiers were systematically moving in small groups up and down the trenches, pitching grenades into bunkers and shooting any Americans they saw. Clifford and Miles spied one such group in an intersecting trench. The Chinese could not see them. Clifford had a perfect shot and took aim with his M1. "As the first one stepped into our trench I pulled the trigger and *nothing happened*. The gun had jammed. The enemy soldier saw me as I pulled the trigger and stepped back to the cover of the intersecting trench, shoved the muzzle of his burp gun around the corner and fired. As we were only six feet apart he could not miss, all of this happened in seconds. The enemy bullets took off the back of my right knee and my right leg became immediately paralyzed. As I went down, I grabbed the edge of the shallow trench and rolled over the side and down the hill." Miles later told him that he too got hit but "fell to the bottom of the trench and played dead. The Chinese walked over him." Medics found Clifford the next morning and treated him. "My leg remains partially paralyzed to this day."[75]

No more than twenty or thirty yards away, a squad of Chinese soldiers neared a bunker occupied by Private First Class Stanley Cahill of the Counterfire Platoon. This platoon was essentially an outgrowth of stalemate warfare. The counterfire soldiers operated in small groups dispersed throughout the regiment. Their job was to locate Chinese artillery as quickly as possible and direct fire on it. They did this with the help of sensitive seismic and sound equipment. Cahill was a college graduate from a family with deep roots in Maine. He got drafted right after his senior year of college and joined the 7th Infantry in the spring of 1953. As a student of history, he was impressed with the lineage of the 7th Infantry as well as the esprit among its men in Korea in 1953. "The first time I ever heard of 'Pride and Honor' in the Army was here at the 7th Regt."

He and the other men in the counterfire bunker debated whether to stay in their bunker or bug out. "The Chinese were all over the place and we didn't want to be trapped inside." They left the bunker and "went a short ways to where the trench split, one part going over to George Co. to our left and the other part went back down the hill to the CP. There were four or five of us there trying to cover all directions. The artillery had done so much damage that the sides of the trenches did not go straight up and down but were more like v shapes with inclined sides." An enemy grenade exploded near them and scattered fragments that wounded Cahill and several men, in spite of the fact that they were wearing their heavy flak jackets. In fact, one man next to Cahill took most of the explosive power of the grenade. "Most of the shrapnel hit me on the outer side of my left leg so I think his flak jacket and body took most of the shrapnel." Like many other wounded men, Cahill made his way down the hill and found medics who evacuated him.[76]

After several hours of inconclusive, bloody fighting, the battle reached its climax around 0300. In several sections of the line, the Cottonbalers contained the Chinese and kept them out in the valley or on the hillside, mostly at bay, where American artillery and mortars could pound them, in tandem with plenty of small-arms fire from unscathed American bunkers. But the 2nd Platoon, on the right flank of the whole battalion, had a real problem. The Chinese infiltrated this platoon's trenches and bunkers and did so in large numbers. Possibly as many as two or three hundred Chinese soldiers poured into the midst of the 2nd Platoon Cottonbalers.

The commander of this platoon was 2nd Lieutenant Lewis Hotelling from Hamilton, Ohio. All night long, he and his men fought nose to nose (almost quite literally) with the enemy in a grueling struggle for existence. "Just the overwhelming presence of the enemy made it impossible to stop them, and they overran our positions. It was back and forth with the Chinese as they overran our platoon until we pushed them back.

The fighting was hand-to-hand combat all during this time. The Chinese taped flashlights to the barrels of their burp guns enabling them to see in the dark. They would come through trench lines throwing grenades and fire into the bunkers using their flashlights to find the entrances. Everywhere you looked there were flashlights, I mean hundreds of flashlights. In fact, the whole area was so lit up it seemed like daylight."

The situation was quickly deteriorating. Hotelling knew that his platoon needed help if any of them were to live to see the morning. Suddenly Hotelling saw his platoon sergeant, Bob Barfield, out of his peripheral vision. "Sgt. Barfield, spotting the break in our line, and armed with a BAR, took some men and personally charged forward, firing as he went and stopping the Chinese dead in their tracks, and forcing them back. Barfield single-handedly killed most of the lead Chinese coming through this break. He then repositioned his squad and laid down . . . effective . . . fire to stop the Chinese from coming any further up the trench lines."

They were not out of trouble yet, though. The Chinese were busy poking around, looking for a way to flank Barfield and Hotelling. The lieutenant's communications were completely out. He sent a runner named Red to the company command post for help. The man made it but found no one there. On his way back the Chinese got him. "One of the Chinese was standing over Red . . . to shoot or bayonet him when Sgt. Barfield bayoneted the Chinese soldier. Barfield then picked up Red and took him to the C.P." He carried Red on his shoulders to the CP, but, like the runner, found it empty, so he brought Red back to Hotelling.

The lieutenant and the sergeant conferred about their desperate situation. They decided to consolidate their few remaining men in the trench, with the officer's group on the right and the sergeant's group on the left. They glanced back in the direction of the rear, down the hill, and noticed an American tank retreating. This was very bad news. That tank had been laying down good suppressive fire on the Chinese, keeping some from getting into the trenches. Hotelling cursed, but in the next instant he saw why the tank was retreating. "I could see the Chinese, like somebody had opened a faucet, coming through the gap toward our positions and down the road towards the tank. There were Chinese all over the tank. We set up machine guns and automatic weapons to try and keep the Chinese off the tank."

Soon they had their own problems. The Chinese were back into their positions, all around them. Hotelling was sure this was the end. The Chinese pitched into the Americans; men gouged at each other's eyes, tried to strangle and bayonet each other. "We . . . engaged in hand-to-hand combat for what seemed like hours, but was probably 15–20 minutes. I remember thinking, 'This is my last night on Earth, you're going to die.'" The Americans mostly triumphed in their primal, hand-to-hand death matches, but they started to run low on ammunition. "I had fired all my ammunition, had thrown all my grenades, and artillery was falling all around me. I remember swinging my Carbine like a baseball bat . . . left and right . . . trying to stop any Chinese I could. I had already been wounded twice . . . when suddenly, a big explosion occurred. The next thing I knew, I was laying upside down at the bottom of a trench. I figured that's it, I'm dead."

Several yards to the left, Barfield saw his lieutenant get hit. A Chinese grenade had exploded right next to him, blowing off his foot and part of his leg. He was bleeding to death, and Barfield knew he had to do something, anything, to help him. Barfield and another man ran to the lieutenant. "He was fighting off the Chinese when we got to him," Barfield said. "His right leg was dangling below the knee. Blood was pouring out of it." Barfield and the other man made it to Hotelling and started to brush rubble and dirt off him, but then the enemy came back. Hotelling had briefly lost consciousness, but now he was alert, taking in the whole terrible scene. "Chinese were running up and down the trenches firing into the positions and throwing grenades. All I could do was lay there and watch. Sgt. Barfield . . . killed at least 5 Chinese on top of the trench who were firing at us. I distinctly remember asking Barfield, 'Aren't you scared?' He answered and said, 'No sir, I have a guardian angel!'"

In that chaotic moment of the most deadly combat imaginable, Hotelling had just heard Barfield's most cherished inner belief, namely, that a guardian angel protected him wherever he went and whatever he did. In fact, Barfield's story was remarkable. After he was born in 1934, his parents divorced and his mother remarried many times. Barfield never enjoyed any semblance of a home or family. He spent much of his youth in orphanages and reform schools, terrible places in which his head was shaved and he was poorly fed and treated. He ran away four times. He dreamed only of turning seventeen and joining the service, so that he could live his own life and be treated like a man. To his horror, his physical examination for the service revealed the existence of a hernia, so neither the Navy nor the Army would accept him until it was fixed. He tracked down his father and convinced him to give him the money for an operation. After two weeks of recovery, he joined the Army.

He had served a Korean tour of duty in the 5th Regimental Combat Team and survived many close calls. In fact, he had already lived through many near-death experiences, the most searing of which had happened just after his twelfth birthday. He was riding in the back of a pickup truck driven by his mother's latest husband. The stepfather would never let Barfield sit in the cab but, on this day, relented for once and let him squeeze into the cab. Moments later a drunk driver smashed into the back of the truck, crushing it. Had Barfield been riding back there, he would certainly have been killed. He believed thereafter in the existence of his guardian angel, and his war experiences only solidified that belief.

So, on this warm June evening at Boomerang, he believed wholeheartedly that his angel, in spite of the terrible circumstances, would protect him. He bent over Hotelling and saw the bloody shreds of his foot and lower leg. The sergeant frantically looked around for a tourniquet and had to settle on an empty ammo bandolier. He tied it to Hotelling's leg, stood him up, and tried to get him to an aid station they believed was nearby. Once again Chinese soldiers materialized. "Barfield laid across me and shot between 8–12 Chinese with my Carbine!" Barfield resorted to dragging the wounded lieutenant. "Several times on the way to the aid station we were fired on by the Chinese. Sgt. Barfield shielded me with his own body while he returned fire. I know if it had not been for Sgt. Barfield I would have died in Korea that night."

The rest of the battle was a blur for Barfield and Hotelling, probably because their adrenaline was wearing off. By the time Barfield dragged his lieutenant to safety, the Chinese attack was beginning to run its course. Two factors conspired to make this happen: First, American artillery and mortars blasted every approach to Boomerang. This meant that the Chinese could not reinforce their troops who had infiltrated the American lines. Second, two companies of Cottonbalers, E and I, accompanied by two tanks, counterattacked and drove the Chinese out of the area.

Private Pat Rampino, a young I Company recoilless rifle gunner from New Jersey, was sleeping soundly in a reserve position behind the lines when a wake-up call came just after midnight. "We were loaded up on trucks and rushed up to Boomerang. When we arrived at the bottom of the hill there was already two or three trucks unloading soldiers from Easy Co. We noticed some guys were praying, some making Signs of the Cross." Rampino and the others gingerly made their way through a path in American minefields leading to Boomerang. Enemy artillery shells were exploding far too close for comfort. "We were told to go ahead but I felt like going the opposite direction. I remember a soldier that was hit and he was hollering out for his mother in the dark. He was saying Mom! Mom! It brings tears to me yet today and tugs at my heart." They spent the rest of the night shooting up isolated groups of Chinese.

The sun rose and revealed a scene of utter destruction, of both landscape and humanity. "The ground was chewed up from so many shells hitting it. It looked like it was plowed. We watched as the medics took the dead and helped the wounded. Medics did a great job; blood was all over them."

Sergeant Barfield also survived to survey the torn landscape. He had delivered Hotelling and several other wounded men to an aid station at the bottom of the hill. "I remember the trenches the next morning . . . looked like a junk yard. Shrapnel, unexploded enemy grenades, etc. I can see it still!" He saw a wounded Chinese prisoner. "Both of his legs were blown off, separated below the knees, a tourniquet was on both legs above his knees." The prisoner said something to Barfield through a South Korean interpreter: "He . . . said, 'Goodbye and good luck.' Later I came back and he was dead." The sergeant earned a Bronze Star for his bravery at Boomerang, but he should have gotten the Medal of Honor.[77]

The Cottonbalers held Boomerang but lost 25 men killed and 79 wounded. Chinese casualties were staggering: 1,255 killed, 865 wounded, and 3 captured, 1 of whom, of course, died. Nine days later the Chinese tried another mass attack on Boomerang, but the 3rd Battalion rebuffed them.[78] It was the last significant battle the 7th Infantry fought in Korea. On July 27 the war finally ended, and the next year the Cottonbalers left Korea for good.

SCARCELY A DECADE PASSED BEFORE the Cottonbalers again found themselves at war. Once more, the U.S. government policy of containment took them to an Asian battlefield, a place every bit as remote and obscure to the Cottonbalers as Korea had been. Once more, the grim reaper of war beckoned the 7th Infantry, as it had done so many times before, this time to a place called Vietnam.

CHAPTER 2

Becoming Grunts

Vietnam

THE PHOTOGRAPH WAS MUNDANE YET so revealing. An anonymous soldier stood in place, not ramrod straight, but quite steady, probably more out of pride or habit than military discipline. His face was youthful, composed, and ordinary. His downcast eyes betrayed little except an odd mixture of sadness, nostalgia, and elation. Other than that, he was unremarkable—a young man you might see walking down the street, sitting at a bowling alley, or in a college classroom, an ordinary, normal person going about his business. In this case, he stood in front of a lieutenant colonel. The officer was pinning a Bronze Star on this unnamed soldier, for an exploit performed in the anonymity of a rice paddy or jungle in faraway Vietnam.

Actually, the soldier's helmet communicated more about him than his ordinary American face ever would. Scrawled on his helmet's camouflage liner were three quick, all-encompassing statements: "Frances: My Love; Oklahoma: My Home; And April: My Month." Those words summed up all he held dear. The first two statements, obviously, referred to his home and family. The last referred to the month he would leave Vietnam, the magical date when he would DEROS (Date of Estimated Return from Overseas), and return to his real life back in the "World," as most Americans in Vietnam referred to their home country. The three statements were so simple yet so emblematic of the Cottonbalers in Vietnam. They were ordinary Americans, of all races, with homes, families, dreams, plans, and property. They were neither imperialist "baby killers" nor gung-ho zealots itching to make the world safe from communism.

Like Cottonbalers before and after them, they wanted little more than to do their job and go home.[1]

Almost to a man, they had little idea just how or why their country became involved in this strange, distant place. The nutshell answer to those questions could be summed up in one word—containment. Once the U.S. government, in the late 1940s, committed itself to the policy of containing communism wherever and whenever possible, the result was involvement in limited wars in places like Korea and Vietnam. The latter country chafed under French rule for much of the nineteenth and twentieth centuries. The Japanese briefly took over during World War II only to give way to the French again after the war. A grassroots army of Vietnamese, led by communists, defeated the French in 1954, effectively controlling the northern portion of Vietnam but not the southern.

This ended the days of European colonial domination, if not the days of strife and warfare in this troubled country. The question now became this: would Vietnam continue as a divided country with a communist north and an anticommunist south (like Korea) or would the North Vietnamese communists, through war, forcibly unite the country under their control? Committed to containment, the United States sought to make sure that communist terror did not spread to South Vietnam. This meant supporting a shaky regime that, in the early 1960s, could not seem to successfully fight its own battles against an increasingly intense guerrilla war of terror and insurgency waged by the communist north. By 1965, the Americans understood that only their direct intervention could prevent the southern regime, based in Saigon, from losing the war.

In the blink of an eye, America needed infantrymen, and lots of them, to fight this exotic war. Where would these men come from? Selective Service and volunteer recruiting mostly. President Lyndon Johnson refused to mobilize the National Guard and Reserves, in any kind of significant numbers, for this war. This was a disastrous, misguided, shortsighted decision because it effectively placed the brunt of the entire war on the shoulders of young (eighteen-to twenty-one-year-old) active-duty draftees. It also cut the vital link the Guard and Reserves had forged between the fighting Army and so many American communities. The Guard and Reserves instead became a domestic haven for the socially advantaged, not a ready force of volunteers to augment active-duty soldiers.

Consequently, army leaders had to build a Vietnam combat and support force, as mentioned, through the draft and recruiting.

What was Johnson thinking? From the beginning, he knew that Vietnam would be a limited war for the limited objective of containing communism, and, thus he did not want to send the wrong signals to the Chinese or the Soviets about American intentions in Southeast Asia.

More than these cold war geopolitical considerations, he was concerned about his domestic programs, collectively known as the Great Society—a War on Poverty through government largesse. Johnson knew that his Great Society programs would never make it through Congress in tandem with a major war footing. For one thing, the country could not afford it. For another, the American people would not be comfortable spending so much money on domestic programs with a major war going on overseas.

So Johnson sent Americans off to war but did everything he could to make sure that life went on without a hitch back home in the United States. The natural divide between secure American civilians at home and their soldiers in combat overseas was always considerable, even in a moment of solidarity like World War II. Johnson's policies—no rationing, no personal privation for the average American, no mass call for national unity—led to an even greater divide than usual between the civilians living their normal, comfortable lives and the soldiers fighting to survive in a country that time seemed to have forgotten.

In spite of these considerable handicaps, the men who did the fighting for America in the Vietnam War proved to be every bit as valorous, every bit as competent, and every bit as tough as their twentieth-century forerunners in Korea and the two world wars. In fact, the American combat soldier in Vietnam, contrary to popular belief, was the best-fed, best-educated, best-trained, best-equipped, best-armed, healthiest fighting man the United States had ever sent into combat up to that time.

Since the late 1940s, Selective Service, generally called the draft, had been a way of life in America. Most Americans accepted that young men, after high school, owed a couple years of military service to Uncle Sam. Millions of American men served in the Army during this cold war era, but as time went on, deferments and rejections became more common. You could get deferred for being a student, a father, even a husband. Stringent physical and mental standards led to the rejection of at least one-third of all potential inductees. Moreover, the available pool of eighteen-year-old men was growing yearly as baby boomers came of age, meaning that the Army could be more and more choosy. All of this meant that the draft was anything but universal by the middle of the 1960s. By 1966, roughly 65 percent of men in their mid-twenties had served in the armed forces, a considerable number but far from comprehensive.

Naturally, draft calls increased as American involvement in Vietnam grew more extensive. Given the established deferments and the low-profile nature of the war, many advantaged young men who wanted to avoid service found ways to do so. The best "out" was a student deferment, given to those who were full-time students at institutions of higher learning. This meant that those who could afford a full-time college education could generally avoid being drafted. Those who could not afford, or did not want, full-time status became prime meat for local draft boards. These men, physically healthy, neither advantaged nor disadvantaged, reasonably ambitious but young, comprised the great mass of those drafted into the armed forces in the Vietnam era.

Historian Ronald Spector, in an outstanding study of who ended up in combat units in Vietnam, described them as "not simply a collection of ill-educated, impoverished youths from the bottom rungs of society. Rather, they represented the solid middle of American society." Indeed they did. More than 80 percent of them had finished high school. Almost all of them possessed better than a grade-school education. One-fourth had some college experience, if not an outright degree (compared with roughly 50 percent high school and 12 percent college for World War II soldiers). Most were white, although blacks were present in disproportionate numbers for the first two years of the war. Spector concluded: "If high school graduates far outnumbered college graduates, they also far outnumbered those with little education. Far from being an army of 'losers,' the Vietnam War Army was an army of achievers, of solid hard workers, men and women to whom society had given no special advantages but who were accustomed to making their own way. If they were not the social and intellectual cream of American youth, neither were they its dregs or castoffs."[2]

In other words, just like the anonymous Cottonbaler in the photograph, the one whose love, home, and month were foremost in his mind (and on his helmet), they were the very embodiment of Middle America. They were the rising youth of small towns, inner-city ghettos, honky-tonk and Levittown-type suburbs alike. They were mostly white, black, and Hispanic. Some volunteered out of a sense of duty or patriotism. Others, the majority, were drafted and served out of the same sense of obligation.

In combat, they fought well and they fought hard. Frederick Weyand, the army chief of staff who so ably had led the 7th Regiment's 1st Battalion in Korea, also served in World War II and Vietnam. Along the way, he came to know as much about combat soldiers as anyone: "What particularly haunts me, what I think is one of the saddest legacies of the Vietnam War, is the cruel mis-perception that the American fighting man there did not measure up to their predecessors in World War II and Korea. Nothing could be further from the truth. It was a hell of a burden our soldiers in Vietnam had to bear. They really had to have their heads screwed on right to survive. Yet throughout it all they performed magnificently. They did everything that was asked of them and more. I have every reason to be proud of their service. And America should be equally proud and grateful to them."[3]

The Cottonbalers in Vietnam fit this mold quite comfortably. In fact, in terms of demographics and performance, they were probably a very typical army infantry unit. They were young (average age between nineteen and twenty), solid, competent, and reliable. "They had my highest respect," a junior officer from the 7th asserted. "They were excellent soldiers; they did what they were told; they did their jobs. I still respect them."[4] The views of one Cottonbaler company commander corresponded precisely with the empirical portrait of the salt-of-the-earth, Middle American combat soldier: "I thought they were pretty decent soldiers thrown in a bad situation and doing the best they could. A lot of them were college graduates. One of my sergeants had already been accepted to law school. He's now a judge in Middletown, Ohio. They came from really good, solid middle-class backgrounds."[5] They were not all that much different from their predecessors. By no means were they products of the affluent upper middle classes, many of whom avoided the war through student deferments or connections. But nor were the Vietnam Cottonbalers, in any significant numbers, from the poorest or most disadvantaged segments of society.

MOST OF THESE COTTONBALERS DID not know that the 7th Regiment's service in Vietnam was somewhat unlikely. In the late 1950s, the Army restructured its infantry regiments and divisions. The three battalion regiments no longer fit the demands of the modern battlefield. The Army needed a high degree of infantry-armor mobility to counter the Soviet threat in Europe. Regiments were phased out as the primary lineage-bearing tactical units, but army leaders were wise enough not to abolish the heritage and tradition of regiments altogether. Now regiments were broken up into various battalions that served with battle groups (mobile armored forces) or brigades (oversize infantry units comprised of at least four different battalions from at least two traditional regiments). Divisions still existed, but they were heavier now. They included multiple brigades and, of course, battalions, augmented by a vast array of supporting logistics and firepower.

Battalions now consisted of five companies (A through E) instead of the traditional four that covered much of the alphabet. For instance, the old regimental organization that had been prevalent throughout much of the twentieth century was set up this way: 1st Battalion consisted of Companies A through D; 2nd Battalion had E through H; and 3rd Battalion I through M (excluding J). Under the new system, the letters did not progress, so each battalion featured companies with the same letters. That meant, for example, that 2nd Battalion and 3rd Battalion both had a C Company and a D Company, and so on.

So the 7th Regiment still existed, but it no longer served as a cohesive tactical unit. Instead, each battalion was parceled into various battle groups or brigades. The affiliation with the 3rd Infantry Division remained. After Korea, the division went back to Fort Benning and then deployed in 1958 to West Germany. Throughout the 1960s two battalions of Cottonbalers, the 1st and 2nd, served with the 3rd Division in Germany on various tours of duty. When the Vietnam mobilization began, most of the armor-heavy divisions, like the 3rd, stayed in Germany. The U.S. Army in Vietnam did not need all that much armor to fight a war against insurgents in a country full of jungles and rice paddies. The Army needed light airmobile infantry to fight this war. Army units like the 25th Infantry Division, the 101st Airborne, and the 1st Cavalry fit this profile. So did a newly organized tactical unit designed specifically for Vietnam—the light infantry brigade. These units, comprised of four infantry battalions, in addition to cavalry and artillery support outfits, were designed to be swift, hard-hitting, airmobile (helicopter-borne) shock troops.

In the summer of 1966 the Army frantically threw together one such unit, known as the 199th Light Infantry Brigade, at Fort Benning. The 199th, immediately nicknamed "The Redcatchers," consisted of four battalions, the 2nd of the 3rd Infantry Regiment, the 4th and 5th of the 12th Infantry, and the newly reactivated 3rd Battalion of the 7th Infantry. The 3rd Battalion had been deactivated in the reorganization of the late 1950s, but now it came back to life. Every Cottonbaler who fought in Vietnam served with the 3rd Battalion in the 199th Light Infantry Brigade. The other two battalions of the 7th Infantry never went to Vietnam, only the 3rd. Among all the infantry regiments in the Army, only the 7th Infantry and three others served in both Korea and Vietnam. Only one, the 7th, served in every twentieth-century war.

During that summer of 1966, as the size of the American military commitment in Vietnam grew by the day, the lonely 3rd Battalion of the 7th was little more than a shell of a unit, not even at half strength, dead last in priority for any troops, equipment, and weapons earmarked for the 199th Brigade. The battalion was at little more than half strength, so personnel officers cast their nets far and wide throughout Fort Benning for soldiers to bring the outfit up to full size. "People with orders to Germany suddenly had their orders cancelled," one private wrote later. "Many had been Officer Candidate School Dropouts. Some had volunteered for Vietnam and a few had just returned. They were all doing something, going somewhere, thinking of a thousand and one things, all of which had nothing to do with the 199th Infantry Brigade. But suddenly the big arm reached out, grabbed them by the back of the neck and said, 'I want you!' The universal response was, 'Who Me?!' "[6]

Private Mike Braun was one of those men who were in the wrong place at the wrong time in the summer of 1966. The son of a career soldier,

Braun was the oldest of five children. Like any military family, the Brauns moved around a lot, from Germany, to the Philippines, to Indianapolis, where young Mike graduated from high school in 1963. Braun worked for a couple of years and then decided to join the Army to become a helicopter pilot. Somewhere along the way, Braun's father, an enlisted man, convinced his son to go to Officer Candidate School at Fort Benning. Mike did so, but in the middle of the course, he decided to apply to flight school. He was assured he would get in, but he had to wait while his orders were cut and his application processed. This put him in limbo and made him a prime candidate for an infantry unit in search of young soldiers. Sure enough, the Cottonbalers snagged him, permanently ending his flying career before it ever got started.

To his mild chagrin, he was now a member of E (Echo) Company and was destined to spend his tour in Vietnam slogging through rice paddies instead of skimming over treetops at the controls of a Huey. He and the other men in the battalion, many of whom had been "recruited" in the same fashion, underwent a haphazard training schedule: "It was a group of young kids, average age probably eighteen or nineteen, and we were just playing war games around Fort Benning and then we did a couple weeks at Camp Shelby, Mississippi. They just told you to march here, move there. We went through a lot of escape and evasion training."[7]

At Camp Shelby, the unit received an influx of noncommissioned officers (NCOs) who became the squad leaders, platoon and company sergeants who led the 7th during its early months in Vietnam. They established authority as best they could. After each day of training, they grudgingly issued passes to their men for an evening of fun in nearby Hattiesburg, home of the University of Southern Mississippi. The young soldiers prowled around the campus looking for impromptu dates with college women. The men met with little success but surprisingly managed to stay out of trouble. "A rash of pipe smoking, book carrying GIs developed over night," one soldier wryly recalled.

Later in the fall they went back to Benning, and the training intensified as the soldiers got used to their weapons. The World War II-era Garands, BARs, and carbines had given way to a new generation of weapons. The M79 grenade launcher, capable of hurling 40mm shells several hundred feet, provided on-site firepower, as did a terrific new "light" machine gun—the M6o, which was based on the devastatingly effective German MG-42. The M6o weighed twenty pounds and spit 7.62mm bullets at an astounding rate. Plus, it came with special gloves and plenty of extra barrels for quick changing under fire. The main rifle was now the M16, a light, nylon weapon that fired twenty round clips of .22 caliber ammo at either full automatic or semiautomatic. The M16, liberally augmented by plenty of M79s and M6os, gave the American rifle squad in Vietnam an effective base of fire at the most elemental level.

Each day in the fall of 1966, the Cottonbalers trained in the Georgia heat. "The field training consisted of marching through thorns, thicket and swamp with full pack, and then saying bang bang or shooting blanks," a Cottonbaler later wrote. "There was little realism we thought, so many did not take the training seriously, although they did try to do their jobs. For in the backs of our minds was the gnawing reality of VIETNAM. The word was heavy with ominous overtones."

As he indicated, everyone knew that Vietnam beckoned. All signs pointed toward a late December departure date, because the men received fifteen-day furloughs in late November and early December. "Your mind was filled with thoughts of home, of a joyous welcome, of a tender smile and tears . . . of the moment when nothing could be said but goodbye."

That sad, but inevitable, moment arrived on December 19 when the first planes began departing for Vietnam. The soldiers had returned from their furloughs, packed up their equipment, and said their final farewells. Over the course of six days each company piled aboard an air force C-141 aircraft and flew to Vietnam. "The trip was 30 hours long. The seating was cramped but the food was good. We spent the time being tense, trying to relax, and occasionally laughing at the whole situation."[8]

They landed at Tan Son Nhut Air Base outside of Saigon. The men got up, stretched their legs, grabbed their equipment, and left the plane. The sights and smells that greeted them were disorienting, like something out of a strange nightmare. "It was just like a wet furnace," Private Braun said. "Hot, humid air came in and we walked down the ramp and it was like walking into a surreal Alice in Wonderland [scene]. They had a guy there in a red Santa Claus suit, standing by a jeep handing out presents as you walked off. Then they put us on trucks and trucked us to the compound at Long Binh [the brigade's base]. You were just overwhelmed by the colors and the sights and the smells . . . the degree of poverty and just the duress of the people and the smell of the area."[9]

The heat almost defied belief. The men sweated night and day. The heat was tangible, liquid, oppressive. It had a kind of taste and an odor. It mixed with the smell of human excrement, garbage, pollution, rot, and human body odor to produce the pungent, nauseating stench of Vietnam. It was awful, revolting, but they got used to it fairly quickly. Their young bodies adapted to the heat, and the powerful odors blended in with the rest of their strange surroundings.

The battalion commander, Lieutenant Colonel William Hartman, immediately put his men into "action" as part of Operation Uniontown, an offensive designed to curtail communist movement in the area north and west of Saigon. Unlike the Cottonbalers' recent wars, this was not the kind of conflict in which the unit moved into a conventional front line and then went into battle. In this war, there were no front lines, just a contest of wits and will against an enemy who was everywhere and nowhere at the same time. Charlie (as the GIs called the enemy) was out there somewhere in the paddies, the villages, the jungles, the high ground, the cities, fighting his hit-and-run war of insurgency, dodging and parrying in an effort to avoid the full force of American firepower.

The enemy came in three varieties: Local Force Vietcong, Main Force Vietcong, and North Vietnamese Army. Local Force Vietcong(VC) were the proverbial farmers by day and fighters by night, local people, lightly armed, who sowed mines and booby traps or sniped at American forces. They were usually organized into small groups of five or six VC and were not particularly well trained or equipped, although they were often dedicated and tenacious. The Main Force Vietcong were more numerous, better armed and trained, more like a conventional unit that fought with guerrilla tactics. These VC came from all over South Vietnam and were often committed communists. The last category, the North Vietnamese Army, were the toughest of all. They were regular members of North Vietnam's Army, superbly trained, well armed and equipped, ruthless as could be. They infiltrated south and fought with whatever tactics benefited them. In reality, they, not the VC, were the backbone of the communist war effort.[10]

Initially, the Cottonbalers faced mainly Local Force Vietcong. In late December, the 7th Infantry began the smelly, dirty, wet process of looking for them in the rice paddies and villages around Long Binh, immediately northeast of Saigon. In truth, the Americans were so new and so green that they really had no idea what they were doing. One private remembered a New Year's Eve patrol in which he and his buddies became "lost after wading in a stream for an hour looking for a familiar crossing. As night fell we were huddled in a small circle covering the avenues of approach. Our New Year's Resolution was to be alive the next morning."[11]

Private Braun's Echo Company platoon was told to set up a night perimeter in a paddy and watch out for a possible strong force of NVA. Intelligence thought that an entire regiment of NVA was moving through the area. Terrified at the prospect of facing massive numbers of enemy soldiers, Braun and the others dug in and hoped for the best: "They left us there all night. You start seeing things in the dark because . . . you don't know what to expect. We saw shadows in the woods. We opened fire. We stayed up all night. We imagined there was the enemy behind every bush." Fortunately, no enemy came. In retrospect, Braun believed that the whole mission was designed to do little more than acclimate the inexperienced Cottonbalers to Vietnam.

After learning the rudiments of the patrol and perimeter routine of Vietnam combat, the unit was transferred in February 1967 from Long Binh to Binh Chanh, located about ten miles southwest of Saigon. The battalion had an area of operations (AO) for which it was responsible. This was standard practice for the U.S. Army in Vietnam. Infantry units constantly and intensively patrolled swaths of territory in search of the enemy. The goal was to find them, fix them, and kill them. While not exactly rare, shooting engagements were not as common as uneventful patrols.

The Cottonbalers' AO around Binh Chanh consisted of small villages and rice farms. About 40 percent of the land was flooded, more so during the monsoon season, which started in May. The rice paddies stank to high heaven because of the moisture and ooze of soggy mud but also because of "night soil." The paddies were interspersed with muddy earthen canals about belly button height. Here and there streams or

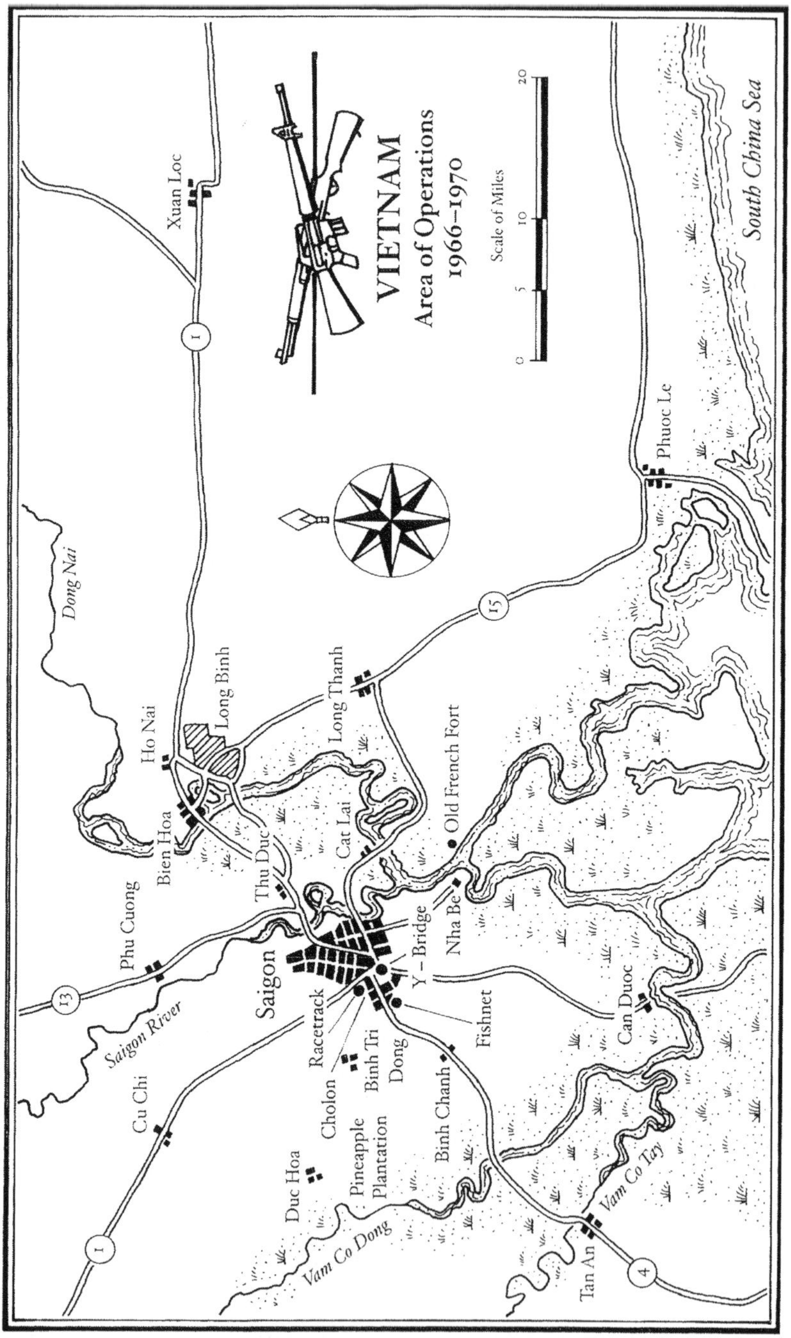
VIETNAM
Area of Operations
1966–1970
Scale of Miles
0
5
10
20
Xuan Loc
Dong Nai
Ho Nai
Long Binh
Bien Hoa
Phu Cuong
Thu Duc
Cat Lai
Long Thanh
Old French Fort
Saigon
Y – Bridge
Nha Be
Saigon River
Cu Chi
Racetrack
Cholon
Binh Tri
Dong
Fishnet
Binh Chanh
Pineapple
Plantation
Duc Hoa
Vam Co Dong
Tan An
Vam Co Tay
Can Duoc
Phuoc Le
South China Sea
1
13
15
4

rivers provided a water source. On the northwest corner of the AO, an abandoned pineapple plantation sprawled along the low ground for several kilometers. During the monsoons, water covered most of the plantation, except for a long raised dike the men took to calling "the Island."

The battalion command group set up a small base camp in Binh Chanh (ringed by sandbagged bunkers and concertina wire), and the rifle companies usually operated from this base, which provided rudimentary shelter and excellent artillery and mortar support. Each day they sallied forth into the AO, living for a day or two in the field, setting up crude bunker perimeters at some of the prominent terrain features. Private Braun's Echo Company spent many days on these nerve-racking missions. "There was different small areas, company size, set up. We gave them names—there was the Island, the Pineapple Grove, the French Fort, and these were just small areas that were ringed by bunkers, holes in the ground, with sandbags around them. You would pull your operations out of there . . . mostly night ambushes."

For American soldiers, night ambushes were to the Vietnam War what amphibious invasions were to World War II—a constant, pervasive aspect of the war. Since the goal was to find the enemy and impede their movement, it made sense to send out and dig in small groups of American soldiers along suspected Vietcong infiltration, movement, and supply routes. In the paddies, the VC moved at night (if they moved in the day, they had nowhere to hide in this open terrain), so it made sense for GIs to "ambush" the enemy during their night movement. Also, ambush patrols were designed to act as the eyes and ears of a combat formation. Rather than allow the enemy to sneak up on the main perimeter, be it a base camp or simply a dug-in platoon somewhere out in the field, it made more sense to establish small groups of men in concealed positions outside the main perimeter. Theoretically, these men on ambush patrol would spot the enemy first and warn the perimeter. Needless to say, any decent squad or platoon leader routinely rotated his men so that no one assumed a disproportionate share of this dangerous duty.

Braun participated in many ambushes in early 1967: "You would go out right before it got dark. You'd be assigned an area. You'd go out maybe a mile or a mile and a half in an area and these were like forks in a wheel. They were pretty well set up along places they thought the enemy might come down—trails, certain river crossings. You would not go directly there because you're right out in the open. So you would bypass it or you would go near it and then you wait until it actually got dark and then you would move into that area and set up. Then, at first light, you would pick up and move back."

Initially, officers ordered everyone on ambush to stay awake all night: "At first they wanted everybody one hundred percent awake." But this didn't work well. Most of the men were "so groggy in the morning that if something happened, we'd be at a disadvantage, so then they allowed us to buddy up. Usually you would do . . . two hours on and then wake your buddy up and he would take over. You'd always want at least two people awake at all times. On an ambush you would form . . . a circle around an area and you would put your heavier weapons like the machine gun . . . facing the direction where you thought the enemy was most likely to come. You also had claymore mines that you'd set up. We had trip flares too."[12]

Claymores were a new weapon that grew out of the Korea experience of human-wave attacks. The claymore was about a foot long and half as wide. The mine came equipped with little legs. A soldier would stand the mine on its legs, point it in the proper direction (very important detail), and string control wires from the mine to a clacker at his position. If he heard enemy troops, he pressed the clacker, detonating the mine and releasing dozens of little ball bearings that did terrible damage to a human body. Each infantry soldier carried one claymore with him on an operation, so GIs routinely ringed their ambush perimeters with these mines.

More than anything, they feared booby traps. The Vietcong concealed mines, trip wires, grenades, and explosives below the waterline or, more commonly, deep within the mud of paddy dikes. "They knew the American wanted to walk on high, firm ground," a company commander recalled.[13] Only through the hard experience of losing people to booby traps did the Americans change their ways. After all, who wanted to walk through feces-ridden, thigh-high brown water unless forced to do so?

Avoiding the obvious dry places, like paddy dikes, made patrolling safer, but it also made it much more miserable and much more tedious. The men squished through the nasty water, holding their rifles aloft. Mud (and who knew what else?) oozed around their boots and stuck to their fatigue trousers. The sun shone hotly above them and sapped their energy. Each step, each motion of bodily movement, was calculated to do one of two things: avoid booby traps or avoid descending into the disgusting, filthy, odoriferous muck any more than necessary. Not surprisingly, the pace of these rice paddy and pineapple plantation patrols was anything but swift. Lieutenant Paul Hindelang, a young rifle platoon leader in Echo Company, reported the results of one such patrol in a letter to his wife in early March: "Today I took 27 men out on a patrol—the tides are running very high—it took 5 hours to travel about a mile, and during that time we crossed eight canals. Generally, you might say we are in wet country."[14]

In the most basic sense, the Cottonbalers, and so many other American infantrymen around Vietnam, were doing grunt work—carrying heavy loads of ammo and equipment, moving through tough terrain, sweating profusely in the heat, keeping a lookout for an elusive enemy, hunting him down in airmobile assaults or cordon and search operations. All of this was tough, physically demanding, mentally challenging "grunt" work. Previous to Vietnam, American infantrymen had generally been known as dogfaces or ground pounders. Now they became affectionately, and respectfully, known as "grunts" because of the difficult nature of their work. The nickname stuck. Infantrymen like the Cottonbalers, from this point forward, were forever known as grunts.

The men of the 7th more than earned this gritty moniker in 1967, as they carried out muddy patrol after muddy patrol, all in blazing heat and insect-ridden conditions. Every time they crossed a stream they picked up leeches. Quite commonly, one group of men stood guard while another stripped down and killed a slew of leeches, usually with cigarette butts or insect repellent. The leeches looked like little black welts on white men; on black men they appeared to be discolored bumps. Sometimes they ended up in the most unwelcome of places—the groin area. In rare cases, they penetrated all the way to the urethra.

Mosquitoes were everywhere. The blood-sucking pests buzzed around ears and landed on exposed arms (most troops rolled up their sleeves to fight the daytime heat). Soldiers could hear the mosquitoes' nasty little zooming and buzzing sounds echo around their steel helmets. Slapping at them did little good. Besides, it made too much noise. Only insect repellent kept them at bay for any length of time. Most of the Cottonbalers tucked their precious repellent into their helmet liners, where it was accessible and would not end up soaked or muddy.

The evidence of ants could be seen everywhere. The little creatures built huge hills, so large that grunts sometimes used them for cover during firefights. It was not at all unusual for men on night ambush to mistakenly set up position near an anthill, feel itching and biting during the night, and discover thousands of ants in their midst come morning. Black ants were the worst, most aggressive kind. They were bigger and nastier than their red cousins. Their bites could cause bad infections.

Then, of course, there was the enemy—tough, resourceful, cunning, and resilient. The Vietcong had intimidated many of the local rice farmers into leaving their farms. Many other farmers had been evacuated by the Saigon government and moved on to evacuee camps in the cities, a controversial aspect of the war. Those farmers who stayed were inevitably caught between the warring forces. At night, the VC infiltrated into villages and shook the villagers down for taxes, rice, or recruits. By day, the Americans or South Vietnamese Army (ARVN) grilled them for information about the whereabouts of the Vietcong.

The whole thing was a mess and, inevitably, the Cottonbalers started taking casualties. Private Braun remembered a day in late February when two grunts lost their lives in terrible fashion: "We had a well-liked squad leader by the name of Sergeant Humphrey and . . . his radioman. We were doing . . . a search and destroy mission. Somebody had declared an area that might be five to ten square miles as enemy territory and everything we found there that could be used by the enemy was to be destroyed or taken back with us. All of the populace had already been moved out, so we would come on to villages that were completely deserted. Most of what we found were isolated little grass huts alongside streams and rivers. It was in one of these that the two guys were going inside the hut to check it out." The Vietcong had booby-trapped the hut: "They had planted one of our own artillery shells. It was planted in front of the door. The sergeant stepped over it and the one behind him stepped on it. Neither one of them were outrightly killed. The one who stepped on it had his legs blown off and the one in front caught all the shrapnel from it, but it took forty-five minutes to get a medevac chopper in there and, during that time, they thrashed around, moaned and cried, and finally bled to death."

Not long after this Braun and the others ran into an even worse situation. On March 3, Echo Company went on a "sweep" to flush out Vietcong near the Island. The men left the base camp and hiked, under a hot sun, for two or three miles. Then the pace slowed down. Private Braun shifted uneasily on his feet and scanned the terrain around them. "We hit an area that had creeks or canals that were running in front of us and on the left side of us." The water in the canals was so deep that they were walking on a dike. "On each side of the dike were these rice paddies . . . about fifty yards square and each one was separated like a checkerboard, if you can imagine a checkerboard having mounds of earth about two or three feet high, and this was what held the water in the rice paddies."

The company commander, Captain Randall Gray, signaled for a halt. He sent a squad from Braun's platoon to check out a tree line on the left. These five men worked their way toward the wood line, as the rest of the American force watched. A moment passed, then another. The men had nearly reached the wood line. Captain Gray thought he might need more men to secure the tree line, so he sent Braun and another man, Private Bob Lee, to join the original force of five. Pushing aside their fear, Braun and Lee left cover and started walking toward the trees. Ahead of them they could see the five men closing in on the tree line.

They were probably no more than ten or twenty yards away from the trees when the sound of AK-47 fire pierced the air. Immediately the five men went down, some of them violently, some of them with little more than a flinch. Braun and Lee splashed for cover behind a paddy dike. They couldn't see the enemy; they just knew the Vietcong were out there in the trees somewhere. Bullets zinged over their heads for several minutes. Then the firing stopped: "The company was about a hundred yards behind Bob Lee and myself on line behind another dike and the company commander wouldn't give them permission to fire because we were between the woods and [the enemy]."

The five men at the tree line were cut off, completely at the mercy of the Vietcong. Braun and Lee were also in a very bad situation, hugging the ground in what had effectively become no-man's-land. Gray hollered orders to come back to the company: "Bob Lee and myself jumped up and we started running back and the shooting started again, right at us. You can tell bullets flying around your head because they sound like bees, but when they get within an inch or two of your ears they crack like a bullwhip would, and these were buzzing and cracking all around us and we made it back to the company line. Only then did the company open fire, but we weren't getting any return fire, so we stopped and the company commander called in artillery into the wood line, and when that was over we got up and walked in."

A terrible sight greeted them. All five of the Americans at the tree line were dead, torn apart by small-arms fire, their bodies already decomposing in the tropical heat. The enemy had even had time to loot them: "They had come out and stripped the bodies and anyone left alive was shot in the back."[15]

Morale plummeted after this awful fight. The engagement was small and brief, but it was one-sided. The Vietcong had inflicted five quick deaths on the Americans and gotten away with, most likely, no casualties of their own. Anyone who still had a "John Wayne" gung-ho attitude quickly lost it. War was not a glamorous quest for glory; it was a deadly, serious enterprise. Young men who tended to think of themselves as indestructible learned differently. This was not a game, not a lark, not a great adventure. Bullets did not distinguish between the "good guys" and the "bad guys." Pure and simple, it was terror and drudgery, just as it always had been in every other war fought in the history of the Cottonbalers. Lieutenant Hindelang, who witnessed the whole debacle from the vantage point of the company position, mournfully wrote to his wife that "it takes about 2 minutes to lose 5 men in this God-forsaken place."[16]

The one-sided battle may have caused ordinary riflemen like Braun to ponder the true nature of war and their mortality, but it made Lieutenant Colonel Hartman think about the quality of leadership in his rifle companies. By any measure, Gray's performance was not very good. As the men saw it, he had sent five soldiers straight into an ambush. Plus, he had unnecessarily risked the lives of Braun and Lee by ordering them to run back to the company when he probably could have called in supporting fire or maneuvered his troops for some kind of flanking shot at the enemy in the tree line.

Truthfully, Gray was never well regarded by his men. He had very little preparation in his background for leading infantrymen. He was seen as a support branch officer who wangled a field command in hopes of furthering his career, a common phenomenon during the Vietnam War. "Captain Gray was not very respected either in the states or over there," Braun explained. "He was really gung ho. He had no military training in infantry. He was what we call medal hungry and glory hungry. He would volunteer us for missions that nobody else wanted or were pretty well useless. He would take us out in the field all day and wouldn't arrange for food or water drop-offs."

Hartman knew that Gray had to go, and in the aftermath of the deadly ambush at the Island he reassigned Gray, with as little fanfare as possible, to a job on his operations staff. The troops were delighted. "We were glad to see him go," Braun said.

Happily enough, Gray's replacement was his exact opposite. Captain Andy Krasnican, the new commander, was extremely well prepared for combat command. In fact, he had spent the previous ten years getting ready for this opportunity. The son of a machinist, Krasnican came from a small town in central Illinois. He loved to hunt and fish but wasn't much for school. He dropped out during his freshman year of high school and spent his time boxing, hunting, and working odd hours in a local foundry. The teenage Krasnican could think of little else besides reaching the age at which he could join the Marine Corps. He tried enlisting at age sixteen but got caught. The next year, 1954, when he turned seventeen he joined successfully and went through boot camp ("twelve weeks of torture and humiliation") in California. At boot camp, he also earned his GED.

He served three years with the Corps but saw no future for advancement, so he left and joined the Army National Guard in Illinois. He eventually went to Officer Candidate School at Fort Benning, earned an active-duty commission, and devoted himself to an army career. He served tours in Germany and Korea. He helped train the inexperienced Cottonbalers for Vietnam in the summer of 1966. When the unit deployed to Vietnam, he served on Hartman's operations staff. But Krasnican's years of military service had afforded him plenty of infantry experience.

Within three days of the Island ambush, Krasnican took over Echo Company. In a very short time, the men saw the upgrade in leadership. Krasnican avoided silly, pointless missions, deployed his men in sensible tactical formations, and, most important, saw that headquarters took care of them properly. In looking out for the welfare of his men, he did not hesitate to go nose to nose with his superiors. "Captain K is really a fine man," Lieutenant Hindelang wrote. "He has extracted from the general a promise of another entire platoon, plus enough men to refill each of [our] platoons, and give us a total of 150. We are going to be a full-fledged rifle company, and be able to hold our own in a rifle company assignment." Most rifle companies in Vietnam did not operate at anything approaching this kind of strength, so Krasnican was able to achieve something unique.

The word of Captain Krasnican's pugnacity quickly spread, courtesy of his radioman (RTO), to grunts like Private Braun: "If we needed something, he got it out there. A chopper would be late bringing in supplies that we needed, and he would get on the horn . . . and chew them out, and chew out people of higher rank than he was. Of course this got back to the troops . . . [who] really appreciated that effort. We felt like we were being backed up . . . better and not just regarded as dispensable pawns."[17]

However, even good leadership could not always prevent tragic accidents that claimed lives. A morose Hindelang sat down in his bunker and wrote a letter about one such accident: "Tragedy struck last night. Something (probably a rat), set off a trip-flare at the far end of our perimeter. That is the end of the perimeter occupied by a platoon from C company. The men claim to have seen a man near the flare, and opened fire, waking everyone in the camp. One of [the Charlie] company men woke up, grabbed his rifle and, confused by the fact that he had moved from an end bunker to a side bunker that night, began to fire at silhouettes he could see in the flare light. Unfortunately, the men he saw were his GI buddies on an end bunker. He only fired two rounds before another man stopped him, but one was deadly accurate! He killed his best friend with one bullet through the back of the head. This is an example of the tragic accidents that make war Hell." Such instances of gut-wrenching fratricide were all too common. Braun even postulated that for the first few months in Vietnam the 7th Infantry suffered more casualties from friendly fire than enemy fire (the official records are, not surprisingly, silent on this sensitive issue).

In essence, the Cottonbalers in 1967 were learning how to function and survive in a Vietnam combat setting. Only experience taught them useful lessons, and the experience came from the daily rhythm of war. Hindelang's letters that spring told the story like nothing else could. "We are now in our third day of the 9–day operation," he wrote on April 12. "We ambush at night, and today we were a blocking force for a sweep of a village. The boys are TIRED. Last night we got a VC who was probing our perimeter. He was wounded, and lay outside the perimeter crying all night. When they picked him up this morning, they also got 3 VC suspects who were trying to get him out." The wounded Vietcong, apparently a company commander, died within hours of his capture.

A few days later, Hindelang's platoon hunkered down in the company base camp: "We are finally settled into a camp for the day, with the 1st and 3rd platoons going on patrol, and my platoon in reserve, building positions, cleaning and caring for weapons and getting some much needed rest. Yesterday, we leveled a small island grove, prodding at every mound, looking for a tunnel system that Gen. Freund [brigade commander] said was there." Five days later Hindelang wrote, with just a touch of exasperation: "My day consists of getting my ass chewed; chewing others' asses; and my nights are filled with keeping bone-weary men awake so they won't be killed in their sleep. Nothing glamorous or exciting to relate most days."

Sometimes they reacted to sightings of Vietcong in the battalion's AO. "Some VC were spotted up near the now-infamous Pineapple Patch." At first another platoon was airlifted on helicopters to get them, but "they ran into a line of bunkers and some very determined VC. They were pinned down and having a difficult time just getting out. We were helilifted in just at dark. We spent a long, miserable night, pinned down in a mud hole. A more miserable night I can never remember. The final count, 3 US dead, 4 US wounded, 5 VC dead and 2 more VC wounded. We swept the line of bunkers and blew up a total of 46 concrete reinforced bunkers."[18]

A day later, Hindelang was transferred to Alpha Company, where he took over command of the 3rd Platoon, all seventeen of them. Infantry platoons were chronically understrength during the Vietnam War. The majority of American manpower went to support duties; even within a rifle platoon, men were constantly coming and going due to rotation, transfers, wounds, deaths, medical evacuations, special duty, and the like.

As a result, platoons usually went out to the field with anywhere from fifteen to thirty soldiers, even though, on paper, they were supposed to have at least forty men.[19]

In spite of his new command, Lieutenant Hindelang began to grow weary of the grind of combat, danger, and responsibility. "I'm really going through a 'down' period, I guess. Nothing quite seems to go right, and everything that comes up rubs me (and everybody else) the wrong way. Tempers flare, and the strain begins to become increasingly obvious as the days wear on." Four days later, on May 6, he and his men were in the middle of yet another operation: "We are on our 4th day of our 9–day odyssey, and ready for a shower. It is hot, everyone is smelly and dirty, the countryside is a mass of mud from the daily rainstorms." Two days before, they had been airlifted south to help units of the 9th Infantry Division that were in contact with the enemy. "On 30 minutes notice, we got up and flew down on a night air assault to help them out. We linked-up, and bolstered their perimeter throughout the night. There were sporadic sniper rounds fired." The next day, they were ordered into an enemy bunker complex. "We made another air assault, guns blazing, on an LZ [Landing Zone] with no enemy. We swept a stream system, blowing 43 bunkers, then air-lifted out and into the base camp we now occupy."

Finally, a few days later they got orders for a stand-down at the brigade's main base in Long Binh: "Passes for the troops, rest and relaxation for all, a chance to throw a drunk and not have a second thought about an alert at 2:00 am. It has been great, and just what the men, indeed all of us, needed so badly."[20]

THAT SPRING AMERICAN AND SOUTH Vietnamese Brass in the 199th Light Infantry Brigade sector agreed to conduct joint operations. Units would buddy up, right down to the squad and platoon level. For the Cottonbalers this meant operating closely with ARVN Rangers in overstrength patrols. On many levels this approach made good sense. The point of the war, ultimately, was to ensure the stability and viability of noncommunist South Vietnam. Only when this country could defend itself could this goal be achieved; ARVN forces, thus far, had not proven equal to the task, but they were not a total loss, especially regular units like the Rangers, who were well equipped and usually well led. If the South Vietnamese could learn from the Americans, they might be able to fight and win the war themselves. To do this, they would have to overcome a tendency toward a defensive mentality. They were too passive, too content to sit in fire bases and fend off the VC or NVA rather than going out and finding them as the Americans labored to do. For all their firepower, professionalism, and determination, the Americans also had much to learn about the culture and the terrain of Vietnam. Operating closely with ARVN units could solve that problem. The ARVN soldiers knew the area and the people (including the Vietcong) far better than the Cottonbalers did.

Naturally there were some language and cultural problems between the Americans and the Vietnamese, but the joint operations worked fairly well. Captain Krasnican was impressed with the proficiency of the ARVN sergeants. "There was a lot of professionalism in their NCO corps. They had primarily Cambodian NCOs." He felt that his unit was a good influence on the ARVN troops. "They didn't like to move at night much, but we broke them of that habit. We'd go into a village and they knew the language and the cultural aspects so they were a big asset to us. They had their own 60[mm] mortars and they taught us a lot about . . . how to control them, and how to fire effectively. Our guys got real good at it by learning from them. And they taught us a lot of stuff about keeping clean and dry, going with the weather instead of trying to fight it."

Krasnican and his men were quite pleased with the arrangement. They befriended the South Vietnamese; worked with them, lived with them, and traded with them too: "They were swapping uniforms and emblems and cigarettes and food. It worked extremely well." In fact, the joint operations seemed like such a good idea that the captain wondered why the whole war wasn't fought this way. "It was their war. We were there to help them, but we couldn't win it for them."

Like many other initiatives in Vietnam, the joint operations ran their course. The unit with whom the 7th Infantry operated was a good, professional force of volunteers. They wanted to be there. They believed in the Saigon government. They wanted to thwart the Vietcong and chase communism from their country. But some other units were not quite as committed. They were poorly led or full of indifferent, untrustworthy draftees. They could not be counted on in combat, and the Americans, frustrated by the Vietnamese's phlegmatic, weak soldiering, came to see them as an impediment to their mission, even an impediment to survival. Most high-ranking American commanders preferred to operate on their own, so that became the norm in Vietnam. Eventually, the Cottonbalers went back to their old routine of working alone.[21]

In late May, Lieutenant Hindelang's platoon was back in the field. One night he went out on an ambush patrol. He and the other men gently swatted mosquitoes, alternated sleeping shifts, and waited warily for any sign of the Vietcong. The night was so dark that he found it hard to see anything, but, for once, that did not seem to matter all that much, because he could hear, even smell, someone coming toward them. It was the VC. "Last night, I killed my first VC," he related to his wife. "My ambush was sprung on 3 VC. We killed two of them and captured the third, a squad leader, though he was very badly wounded. I triggered the ambush, and am sure I killed the first one. After having seen what happens to a GI who trips a VC booby trap or is killed by small arms fire, you'd be amazed how easy it is to aim and fire at a human. Actually, you need only convince yourself that he's not human. It makes your heart beat faster for awhile, but that's about all. I never thought I'd sound that cold-blooded!" Combat, as always, left little room for mercy.[22]

By now, Braun, the army brat, had been promoted to squad leader. A calm and resolute person, he took to the job fairly easily. His green edges had worn off, giving way to the veteran's keen sense of how to stay alive. He and many others were coming to believe that this war was pointless, perhaps even unwinnable. Like many other American infantrymen, they began to think more in terms of survival than victory. Braun and the other Cottonbalers simply existed from day to day, doing their jobs as best they could but taking no unnecessary chances. They established a comfortable, proven routine in the field. "At that time we were just over there to put in the rest of our year and get home . . . so the attitude of the squad leaders was basically, 'let's just do this as safely as we can.' The squad leaders . . . were called in [during] the afternoon and [the captain or the sergeants] would tell you where they wanted you to go. They would point to a stream and say, 'Squad number one, you set up here,' or they'd point to a road intersection and say, 'Squad number two, you set up there.' They were usually within the umbrella of our mortars which were half to three-quarters of a mile away.

"The squad leader then went back and informed the squad that they had a mission that night. The men pretty much knew what to take and what to do. You didn't have to really check to see if they had enough ammo or hand grenades." Each man carried extra ammunition for the M60, a weapon that consumed immense amounts of ammo in a firefight: "Once the squad left the base camp, a whole new set of rules came in. Where they had told you to set up the river might have changed, or you might find there was a river right where you were supposed to set up. So, the squad leaders pretty well took it upon themselves to set up in areas that they considered safe, not an area that you would think, 'Well, this is the best area that I'm going to engage the enemy.' I would pick an area where I could keep my squad safe for the night. Now, if you happened to hit an enemy—I wouldn't say you were looking for a fight, but you didn't run from one. You took it on, and you called in what it took to take care of them."[23]

Most days and nights were calm, albeit tense, but each man lived with the possibility that the calm could give way to chaos in a blink of an eye. One man's uneventful day could be another man's doomsday. For instance, on June 20, 1967, Lieutenant Hindelang took his men on a routine village sweep. "We were up and moving at 4:30 this morning, off to seal and search a village about a mile from here [company base camp], but after that was accomplished, about 9:00 am, we came back here with nothing to do. Troops are bathing, washing clothes, cleaning equipment, taking naps and writing letters. Our next activity will be ambushes tonight. The area we are in is beautiful country, but is crawling with flies. The natives haul garbage from Saigon to spread on the fields as fertilizer, which breeds flies, of course. We have someone all day spraying chlordane powder with a backpack sprayer. That is making some headway, I think."

At the same moment Hindelang was worrying about the ebb and flow of the fly population, Captain Krasnican flirted with his own, personal doomsday. He and his men were sprawled out on the deck of a Huey, feeling the pleasant sensation of cool air tickling over their bodies, on the way to help out a unit of the 9th Division that had apparently run into some Vietcong. The landing zone was "hot," in other words, under fire. The 9th Division artillery was hurling 105mm rounds into the area in an effort to provide fire support to the grunts. Krasnican and his men were in the process of jumping off the helicopter when they heard shooting and a terrific explosion. A shell, possibly American, had landed somewhere very close and scattered shrapnel all over the place, hitting Krasnican, one of his lieutenants, his RTO, and two ARVN officers.

Krasnican was stunned and numbed by the explosion. He quickly saw that he was badly wounded. "The explosion blew out my right eardrum. I was hit in the stomach and the right hip, and got nicks and cuts on the arms." The shrapnel had done considerable damage, tearing off part of his hip and embedding into his abdomen. He looked around and saw that the others were not in much better shape. Lieutenant Jim Jarrett, a rifle platoon leader, was hit in the right leg. The shrapnel came close to taking off his leg at the knee. He lay bleeding and groaning in the mud, as blood coursed dangerously from the wound. Nearby, the RTO, Specialist Kenneth Wells, was in even worse shape. Krasnican saw that shrapnel had cut Wells's throat. Bright red blood spurted in great gobs from his jugular vein. The captain tried to help him, but there was nothing he could do. Wells died very quickly. "He bled to death right there." The dead RTO's blood stained the soil and splattered over the other men, leaving behind only a sticky, almost sweet smell.

Medics arrived on the scene and saved the lives of Krasnican, Jarrett, and the two ARVN officers. The firefight seemed to fade away, recede in importance. The medics gave the captain a shot of morphine to dull the pain that would inevitably follow his traumatic wounding. He would not allow himself to be evacuated until he fully briefed the lieutenant who would now take over Echo Company. Later a medevac helicopter "dusted off" (evacuated) Krasnican to a field hospital where he underwent two operations to dig out shrapnel and stabilize his condition. He went to Japan and endured yet another surgery. It took him months to recover from these wounds, and he never returned to Echo Company—at least not officially. In Japan, once he started to feel better, he hitched a plane ride back to Vietnam so he could check on his old company. At heart, he still felt responsible for them, and he missed the brotherhood of infantry in combat: "You didn't worry about national policies—is Johnson doing this right, or is Westmoreland doing that right. You only worried about staying clean, dry, and healthy, taking care of the guy next to you, and doing your share." Krasnican received a warm reception, but eventually he had to leave to fully tend to his wounds. He served a long military career, but once he retired he ended up getting both hips replaced (a direct consequence of his wounding) and even lost part of a leg to cancer.[24]

SUMMER TURNED INTO FALL, AND the frustration of dealing with an elusive enemy, a disinterested populace, and a deadly war set in among the men. Very few veterans went out of their way to tangle with the Vietcong, but when they did find Charlie, they resolved to give him a full taste of American firepower—payback for all the booby traps, sniper harassment, and sleepless nights on ambush. Sergeant Braun noticed this mind-set taking hold among his men: "We tended to get frustrated because we couldn't engage them on our terms, and so when there was an incident where you did engage them and could do damage to them, you tended to go a little overboard." Lieutenant Hindelang illustrated this point perfectly in a letter to his wife. A small ambush patrol contacted the VC one night in late July and called for fire support. The base camp "shot 650 rounds of artillery, 130 rounds of mortars, and thousands of rounds of small arms ammo, but no body count in the morning."

Under these challenging circumstances, the soldiers' discipline held up fairly well. Still, the hankering for payback kept tempers on edge. "We never had a My Lai incident . . . but I can see how that would have happened," Sergeant Braun said. "We actually at times were ashamed of what we were required to do over there. We didn't shirk from the fighting. It was look after your buddy . . . but you had to go into areas and burn houses, shoot livestock. It's something you look back on and say we didn't make a lot of friends with the people over there." Essentially, the Cottonbalers had to make war against anyone, or anything, that helped the Vietcong. The popular image of bloodthirsty GIs wantonly killing innocent people was simply not true. Such atrocities seldom happened. However, the grunts did have to destroy plenty of property and detain innocent people as VC suspects. The soldiers disrupted lives and sometimes did irreparable damage to farms, homes, and villages. Very few Cottonbalers looked back on that aspect of the war fondly.[25]

In September, Sergeant Braun's squad assisted a mechanized unit from the 25th Infantry Division. This outfit had been taking VC sniper fire for several days and needed light infantry to patrol the area around their base. On the first night there, Braun's squad and another squad, about twelve men in all, set up an ambush: "We hiked out about a mile and it was getting dark and we came to a little canal and we decided that this should be far enough. We were deciding how to set up, where we were going to put the machine guns, where were we going to put the radios and so forth, and it was raining that night. Down this dike came a line of guys and they had ponchos on and floppy hats."

Braun studied them for a moment and then asked the other squad leader, "Who are these guys?"

He said, "I don't know; they must be ARVNs."

Something about them seemed strange to Braun. "Well, nobody told us there would be South Vietnamese Army out here."

They weren't ARVNs. "These guys literally walked within three feet of us. The other squad leader called out, 'Dung Lai!' which meant 'halt.' The guy in front looked up and backed into the guy in back of him. At this time it was getting so dark, we could only see for about ten feet. Well, somebody fired off a round and then everybody started shooting. The guys that we saw coming down the dike . . . took off into this rice paddy in front of us. We dropped down behind the dike. At that time all you could see was muzzle flashes. We had no idea how many they were. They probably had no idea how many we were. Obviously they were just trying to get the hell out of there. But people were getting hit out in the middle of this rice paddy because you could hear screaming and crying. Then, we were on the radio with the 25th to get some support out there and then the firing stopped."

About fifteen minutes later, a 25th Division armored personnel carrier (APC) showed up and beamed a spotlight into the rice paddy where the enemy had fled. "They lit up the field and then we walked in front of it. I found a World War II Carbine. On the other side of the field, we found an old man. He'd been shot in the back of the leg—the leg was broken—and he'd been shot in the shoulder. Apparently, he was too badly wounded to take with the rest of the group and was left behind."

The man passed out. The Cottonbalers lifted him up and placed him on the APC, only to see the 25th Division soldiers loot him: "The first thing they did was search through his pockets. They took a watch off him and his wallet and so forth. For some reason that . . . made me angry, because these guys were just interested in souvenirs and this was an old man, probably in his seventies or so, and bleeding. "The prisoner did not care about being looted, though. Actually, he was angry at his comrades. "He was so mad that the other ones left him, he told us where they were, where they had their weapons."

This fight was the last significant one of Braun's tour of duty. In November he had just come back to base camp after a two-day platoon sweep, slogging through an especially nasty cluster of malodorous paddies, when he received some welcome news. "I was called up to the CP and I thought, 'Now they want me to take an ambush out tonight.' I was totally exhausted." He was not at all sure he had the mental or physical resolve for another night in the paddies, but he need not have worried. At the command post they gave him joyous news. "Get your gear together; your time's up; you're going out on the next chopper." Braun felt like he had been given a new lease on life. "Every ache and pain just left me. In no time, I had everything packed up and ready to go." He left Vietnam on November 15 and never returned. [26]

THE WAR SEEMED TO BE winding down, but it wasn't. American generals and civilian policy makers kept talking about a "light at the end of the tunnel" and hinting that the communists were on the brink of defeat. Cloaked in these optimistic forecasts was the possibility of American withdrawal by 1969.

Meanwhile, the enemy was planning an all-out offensive aimed at winning the war in 1968. After more than two years of mostly hit-and-run warfare, the communists decided to spring a surprise offensive throughout the entire expanse of South Vietnam. They planned to draw American combat outfits west, into the remote areas near Cambodia and Laos, while they infiltrated Main Force VC and NVA units into the cities. The infiltrators would spring their surprise on Tet, the Vietnamese New Year, one of the country's biggest holidays. Previous years had seen a wary truce during Tet, but not 1968. The communists would use surprise and proliferation to overwhelm ARVN forces, rally the South Vietnamese to their cause, and destroy the Saigon government.

In conceiving this offensive, the North Vietnamese believed what they wished to believe. They believed that they could go toe-to-toe with American firepower. What's more, they believed their own propaganda that the people of South Vietnam were itching to be rid of their "imperial" American overseers and would welcome their northern countrymen with open arms. As it turned out, the North Vietnamese were dead wrong in both beliefs. The Americans rallied quickly and decimated the enemy attackers in a conventional style of battle that played right into American hands. Moreover, ARVN units, often fighting for their homes and families, were quite effective, and the people of South Vietnam did not even come close to a popular, pro-communist uprising. Quite the opposite was true. Many of them were as determined as ever to reject northern rule.

On January 31, the enemy struck all over Vietnam, in every major city and province capital. The Cottonbalers were still in their Binh Chanh AO, although Hartman's successor as battalion commander, Lieutenant Colonel John Gibler, had moved the unit's main firebase a kilometer west of the town. In the days leading up to Tet, Gibler felt a powerful sense of uneasiness about the enemy's whereabouts and disposition: "We knew something was up. We had several contacts in the last few days before Tet, but none of the enemy wanted to join battle. You'd see 'em, you'd go after 'em and they'd fade—and that wasn't like the enemy we knew." Gibler had been in command since September. In his experience, when the Vietcong outnumbered an American unit, they usually closed quickly to point-blank range ("grabbing the Americans by the belt" so as to negate American fire support) and tried to inflict as much damage as possible before moving on. They weren't doing that now, and that alarmed him.

Perhaps Lieutenant Colonel Gibler was influenced by the attitude of General Weyand, the old Cottonbaler. After commanding the 25th Division in Vietnam, Weyand had moved up to the number-two position in the Allied command structure, second only to General William Westmoreland. In the days leading up to Tet, Weyand became convinced that the enemy was about to strike the cities of Vietnam. He vehemently, and successfully, urged his boss to redeploy significant numbers of American troops in such a way that they could react to an attack: "Our radio intercepts began picking up the movement of units toward Saigon, which caused us to cancel a major multi-division operation we had planned to launch . . . about 100 miles north of Saigon. That really proved to be a stroke of good fortune, for if those units had gone north, the VC would have had a field day in Saigon."

Gibler, meanwhile, was feeling spooked on the eve of Tet. He told his operations officer, Major James MacGill, to issue orders to every company to return to the firebase. MacGill wondered why. "I don't know; I just want 'em on their way back in," Gibler replied. Late that afternoon, Gibler's eyes kept wandering to a map of Saigon. He could not escape the feeling that a fight would soon break out there. That night, he ordered his newly returned company commanders to instruct their troops in urban combat tactics.[27]

In the morning, at the beginning of the Tet Offensive, the communists attacked the brigade base at Long Binh with 122mm rockets. They also hit Bien Hoa Air Base very hard. They infiltrated and attacked Saigon, including, most famously, the U.S. embassy. The Cottonbaler compound near Binh Chanh was still quiet, but Gibler soon received word that the embattled forces in Saigon needed help. VC attackers had captured Cholon, the western suburbs of Saigon, including the strategically important Phu Tho Racetrack. This horse-racing facility was located at the hub of many streets. It also comprised an ideal landing zone for helicopters. If the Vietcong could hold the track, then they would have a good chance of remaining in Cholon. Gibler's Cottonbalers received orders to retake the track.[28]

For obvious reasons, then, this would not be an airmobile attack. It had to be carried out on the ground, and it could only be supported by a limited number of vehicles. That meant only one company could go in at a time. Gibler chose his best company, Alpha, for the difficult task of going in first. Alpha was led by one of the best and toughest junior officers the Cottonbalers had in Vietnam—Captain Antonio Smaldone. Smaldone hailed from Cohoes, New York, and was already a veteran of three Vietnam tours. He had been wounded four separate times over the course of three years in Vietnam. He was the perfect leader for an infantry company in combat—resolute, fair-minded, tough, smart, no nonsense, and brave. One general called him "the best damned company commander I've ever seen." Dan Shaw, an Alpha Company grunt, remembered Smaldone as a "tough, honest leader." Never one to back down from a fight, Smaldone settled differences with his men in an unusual way. Whenever one of the men had a disagreement with the captain, the two of them settled it back at base camp with boxing gloves. If the man could outfight Smaldone, a former Golden Gloves boxer, his view prevailed. If not, the captain's opinion would be law. In Shaw's memory, only two men ever beat Smaldone.

Now, Smaldone's Alpha Company Cottonbalers paired up with a platoon of APCs from the 17th Cavalry. The infantrymen loaded on deuce-and-a-half trucks and the cavalry APCs, totaling eight in all, shepherded them on the short drive to Saigon. Two APCs led the column, two wedged in the middle, and two brought up the rear. Immediately overhead, Major MacGill guided them in an observation helicopter. At 0800 they left the base camp and started their odyssey down Highway 4, which led straight from Binh Chanh to Saigon.

They rumbled uneventfully for about an hour until they reached the outskirts of Cholon. Here they could see evidence of fighting. "As we got into the outskirts, we started passing bodies along the road," a cavalry gunner remembered. "You'd see a smashed moped, and a Vietnamese would be laying there shot up. They might have been civilians, or ARVN returning to their units—or running away." This sight was grim enough, but soon they saw the sprawled remains of American bodies, blood still trickling from multiple gunshot wounds, flies buzzing and dancing around them. Hovering overhead, MacGill studied the grisly spectacle. "They were in khakis and had obviously been going into Tan Son Nhut or another duty station . . . in Cholon. They had just been slaughtered in their jeeps."

The Cottonbalers kept going deeper into Cholon. Buildings, most of them wooden two-story structures, flanked them on either side of the road. Small numbers of Vietcong began shooting from the rooftops. The cavalrymen opened fire on them with a 106mm recoilless rifle they had mounted on one of their tracks. The rounds impacted and exploded, driving the VC away. The column continued for a few more blocks.

When they were within six blocks of the racetrack, an enemy soldier opened fire with an RPG (rocket-propelled grenade). Like an out-of-control Fourth of July rocket, the RPG round streaked ominously through the air and smashed into the lead track. The front of the APC exploded, showering sparks and debris everywhere. The cavalry platoon leader and two other men were dead. Their bodies had been reduced to raw, bloody pulp. A split second later, a cacophony of enemy small-arms fire pierced the air. The enemy seemed to be everywhere. The shooting came from both sides of the street, straight down into the Americans.

Immediately the GIs sprang into action. The cavalrymen returned fire with their 106s and machine guns. Smaldone's infantry scrambled off their trucks and raced into the buildings. Others took cover behind the tracks and returned fire as best they could. They went through ammo clips in no time, often shooting their rifles on full automatic ("rock and roll"). The infantrymen had long since learned an effective way to forestall the M16's propensity to jam when fired continuously. They loaded their clips with eighteen bullets instead of the prescribed twenty. For some reason, that seemed to solve the problem.

After the first few bewildering moments of the firefight, when enemy rounds ricocheted off the street and APC treads, the battle settled down into a kind of routine. Smaldone took charge and began methodically working his way through the buildings. He knew the area well from an earlier tour of duty. His infantry worked closely with the APCs. The tracks blasted away with their 106s while the infantry laid down a terrific base of fire on the rooftops. Enemy soldiers went down or fled. Shards of wood, glass, and tin sprayed all over the place. Empty casings from machine guns and rifles jangled on the street. MacGill pointed out targets to helicopter gunships hovering in the area. They added their immense firepower to the noisy, hellish scene.

Inside the buildings, the Cottonbalers used hunks of C-4 plastic explosive to blast holes in walls. This allowed them to advance from building to building without exposing themselves in the street. At close range, the soldiers shot up any Vietcong they saw. The tumbling M16 bullet did terrific internal damage to enemy bodies, even though it tended to leave small, unimposing entry wounds. The whole area smelled of cordite, urine, rotten fish, and recent death. Several times, the Americans held their fire as frightened, fleeing civilians ran past them on the street. Other times civilians got killed in the cross fire.

For just over two hours, the grunts and their cavalry counterparts slowly advanced five blocks. By 1300, they were only a block away from the racetrack and could see it, but enemy resistance got tougher. The Vietcong, lying prone behind and under the concrete benches of the track, sprayed the area with automatic weapons fire. To make matters worse, the enemy also had several machine guns spewing deadly fire from a building that covered every approach to the racetrack. The Americans retreated into the buildings opposite the track.

Tired and hungry, the soldiers took a break while helicopter gunships refueled and the officers decided what to do. MacGill's command helicopter landed on a rooftop and the major spotted two American military policemen firing away at the Vietcong across the street. MacGill jumped out and joined the MPs, who were thrilled to see him. He gave the MPs some ammo for their M60 and watched as they shot at random VC running here and there among the buildings. Then MacGill saw a VC come out of a building, hide his rifle, remove an identifying red armband, and raise his hands in an attempt to pass for a civilian. The major leveled his rifle and squeezed the trigger, dropping the man like a sack of wheat.

Smaldone, meanwhile, used the downtime to cautiously scout the building that commanded the approach to Phu Tho Racetrack. He felt very confident that a 106 round or two could reduce the place. He collared two cavalry crewmen and took them on foot to his concealed observation spot just opposite the building. Once there, he showed them exactly where he wanted them to drive up with their APC and how they could get a shot at the building.

At 1630, he set his plan in motion. His infantrymen opened up with everything at their disposal. Rifles, M60s, and M79s riddled the building. The Americans, as was their tendency, poured out an incredible, almost gaudy volume of fire. They wanted to make damned sure that the Vietcong kept their heads down and that they would have no chance to aim or shoot an RPG when the APC rumbled forward into the street. In the meantime, the APC crew drove their track up, positioned it in the street, and opened fire as fast as they could.

In his helicopter, Major MacGill was just taking off from the roof of his building when "they fired the recoilless rifle. Debris from the [VC] building went about a hundred feet in the air right in front of the chopper. It scared the shit out of us. The secondary explosions started a horrendous fire, and I got on the radio . . . requesting that they call the fire department. I was worried about burning down all of Cholon!"

In a frenetic rush, Smaldone led his men across the street into the racetrack. Adrenaline coursed through their veins. They sweated and roared. They were locked in, psyched up, ready to kill at close range. But, the enemy fire was desultory at best. The Vietcong, with their machine gun strongpoint obliterated, chose to melt away into the rest of Cholon. The Phu Tho Racetrack belonged to the Cottonbalers, at the cost of one man killed and several others wounded. The racetrack proved to be an ideal helipad and a nice base from which to operate in Cholon. Shortly after dark, helicopters brought in reinforcements, Cottonbaler grunts from Bravo and Charlie Companies.[29]

In the morning, they began a methodical, street-by-street battle for Cholon. It was the kind of fighting their World War II veteran fathers would have recognized from their own combat experiences, but nowhere near as costly. True to form, the Cottonbalers made no impulsive moves or reckless charges. They simply worked their way from building to building, blowing holes, clearing out rooms and rooftops. Every step of the way, they called on a wonderful coterie of support from APCs and helicopter gunships. At one point on February 1, the Vietcong tried taking Phu Tho back. American machine guns, small-arms fire, and gun ships cut them to ribbons. The enemy's best hope now was to hole up in buildings and look for good ambush opportunities. They were tough and did the best they could, but this kind of fight did not play to their strength; it played to the Americans'.

For five days, the Cottonbalers slowly and inextricably cleaned the Vietcong out of Cholon. The work was dirty and exhausting. Soldiers choked and coughed in the dust of ruined buildings. They sweated and bent under the exertion of endless building assaults. Everyone worried about the possibility of that one Vietcong sniper who might be well hidden somewhere, staring down the sights of his AK-47 right at them. The grunts took no chances; they sprayed the place with as much ordnance as they could, engaging the enemy in the American way of war—firepower, bullets not bodies.

Cholon was a mangled mess of destruction. Everywhere there were ruined businesses, ruined homes, smashed-up cars, broken windows, blown-out walls, and dead bodies, both civilian and Vietcong. Actually, sometimes it was hard to tell the difference between the two, which was exactly what the communists wanted. They tried to blend in with the population of Cholon, but most civilians fled as quickly as they could. They wanted no part of their supposed "liberation" from the Saigon regime.

Within days, the Americans and South Vietnamese had a major troop presence in the Saigon area. The ARVNs had committed five Ranger, five Marine, and five airborne battalions, and the Americans had seven infantry, one MP, and six artillery battalions fighting in the city. The battle had turned against the communists. Their element of surprise (their best asset) was gone, and their soldiers in the city were in a difficult spot, fighting on Allied terms in a bloody struggle for each block. The South Vietnamese, for political reasons, requested that American troops be withdrawn. They wanted to prove to the world that they were strong enough to win back their own capital without any more help from their American partners.

The Cottonbalers, dirty, tired, and red eyed, piled aboard helicopters and flew back to Binh Chanh, where they went back to their patrol routine. For several days, they humped through the paddy country and took sniper fire from individual VC troops who had managed to escape Saigon.

Try as they might, the South Vietnamese could not quite administer the coup de grâce at Cholon. The stubborn Vietcong, augmented by a few NVA, were hanging in there, dealing out death to many ARVNs. The Cottonbalers got the call to go back into Cholon. On February 10, the whole battalion boarded helicopters at Binh Chanh (always a windy, eye-stinging experience in the rotor wash of so many helicopters) and flew into Cholon. The operation was a bit bizarre. The Americans did not seem to know that the VC had taken back the Phu Tho Racetrack and landed their choppers right on the main field, on top of the VC command post. What could have been a bloody tragedy turned out instead to be a fairly quick victory. The M60 fire of the helicopter door gunners kept the enemy at bay while the grunts hopped off the choppers and into the strangest landing zone any of them would ever experience. They stumbled and staggered into positions and laid down fire on the stands, sending chips of concrete and dust everywhere. Within minutes, the Americans had Phu Tho back.

From there they repeated the routine of a week ago, cautiously securing buildings, blasting Vietcong, and warily watching one another's backs. The fighting lasted for the better part of four days. This time the VC was not as well armed or as determined. Some fought to the death, but others retreated into the city, assuming their other identities, hoping to fight again another day. They were the lucky ones, though. Most of the VC who infiltrated into Saigon, amid so much hope and expectation in late January, were dead by the middle of February. The capital remained firmly in Allied hands. The 7th Infantry later received a Valorous Unit Citation for its performance at Cholon and even claimed, incorrectly as it turned out, to have killed the VC commanding general in addition to destroying his command post.[30]

In pure military terms, the Tet Offensive had been a disaster for the enemy. They held on to no major objectives, incurred tens of thousands of casualties, and saw the Vietcong decimated in the kind of open, conventional fighting that guaranteed their demise. From this point forward, the NVA, by necessity, carried the weight of the war. Basically, the communists had decided to eschew their hit-and-run war of wits in favor of an all-out battle of firepower and maneuver, the exact kind of fight at which the U.S. Army excelled. For this bravado the enemy paid a heavy price. "I think the VC made two major mistakes," Weyand later ruminated. "First, by attacking everywhere at once, they fragmented their forces and laid themselves open to defeat in detail. Second, and most important, they believed their own propaganda and thought there would be a 'great general uprising' wherein the South Vietnamese people would flock to their banner. There was a general uprising all right, but it was against them rather than for them. The vast majority of the South Vietnamese people wanted nothing to do with the VC."[31]

In fact, the Tet Offensive succeeded in only one subjective area: it broke the will of the American people to continue the war indefinitely. The furious offensive seemed to negate all the optimistic talk about an imminent end to the war. It seemed to many Americans that the war was just beginning, and they wondered about the feasibility of winning. What's more, they began to wonder if Vietnam was worth losing the lives and futures of so many young Americans. Public opinion now favored scaling down the war and finding a way out, ushering in the phase of the Vietnam War known as de-escalation (roughly 1968–73).

BE THAT AS IT MAY, the fighting in Vietnam continued at a furious pace, at least compared to the two previous years. In fact, 1968 was the most violent year of the conflict. Spasms of bitter, costly fighting broke out all over South Vietnam throughout the year. American casualty rates for several months in 1968 actually exceeded the rates suffered by combat units in Korea and World War II.[32]

The 7th Infantry's AO was not one of the busiest or most violent, but the Cottonbalers did find themselves involved in a very tough engagement in May. In the months leading up to that time, the 199th Brigade functioned as a kind of "fire brigade" reacting to trouble spots but rarely encountering any kind of sizable battle. The generals fully anticipated that the enemy would make another grab for Saigon and believed such a move was imminent in early May. The Cottonbalers left their AO in Binh Chanh and took up blocking positions along the western approaches to Saigon.

The commanders were absolutely correct. Parts of three NVA regiments tried to get into Saigon from the west. Some of them ran into soldiers from the 4th Battalion, 12th Infantry, another unit in the 199th Brigade. The NVA tried to overrun the 12th Infantry's base camp, with little success. The soldiers of this regiment, another of the oldest in the history of the U.S. Army, stopped the enemy cold. The NVA kept probing around the base camp, looking for a route into Saigon. This brought them out in the open, straight into the crosshairs of American helicopters and jets. Light fire teams (one observation helicopter combined with two gunships) dived at the NVA and blasted them with rockets and machine-gun fire. The Air Force got into the act too. Their jet fighter-bombers, F-100s, roasted the NVA with napalm. "Spooky" gunships, C-47s modified with rockets and miniguns—most grunts called them "Puff the Magic Dragon"—poured 18,000 rounds per minute into the enemy ranks.

In the face of this kind of firepower, the NVA could not find a viable route into the capital, so they contented themselves with digging in and extracting casualties from the Americans in a defensive contest. The Ratcatchers, including several companies of the 7th Infantry (Alpha, Bravo, and Delta), turned west and tried to force them from those positions. Once again, this was exactly the kind of situation American commanders wanted. Their soldiers had found and fixed the NVA; now it was time to kill them.

The Cottonbalers on May 7 once more went into battle with 17th Cavalry troopers at their side. The men were sweeping west with the intention of taking Binh Tri Dong village, a motley collection of hootches and palm trees three miles west of Saigon. They approached the village over open fields and paddies; the ground was dry for once. Suddenly, the village erupted with small-arms and RPG fire. A few Cottonbalers and cavalry troopers got hit in the initial volley. The bullets striking home made the ugly, fleshy "thwack" sound so familiar to the combat veterans. The wounded sagged and keeled over. The Americans returned fire with everything they had. APCs lit up the village with .50-caliber machine gun fire. Grunts raised their M16s and fired off clip after clip on full rock and roll. M79 grenadiers blooped their 40mm rounds into the hootches. M60 gunners and their loaders took up whatever positions they could find and belched out a terrific base of fire. The M60 emitted a rhythmic sound that could be heard above the din of battle—"tu tu tu tu tu, ta ta ta ta ta."

Captain Smaldone was wounded by a bullet in the gut, but he could not be readily evacuated because the enemy was shooting at medevac choppers. He and the other wounded men could do little else besides lie still, fight the pain of their wounds (with a little help from morphine shots), and hope for the best.

The battle stalemated. The NVA had built impromptu bunkers in the village. They could not be dislodged by infantry or APC fire alone. Moreover, if the Americans wished to assault the village, they would have to attack over flat ground, right into enemy guns. Nobody was going to attempt something that foolhardy, at least not without tremendous support. The grunts found a drainage ditch that afforded them pretty good cover. They took up position and traded shots, at a distance, with the enemy.

Up above, helicopters, including the one carrying the latest battalion commander, Lieutenant Colonel Kenneth Hall, overflew the battle area. Hall called for supporting fire. In moments artillery shells, originating from the brigade base camp, roared into Binh Tri Dong. The explosions sent trees flying and set hootches afire. Then came the air force F-100s. The grunts threw marking smoke grenades in front of their positions. Then they ducked down as far as they could in their ditch and heard the jets overhead. The planes were awesomely loud. They dropped bombs and napalm right on target, within "150 meters of our positions," one captain later claimed. At such close range, the Cottonbalers could feel the massive concussion of the bombs and the heat of the napalm. The air strikes did some damage but nowhere near enough. Every time the infantrymen showed any inclination to move forward, the NVA opened up with smothering RPG and small-arms fire.

The stalemate lasted two more days and approximately thirty more air strikes. Try as they might, the Cottonbalers could not get into that village. Every time they attempted to do so, they took casualties. The enemy was cornered, but he was very dangerous. However, in this case, time was on the Americans' side. The longer the battle went on, the more fire support the United States could use. The repeated air attacks, from jets and helicopters, wore down the NVA's fighting capability, and they chose to melt away on May 9. Against "only" sniper fire, the cavalrymen and Cottonbalers finally left their pinned-down positions and swept into the battered, burning village. They found some dismembered enemy bodies, along with gobs of blood and discarded equipment. For whatever it was worth, Binh Tri Dong belonged to the Americans. Intelligence believed that an entire enemy battalion had been shattered.

Clearly, the NVA was in disarray. They had hoped to sneak past the 199th Brigade, get into Saigon, and wreak havoc. Instead, they had been forced into battle in the small villages and paddies west of the capital. Groups of enemy soldiers wandered around the brigade's AO, looking for infiltration routes, looking to ambush smaller groups of Americans, or perhaps just looking to escape the maze in which they now found themselves.

Throughout May, they ran into various companies of Cottonbalers who were busily searching for them. On three occasions, the Cottonbalers pinned them down and practically annihilated them. In the first instance, Alpha Company saw a group of NVA heading straight for their perimeter positions and opened fire. Helicopter gunships and "Puff the Magic Dragon," flying on station, soon nailed the NVA with a terrible display of killing power. Only pieces were left of many of the enemy dead. The fortunate NVA survivors fled southwest, as far away as they could go. The second time, Charlie Company spotted a platoon of NVA, about fifty men, retreating west. The Cottonbalers shot at them, dropping several, and called for artillery, which killed even more of them. The third firefight involved Bravo Company, which had fought so hard at Binh Tri Dong. Men from Bravo saw fifty enemy soldiers hurrying along an open plain. They made perfect targets. In a familiar ritual, the infantrymen shot at them with every weapon at their disposal and then called for air strikes, which further pulverized the enemy. Bravo Company soldiers believed they had killed at least seven enemy before the rest got away.[33]

BY JUNE THE FRENZY WAS over and the situation in the Cottonbalers' Binh Chanh AO settled back into the usual cat-and-mouse routine. Unquestionably, the communists had been bloodied terribly over the last several months, but they had not been beaten, not even close. They were as resolved as ever to keep fighting, no matter the considerable cost.

The Cottonbalers spent the summer and fall conducting the usual missions: sweeps, ambushes, patrols, cordon and search operations in villages, bridge security, riverine amphibious duty, and firebase security. The climate was hot and miserable, the terrain disgusting and mosquito ridden. Day after monotonous day, the soldiers carried out their mundane, dangerous tasks. They were quite a sight. Small groups, anywhere from thirty to one hundred green-clad Americans, helmets adorned with slogans ("Don't shoot, I'm Italian," "Peace," "Short!" or the ubiquitous "Yea Though I Walk Through the Valley of Death I Shall Fear No Evil . . . Because I'm the Baddest Motherfucker in the Valley"), bandoliers of rifle or M60 ammo crisscrossing their chests, sleeves rolled up, towels around their necks, rucksacks, usually weighing as much as fifty pounds, digging into their shoulders. Their trousers were filthy with mud and grime, their boots inundated with slime. The white guys were sunburned or tanned, the black guys sometimes burned too. Veterans wedged insect repellent into their helmet liners or sometimes packs of cigarettes—bright red packages of Marlboros or Winstons, green-lined packs of Kools or Salems. All of them had the locked-in look of the grunt in Vietnam, a mixture of concentration and blankness, as if they were there but not really. The experienced among them knew how to look out for danger and still compartmentalize—perhaps even ration—other thoughts during these long, boring, hot and dangerous days.

"It was soggy and slimey and steamy from the sun," one soldier later wrote of the terrain, "flat, hot, and seemingly endless, it was covered with rice paddies, elephant grass, nipa palm, and succulent fruit-all peppered with bomb craters and a liberal supply of enemy bunkers. The men who worked there were always wet, but their throats were dry; they were never comfortable and always dirty."[34]

Day after day, week after week, month after month, the Cottonbalers' war dragged on. In Alpha Company, somewhere in the midst of the anonymous crowd of American soldiers carrying out their daily patrol, a twenty-year-old college dropout from Florida, Private Jerry Lyons, fixated on the man in front of him, moving ahead one step at a time, right in the tracks of the next man, if possible. Shorn of his student deferment, Lyons had been drafted early in 1968 and, by fall, ended up in the 7th Infantry. He adapted as quickly as he could to this life-or-death world in which the main objective was to live until your DEROS date: "I saw my share of boredom, terror, physical and mental stress, waste, B.S. and confusion. I came up with a plan. I . . . made a conscious decision to try to control as much of my destiny as possible. That boiled down to the following: stay alert, do things right, have faith and don't dwell on the bad stuff." His leaders were good. They had the same attitude.

As usual, the number-one fear of many soldiers was booby traps. These demoralizing weapons inflicted a steady stream of casualties on the battalion. "They were well concealed antipersonnel explosives, often detonated by an unsuspecting GI on patrol who snagged a trip wire attached to a grenade (ours or theirs), claymore mine or artillery round. Our grenades had a 15–meter 'kill radius' so you can imagine the damage that could be done. 'Spread out! One round will get you all!' The bigger the explosive, the more serious the casualties would be. I can remember seeing the x-ray of one GI who got hit with a homemade VC booby trap. There was no mistaking the image of . . . 6–penny common nails in his back. He and I later joked about it. Too many more serious injuries, we did not joke about. It was frustrating, to say the least, that the enemy soldiers who were responsible for these things were usually nowhere to be found when the damage was done."

Lyons volunteered to be a point man so that he could control the pace of movement and also so that he would not have to carry extra ammo for the M60 (the men called it the "pig" because it ate ammo so voraciously). In his capacity as point man, he had some close calls: "On Christmas day 1968, I stepped on a grenade that was set into the mud for an unsuspecting American to kick by accident. The pin was pulled so the handle should have flown off and set the fuse when I kicked it. Thank God for dry weather. The mud was dried and the handle didn't move."

Another time, one of Lyons's buddies, an accomplished point man himself, saved his life: "He spotted a trip wire caught on my flak jacket zipper one morning in the Pineapple Grove. I hadn't noticed the thin monofilament fishing line caught on my flak jacket until he told me to freeze. The booby-trapped artillery round at the other end would have done major harm to more than just me, had he not seen it." Such terrifying close calls could work on a man's mind ("when will I get it . . . will it be today?"), but in order to survive and function, the grunts had to force these kinds of thoughts from their minds.[35]

TROUBLED, CHAOTIC 1968 GAVE WAY to 1969. The 7th Infantry, at the end of January, had some success in trapping an enemy formation in a cordon and search operation. This kind of thing happened occasionally but, of course, nowhere near as much as American commanders would have liked. At any rate, on January 27 Alpha Company drew an airlift mission to a landing zone (LZ) in which Vietcong had apparently been spotted. As was the standard procedure, artillerymen lobbed shell after shell into the LZ and gunships scouted the area. The Cottonbalers boarded their helicopters, took off, and waited apprehensively in the windy, noisy wash of the chopper interiors. At times like these almost everyone felt a slight twinge in the pit of his stomach. You never knew when an LZ would be hot, and something about this one felt dangerous and foreboding.

Sure enough, one of the escorting helicopter gunships spotted a VC bunker about fifteen hundred meters north of the LZ. The gunships opened fire on the bunker as well as a few Vietcong they spotted moving on foot near the bunker. Machine-gun and rocket fire sizzled into the area. The pilots thought they saw their rounds hit several of the VC.

Since the original landing zone was obviously unsafe, the helicopters carrying Alpha Company diverted to a secondary LZ located nearby. The grunts landed in four waves. The helicopter pilots hovered their birds several feet off the ground, and infantrymen jumped off the skids into the swirl of mud and dust below them. Helicopter door gunners fired over their heads, in the hopes of suppressing any enemy fire. The Cottonbalers moved as quickly as their heavy equipment loads permitted. They fanned out, ducked, and rolled. They could hear shooting coming from somewhere and it did not sound like the door gunner's M60 fire. In actuality, it was AK-47 fire coming from somewhere up ahead, somewhere in the muddy bramble of this LZ. Enemy rounds stitched one helicopter, slamming into a door gunner and then a pilot. The helicopters, even the ones with these wounded crewmen, took off and flew away.

As the grunts spread out and took cover, Alpha's commander, Captain James Smith, assessed the situation. He believed that his unit faced approximately seven or eight lightly armed Vietcong dug into one or two bunkers. He decided to go after them in skirmish formation. Shouting orders rapidly, he spread his men out (150 meters from one flank to the other) and led an assault on the bunker some five hundred meters away. The Americans ran as fast as they could, maneuvering, ducking, firing here and there from the hip. They were engaging in the age-old role of the infantry—close with the enemy and destroy him—a mission common to so many generations of Cottonbalers.

To this point, enemy fire was pretty light, but that soon changed. The Cottonbalers closed to within twenty-five meters of the bunker and found ideal cover behind a rice paddy dike. All of a sudden enemy fire intensified—machine guns, small arms, and hand grenades primarily. Enemy bullets and shrapnel whizzed and buzzed all over the place. The soldiers ducked behind the relative safety of the dike, and the bravest among them tried to ascertain the origin of the VC fire. One brave soldier, Private First Class Richard Clark, spotted a machine-gun position.

He could see the muzzle blast of the enemy gun. Clark crawled over the dike and plopped into a shallow, muddy crater. "Clark stood and fired a magazine of M16 ammo into the position, turned to return to his platoon, and was hit by enemy fire," one soldier recalled. The VC machine-gun bullets tore through Clark, killing him instantly. One other man had also been killed and several others wounded.

Captain Smith now realized that he was dealing with more than one bunker. He ordered his men to pull back. Many were doing little more than quaking with fear behind the paddy dike. The soldiers roused themselves, grabbed their wounded, and ran for their lives. Clark and the other dead man had to be left behind, at least for the moment. The noise of the fight was terrible. Enemy machine guns and AK fire raised a terrific din, as did the American return fire. The U.S. soldiers lit up the enemy bunker line with every weapon in their arsenal. The bloop of M79 rounds mixed with the steady clatter of M60 fire. Dust-off helicopters, circling above, waiting for the right moment to swoop in and evacuate the wounded, added to the wall of sound.

After several minutes of this inconclusive standoff, Smith ordered another assault. Once again, the Americans reached the vicinity of the dike only to be repulsed by thick enemy fire coming from many bunkers. Three more Americans dropped dead, their hearts forever stilled, their blood staining the soil of a faraway land they knew so little about. Like the two other KIAs, these dead men could not be evacuated when Alpha retreated back to a safer position. Alpha had lost five brothers and several more wounded. No one, including Smith, saw the point of another assault. Alpha was critically low on ammo. Smith ordered another retreat so that the wounded could be evacuated and his company resupplied.

In the meantime, the brigade commander, Brigadier General Frederick Davison, flying high above in his command chopper, had set plans in motion to encircle and crush this stubborn force of hunkered-down Vietcong. Since the enemy had decided to stand and fight, Davison proposed to make them pay for their valor. He ordered reinforcements to be moved into the area; they would carry out a classic cordon, or hammer and anvil, operation. Within hours, units from all over the brigade, including two companies of Cottonbalers, descended on the area. They dug into positions all around the enemy bunker complex.

The men sat all night in two-man foxholes, alternating watch. American flares burst in the night sky, illuminating the area all night long. Here and there, small groups of enemy tried to escape the cordon. Two of them ran right into Bravo Company of the 7th, which had set up its positions on the north end of the cordon, exactly opposite Alpha's positions in the south. The alert Bravo soldiers opened fire and killed the two Vietcong. Later, at 0800, another Bravo man spotted a VC who had crawled to within ten meters of his position. The American rose from his foxhole, leveled his M16, and shot the enemy dead.

Half an hour later, Davison coordinated massive strikes on the enemy bunkers. For three hours on the morning of January 28, American artillery, gunships, and jets pounded the enemy. The bombs and shells seemed to shake the earth. The GIs watched the fireworks intermittently and thanked heaven that they were not on the receiving end of that hellish theater of death. Late in the morning, the barrage ended.

The men from Bravo left cover and slowly advanced into the wet, sticky rice paddies leading to the bunker complex. The water was thigh high. Mud and slimy, gooey moisture splashed all over everybody's trousers and tops. The smell was nauseating. Similar to Alpha Company the day before, the Bravo soldiers closed to within twenty-five meters of the bunkers—helicopter crewmen above could even see the bodies of the five dead Alpha Cottonbalers—and met a hail of fire. The Americans splashed into cover behind dikes and returned fire, but they were not going anywhere. The bunker complex could not be taken without incurring prohibitive casualties. Davison wisely decided that it made more sense to pull back, tighten the cordon around the Vietcong, and let them walk straight into the muzzles of his guns if they wished to escape.

That night the Americans lobbed more than thirteen hundred artillery rounds at the VC bunkers. All night long the shells exploded in a continuous orgy of violence, flashing and crashing, spraying mud, water, and debris all over the place. Flares again lit up the night sky. The artillery rounds collapsed many bunkers and undoubtedly killed many Vietcong.

In the morning a heavy fog enveloped the entire area, oozing humidity and rot. Men could not see more than two or three feet in front of them. Bravo's commander, Captain Eugene New, waited for the fog to lift and then sent his men forward with orders to proceed with extreme caution.

Slowly, they trod forward, a lump in their collective throat. The area was quiet, even eerie. The men did not like the idea of nosing around in the bunker complex again ("bad karma"), but they had little choice. Luckily, the enemy was gone, but the Bravo soldiers found plenty of evidence that they had been there in strength. Decomposing, dismembered bodies, clad in VC-style pajamas and NVA-type fatigues, lay everywhere. Maggots and flies inundated the bodies. Parts of their heads had been blown off. Some of them stared at the Cottonbalers through half-opened lids; their faces were bent into crooked death-mask grins. The sickly sweet stench of recent death hung everywhere.

Immediately the Cottonbalers searched for the five dead Americans, but they only found three of the bodies. The two others were never recovered. Officers believed that the two other bodies had been pulverized, atomized in the artillery barrage. In addition to the five dead, the Cottonbalers had suffered twelve wounded in the three-day battle. The Americans claimed sixty-two enemy dead (forty-two actually counted and another twenty "probable"). According to the official records (at times a questionable source), only ten enemy escaped.[36]

Without any doubt, the cordon battle was a victory for the Cottonbalers, but even when the Americans inflicted casualties on the enemy, it did not seem to change the pace or rhythm of the war. The enemy still kept fighting and the Americans, stung by growing domestic opposition to the war, thought increasingly of turning it over to the South Vietnamese. Still, as summer approached, the Cottonbalers fought plenty of small battles against irregular mixed groups of NVA and VC, in the paddies and river deltas around Binh Chanh.

Moreover, plenty of American boys were still being sent to fight in Vietnam. One of them was Private First Class Jim Norris, a dark-complected, beefy kid from New York City. Born in 1950, Norris was the son of a Manhattan longshoreman. After graduating from high school in 1967, Norris, the eldest of three children, spent a year at St. John's University, but he did not do well. He did not yet have the maturity and focus for college. Many of his friends without student deferments were living lives of inertia, "sitting around watching *Laugh In*," just existing and hoping their draft numbers did not come up. Others were dodging the draft or getting into heroin, flirting with overdoses, "wasting their lives," in Norris's view. He had no interest in any of that stuff. He did not know what he wanted to do with his life; he only knew what he didn't want. Norris felt that he needed to grow up, become a man, and prove himself: so, he joined the Army.

In October 1968 he left home for basic training at Fort Jackson, South Carolina. Sheltered and naïve to the ways of the Army, he was absolutely shocked by the rigors and abuse of basic training. One day Norris even called his father and asked him to send money so that he could escape, go AWOL, maybe go to Canada. His father squelched Norris's evasion plans. Basically he told him, "You got yourself into this and you're going to make the best of it. Deal with it." In many ways, the rebuke was the best thing that could have happened to young Jim. He knew he had no recourse but to endure basic training the best way he could, and he did exactly that. Slowly but surely, he matured both mentally and physically. Norris began to feel more pride in himself, began to have more confidence. He decided that the Army was not so bad after all.

By the time he graduated from basic, he had lost forty-five pounds. He was now lean, focused, and tough. He went home on a furlough and found himself disgusted by the dead-end lives of so many of his friends. He knew that he would soon be sent to Vietnam but felt that somehow it was his duty to serve there. He was curious about war, and like so many males of his generation, he was greatly influenced by the swaggering, glamorous John Wayne portrayal of maleness and combat.

In May 1969, Norris joined Alpha Company of the 7th Infantry as an FNG (Fucking New Guy) replacement. He and five other men joined Alpha's 2nd Platoon. The veterans gave him the most rudimentary of welcomes. "Guys didn't talk to you. Nobody talked to you. You were just the new guy in a brand-new uniform and your helmet liner . . . had not been dyed out by the sun. You learned . . . when you got to the company . . . that your life wasn't worth as much as the guy who had been there the day before you." When the vets did talk to him, they conveyed the grunt's mind-set at this latter stage of the war: "We're not petting kids on the head; we're not taking their pictures; we're trying to kill them. We're not going to get friendly with the locals. We're not here to win the hearts and minds of these people, we're here to survive, and if you're lucky you'll get home a year from now."

Almost immediately, Norris went out on a daytime ambush with five other soldiers: "We went out and walked through the elephant grass. We got to a stream and . . . the squad leader said there could be booby traps on the other side so we were going to recon by fire. He had the M79 guy fire a round across the bank and I had gotten down in the prone position. The grenade went off and wounded two guys in the squad." The two soldiers were dusted off. As Norris watched them go, he pondered the absurdity of what had just happened: "I looked around and I said, 'Boy, this is a crazy place.' "

Private First Class Norris and the other grunts spent many of their days being helicoptered from place to place throughout the AO—commanders called this "The Jitterbug"—constantly seeking to find and pin down small groups of Vietcong. Usually nothing happened. Then, at night, they would go back to the base camp, eat a hot meal, and sleep in bunkers.

Sometimes they patrolled on foot in the misery and muck of the paddies. They carried incredibly heavy loads of equipment and ammo. "My load as a rifleman would be twenty magazines of eighteen rounds apiece . . . plus a couple of frags, plus a smoke grenade, three days' worth of chow, seven quarts of water, a claymore, your bedroll, T-shirts . . . probably around seventy pounds . . . all on your rucksack." The weight of the equipment made them sink even deeper into the mud. The hot sun beat down on their heads—they had no shade in the open paddies—and produced a kind of sauna effect, made worse by the weight and mass of their steel helmets. They consumed water voraciously. Most days a helicopter would resupply them with water. Other days, they had to settle for foul-smelling, grainy, muddy river water, liberally sprinkled with halazone tablets.

They rarely encountered any Vietcong but found much evidence, in the form of booby traps, that they were still active. One day, somebody in another squad tripped a mine the VC had planted in the mud. "We had stopped for a break. When we got up . . . a guy took one step, and stepped on it. It killed him and wounded three or four other people. I was probably four or five feet away from them. We were in two columns. I was in the lucky column." In addition to the man who had been killed instantly, another man, who had joined the unit with Norris, died later: "That's when I realized this wasn't a game. I thought about it all night." The finality of death hit home to Norris. He realized the deadly seriousness of the war—it wasn't *The Sands of Iwo Jima*; it wasn't guts and glory. It was real, graphic, death, dismemberment, and tragedy.

When they did run into the Vietcong, the engagements were quick and usually inconclusive: "It was five minutes, ten minutes, maybe thirty minutes, but it was over, they withdrew, and that was it. They were very good at the war they were fighting. If you caught them . . . out in the open, that was it, it was all over [for them], but if they could pick the time and the place, they would let you get as close as you could because then you couldn't bring . . . the might that you had there to overwhelm them." Thus the firefights often took place at close range, within twenty to thirty yards of one another. The VC would take a few shots and then go. "You would have . . . the unreal din of everybody shooting at God knows what, something you couldn't even see. Then you would do the old fire and movement thing, but by then they've disengaged and moved on." The Cottonbalers would usually fire their magazines on full rock and roll (somehow it was comforting to do so), and then they would fire aimed shots until someone yelled to cease fire.[37]

All summer long, the elaborate high-stakes game of hide-and-seek continued. Captain John Parker commanded Bravo Company that summer. "The nippa [*sic*] palms and the villages were where Charlie hid during the day. In order to flush him out, and kill or capture him, we came up with a form of heliborne assault called 'The Jitterbug.' We broke our companies into several three-chopper sized units and set out to make numerous insertions at predetermined sites. Each of these sites was near a village, or a patch of nippa [*sic*] palm. We would roar in, the troops would dismount, and the choppers would circle overhead. If the VC were in the nippa or the village . . . they would invariably run out the other side, and our choppers would swoop in and let them have it. If we made no contact with the enemy within about 10 minutes, we would call the ships down and try a new spot."

One day they diverted to cover a helicopter that was forced to make an emergency landing: "It seems that several VC had snuck up to the downed chopper and had gotten within about 30 yards of the ship when we arrived. They were now hiding in a small depression just outside grenade range." Parker and the other Bravo Company men maneuvered ever closer to the enemy soldiers. "I was the first to get to where the VC were hiding, and I finished off one. I then turned and saw the third one running across a field, only about 40 yards away. I started firing at him with well-aimed single shots, but a [CAR-15 light rifle] is not much good at that range. My machine gunner then arrived, took up a firing position, but could not see the VC because of . . . smoke." It was the enemy soldier's lucky day. The Americans could not get a good shot at him, and he escaped.

Luck, or random chance, mostly determined if the Americans found the enemy. On a typical hot summer day, Parker's company was flying around in helicopters and had assaulted several locales with no contact. Then, on another sortie, they caught two NVA soldiers flat-footed: "A gun ship opened up two hundred feet from my location, and reported that they had a kill. [We] rushed to the spot to find an NVA soldier floating in a small pond. I waded in and drug him half way to shore, when I realized this was not really a job for a company commander." He ordered two replacements to drag the body to shore. They heaved the body onto a paddy dike and discovered a pistol. The new guy had himself a souvenir. The dead man was an NVA mortar captain. Minutes later they found the captain's first sergeant. "He had a serious wound in his shoulder, but he gave no indication of pain. He seemed to be resolved to the belief that we were about to shoot him." Parker told the NVA sergeant he would be evacuated to a hospital. A dust-off came and took him away, but not the dead man. A new policy dictated that any dead enemy officer must be photographed, but no photographers were available to helicopter out to the grunts, so the grunts had to drag him part of the way back to their base, until helicopters came for them: "We unceremoniously dumped the dead guy on the grass next to the air strip." The photographers came and shot their pictures. Somebody later buried the body.[38]

In late August, Bravo and Charlie Companies of the 7th Infantry stumbled upon an extensive enemy base camp about seventeen miles south of Saigon. The Cottonbalers were sweeping the paddies and river deltas of that low country, working with ARVN troops and the American 9th

Infantry Division, which had been modified into a riverine combat force. Charlie Company was operating in conjunction with river gunboats (called "Zippos" because they shot flaming napalm at targets). The grunts exited the boats and set up ambush sites. At first they found nothing, but later they were choppered into a landing zone near a village about a mile away. "There was about 400 yards of open rice patties [*sic*] between the village we took and the area we were headed," Private Larry Compton remembered. "The VC let the first squad get about half way to the nipa palm before they opened up." Everyone took cover and returned fire: "We called in an air strike. They riddled the place. The squad moved ahead about 50 more yards and the VC hit them again. We called in another air strike. Our squad moved out and around to the south of the first squad. We didn't get 150 yards before the VC hit us. We laid down and another air strike was called in. This went on for 3 days. Back and forth, back and forth. We were hitting them from four different ground areas, from the air and from the boats. After the 3rd day we were able to move in. Lots of bloody gear, no VC. Underground was a complete village consisting of multiple levels, complete with a hospital on the third floor and a major communications center."

The whole complex was spooky, almost surreal, especially after it had been pounded by so much American firepower. Another Charlie Company grunt, Private First Class Gary Moffitt, stared in wonder at the place. Moffitt had walked point many times, but he had never seen anything like this: "I just couldn't believe it. The area didn't even begin to resemble the one I had seen [the first] morning. After they were done pounding it, the whole area had sunk about eight feet." Moffitt's company commander, Captain George Watts, also shook his head in amazement. "The main body of one tunnel alone was large enough to hold over 100 soldiers." He even found one bunker that was reinforced by sturdy concrete. "A passageway from this bunker led into the tunnel complex."

The men were glad to have found the place and taken it from the enemy, but more than anything, they wanted to get away from it. Extensive bunker complexes like this one were creepy and foreboding. Somewhere in the back of everyone's mind was the disquieting thought that a dedicated enemy had built such a well-conceived complex right under the very noses of the Americans and the ARVNs. For every one they found, there were probably three or four others out there, full of ruthless enemy troops, just waiting to set an ambush. Cottonbaler records claimed that the soldiers found thirty-four enemy bodies in this complex.[39]

IN A WAY, THIS WAS the 7th Infantry's last hurrah in the low country AO it had patrolled for almost three years. Throughout September, the Cottonbalers moved to a new AO near Xuan Loe, northeast of Saigon, in remote Long Khan Province. This new AO featured radically different terrain. It had a few rubber plantations, but mostly it was virgin jungle, the triple-canopy type providing ideal cover for the communists. The area was a resupply and infiltration point for enemy units around Saigon. For years, the VC and NVA had been left to roam at will in the jungles of Long Khan, so much so that one American soldier claimed that "uniformed NVA troops were seen nonchalantly walking along highways and crossing fields without fear of being engaged." The Cottonbalers built a camp, known as Firebase Mace, east of Xuan Loe. Sallying forth from Mace, they patrolled deep into the jungle, searching for Charlie.

Alpha Company now had a new commander, Captain Roland Merson. Merson had taken over the company in late June. As much as anyone ever can be, Merson was born to command an infantry unit in combat. "I have always believed that my mother mixed gunpowder with my pabulum," he once wrote. Born in 1939 in Baltimore, Merson was the son of a construction foreman/manager with a degree from nearby Johns Hopkins University. As a child, Merson was heavily influenced by World War II. He followed the war from the vantage point of a small boy but dreamed of growing up to be an infantry soldier. In fact, he yearned for little else. One of his earliest memories was a visit from a Marine veteran of Iwo Jima who was a friend of his mother's. The man sat in the Merson living room drinking beer and talking. Periodically he would turn to little Roland and urge him to one day join the Marine Corps: "I always answered that I wanted to be a soldier." The Marine chuckled and gave him a copy of the *Marine Corps Manual*. Merson devoured it; soon he knew it practically by heart.

Merson also had an uncle who had served as an artillery forward observer with the 29th Infantry Division in World War II. Roland revered this uncle and, partially because of his influence, joined the Maryland

National Guard in 1956, before he had even graduated from high school. He spent several years in the Guard and got some college under his belt before deciding to go on active duty in the Army. He went to jump school and joined a Special Forces unit. Around the time Vietnam started heating up, his superiors sent him to Officer Candidate School at Fort Benning. They had recognized his inherent leadership abilities and knew the Army would soon need good junior officers to lead infantrymen in combat.

Merson thrived at Officer Candidate School. His years of military experience and his lifetime of preparation served him well. He breezed through the difficult course and earned the coveted distinction of Honor Graduate. In 1966 he went to Vietnam and served a tour of duty as an adviser to a Regional/Popular Force (RF/PF or "Ruff Puff" in American parlance) battalion. The Ruff Puffs were local South Vietnamese militia, usually poorly armed, poorly trained, and poorly motivated. He managed to survive the experience of "advising" the Ruff Puffs for a year and went home. In spite of the fact that he had a wife and three children, Merson volunteered for another tour of duty—in the back of his mind he believed he would not survive this tour—only this time he wanted to command American soldiers. In 1969, as a captain, he got his wish when he took over Alpha Company.

Thanks to a combination of fortune, good leadership, professional expertise, and good soldiers, Merson led Alpha on a remarkable eight-month streak in which no one was killed. He did not achieve this by hunkering his soldiers down in bunkers at base camp. They participated in a dizzying array of operations. "We moved by day, and were required to put out two ambushes per platoon at night. We also conducted airmobile operations, but mostly as a means of transportation. We were taken to the drop off point by truck or helicopter, and extracted by same."[40]

One of Merson's Alpha Company soldiers was none other than Private First Class Norris, the kid from Manhattan, who was still humping a rifle and rucksack. He had no sooner gotten used to the paddies when the unit was transferred to the jungle. "We humped more in the jungle than we did in the paddies. I think we were expected to cover more ground. In the jungle . . . you weren't going to see a helicopter until you were picked up." Generally the men walked cautiously at five-foot intervals in the jungle, taking care to avoid trails that were ideal ambush and booby-trap kill zones. "If it was real . . . thick triple-canopy-type stuff you tightened up, and if it was more open, you'd open up, so it all depended on the terrain. It was more of an endurance test. You would hump all day and then you would set up . . . probably at four or five o'clock. You'd set up your night defensive perimeter. You were usually operating not in squads but in platoons. You'd set up in an oval for the night. You knew you were going to get up at five or six in the morning. You'd start humping again by seven thirty. It was kind of like a nine-to-five job." Norris and many others actually preferred the jungle because the heat was not as intense—the jungle canopy often shaded them from the sun—and booby traps were not as common.

Merson believed in the command philosophy common to most good American small-unit commanders in Vietnam: do your job, be tough, be competent, but don't do anything stupid; don't go out of your way looking for trouble. Private First Class Norris and the other men quickly noticed Merson's sensible attitude and soon grew to admire their captain. "Roland Merson was a great CO. He was a guy who cared for the troops, who paid attention to what was going on."[41]

In October, Merson's Alpha Company began finding evidence of an NVA bunker complex. The bunkers were well camouflaged, built almost right into the jungle with layers of logs and mud, and protected by brush and vines. The men almost had to bump into them to see them. On the eighteenth, the men found several bunkers and a trench line, along with a grenade and some NVA mess equipment. Merson possessed a keenly honed internal radar for danger. He could sense the presence of the enemy, feel them, almost smell them. He referred to this subjective warning system as "getting spooked." The next day, as his soldiers hacked their way through the jungle, fighting vines, ants, and mosquitoes, the "spooked" meter kept buzzing. The enemy was very close, and Merson knew it.

The morning air was dank and moist. The jungle was quiet except for the sounds of shrilling birds, buzzing insects, and softly trodding American soldiers. Each man scanned the jungle with his eyes, looking for bunkers, trip wires, enemy soldiers, looking for danger. All of a sudden, small-arms fire shattered the rhythmic sounds of the jungle. The Cottonbalers bolted for cover and returned fire, mostly on full rock and roll. Bullets ripped through the leaves and skinny trees of the jungle. M79 men blooped their rounds into the green wall in front of them, in the vague direction of the unseen enemy.

Up front, with the point element, Private George Sheehan, a replacement rifleman who had only been with the unit a few weeks, found himself right in the enemy line of fire. An Irish Catholic kid from Queens, he had dropped out of community college only to find Uncle Sam knocking on his door. Now he recoiled in horror as an enemy round slammed into him: "All hell broke loose. I got hit in the [left]forearm." The bullet tore through his arm, knocked him down, and left an ugly, open wound: "There was dirt kicking up. There was branches breaking." Private Sheehan propped himself up and fired back as best he could: "I remember firing my M16 with my right hand. I couldn't move my left hand." Sheehan fired a full magazine. Another man, Sergeant Robert Perkins (nicknamed "Perk") was pinned down five feet away from Sheehan. Perkins was a skilled M79 grenadier, by all accounts the best in the company. Perkins pumped shell after shell at the unseen enemy. His 40mm shells, combined with the rest of their squad's fire, allowed the two of them to crawl over an embankment. "We kind of backed on out of there over to the other side of the embankment," Sheehan said. "The platoon leader came out and got us . . . and brought us back." A medic gave Sheehan first aid.

Almost as soon as it began, the shooting stopped. The enemy disappeared into the jungle. Merson ordered a search of the area, but the men only found a couple of rucksacks. Private Sheehan and the other wounded man were medevaced as soon as possible. At the hospital, Sheehan later noticed that a bullet had torn a hole in a paperback book he was carrying in the trouser pocket of his left leg, saving him from a more extensive injury. He kept the remnants of the book as a kind of sentimental talisman.[42]

Later that day, Alpha found yet another bunker complex. The men were blowing the bunkers up when someone spotted several enemy soldiers. Once again, the terrible racket of modern weapons filled the air. The amount of violent noise produced by so many rapidly shooting M16s, M60s, and M79s was nearly ear shattering. Cottonbalers blazed off clip after clip of ammo. Machine gunners went through belts of ammo in a matter of seconds. Merson's forward observer, Lieutenant

Gary Masuda, called in accurate artillery fire that killed several enemy soldiers. Masuda, a Hawaiian of Japanese ancestry, knew his craft well. A 1967 graduate of Western Washington University, he had joined the Army and survived Officer Candidate School and the advanced artillery officer's course at Fort Sill before spending several months as a forward observer with an airborne unit in Vietnam. By this time, he was a veteran and understood the nuances of artillery quite well. Rather than rely on compass readings alone or sheer dead reckoning, he counted each and every step he took. "Every hundred meters I would put a mark on my watch and keep track that way." This compass and pace system succeeded mightily. He had an uncanny knack of knowing exactly where they were in the bewildering jungle. So when the shooting started he was able to call down accurate artillery fire: "You call in your artillery about one thousand meters out and then you bring it in to you, so you kind of fan where you think the enemy is at and then you bring it in, almost literally on top of your position."

Lieutenant Masuda's artillery was devastating. The rounds shrieked into the thick, lush jungle, probably only a couple hundred meters away. The explosions came quickly, one after the other, flashing and bursting. Then everything was quiet. No one could be entirely sure, but Alpha Company had probably killed at least five enemy soldiers, one or two by small-arms fire and the rest by artillery.[43]

A few days later Captain Merson received some intelligence information that, for once, allowed the Americans to get the drop on the enemy, rather than the other way around. "I got an Intel report, with coordinates, that a [VC] pay officer was to cross a certain stream, on a trail, at a certain time." Alpha Company moved to the area and found the terrain exactly as described: "I had the company spread out along the stream, and the 3rd Platoon set up a point ambush in a bend of the trail. I pulled my CP off to one side, and settled down to catch a nap. About the time I closed my eyes, the M60 opened up." At the appointed time and place, the enemy pay officer appeared. The American machine gun quickly found its mark. At least one bullet shattered the man's abdomen and he was lying still, bleeding profusely. "He was carrying sacks of money and reams of documents. He was gut shot and dying. We stood around him and my soldiers just looked at me—what next Captain?" Merson briefly contemplated shooting the wounded enemy but thought better of it. "I . . . called for a dust off." The helicopter came several minutes later, lowered a jungle penetrator, and the Americans loaded the wounded Vietcong onto it. On the way up to the helicopter, the penetrator got caught in a stand of tall trees. The prisoner fell out and plunged to his death.

The presence of the Americans did not exactly scare the enemy away. The communists, VC and NVA, were still out there in the jungle, shadowing the Americans, most likely determining the right time and place for an ambush. Merson could feel their presence. "I knew there was a sizable force in the area. The signs were everywhere. I [kept] asking battalion to send in additional forces so that we could turn this into a real show." The rest of the battalion was busy with other missions, though. "I was told that they couldn't pull assets away without brigade approval, and that brigade wouldn't approve until I locked them in sustained combat." This was a catch-22. "I said 'Right, and by the time you get here Alpha will be wasted—I don't think so.' So, we played cat-and-mouse. I couldn't fix them and they couldn't fix me."

The tension of each day was enormous. Moment by moment, the men did not know if the enemy would materialize, just as they had so many times before. The filth, heat, and privation of the jungle also took their toll on the soldiers. They had not eaten a decent meal or bathed in days. They had been sleeping in muddy foxholes and spending their days carrying out the exhausting task of humping through tough terrain. Many of them had numerous small cuts up and down their arms and all over their faces. These cuts were caused by tall grass or jungle foliage. They were almost like paper cuts. It was almost impossible to keep them from getting infected in the fetid climate; many of the cuts oozed with pus. Most of the soldiers were exhausted and irritable, but also deathly wary of the enemy's unwelcome presence.

Merson knew his company was in real danger, and, in light of the "cat-and-mouse" situation, he saw nothing to be gained by thrashing around in the jungle, moving toward yet another worthless objective. He ordered a halt and instructed his men to dig a hasty perimeter. He met with his lieutenants: "I told them to put out one LP [listening post] per platoon, and get a fire team ready to start clover leaf patrols." Several minutes passed while they carried out his orders. Most of the men were only too happy to comply. They were sick and tired of humping: "About the time we were getting into position the word was passed—movement! I thought 'O Shit; they've got me fixed.'" A terrible shiver of fear and apprehension crawled down Merson's spine. He looked at Masuda and nodded. The forward observer immediately began cranking up a fire mission. Then the captain found a good observation point. "I found a tree on some high ground in the approximate center, and sat down with my back to the tree. I put my rifle on my lap and took off my helmet to hear better. My RTOs were right there and I took a hand set from each."

Adrenaline pumped through his bloodstream. He and his command group were alert and coiled, ready for action. "Then I saw it—almost in slow motion. Soldiers all around me were going down to the prone [position]. They dropped on their knees cradling their rifles, and reached out with their left hand to break the fall. They tapped their magazines, hit the charging handle, and made sure their weapons were on FIRE. I thought WOW; I've got me a real . . . living, breathing, line infantry company." Seconds later, Merson and his men heard the sounds of steady thrashing in the jungle. Everyone's heart was beating furiously now. The approaching footsteps were heavy and loud. It sounded like a large group of NVA was right on top of them.

But an instant later, they watched in bemused silence as a pack of monkeys emerged from the jungle and ran by them. They stared as the monkeys ran by them and out of sight. "I'm sure the sigh of relief rocked the Golden Gate Bridge," Captain Merson cracked. No one fired a shot. They just grinned, shook their heads, laughed, and expressed relief and wonder. The "monkey sighting" effectively punctured the tension. Maybe this place was not so bad after all. Maybe they would survive without a big showdown with the NVA. They did. Alpha Company went back to base camp with no further casualties on this operation.[44]

OTHER COTTONBALER COMPANIES WERE ALSO tromping around the bush that fall, reacting to reports of large NVA troop concentrations. The NVA sought to avoid large-scale contact, but, inevitably, they and the Americans bumped into one another. In one instance, a platoon-sized group of enemy soldiers ran straight into a Bravo Company ambush. Second Lieutenant Roger Soiset was a rifle platoon leader in Bravo. A farm boy from North Carolina, he grew up with martial ambitions and attended the Citadel in Charleston, South Carolina. He graduated, earned his commission, and joined Bravo as a replacement officer in September 1969. On the night of the ambush, he was taking full advantage of his turn to sleep when the bark of M60 fire rudely awakened him.

He grabbed his rifle, took up a firing position in the mud, and searched for targets. However, most of the shooting was from the other side of the perimeter. He settled in and listened to the firefight. "It was not possible to distinguish anything other than one long explosion as the M60s and several M16s fired on full automatic simultaneously." He could hear the forward observer calling in fire, and muffled "crump" sounds as the shells exploded in the jungle.

In a matter of moments, the shooting petered out and the area was absurdly quiet. Bravo Company's commanding officer, Captain Michael Murphy—Parker had rotated out of the field a month before—issued orders to search the area for enemy bodies. Before the men could do so, strange-sounding Vietnamese voices could be heard on the company radios. "Yankees, we have you surrounded. You are all going to die. Yankees, we are going to take you prisoner. We will take you to Hanoi. You will die." Like so many other aspects of Vietnam, the voices were creepy. The Americans silently listened to the radio threats.

Captain Murphy went ballistic when he heard the voices. He got on the horn to battalion and called for fire support—air strikes, gunships, artillery, everything. He spewed obscenities and hollered into the phone, "Goddamn it! I want some aerial support! I don't know what's out there beside the seven gooks we just killed, but they're not going away! I want some gunships! I don't mean in the morning! I mean right fucking now!"

Moments later a lone "Puff the Magic Dragon" overflew the area. Soiset watched it circle and then unleash its deadly cargo. "The sound of the guns was a continuous, high-pitched roar. It was an unforgettable memory for those lucky enough to be watching and a deadly event to anyone unlucky enough to be caught in its path." The fire may have killed some of the ambushed NVA, but it did not shut up the radio interloper. He continued his threats even as the airplane shot up the area. Most likely, he was far away, sitting in a hootch, talking into a shortwave radio in hopes of unnerving the Americans.

In the morning, Bravo found four enemy bodies. Somehow the NVA had dragged the other three away. The air smelled acrid and pungent, a mixture of the stench of gunpowder from expended ammo with death and the rot of the jungle. Soiset reluctantly sidled up for a look at the four dead enemy. He was surprised to see that the dead bodies were not very bloody; their blood had seeped into the ground. "Later I realized that when the heart stops pumping, the blood stops flowing. Dead men don't bleed. We left the enemy dead in a pile, booby-trapped with grenades in case their friends returned again." Some of the grunts took pictures of the ghastly spectacle. Lieutenant Soiset had no interest in doing so, but he never forgot the sight of those torn enemy bodies.

Several weeks later, Soiset's Bravo Company was choppered into the northwest edge of the battalion's AO. The helicopters dropped off the grunts in a small, elephant-grass-covered clearing at the edge of triple-canopy jungle. "There seemed to be some sort of magnifying effect of the sun's rays. The temperature in that clearing must have been over a hundred and twenty." Three men collapsed from the terrible heat and had to be medevaced out. Finally, after sweltering in the miserable and dangerous clearing, the Cottonbalers entered the jungle. "The immediate drop in temperature was like a tonic. Under the trees in the jungle, it was probably ten degrees cooler. We were all soaked in our own sweat by that time, but there could be no rest."

They had to move quickly, so they followed a network of logging roads. "It made a world of difference if you could walk at a normal pace rather than claw your way through thorns, vines and mud. Of course, following a road is also a quick way to walk into terminally bad news. Sometimes, you have to push your luck a little, and on this day we got away with it." At noon, Captain Murphy split his unit up into platoon-sized ambush formations along the logging road. Soiset's platoon was situated along the westernmost approach to the road. He and his men were settling down for a C-ration lunch. "We had barely set up, and were just starting to break open cans of fruit cocktail, cheese and crackers, beefsteak and gravy, when we heard a solitary M16 fire a burst. Then we heard firing from a M60, followed by silence."

One of the other platoons, about seventy meters away, had spotted enemy troops and opened fire. Soiset could hear the men of the other platoon yelling at one another, calling out positions and targets. He made a move for his PRC-25 radio (the men called it a "Prick 25") in the expectation that he would soon get a call from Captain Murphy. As he did so, one of his men edged up to him and hissed, "Lieutenant!" Soiset looked up and saw the man gesturing with his eyes at something along the road. "I snapped my head around and saw three Vietnamese men rushing down the road between us and the second platoon." Soiset could tell that the three enemy soldiers were planning to spring an ambush on one of his squads that was facing away from them. "Without taking my eyes off the scene in front of me, I reached for my CAR-15. My fingers couldn't find it, so I looked down. It wasn't there."

After a brief nanosecond of panic, he saw it sticking out of his rucksack and retrieved it as quietly as he could. Meanwhile, two of his men, including an M60 gunner, carefully took up firing positions. "I knew we were enjoying an instant of luck as our opponents had not seen us." A second or two passed while Soiset and the other men aimed their weapons. "By this time the Vietnamese were in motion, their eyes still transfixed" on the vulnerable squad. "One with a AK-47 had stepped to the front and was taking aim. I sighted on his head and said, 'Now!' I heard the first two shots of my usual four-shot burst, after which [the M60] drowned everything else out. I knew that only my first round had any chance of going where I wanted since accuracy with a hand-held automatic weapon is a joke. You just point in the general direction and hose down the target. My first bullet must have been on the money because the man dropped like an inflatable toy that had its air suddenly sucked out. The second man was being knocked backwards by the combined fire. He seemed to be flailing at the air. The third man must have thought he would be safe if he dropped his rifle, as he threw it down and took off running. I sighted ahead of him and fired another burst. This time I held the trigger a little longer and let him run through the invisible stream of bullets." The Vietcong sprinted away, seemingly impervious to the fire until he was out of sight. "I was embarrassed and angry. How the hell could I have missed?"

Soiset ordered a cease-fire and took stock of the damage his men had wrought. As it turned out, one of the other squads hit and wounded the third Vietcong. The lieutenant's ears were ringing from being so close to the muzzle of the loud M60; the noise permanently damaged his hearing. Soiset checked out the two VC he and his men had shot and found that one was still alive, albeit in very bad shape. He was full of holes; his leg had been practically sawed off by M60 bullets. The man had a pistol indicating that he was an officer. The grunts modified a makeshift tourniquet out of empty ammo bandoliers and tied it to his leg. Soiset's machine gunner claimed the pistol as a souvenir.

The two enemy wounded were medevaced out, thanks to jungle penetrators, and the grunts rifled through their packs and possessions. One sergeant found a plastic envelope with maps and papers. Soiset inspected it: "I noticed a glint of gold inside the envelope. I reached in and fished out a medal, with an enameled picture of a man holding a AK-47 and a woman behind him in a blue background, encircled by a red border, with a ten-pointed gold star forming the overall shape." One of the men recognized the medal. "It's an award the NVA cadre gives to VC regulars who have been credited with killing three Americans." They found another such medal in the man's pack, indicating he had killed as many as six Americans. They also found evidence that he was a first lieutenant. "I was thankful he did not have a full platoon with him when he and his companions walked into the middle of us."

That night, as Soiset and his men sat in the jungle and kept the usual evening watch for enemy soldiers, the young lieutenant played the firefight over and over in his head. "I had killed a man, possibly two. I didn't feel a thing. I supposed this was in part due to our unconsciously imposed psychological cocoon which we all had to keep from going nuts. I had expected something, although I did not know what. I was a little surprised at how easy it was. The only sensations [were] relief and numbness. The relief from having survived and having done all that was required; the numbness from the mental shield our subconscious imposes to save our sanity."[45]

SOISET'S PLATOON HAD GOTTEN THE first shot on the day of that firefight, but more often the enemy got the jump on the Americans. This especially happened when grunts were tired, hot, and generally not very alert. Case in point, one day, while Alpha Company was deep in the jungle, an enemy soldier snuck up on a listening post man pulling perimeter security along a trail and shot him. This happened early in the morning when the company was about to move out. "Guys were pulling in their claymores. They were having breakfast," Captain Merson recalled. "I was getting ready to move when the next thing I know I hear 'Bang, Bang, Bang' . . . right up the trail. We put some M60 fire out." Moments later, they moved in the direction of the shooting and found out what had happened. "There was this young soldier shot right in the face. He was on listening post and was supposed to be our early warning, but he was sitting there reading a goddamn comic book. Charlie walked right down the trail and shot him at point-blank range."

Merson speculated that the enemy soldier "probably came around a bend in the trail, saw the GI there, shot him, and moved out." The bullet slammed into the GI's jaw and exited without hitting his brain or skull. Amazingly, the man lived. Merson was very relieved that the man survived but was enraged at the man's lack of vigilance. "He was not killed by the incident, and he damn well should have been." Merson gave his sergeants an earful. "I used it as a teaching point. I said, 'Goddamnit, this is your responsibility.' It's a sergeant's business, not a company commander's, not even a platoon leader's . . . to make sure that the guys you've got out there know what . . . they're doing . . . and that they're not smokin' and jokin'. I reamed 'em out." Comic book reading came to an end.[46]

Unfortunately, the same could not be said of the war. It continued through yet another Christmas and another New Year. Vietnamization was now in full swing, and platoons from the 7th Infantry routinely operated with Ruff Puff outfits of varying quality and motivation.[47] Many Americans, by now, were heartily sick of the war and wanted it to end as quickly as possible. American leaders, civilian and military, no longer thought of victory. They were more interested in a phased withdrawal; "peace with honor," they called it. The troops in the field were left to get along as best they could, carrying out the same missions they always had, but with precious little national will to support them. The war had torn the American people apart, setting them at odds with one another; the country was plagued with racial and cultural strife.

Inevitably, these problems affected the Army. By the end of its involvement in Vietnam, the U.S. Army was on the verge of disintegration stemming from low morale, drug use, and racial tension. These problems were much more acute in the rear areas than in combat units like the Cottonbalers.[48] Drug use went on in the 7th Infantry but almost never in the field. "In a line company that would never be tolerated to be out in the field or back at a base camp and doing drugs," Private First Class Norris said. "Everybody in a line company depends on the other person. You fight a war not for the cause but for the guy next to you. You rely on the person next to you, so none of that went on. There was definitely marijuana when you went on stand-down, but . . . there was never, ever anybody smoking dope or doing drugs in the field. You would be ostracized. You couldn't do that. You lived on the edge."[49]

As Norris indicated, drug use was mainly limited to marijuana smoking on stand-down in a secure area. This had gone on in the Cottonbalers as early as 1966 (Lieutenant Hindelang mentioned it several times in his letters). Lieutenant Masuda never saw any drug use in the field, but he did see it from time to time back in the larger base camps that passed for rear areas. "A lot of them smoked dope when they were back at base camp. I remember walking around . . . as officer of the day and I'd check the bunkers. I'd open the door and they were all stoned in there, but I knew that when they went out [to the field] no one smoked. Out in the field no one smoked, because everybody depended on each other."[50]

What's more, the Cottonbalers, along with most other grunt outfits, were remarkably devoid of racial tension, at a time when America seemed on the verge of a race war. In fact, it is quite possible that the most racially harmonious place to be as an American in 1970 was with a combat unit in the field in Vietnam. In the rear, blacks and whites sometimes went their separate ways, but in the field race did not matter a lick, only dependability and brotherhood. "We made no distinction," Merson said. Lieutenant James Edwards, a natural leader and an ROTC graduate of Norfolk State College, was one of the few African-American officers in the 7th Infantry in Vietnam (racial mores had changed for the better, but not all the way). In his Alpha Company rifle platoon, race meant next to nothing. "I think guys actually forgot, while you were out there fighting for your life, the color of the person next to you. You only thought about whether that guy was going to pull his responsibility . . . whether he could cover you if you got into some trouble. If he could do that then he was alright."[51]

IN EARLY FEBRUARY, ALPHA COMPANY lost a good commander when Merson rotated to a staff job as the battalion supply officer. This was common practice for officers. Most served no more than six months in the field. The policy guaranteed that many officers got combat experience, but it also guaranteed that combat units were constantly breaking in new commanders. Most of the grunts thought of it as "ticket punching" at their expense. Career officers needed combat experience to advance, even those in support branches, so they did their time in a combat zone and "punched their ticket" for promotion, even though they were not qualified to lead men in combat and sometimes got them killed.

In Merson's case, though, he was finally ready to leave his beloved Alpha. "By this time I was brain dead; and couldn't give you my name, rank, serial number, or date of birth." His first tour of duty, in addition to the months of life-and-death responsibility of leading Alpha's soldiers, had weighed heavily on him. "It's a fine line and tightrope walk, and a damn lonely job. No one will ever understand the weight of this responsibility unless they've been there." By the end, he could not stop thinking about the fact that he had never lost a man killed. This win streak worked on his mind and, quite possibly, cut into his effectiveness as a leader. He was ready for a change. He served out the rest of his tour and went home. At the San Francisco airport he, like many other returning veterans, was spit on. Naturally, he was stunned and angered. The assailant was a young woman who quickly disappeared before Merson even knew what had happened. He stayed in the Army for a time but became disaffected with the Army's post-Vietnam malaise and got out. He went back to college, earned two degrees, and enjoyed a long career as a cartographer for the National Forest Service.[52]

Merson's exit meant that Alpha was now in the hands of one of the ticket punchers. Captain Osualdo Iszqveirdo, a native of Puerto Rico, was a quartermaster officer totally out of his depth as the commanding officer of a rifle company. He had precious little infantry experience and no command presence. Many of the Alpha soldiers understood this and felt that he had no business being in the field. "He was a rear echelon captain," Lieutenant Masuda explained. "He needed his field experience; it was his first time out in the field. He was telling me how to run artillery by the books." This led to plenty of tension and several arguments between Masuda, who knew his business when it came to calling in artillery, and the previously deskbound quartermaster captain. Lieutenant Edwards claimed that Iszqveirdo was so scared he could hardly function. Soldiers could easily pick up on that kind of fear in an officer; it ate away at their resolve and spread like a virus from man to man.[53]

On March 1, 1970, Captain Iszqveirdo's lack of combat expertise led Alpha into a deadly ambush. In fact, the ambush that day was a defining experience for many of the grunts, including a twenty-one-year-old M79 man, Private First Class Philip G. Salois of the 2nd Platoon. Salois was an only child, born in Rhode Island but raised in California. His father was a World War II veteran who had married a French bride. Phil went to college for a year at Cal State-Fullerton but flunked out. In truth, he had no interest in college at that point and flunked out deliberately. An incurable optimist, he erroneously believed his draft number would not be called. Like many other young men of his generation who went to Vietnam, he was not involved in the counterculture or particularly aware of the war. He was simply living his life, working at an insurance company, when the draft call came in early 1969.

He joined the 7th Infantry in September of that year, went through the usual FNG routine, and served as an RTO for a couple months before becoming an M79 man. In late February, he and the other Alpha grunts were patrolling an area that intelligence said was infested with NVA bunkers. "The afternoon of February 28 we . . . found the bunker complex. It was about 5 o'clock . . . in the afternoon. It was getting dark and we didn't want to start any mess that late in the day, so we headed off in an opposite direction for a couple of clicks and set up a night defensive perimeter. At first light we would assault the enemy bunkers."

That night the men wrapped themselves up in ponchos, slept, pulled guard duty, and thought about what might happen the next day. Salois, filled with a deep sense of foreboding, did not sleep at all that night. As a veteran, he knew that bunker complexes were dangerous. The enemy often built them for the express purpose of luring Americans into them. They were usually well constructed, with tunnels and firing ports; almost always they were difficult to detect until the Americans walked right on top of them. For all these reasons, the enemy liked to defend bunker complexes whenever possible, and Salois knew it. Basically, the best thing that could happen the next day would be that Alpha Company would find empty bunkers, blow them in place, and risk an enemy ambush from elsewhere in the jungle.

In the morning, the men munched on C rations, policed up their weapons and equipment, and prepared to move out. Salois's 2nd Platoon was in the lead. Captain Iszqveirdo now made a major error. According to Salois, "He was looking for his promotion to major—and a body count. He said, 'Let's go down [to the bunkers] the same way we came up. Let's not bother blazing a new trail.' He did not want to waste time breaking a new trail. That was a real bad mistake."

Actually, it was an egregious mistake. Any infantry commander knew never to tread the same path to and from an objective on any patrol, no matter the situation. To do so was to beg to be ambushed, but Iszqveirdo did not seem to understand this. The NVA made Alpha Company pay dearly for this fateful oversight. The enemy set up a U-shaped ambush along the previous day's approach to the bunker complex.

The Cottonbalers came along and walked right into the ambush. The point element had just crossed a small clearing when the enemy opened fire. "All of a sudden I could hear the crack of rifle fire. We immediately formed a defensive perimeter. It seemed as if the fire was coming from everywhere. They had us surrounded on three sides. At the beginning, we were shooting back over each other's heads until we were able to get into fighting positions. There was so much chaos. It's lucky that we didn't kill some of our own guys." The whole situation was awful. Men were screaming and cursing; men were getting hit. Enemy fire was coming from seemingly everywhere. "When we finally got our act together, there was a visible line that we had formed."

The six men of the point element, including Private First Class Salois's platoon leader, Lieutenant Terry Bowell, were cut off, probably no more than fifty feet away from the enemy. "They were trapped in [the] clearing, maybe 20 yards all around. We couldn't see any of the forward element because of a tree line in front of us." Frustratingly, Salois and the 2nd Platoon had to be very careful where they shot for fear of hitting the pinned-down point element somewhere ahead, through the trees. "We could only fire from . . . about one o'clock to five o'clock because we . . . didn't want to shoot . . . where our guys were over there."[54]

The men of the point element were in the midst of a living nightmare. Most all of them had been hit. They were bleeding and cowering, shrinking from constant enemy fire—rifles and machine guns mostly. They were cut off from the rest of Alpha Company, lying out in the open, at the mercy of the NVA. To make matters worse, Lieutenant Bowell took a round through the temple and died quickly. He was one of the most popular and respected officers in the company. The man oozed integrity and decency.

Jim Norris had been promoted to sergeant and squad leader by now and, as such, had the opportunity to work closely with Bowell. "Terry Bowell was a great guy, absolutely the most outstanding officer. I had three platoon leaders while I was there and he, beyond a doubt, was the most outstanding, caring individual that I worked for. He cared about the people that worked for him. He had a lot of compassion . . . a tremendous person." Lieutenant Masuda considered Bowell his best friend in Vietnam. "He was just a nice guy. When we came back to base camp . . . we'd go to a bar, have dinner. We just basically hung around. We had a lot of things . . . in common. He was . . . just a gentleman. I don't recall anybody in his entire platoon not liking him. He always took care of his men first."

The NVA might well have braved a dash into the clearing to finish the rest of Bowell's men if not for Lieutenant Masuda. Fifty meters back in the column, hugging the ground with the company command group, he cranked up a fire mission: "I saw bullets tearing the trees above me. We just hit the ground and . . . called in artillery." The forward observer could not see anything beyond the confusing foliage in front of him. "It was complete jungle. I called in artillery by sound." Considering how little chance he had to view his target, the rounds were pretty accurate. They screamed into the NVA-held positions along the U shape of their ambush, probably inflicting few casualties but definitely keeping them at bay.[55] The firefight settled down for probably at least half an hour.

In the meantime, at the edge of the tree line near the fateful clearing, Private First Class Salois felt a distinct sense of rage welling up inside him. He could think of little else besides those six unfortunate men of the point element, pinned down and bleeding under the hot sun and the NVA's bullets. The shooting had died down a bit, but the situation was just as desperate as before. "I became very angry over the whole situation. It seemed like a long, long time. I really got very disturbed that no one was making any attempts to rescue them. We had lost radio contact with them." Salois made up his mind that, danger or not, he would make an attempt to rescue the forlorn men. He took a moment and bowed his head in prayer. "I said to God, 'If I were out there, I would hope someone would make an attempt to rescue me. I'm going to go out and do something. If you get me out of this mess, safe and sound without a scratch, I'll do anything you want.'" Salois's parents were devout Catholics and made sure he went to Mass each Sunday, but aside from that, he was not especially religious, at least not until this fateful moment.

Private First Class Salois finished his prayer, grabbed his M79, and went up to the front of the perimeter. He told the other men he was going to save the point element. The others looked at him a bit quizzically and tried to talk him out of his mission of mercy. They knew he would need more than an M79 if he hoped to succeed. "It was kind of a useless . . . weapon in the jungles, but that's what I had, with my vest with all the grenades in it." Salois was adamant. He was going out there to get those men.

Seeing Salois's resolve, another man, Specialist Fourth Class Herbert Klug from Dayton, Ohio, said, "If you're going to go out there, I'll go with you. But let's develop a plan." For a few minutes he and Salois talked. Soon they agreed on a plan.

"Well, there were two huge boulders to the right of the forward element," Salois said. "We would just kind of barrage that whole right flank with everything we had to kind of distract the enemy long enough . . . so that the guys in the front element could run back." So the front or point element would be on the left and Salois and Klug on the right, near the boulders.

Salois clutched his M79 and Klug his M16. They prepared to run from cover into the terrifying abyss of the NVA kill zone. At the last moment another soldier, Private Edmund Killingbeck of South Carolina, joined them and lent the firepower of yet another M16. With no more fanfare, they glanced at one another and took off for the rocks. Immediately the area came alive with rifle and machine-gun fire. Bullets zipped and crackled everywhere. The three American soldiers ran as fast as they possibly could, adrenaline pumping through their veins and arteries. The firefight was noisy as could be, but they almost couldn't hear it. More pervasive was the huff and puff of their frenzied breathing, the pumping of their hearts, the sound of their boots and trousers whipping through the foliage.

About halfway to the boulders, Salois saw an enemy bullet smash into Killingbeck's shoulder. He staggered, turned around, and ran safely back to the perimeter. "Herb and I continued on. Once we got to the boulders, he sprayed the area with automatic fire and I kept lobbing grenades at the enemy's position. And it worked! We saw four guys [from the point element] run back." Just as they had hoped, the boulders provided adequate cover, and for a few minutes Salois and Klug waited to see if anybody else among the point element was still alive and able to get back to the perimeter. "After a while, when we saw there was no one else moving, Herb said it was time for us to get back to our perimeter. We both started to low-crawl on our bellies; he was on the inside, and I was on the outside. We were shoulder to shoulder. I made it all the way back."

Only then did Salois notice that Specialist Klug was not with him. "I was so focused on looking ahead to reach the safety of our lines. I still feel guilty about that. I gazed over the berm and saw him lying out there . . . face down in the dirt. Without even thinking, I ran out to get him. We were still receiving fire. I grabbed him under the shoulders to drag him, but I couldn't budge him. He was just so heavy. A couple of soldiers from my platoon noticed my struggle and ran out, and we dragged him back."

Coughing and sputtering from the exertion, excitement, and danger of retrieving Klug, they caught their collective breath, turned Klug over, and finally got a good look at him. Klug was not wounded; he was dead. "He had received a round in his chin, that ricocheted off the ground . . . entered under the chin and exited through the top of his head, killing him instantly."

Moments later some other soldiers asked Private First Class Salois if he would be willing to go back out again. Lieutenant Bowell and his RTO were still out there, presumed dead, but their bodies had to be brought in. Salois was the only person who knew where their bodies were, so he agreed to go. Luckily, the NVA, possibly prompted by Masuda's artillery, had decided to disengage. "The firing had ceased and the enemy had scattered." Salois and the other men quickly found Lieutenant Bowell and his RTO. "I led them to the spot and found the radio operator severely wounded and Lieutenant Bowell dead. We brought the L-T back and the [RTO] who was too injured to move. We carried them back to the perimeter . . . and we dusted everybody off using the jungle penetrator."

There were quite a few to dust off. At the beginning of the day, 2nd Platoon's strength was twenty-seven men. Now it had seven. The platoon had lost two men killed and another eighteen wounded. The survivors watched as U.S. artillery and air strikes torched the jungle where the commanders thought the NVA had gone. Then Alpha moved out again. Salois felt damaged and morose. He could not believe he was unscathed. "Not a scratch. To me that was a miracle. We did a recon into the bunker complex and found some maps. Then we threw grenades into the bunkers and destroyed them. For the rest of the afternoon I was in a daze."

Lieutenant Masuda was also in something of a daze, stricken with grief over the loss of his friend Bowell. "It really hit me hard when they brought his body back. I can still visualize it. I knew he was gone. I remember sitting after everything was over. I just sat behind a big tree for I don't know how long. I was fairly numb." Sergeant Norris was getting very short by now (near the end of his tour) and was not with Alpha that day, an absence for which he always felt a bit guilty. He had just returned from R&R and was in the process of being reassigned from field duty to a rear job. Quite by accident, he saw Bowell's body when it was helicoptered back to the base camp. Like the others, he felt completely numb. "Just like I did with the rest of the war, I just put it out of mind. I just didn't deal with it. I just put it away and put it in that compartment where I had shelved everything else I had seen for the last eleven months. It enabled me to just go on with my life."

That night Alpha Company set up a defensive perimeter. The captain quizzed Salois about his experiences while they were still fresh in his mind. The young soldier—along with many of his buddies—resented the captain for the terrible mistake he had made but nonetheless told him everything he wanted to know. Iszqveirdo wrote up citations for both Salois and Klug. Salois won the Silver Star, and Klug the Distinguished Service Cross.

But as he sat in the perimeter on the evening of March 1, Salois could not have cared less about medals. "I started running the events over and over in my mind, like a newsreel. That's when I started getting scared. When the adrenaline started going away to wherever it comes from, I really got scared because I thought they were going to come back and finish us off. It's dark, you can't see, there's no control." Salois did not sleep at all: "I couldn't wait for the morning. Then the morning came and we got out of there."

Salois continued with the daily survival chore of being a grunt. He tried to force the memories of that terrible March 1 from his mind including his promise to God—and focus on the future. Two years later, back in the World, he was reading the newspaper one Sunday afternoon in his apartment. "An article caught my eye that said the Catholic Church would be in trouble in 20 years because of a growing shortage of vocations to the priesthood. I left the newspaper on the dining room table and kept going back to that article every day." He started reading the Bible he had kept in Vietnam and finally asked himself, "Is God calling me to the priesthood?" Salois believed so. He went back to college, attended seminary, became a priest, and dedicated his life to ministering to veterans.[56]

TWO WEEKS AFTER ALPHA'S AMBUSH, Charlie Company got a little payback. On March 15 they were investigating reports of yet another NVA bunker complex somewhere in the jungle east of Xuan Loc. They quickly found what they were looking for, an elaborate series of hootches and bunkers, including a hospital with nineteen bamboo beds. The Americans spent the day destroying the bunkers and gathering up stray enemy weapons and equipment.

As always, where there were bunkers, there were often enemy soldiers. That night, an ambush patrol from Charlie Company set up shop along a dry streambed near the complex. They had barely gotten settled in when they noticed movement. "We had just finished setting up," First Lieutenant John Chryst explained, "and we were about to break for chow when our machine gunner heard someone walking."

The machine gunner, Private First Class Dennis Boryla, clearly saw enemy soldiers walking right into his kill zone. "I saw three enemy walking into our ambush. I hooked up the claymores and waited for them to come. I waited for them to get further along so that we would be able to get them in a cross fire, and finally I thought the time was right, so I blew the claymores."

In no time, the entire ambush patrol opened up with the usual devastating array of firepower. They swept the streambed with hundreds of machine-gun and rifle rounds. M79 men shot grenade after grenade into the bed. Fragments and bullets tore everywhere, dealing out death with impunity. After several moments of this, the grunts heard the enemy screaming, "Chieu Hoi!" a phrase indicating surrender. "Then we saw two arms raised above the stream bed wall," Lieutenant Chryst recalled. He ordered a cease-fire and the terrified enemy soldier surrendered. Chryst and his men searched the streambed and found twelve dead, bloody, shredded remnants of human beings who were once NVA soldiers. It was a little victory, but it bolstered morale in the company and the battalion. The war was devolving; it was unpopular and most Americans, soldiers and civilians, wanted it over with as soon as possible, as sensibly as possible.[57]

When Alpha Company lost Lieutenant Bowell, Jim Edwards took over for him and, in no time, proved himself to be a fine platoon leader. He blended with his men, wore a bandanna under his helmet, and made no distinction of rank in his appearance. His soldiers, including Salois, called him "L-T," a grunt salutation of respect for an esteemed officer. Edwards had a wife and two daughters back home in Norfolk, but he tried to put them out of his mind when he was out in the bush. He knew he had to stay locked in, focused, and alert, so much so that he did not even read letters from home until the platoon went back to the relative safety of base camp.

On the day Bowell was killed, Lieutenant Edwards was still fairly new to the 7th Infantry. He was back at battalion headquarters waiting to be assigned to a line unit. At first, his superiors wanted to send him right out to the site of the ambush to take over for the fallen Bowell. "I had never met him. They told me to get my gear together to replace him. All these thoughts were going through my mind: 'They are in an ambush. They don't know me. I don't know them. I don't know nothing about Vietnam. This is crazy.' They told me they were going to helicopter me in and . . . drop me down in the triple canopy. I said, 'Now, this is crazy.' But that's what they intended to do." Luckily for Edwards, Alpha Company moved on and that negated the dubious idea of plopping him down into an ambush situation. The lieutenant breathed a huge sigh of relief. He took over the 2nd Platoon in a little ceremony when it came back to base camp. "I had this premonition that I was not going to come back home." Fortunately, Edwards was wrong.

In March and April, he led the 2nd Platoon through many small firefights. In one of them, in March, he got wounded in the jaw—a piece of shrapnel lodged near his chin. He had it removed and soon returned. Then, in April he got hit again. His platoon got mortared by an unseen group of NVA. For a few terrifying moments, the rounds came in one after the other. One of them exploded somewhere right behind Lieutenant Edwards. Two fragments hit him, one in the shoulder and one in the back, but it all happened so swiftly that Edwards hardly understood that he had been wounded. "I didn't even realize I was hit. Unless [the wound] is something major that prevents your movement or your thoughts, you don't even know what's going on. Your adrenaline is so high." At that point he realized he had been hit, and the medic gave him first aid. "After things calmed down, I can remember one of the guys saying, 'L-T, you got your job back in the rear now.' " Usually if a man was wounded twice, he rotated out of the field, but not in Edwards's case. As an officer he was expected to go back to combat, provided he was physically able. A medevac evacuated Edwards and he spent a few days at a hospital. The doctors dug the small fragment out of his back but left the other fragment in his shoulder, on the premise that it would be more trouble to take out than leave in.

When Lieutenant Edwards recovered and returned to the unit, he asked about the possibility of rotating out of the field. "The point was made that as an officer, and since mine weren't major wounds, I shouldn't even be asking that. I was highly irritated." He didn't waste time complaining, though. He simply continued leading his men on various operations, praying often that he would not screw up and get anyone killed, and left the field a few months later on the usual officer's rotation. He was more than a little relieved that none of his men got killed.[58]

EVER SO STEADILY THE U.S. Army was scaling back its forces in Vietnam. One by one, units were deploying home. Normally, the unit's logistical staff and colors were sent home first, mostly for PR reasons, so that politicians and generals could brag about the extensive withdrawal from Vietnam. However, anyone in a homeward-bound unit who had significant time remaining on his tour transferred to another unit. In the summer of 1970, even as the Cottonbalers moved to an AO farther east at Ham Tan in Binh Tuy Province, the 199th Light Infantry Brigade received orders to go home. All summer long, the brigade, including the 3rd Battalion of the 7th Infantry, scaled back its operations and prepared to deploy to the states.

Newer men were transferred to other units, but many of the veterans, including Lieutenant Masuda and Sergeant Norris, finished their tours by the summertime and went home. Masuda returned to Hawaii, got married, and went on to a quiet, productive life as an insurance adjustor. Sergeant Norris met and married a girl from Queens in 1972. For a time he worked as a firefighter in New York, but he was laid off during the city's bout with bankruptcy in the mid-1970s. He ended up moving on to New Hampshire, where he embarked on a long career as a state trooper and investigator for the attorney general's office. Lieutenant Edwards, after rotating out of the field, served out the rest of his tour with the Americal Division, went home, left the Army, and worked in the circulation department of a Norfolk newspaper. Much as Salois had, Edwards remembered a promise he had made to God while in danger during a firefight in Vietnam and got involved in the Baptist church in which he grew up. He ended up becoming a full-time minister and pastor of that church.[59]

In September 1970, after almost four years of fruitless fighting, the Cottonbalers' colors left Vietnam for good. By now everyone who had once populated the unit had either moved on to another unit or gone home. Phil Salois spent his last few months as a clerk in the rear. He came home the day after the 7th Infantry's colors left Vietnam. In a sense, his homecoming was symbolic of the regiment's homecoming. Like so many other Cottonbalers, he went home alone, almost anonymous. "I was feeling pretty alone. There was nobody left in the unit. Everybody had either been reassigned or gone home." He rode a bus to the airport, and when it was time to go, he reveled in the wonderful sight of a Northwest Orient aircraft—his personal freedom bird. "When I got on that plane and it took off, it was a big, big sigh of relief."

The trip was uneventful. The plane landed in San Francisco late at night. The airport was quiet and mostly empty. There were no protesters and no one spit on him. He hopped a flight to Los Angeles. "I didn't tell my parents I was coming home. I grabbed a cab . . . and it took me home. I wanted to just . . . walk in the house and surprise them. I told the cab . . . to leave me off a couple doors down. I went right in the house. They were watching TV, my mother sprawled out on the couch. I thought she was going to have a stroke when she saw me." His parents jumped up and mobbed him. The three hugged and his mother cried. "It was good and it was worth it." They basked in the joy of his homecoming. Salois, the future priest, felt an overwhelming sense of joy and sheer relief at having survived the war when so many others had not.[60]

He and so many other Cottonbalers had done their best in what was ultimately a doomed war effort. They were among the finest combat infantrymen ever to serve under the colors of the 7th Infantry. Now, like many generations of Cottonbaler combat veterans before them, the rest of their lives beckoned, lives to be spent in building, working, struggling, soul-searching, and renewing.

The Cottonbalers were home.

CHAPTER 3

The Triumph of Professionalism

The Persian Gulf War

IN THE YEARS FOLLOWING VIETNAM, the Army bottomed out. Seven years of fighting an ultimately futile war ate away at the Army's vitality, its morale, and its soldiers. The unpopular, divisive nature of the war, combined with the social upheaval of the 1960s, led to a steady corrosion of morale, fighting power, readiness, and quality among America's soldiers. Tragically and unfairly, many Americans blamed the military for the Vietnam debacle. The soldiers who fought there were sometimes branded as baby killers, losers, imperialists, or, at best, exploited dupes of a terribly misguided, morally corrupt government. Anti-military feelings ran high among the American people, especially in intellectual circles. Universities abolished ROTC programs. Reporters wrote muckraking stories exposing the many problems of the military. Soldiers went out of their way to avoid wearing their uniforms in public. Filmmakers who had once produced hero-worshiping movies extolling the virtues of men in battle now avoided military topics altogether.

The American citizenry had, of course, always been a bit uneasy about the soldiers who wore the country's uniform. In the 1970s, the citizenry decided, in a general sense, that they did not like them one bit. Anyone or anything military was suspect, scorned, outcast, at least in the view of a rising number of Americans. These civilians, in the wake of Vietnam, Watergate, and the social activism of the 1960s, were no longer sure their country stood for honorable values, so it is not surprising that these anguished, soul-searching people often viewed soldiers—those who dedicated their lives to defending America and its values—as suspect, perhaps even dangerous. To wit, a 1973 Harris poll asked Americans to rank occupations from most to least respected. The military finished perilously close to the bottom, only above garbagemen.

In a very real sense, then, society's problems were spilling over into the Army. More than 40 percent of the U.S. Army in Europe used drugs. Seven percent were addicted to heroin. Crime and desertion were out of control. In some instances, renegade bands of soldiers ruled their barracks in defiance of their officers and NCOs, functioning as little more than gangs in uniform, all on the taxpayers' dime. The poison of racial hatred also debilitated the Army. Mass brawls between black and white soldiers broke out in such places as Fayetteville, North Carolina, and Bamberg, Germany. Forty percent of the Army's soldiers had no high school diploma, and 41 percent scored in the lowest mental category on the Army's entrance test.[1]

In addition to changing the public's view of the military, the Vietnam War also eroded any significant popular support for the draft. In fact, the only thing more unpopular than the military itself was the draft that forced young men to serve. Congress phased it out by 1974. On the surface this seemed to compound the Army's problems. The U.S. Army of the 1970s had had enough problems filling its ranks with the draft, much less without it. Given the antimilitary tenor of public sentiment and the Army's declining reputation, how in the world could the service hope to attract quality manpower? When seen in this context, the end of the draft seemed like the coup de grace to a dying, aimless army.

In actuality, it proved to be the complete opposite. If the Army no longer had a large number of well-trained, quality soldiers in the 1970s, it certainly did not lack for visionary leaders in the top positions. Army Chief of Staff General Creighton Abrams led a reformist crusade that eventually turned the U.S. Army into the best in the world. Abrams was a tough, cigar-chomping, passionate armor officer who had carved out a lasting legacy as a tank battalion commander in George Patton's 3rd Army in World War II. Abrams led the armored task force that broke into Bastogne during the Battle of the Bulge. Later in his career, he commanded U.S. forces in Vietnam. Abrams knew that an unfortunate byproduct of pacifism was unpreparedness; he knew from his World War II experiences that such unpreparedness inevitably led to a terrible price in

American lives. He understood better than anyone that the best way to prevent war was to prepare for it.

He strongly believed that the Army was better off without the draft. In his view, most of the problem soldiers were draftees. Remove them and you removed many of the troubles. Shorn of such recalcitrant millstones, he and other officers could now build a modern, all-volunteer force of some 780,000 soldiers around one unified, simple, effective concept-quality soldiers armed with superior weapons. Abrams devoted his considerable energies laying the groundwork for this goal. In the process he devised a total-force concept that made sure the Army could never again be committed to combat without a call-up of the reserves and National Guard. This prevented the unhealthy division of forces and responsibilities that had developed during the Vietnam era.

Abrams's reformist fervor bolstered morale among his fellow senior officers and imbued them with a similar zeal for change. When he died of cancer in 1974, his successor, General Fred Weyand (the man who had once been a Cottonbaler), picked up right where Abrams left off. Weyand made sure that troublemakers were weeded out of units, drug offenders prosecuted or kicked out of the service, and training standards raised.

Still, this "spring-cleaning" mentality was not enough to solve the Army's serious problems. In the long term, only two things could really bring about the renaissance Abrams, Weyand, and so many others (including future senior leaders like Norman Schwarzkopf and Colin Powell) wanted: a change in society's attitude and more money from Congress. One inevitably led to the other. The Army did attract some good volunteers—of both sexes—during the 1970s, but it had serious problems keeping them, mainly because society still held them in low esteem and, as a result, they were paid abysmally. Enlisted soldiers moonlighted or went on food stamps; they often lived below the poverty level. Even officers had real difficulties supporting their families.

Although waste has always been a serious problem in American defense spending, it is an indisputable fact that when it comes to the U.S. Army, the American people usually get exactly what they pay for. When the Army has been deprived of even basic operating expenses such as during the antebellum period, the peacetime years of the early twentieth century, or the 1970s, then its fighting readiness and the quality of its soldiers decline. But when Congress has been willing to spend money on the Army, the result has generally been a powerful, well-armed, well-trained fighting force—the armies that fought the Civil War, World War I, World War II, Vietnam, and, eventually, the Gulf War exemplify that point.

By the end of the 1970s, the ineffectiveness of American foreign policy, combined with the Army's poor state of fighting readiness, its retention problems, and its horribly botched rescue mission of the American hostages held in Iran, led to a change in public opinion. Hungering for an end to the demoralizing malaise that had settled over American life in the 1970s, many Americans longed to believe once again in their country's greatness as well as its moral ascendancy in the continuing struggle against communism; a strong military seemed to embody these values of American greatness. Ronald Reagan's landslide victory in the 1980 presidential election partially stemmed from the voters' belief that he would rebuild the American military, in so doing providing American servicemen and -women with the funds, weapons, and esteem they needed to defend the country effectively.

Indeed, things did change in the 1980s. The reformist ideas of officers like Abrams, Weyand, and such tactical thinkers as General William DePuy were really just a blueprint for change, roughly similar to an architectural design for a splendid house but without the funds for building materials or construction crews. All of a sudden, the money for such building materials and construction crews became available. During the Reagan years, defense spending more than doubled from $140 billion in 1980 to over $300 billion in 1989. Clearly, the president and an increasingly military-friendly Congress were now committed to creating a powerful, all-volunteer defense establishment.

The Army spent some of the money on new training facilities designed to make sure that American soldiers would never again go to war unprepared. The best, most influential, and most innovative of these new training areas was the National Training Center located at Fort Irwin in the Mojave Desert of California. The National Training Center (generally called the NTC) used laser-guided technology to determine the shooting and tactical effectiveness of tanks, APCs, and even individual riflemen. Units from the combat branches rotated to the NTC for training cycles, fighting realistic "battles" in the same kind of heat, dust, privation, and confusion they might experience in a real war, against an opposing force ("OPFOR") that was superbly trained, even schooled in the latest Soviet tactics.

Officers and noncoms underwent constant After Action Reviews, in which instructors critiqued (and sometimes humiliated) them in front of their troops. The AAR sent the not so subtle message to American soldiers that the Army cared more about producing good leaders than large egos. "As a company commander it was great," Captain Rick Averna, a company commander in the Cottonbalers during the Gulf War, later said. "It was a stressful, twenty-four-hour operation in the desert. At the end of it I was dog tired. I learned a lot about my company, my platoon leaders. We learned a lot about our war fighting skills. You're tired; you're hungry; you're hot." Another man who would one day lead Cottonbalers in the Gulf, Lieutenant Alan Huffines, also found NTC to be a remarkable training experience: "It replicates so much of what we do in combat. I think the National Training Center changed the United States Army to . . . what it became during the Persian Gulf War. What units learned in blood in World War II, we learned in the Mojave." That did not mean the experience was fun for him as a junior leader; it wasn't designed to be. "I hated it. It was tough. There's just this pressure of the moment." The instructors were unforgiving. "They were pretty merciless. You're there in front of your whole platoon. They sit down and say, 'OK, Lieutenant, what were you doing right here?' And you have to fess up in front of your entire platoon that you really don't know what you're doing, in front of God and everyone. That's where I learned, in that environment, I wanted to do the right thing the right way. You really don't know it until you're doing it. I'm really grateful for that experience."[2]

Army leaders were determined to prevent the tragedy of unpreparedness. They knew that the United States had not been prepared for any of its major wars, resulting in unnecessary bloodshed, as Americans learned under fire. The NTC was designed to make sure that such bloody "OJT" would never happen again, and it worked. The Persian Gulf War was the only major war in American history for which American soldiers were truly prepared. The resulting lesson was quite clear—overwhelming victory at minimal cost in American blood.

The Army needed more than good training for such positive results, though. It also needed superior weapons. The Army spent a tremendous amount of money in the 1980s on a new generation of weapons designed to be used in a synchronized approach called Air Land Doctrine. The M1 Abrams tank, heavily armored, heavily gunned, beautifully designed, became the main battle tank of the U.S. Army. The generals hoped that the qualitative edge of the Abrams would offset Soviet numbers in a prospective superpower showdown in Europe. A new generation of APC, the M2/3 Bradley, came into service. The Bradley mounted a turret with a devastatingly effective 25mm chain gun augmented by a coaxial machine gun and an antitank projectile known as a TOW (Tube-launched Optically-tracked Wire-guided) missile. The old UH-I Huey that so many Vietnam-era Cottonbalers rode into battle gave way to two new helicopters: the UH-60 Black Hawk designed for transport and fire support and the AH-64 Apache, which proved to be the best tank-killing helicopter in existence. These new air and land weapons, working together in battle, gave American infantrymen and tankers a firepower edge, especially when combined with the vast complement of artillery, engineering, antiaircraft, and air support so typical of the American military in the modern era.[3]

These new-era soldiers were now equipped with Kevlar helmets (coal scuttle style reminiscent of the old German Army), flak vests, chemical overgarments (MOPP suits), and battle dress utilities ("BDUs") designed to hold up in nearly any climate. Their small arms were mostly the same as those used in Vietnam; they were modified, improved versions of the M16 rifle and M60 machine gun, with one important addition, the new Squad Automatic Weapon (SAW), a machine-gun-type weapon that could spew even more reliable, deadly firepower than the M60.

But what of the soldiers themselves? Marvelous new weapons and burgeoning budgets meant nothing without well-trained, disciplined, courageous troops who would fight hard and fight well when America needed them. Finding and training such soldiers was a more difficult challenge than pumping money into military coffers or conceiving effective weapons. As late as 1980, only 50 percent of the Army's new recruits had finished high school. After a decade of neglect and troubles, the Army was still perceived by American youth as a place for losers and ne'er-do-wells.

Only effective, ingenious, innovative marketing could change that perception and attract the kind of motivated, educated young people the Army so desperately needed to make the all-volunteer concept work.

Enter Major General Max Thurman, the head of Army Recruiting Command. More than anyone else, this vigorous, affable man changed the Army's image and attracted quality people to the service. He assigned the Army's best soldiers to recruiting duty, stepped up recruiting at high schools, demanded that new recruits earn their high school diplomas (an indicator of future success in the service), and employed advertising brilliantly. Armed with a congressional agreement to free up half a billion dollars for recruiting bonuses, a new GI Bill, and an Army College Fund, Thurman appealed to American youth to use the Army as a steppingstone rather than a resting place. He presided over the implementation of the "Be All You Can Be" slogan, a powerful challenge to upwardly mobile young people searching for independence, maturity, or just a good place to start adult careers.

Thurman's new recruiting direction worked extremely well. In the space of a few years, the Army's image changed from a sad-sack organization time had left behind to a caring, committed high-tech organization full of intelligent, tough soldiers. By the end of the 1980s, the Army was completely transformed. Hundreds of thousands of quality young men and women had joined throughout the decade. By 1991, when this new Army fought in the Gulf, over 98 percent of army recruits had graduated from high school, 75 percent tested in the highest mental categories on the Army's aptitude tests, and 41 percent were enrolled in the Army College Fund. Discipline problems had practically disappeared, as had drug abuse; fewer than 1 percent of the Army tested positive for drugs. Those who ended up in the combat branches like infantry (still all male) were generally the toughest, best-conditioned, most motivated troops. Nor were they lacking in intelligence. Manipulation of high-tech weaponry, survival on the modern battlefield, and the tactical demands of late-twentieth-century infantry combat meant that the United States needed bright soldiers, and it now had them.

In fact, the combat soldiers of this new Army of the late cold war period eclipsed their Vietnam-era fathers in terms of training, education, motivation, and weapons. American infantrymen of the Gulf War were the brightest, best-armed, best-equipped, best-prepared, most professional soldiers the United States had ever produced. "Most of the troops were pretty smart kids," one 7th Infantry officer explained. "Most of them just out of high school, not sure of the direction they wanted to go, different backgrounds. Ninety-five percent of them wanted to do a good job every day."[4] They were from all races, all regions, all socioeconomic backgrounds. Their reasons for joining varied—money for college, adventure, career, escape from broken families, escape from dead-end lives of crime and drugs, perhaps a sense of duty or responsibility. No matter what the motivation for joining, the Army turned them into solid, professional combat soldiers.

More than the generals, the people who made that happen were the noncommissioned officers (NCOs), those who really prepare soldiers for battle and lead them when bullets fly. The long years of ponderous fighting in Vietnam had eroded the Army's NCO corps. Far too many of them got killed or wounded or left the Army. They could not be replaced. More than anything, experience makes a good noncommissioned officer, and the fresh-faced graduates of "shake and bake" NCO schools in Vietnam did not have enough of it. During the reform period of the 1970s and the renaissance period of the 1980s the Army placed a premium on the development of good NCOs. It did so by strengthening the NCO academies, identifying leaders early in their army careers, and affording greater responsibility to experienced sergeants.

The positions of platoon sergeant, first sergeant, and sergeant major were among the most important in the Army, and the service began to treat them that way. Physical and mental standards became far more stringent. For instance, of those who graduated in the Sergeant Major Academy's first class in 1973, only 8 percent had attended college. By 1991, 88 percent had attended college and half had earned their degrees. By that time, noncoms had become, in a way, almost a parallel officer corps. The beefy, dough-faced top sergeant of yesteryear gave way to the lean, tough, combat-experienced (usually in Vietnam), intensely professional first sergeant of the new Army. By and large, these products of the new NCO culture performed extremely well in the Gulf.

Thus by 1990, the Army's rise from the dead was complete. One soldier summed up this redemption process well: "A visionary cohort of soldiers who stayed with the institution during the difficult years following the war in Vietnam was responsible for launching the Army on its path to reform. They saw in the volunteer Army concept the opportunity to create a new-style Army capable, for the first time in its history, of winning the first battle at the lowest possible cost in human life. The small, professional Army they created would be able to maneuver with unprecedented agility and speed. Its leaders would possess the independent spirit to make decisions on their own initiative. This new Army would seek to outthink rather than outslug its opponents. It would be peopled by a new style of soldier whose intelligence, skill, and esprit would allow him to take on and defeat a more numerous foe."[5]

This new Army's test came in the broiling deserts of Southwest Asia. The soldiers who led the Army's rejuvenation had expected to test their ideas and competence against the Soviet Union's Red Army amid the rolling plains and forests of Europe, but the end of the cold war precluded that possibility. Instead, their proving ground was the Middle East, a bubbling cauldron of modern terror.

After a costly victory in a war against neighboring Iran in the 1980s, Saddam Hussein's Iraq sought to rebuild its oil and economic resources. Hussein dreamed of turning his country into a regional superpower. Possession of the lucrative oil fields owned by Iraq's southern neighbor, tiny Kuwait, would provide Iraq with the ability to pay off the debts it had accrued during the Iran war, in addition to giving Hussein control of a substantial portion of the world's oil-producing capacity. To that end, in August 1990 Iraqi soldiers invaded Kuwait and took over the country in a matter of days. They quickly established a nightmarish and exploitive occupation of this helpless, albeit wealthy, country. Iraqi soldiers looted, raped, tortured, and stole.

President George H. W. Bush decided that the Iraqi takeover of Kuwait was intolerable and must not be allowed to stand. He believed that it was morally wrong for one country to simply invade another, erasing it off the map. Such unchecked aggression could set a bad precedent. Far more important, though, he worried about the free flow of oil. Hussein's possession of Kuwait, and the implicit threat against its even larger oil-producing neighbor, Saudi Arabia, might lead to terrible consequences for the world's oil supply. What if Hussein made a move on Saudi Arabia?

He possessed a well-equipped army, the world's fourth largest, and could defeat the Saudis without much trouble. In that unthinkable scenario, this cruel, sadistic dictator would enjoy such rich oil resources that he would have the rest of the world by the throat.

Bush's foreign policy stressed stability in the Middle East to keep the oil flowing and squelch the troubling, and rising, phenomenon of Islamic, anti-Western terrorism. Saddam's aggression, if left unchecked, would, in President Bush's view, destabilize the region. The president felt this would seriously damage the world economy and abet terrorism. Bush remembered well the OPEC oil embargo against the Western nations in the mid-1970s, the way it had come close to paralyzing the United States and led to a deleterious rise in heating and fuel costs. He could not risk that happening again. In spite of his despicable nature, Hussein had been useful to the United States in the 1980s as a check on Iran's hyper-Islamic terrorist fundamentalism, but now the situation was different. Now he was a threat to the entire world economy, and, in Bush's view, Hussein's forces had to be thrown out of Kuwait—by force if necessary.[6]

Bush's decision meant that U.S. troops would be deployed to Saudi Arabia as a deterrent to Saddam. Even as the Bush administration cobbled together a multinational coalition against Iraq, troopers from the 82nd Airborne Division went to Saudi Arabia in August 1990. In the months that followed, thousands of American, British, French, Egyptian, and other troops poured into Saudi Arabia while an uneasy standoff developed between the Iraqis on one side of the Kuwaiti border and the coalition forces on the other.

In the meantime, the Cottonbalers were spread out in two places, geographically far apart. As mentioned in a previous chapter, the Army no longer employed the regiment as its primary tactical organization, but it did continue the regimental lineage of each battalion, within each brigade and each division. Four battalions of Cottonbalers existed as of 1990. The 2nd and 3rd Battalions (now called 2-7 and 3-7) were part of the 24th Infantry Division (Mechanized) based at Fort Stewart, Georgia. Two other battalions, the 1st and the 4th (1–7 and 4-7), resided in Germany as part of the 7th Regiment's old divisional home, the 3rd Infantry Division. The 7th Regiment, in both Europe and the United States, was now a completely mechanized unit. Its soldiers rode into battle in Bradleys and often called themselves "crunchies," "grunts," or "11 Mikes," in reference to their Military Occupational Specialty—11M, meaning mechanized infantryman.

On a hot Georgia evening in early August, the soldiers of 2-7 and 3-7 got word that they were deploying to Saudi Arabia. First Lieutenant Huffines, a twenty-six-year-old platoon leader in 3-7, had been in the Army for three years. Huffines hailed from Graham, Texas. An orphan and eighth-generation Texan who was raised by his maternal grandparents, he decided during his senior year of high school that he wanted to be an army officer. He believed he possessed intrinsic leadership capabilities, and he cultivated them during four years of college at Western State University in Wichita Falls, Texas. Upon graduation, he earned a commission and successfully completed the infantry officer's basic course, in addition to Ranger school, before eventually joining the 7th Infantry as a rifle platoon leader.

By 1990, he had earned a reputation as a fine officer. The proof of this was his appointment to support platoon leader, one of his battalion's key positions. Huffines was responsible for seventy-three soldiers, as well as dozens of fuel and supply vehicles. It was his job to make sure the unit had enough fuel, food, and ammunition in combat, a challenging logistical responsibility under adverse conditions. Generally, battalion commanders chose their best, most experienced lieutenants to lead either the support platoon or the scout platoon.

When Huffines heard about the deployment order, he knew he had a lot of work in front of him. His many responsibilities included overseeing the movement and deployment of the battalion's vehicles to Saudi Arabia. On the morning of the order, his immediate superior, headquarters company (HHC) commander Captain Mark Perry, turned to Huffines and said, "Al, deploy the battalion by land, sea, and air. Any questions?" Huffines shook his head, saluted, and moved out.

A few minutes later, he addressed the men of his platoon and told them they were going to war. As he was a professional officer to the core, the imminent danger of his near future sank in quickly, rather matter-of-factly to Huffines but not necessarily for his soldiers. "For the kids who had come in for college, that's the worst thing that could happen." The members of the support platoon sat around picnic tables in the dark and Huffines told them, in frank sentences, that they would soon deploy: "I just remember looking at those saucer eyes looking back at me. They were like, 'Well, hero, that may be what you joined up for, but it's not what we joined up for.' " They soon resigned themselves to the inevitable. They had no other choice.

After alerting his platoon, Huffines spent the next couple weeks attending to a myriad of details necessary for deployment overseas. "Pretty much from that point on I was leading convoys to the port and loading boats. Once the boats were loaded I was selected to be in the advance party for the battalion. We manifested at Ft. Stewart and shipped to the airfield. Once there, we remained in hangars for a few days waiting on lift to carry us to the theatre. Around the hangers were hurricane fences and many families of the departing, not able to say goodbye, waited at the fence, crying, visiting, etc. We called it the wailing wall."[7]

Lieutenant Huffines, and most of the rest of 3-7 and 2-7, arrived in Saudi Arabia by the end of August. Their heavy equipment and vehicles traveled by ship; the soldiers, by plane. They landed at the port of Dammam and disembarked in 105–degree heat. Crude tents had been set up for them, and they settled down to wait for orders. "You had your choice of baking in the tent or broiling in the sun," Huffines recalled. Support troops set up smelly latrines "reminiscent of 'Nam, open air with 4 sawed off 55 gallon drums inside brim full of bile. Nauseating." Some soldiers puked from the disgusting stench. Thankfully for everyone, they soon boarded buses that took them to an abandoned cement factory. At the factory they established a physical training routine, subsisted on Hardee's fast-food fare, drank bottled water, and generally tried to stay cool.

Lieutenant Huffines spent much time in Dammam looking after many supply-related details. He was not impressed with Saudi Arabia or its inhabitants. In his spare moments, he vented his feelings in a private diary: "Locals are a filthy people, we are using common bathrooms at the port, a public bathroom consists of a room with a hole in the floor & you defecate in the hole. Filthy. Town has a Las Vegas appeal, lots of neon. Not hardly any women on the streets, see a few in cars all covered up except their eyes. Most of the men wear sandals, long Nehru type jackets going all the way to the ground w/high collar and long sleeves. On their head each wears a turban."[8]

The vehicles and equipment arrived and were off-loaded on August 31 and September 1. Immediately the two battalions of Cottonbalers left the Dammam area and drove to a desolate spot in the Saudi desert roughly thirty kilometers north of As Sarrar.[9] On the way there, Lieutenant Huffines witnessed something truly surreal. As he passed through the town, he stopped to chat with a fellow officer who seemed transfixed by something. "What's up?" Huffines asked. The other lieutenant pointed to a small courtyard that was neatly nestled behind a cinderblock house: "There was a group of . . . old men with a little bitty black-and-white TV set watching *I Love Lucy* in Arabic, with a giant . . . eight-foot bong [hooka] in the center with all these pipes coming off it. They were just sitting there blowing their brains out watching *I Love Lucy*." Fascinated, Huffines watched them for several moments. An intelligent, perceptive man, and an avid historian in his own right, he recorded the mental image of that odd sight in his mind forever after.[10]

A couple weeks later, the Cottonbalers moved on to yet another forlorn spot in the barren desert. By now, they were located at about the midpoint of the Saudi peninsula. They set up perimeter-style camps right in the middle of the desert and did their best to adapt to the harsh environment. The sense of isolation was strong. The companies were spread out far and wide throughout the featureless desert. Men from different companies rarely had any interaction with one another. Some of the 7th Infantry rifle companies were cross-attached to tank companies. In a general sense, each 120–man combat company comprised its own minicamp, not quite self-contained but certainly physically separated from the other companies.

That fall, somewhere within 2-7's area of responsibility, the commander of Charlie Company, Captain Rick Averna of NTC fame, spent his days preparing his soldiers for the possibility that this stalemate could lead to war. Averna, a Midwesterner from Gearing, Nebraska, had been in the Army for almost ten years. He originally joined in 1979, fresh out of high school, and served as an enlisted infantryman. Deciding that he wanted to become an officer, he went to New Mexico Military Institute on a two-year ROTC program and earned a commission. From there, he moved on to the University of Nebraska and finished his bachelor's degree while serving in the National Guard from that state. He also met his wife, Elaine, at the university. They married just after graduation in 1984, and the newlywed second lieutenant, barely pausing to catch his breath, went to Fort Benning for airborne and Ranger training.

In April 1989, Averna, promoted to captain by now, assumed command of Charlie Company at Fort Stewart. He loved the job. His soldiers were bright, motivated, and quite proficient at their trade. Training day after day, week after week, Averna got to know his lieutenants and his NCOs inside and out. Charlie Company spent plenty of time in the field, training with their Bradleys, refining tactics, getting to know one another almost intimately. By mere chance, 2-7 had served an NTC rotation in July 1990. This training was absolutely perfect preparation for the fighting they would do in the Gulf. They had no sooner returned from this stressful, challenging, exhilarating experience when they got the call to deploy to Saudi.

Captain Averna knew that he commanded an excellent company. He also knew that upon deployment to Saudi his men were pretty well prepared for war, but he wanted to leave nothing to chance. When and if the order for war came, he wanted his men to be so finely honed, so well prepared, that war would almost seem like just another exercise. "We'd get up in the morning and we'd have stand-to and I'd frag [fragmentary or impromptu order] one of my platoons to go out and do just a quick recon somewhere . . . kind of a quick exercise in the morning just to get them up and to keep them busy, maybe go recon something about ten or fifteen miles away." He did it "just to keep them active and also to test them at different skills that we'd been training on. I think you had to keep them busy."

If not, then morale problems sometimes developed. Soldiers had too much time to think and brood, too much time to ponder their empty, strange surroundings. They snapped at one another, blew up over trivial matters, bitched about the lack of letters from home, wondered if wives were being faithful, or, in truly melancholy moments, ruminated as to whether they would die anonymously in a desert thousands of miles from home. Such thoughts had always been part of the panoply of war, and Averna's professional, disciplined soldiers were by no means immune to them.

The captain himself struggled with his moods. In a way it was tougher for him. As the leader, he had to put on a brave face for his troops. Like a coach who sets the mood for his team, Averna always had to be mindful of how his behavior would affect the morale of his men. If he seemed down or distracted, they probably would be too. If he was upbeat and professional, they would follow his lead. He tried to convey a sturdy sense of quiet efficiency and purpose, but it wasn't easy.

He may have been a highly trained infantry captain, but he was also a man far away from his wife, Elaine, and his young son, Nathan, who had yet to reach his first birthday. The mail was irregular, but every few days the captain received a letter from Elaine. She chatted about how she filled her days at Hinesville (just outside Fort Stewart), taking care of their son, interacting with other military wives, sharing whatever they knew about the Cottonbalers in the Gulf. More than anything, she pined for him. "I just really miss you, Rick," she wrote just after Labor Day. "I wish that I could know what you're going through, honey. What your company does has been so much a part of my life and now you're so far away." At times, she listened to their answering-machine greeting just to hear his voice. In the evenings, she took Nathan and the dog and let them play at a nearby park. "Nathan loves you and misses you too. Every night before he goes to bed we pray that God will Bless Daddy and I give him a kiss for you and one for me and tell him that you love him & that I love him too."

For several months, letters were the captain's only connection with Elaine. Then AT&T set up phone banks for soldiers to call home. The phones were located far behind forward-deployed infantry units like the 7th, but occasionally the Cottonbalers got the chance to use them. "It was about fifty miles away," Averna said. "The battalion would put us on a rotation plan. A company would get [access to the phones] for a three-day period. You can send one truck back with each platoon over a three-day period once a month and use the phone. When you got there sometimes the phones were up, sometimes they were down. Sometimes you got an answering machine. So, you knew when the soldiers came back which ones had talked to their families. Mail and those phones were the two morale support things we had."

The phones, in particular, were a nice, albeit temporary, link to home, but hanging up, switching your mind back to Saudi, and going back to the forward areas could be very tough. Averna had a difficult time keeping his mind straight after he spoke with Elaine for the first time. "That was probably the hardest right there—the first time I talked to her. The first time you hear her voice, what do you say? You don't want to do any talking, you just want to listen to her talk . . . so there were a lot of awkward moments and you just wanted to catch up on everything happening, because a lot happened to my son at that time."[11] Each soldier only received about ten minutes to talk and the time flew by. Polite but insistent sergeants would inform the conversationalist that his time was up and then quickly usher the next man into the phone booth.

To some, the experience of talking to loved ones on the phone seemed almost cruel, as if they had been shown, for a few brief moments, what they were missing and might never see again. Lieutenant Huffines went with a few other soldiers to As Sarrar one day and paid a Saudi businessman for the use of his phone so that they could call home. The lieutenant called Caroline, his wife of less than two years. Far from raising his morale, it practically tore his heart out. "Only talked about 10 minutes and it did break my heart," he confided to his diary. "I don't think I'll call again. My morale is shot. I miss her so bad. I never really noticed just how much I loved her till she was gone from me." As days passed, he felt better and he eventually did call her again, but the experience was very difficult for him.[12]

For his part, Captain Averna found solace in his work. This was the most professionally rewarding time in his life. He had worked ten years for this opportunity. The juxtaposition was striking. On the one hand, he missed his family terribly. On the other hand, there was nowhere else he would rather be than in charge of Charlie Company in a potential theater of war. Even the heat and the lousy conditions did not quell his love for his job, a substantial statement considering the nuisance the desert and its climate posed. "The heat played with filters and that kind of stuff [on the Bradleys], but really for the most part they were pretty good. The people, on the other hand, were different. There was not a lot of sickness and not a lot of bites from animals that I thought we were going to have because there was a lot of weird stuff in the sand and we didn't really have cots or stuff like that. We dug bunkers and stayed in the bunkers. But I learned a lot about human conditions."

If idleness risked morale problems, then the opposite problem—too much training—risked burnout. "About every third or fourth day, you had to stop training because you'd burn people out." The heat was just too intense during the day. "It was like being inside a dryer. That's how I would describe it. It's just so dry. It's so hot. You could drench yourself and literally ten minutes later your uniform would be dry. It's like living in a dryer. When you added the *shamals*, the dust storms, it was like living in a dryer with sandpaper. Hotter than anything I'd ever experienced."

Sand wore out boots, got into blankets, helmets, food, sometimes even drinking water. Most men only had two BDU uniforms, and they got dirty rather quickly. In this environment of heat and filth, the Cottonbalers tried to stay clean as best they could. They rigged up makeshift showers. "All the platoons had what we called an Australian shower. It's a collapsible bucket with a showerhead on it." Averna's men filled the bucket with water and hung it on a Bradley gun tube. "Traverse the gun tube and that was basically how we took a shower. Once in a while, if you went back for the phones, they had set up hot shower and bath units there, but by the time we would get there in the middle of the night, guys would just want to talk on the phone and get back. So, really for us, it was just the Australian shower off the gun tube of the Bradley . . . which was OK." The heat in this instance worked to the soldier's advantage because it was easy to heat water for showers. "At the end of the day, you could take a nice hot shower and it was not a big deal. You threw a piece of plywood on the ground, traverse the turret over . . . took your shower, and it was good. A whole squad could use that."

They also did their own laundry. "Everybody washed their clothes with bottled water. You took a cardboard box, put one of your waterproof bags in there, filled it with the hot water of the day, put your clothes in there, and you got soap powder . . . or shampoo in there, and it was like stomping grapes. You just stepped on your clothes. When it was relatively clean, you pulled it out, shook it out, and in about thirty minutes . . . with a little bit of breeze and hundred degrees it was dry." If they wanted hot coffee, they simply stuck a bottle of water out in the sand all day and mixed it with the instant coffee that came with their rations. Logistics and climate negated the possibility of getting ice to combat units like the 7th Infantry, but the Cottonbalers nonetheless figured out how to cool water for drinking. "We learned that if you take a bottle of water . . . then take an old sock and drench the sock in water and tie it to your vehicle and drive around . . . as you're doing training, the water evaporates off the sock and cools your water down. It's not ice-cold, but it's cooler than the air temperature and it feels like it's cold."

Deeper into the fall, the nights grew colder, especially in contrast to the broiling days. "It got extremely cold. It rained and it would frost. It would plummet fifty degrees and . . . get down to thirty or forty degrees. That change in temperature was just unbelievable. You would literally be freezing when that sun went down because that temperature plummeted very quickly." The soldiers bundled up as best they could. "Guys were wearing everything. We were in our MOPP suits, which is kind of like this insulated suit anyway." (MOPP suit stood for Mission Oriented Protective Posture, a specially designed overgarment to help soldiers survive nuclear, biological, and chemical weapons. The suits were charcoal-lined and quite stifling.) "Guys would put on their waterproof suit, which is plastic, so that helped hold in the heat. Once you're inside the Bradley it's OK."[13]

On one of those chilly nights in the middle of November, Captain Averna felt the crushing weight, not just of loneliness but of command. In private, quiet moments, while his men thought about the privation of living in the desert, waiting for whatever might happen, he thought about the fact that he was responsible for their very lives. Those other 120 men depended on him to know what he was doing when the shooting started. If he didn't, some of them would die. In that sense, their blood would be on his hands, a terrible thing to live with. Averna was very confident in his abilities, but he had never been in combat, which meant that he did not know with 100 percent certainty just how he would function.

In his bunker, he sat down at his writing table and wrote to Elaine about his command worries, saying the kind of things he could not discuss with his men: "Elaine, I need to share this with you because as a Commander I cannot . . . show my real feelings to my troops but to you I can. You are most definitely the one true friend I can trust in and talk to that will understand. At times I am scared of what can happen over here. I do not want to go to war, I do not want to see combat but if it comes I will most definitely return safe and sound. What scares me is that my decisions affect so many lives, the lives of sons, husbands and dads of Moms/Dads, wives and children. I feel this responsibility every now and then when I . . . talk with my soldiers [something he did every day] and the weight is heavy at times. I have gotten on my knees in the late hours of the night and prayed for the strength of God so that I might make the right decisions."

A day later he lost his St. Mary's and St. Christopher's medals. When he could not find them, he worried that their loss might be a bad harbinger. "I'm not really a superstitious guy by nature but I have come to rely on these two pieces of steel for protection and mental confidence. Will you please get me another St. Chris medal from you & Nathan. Without them I feel uneasy and as if I am susceptible to great harm. Funny, huh? Situations like the one we're in make people rely on strange things. I hope you can understand." He did not get a replacement medal until many weeks later.[14]

The life of waiting, training, moping, sweltering, shivering, and ruminating settled into a routine of sorts. The soldiers may not have liked it, but they got used to it. After all, they had, each and every one of them, volunteered for this. Some of them may have regretted doing so, but even so, they were here willingly. Corporal Bryan Crochet, a Bradley gunner in Alpha Company 3-7, did not much like desert life, but something deep within him, perhaps an adventurous spirit, was curious to experience war. A Baton Rouge native with deep Cajun roots, Crochet joined the Army in 1988 a few months after he graduated high school. He wanted to be a paratrooper, a rugged, lean soldier. His father, a graphic artist at LSD Press, had served in the U.S. Air Force as a munitions sergeant during the Korean War. Bryan's mother was a registered nurse, the most educated daughter from a sharecropper Cajun family. Bryan thought the Army would prove to be a maturing, enriching experience. "I wanted to serve. I wanted some time to grow up. I had gone through ROTC all through high school. From junior high I wanted to join the Army. I was one of those kids who played army. It was something I always wanted to do." Crochet came from a large family—he was the only male among six siblings—and he saw the Army as a way to pay for college, so, upon enlisting, he enrolled in the Army College Fund.

As a gunner, he usually slept in his Bradley, as opposed to the "dismounts" (riflemen and machine gunners) who bundled up in sleeping bags and went to sleep in bunkers or holes. Crochet got used to curling up in his station within the turret or in the rear compartment of the cramped APC and found that he slept fairly well ("I was twenty-one then and didn't have the same aches and pains I do now"). Each morning he watched the foggy desert come to life. "With all the moisture from the fog it basically came alive. You'd see all these insects that were out collecting moisture and you'd see their tracks in the sand. The things that you didn't notice before suddenly became obvious." One day, light rain began to fall. The soldiers had not seen any significant rainfall in months. "When it started raining, it really caught us off-guard. I remember it being depressing because it kind of made me homesick. In Louisiana we get a tremendous amount of rain."

The rain went away almost as quickly as it started. Corporal Crochet spent much of his time maintaining his guns—sand got into everything—and his section of the Bradley. "As the gunner, I basically had responsibility for maintaining the turret. I also supervised the driver. Together we supervised the dismounts who were assigned to us, such as where they hung their gear and tied things on to the Bradley. Maintenance-wise, the driver had to make sure that the tread on the Bradley was serviceable." Crochet made sure the driver kept the treads in good shape and spent a lot of time cleaning and lubricating his bread and butter, the 25 mm chain gun. "It's made by General Electric. You keep it maintained and it's clean, it behaves well." Luckily for Crochet and his buddies, the Bradley had a decent circulation system that kept the Bradley pretty well ventilated in the heat and warm enough when the winter months began. Every night he stood guard for a couple of hours, watching anything beyond the perimeter, before going to sleep.

Every ten days or so, his platoon got to go to the battalion base camp for R&R. "Each company was arranged in a circle covering a couple of miles and then in the center of that was the base camp. You'd shower, do laundry, watch videos, play volleyball . . . they had tents with cots." After a day or so at the base camp, the platoon rotated back to its forward positions, where the guarding, training, cleaning, waiting routine resumed.

The men subsisted on Meals Ready to Eat, the modern Army's version of prepackaged rations. These rations, generally called MREs (soldiers liked to call them "Meals Rejected by Ethiopians"), featured the typical American array of beef and chicken entrées. Packaged in thick plastic, they could be torn open and heated up. Like most rations of this ilk, they were nutritious but monotonous. "For the first month," Crochet recalled, "we had MREs three meals a day, and that got old pretty quickly." When the unit got more established, with camps and perimeters, cooks began feeding the Cottonbalers tray rations in the mornings and evenings. These meals consisted of containers of food heated up over garbage cans full of boiling water. They at least presented some semblance of a hot meal. "The breakfast T rat would be like scrambled eggs. It would be a big pan of scrambled eggs . . . and they'd have these things called submersion heaters that were like big garbage cans and a doughnut-shaped heater element that you drip gasoline into it and it'll boil a garbage can . . . full of water. You could boil it in a few minutes and then take these pans . . . and just throw them in there. They're cake pan size . . . rectangular shaped. The cooks would just throw them in there and boil them, take them out, throw them in a . . . thermal box and then ship them out to the different companies to eat." Sometimes, though, the cooks goofed. They sent only the submersion heater and the can, not the food. When this happened, Crochet and the other Cottonbalers shook their heads in hungry exasperation at what they considered to be unpardonable cook stupidity. "My opinion of army cooks is pretty low. Extremely low."

Not surprisingly, the men longed for the kinds of goodies they could only get in the states—candy, chips, ice cream, snack food, and the like. Crochet's family took it upon themselves to collect all sorts of items from businesses around Baton Rouge, including junk food, and send a stocking full of goodies to each man in the platoon. In that sense, the Crochet family "adopted" the 2nd Platoon—Crochet's father even designed a special platoon logo consisting of a two of diamonds and a wolverine—something for which the soldiers were quite grateful, especially those who were single and rarely received any mail. "It was just a really nice thing. I feel like I generated a debt to my family that to this day I still have not been able to pay off. It was tremendous to me how much my family got behind us."[15]

The Crochets simply wanted to send a little slice of America to the soldiers who had left home to defend it. At Thanksgiving time, the brass tried to do the same. The commander of 3-7, Lieutenant Colonel Dave Jensen, issued orders for his unit's bivouac, Assembly Area Cotton, "about as far out in the desert as you can get," to be transformed into a virtual fun house: "Instead of having the soldiers spend the day thinking about Thanksgivings of the past, we wanted to give them a Thanksgiving they'd never forget." Work parties scraped out a track in the sand for foot races, an eighty-yard football field, and a route for a mock "parade" in imitation of the great Macy's Thanksgiving Day parade in New York City. Considerable time and effort was devoted to the task of preparing the bivouac area for such entertainment. "Thanksgiving involved more stress than the rest of the war combined," Lieutenant Huffines sarcastically wrote. "We had huge festivities planned, a float parade, impressive dinner, bowl game and VIP's." Rumors flew that President Bush himself was coming. Lieutenant Colonel Jensen, perhaps with this possibility in mind, supervised with a heavy hand. "[He] was hammering people; everyone who briefed [him] missed something and got slaughtered by him. At the conclusion, he asked if anybody . . . had any question[s]." A lieutenant raised his hand and asked, "What will the Iraqis be doing?" Jensen "was not amused."

Jensen, a well-respected battalion commander, need not have worried. The rumors about Bush were untrue, and the holiday went off without a hitch. The soldiers had a great time. They enjoyed a feast of ham, turkey, roast beef, mashed potatoes, sweet potatoes, rice, salad, stuffing, cakes, and pies. They enjoyed watching the parade full of makeshift floats, especially Jensen's. It consisted of a boxing ring. Jensen, wielding a golf club and a fishing pole, masqueraded as Bush, warily eyeing someone posing as Saddam Hussein, wearing a villain's cape. Another float featured Santa Claus with eight human reindeer using tree branches as antlers. A Cottonbaler band called "The Lynch Mob" utilized MRE boxes, five-gallon water cans, and cot legs to screech what passed for music.

The main event was the football game, billed "The 'Baler Bowl," a contest between Bravo Company and an attached medical unit. The soldier-football players ran, scuffled, and rolled around in the sand, much to the delight of their buddies. At halftime a group who called themselves "The Breech Boys" sang tone-deaf versions of two parodies. "Saudi Bedouin Babes" sung to the tune of "California Girls" and "Bomb Iraq" sung to the tune of "Barbara Ann." The first song reflected the American GIs' disdain for the veiled, sexual taboo culture of the Saudis. The second was a popular parody among both American soldiers and civilians alike during the fall of 1990. Bravo Company did its best in the second half of the football game, but it could not pierce the goal line. The medics won the 'Baler Bowl 6–0. The spectators drifted back to their bivouac areas, digested, rested, slept, and then went back to their usual training routine the next day.[16]

EVEN AS THE TWO BATTALIONS of Cottonbalers with the 24th Division (2-7 and 3-7) guarded Saudi Arabia and prepared for a possible war with Iraq, the other two battalions of Cottonbalers in Germany wondered if they would deploy to the desert. At first, when coalition leaders envisioned a defensive war, the German-based Cottonbalers of 1–7 and 4-7 did not believe they would be needed. However, President Bush decided in early November to send thousands more American troops to Saudi, so that the commander in chief, Schwarzkopf, would have the offensive capability to kick the Iraqis out of Kuwait. The president and his generals chose the VII Corps, under the command of Lieutenant General Fred Franks, to be this offensive force; the corps deployed to Saudi Arabia by late December. This powerful force of 142,000 soldiers consisted of the 1st Infantry Division, the 1st Cavalry Division, the 1st and 3rd Armored Divisions, and, eventually, the 2nd Armored Cavalry Regiment as well as the British 1st Armoured Division.

The Cottonbalers of 1–7 and 4-7 ended up with the VII Corps almost by accident. It so happened that the mechanized infantry battalions of the 1st Armored Division did not have Bradleys. These infantrymen of the "Old Ironsides" division were still using M113 APCs that dated back to the Vietnam era. The division's commander, Major General Ron Griffith, did not want his soldiers to go to war with antiquated equipment. He wanted two battalions of trained, prepared, Bradley-equipped infantry to meld with his tank battalions. He did not have the time to transition his

1st Armored mechanized infantry from their old M113s to new Bradleys. He needed Bradley-experienced infantrymen and he got them when the 3rd Infantry Division agreed to loan him its "Phantom Brigade," two battalions of Cottonbalers and a tank battalion. On November 18 the commander of this brigade, Colonel Jim Riley, officially got word that his unit would soon go to Saudi as part of the 1st Armored Division (specifically, 1st Brigade, 1st Armored Division).

The news spread like wildfire among the soldiers. "Notification was received on a Friday afternoon," Lieutenant Colonel Stephen S. Smith, the commander of 1–7, later wrote, "and the information was quickly passed to each company to tell their soldiers before they were released for the weekend. Commanders and staff were brought in and over the course of the weekend a tentative work schedule for initial planning was outlined."[17]

Strangely enough, the gravity of the situation did not immediately sink in to some soldiers. The deployment order seemed like just another exercise. Captain Dave Sutherland, the HHC commander of 1–7, sensed this mood among the soldiers of his company and, for a brief moment, he snapped. Sutherland grabbed one of his privates by the collar and started screaming. "This kid could be in danger. This kid could be killed!" Sutherland then glared at his soldiers. "Everybody just shut up. Reality set in. I was a nervous wreck when I did that." His soldiers got the message, though. They were going to a real war. Their captain would accept nothing less than total preparedness and total concentration on the mission at hand.[18]

Before they could go, they needed to brush up on their gunnery skills. The Cottonbalers spent a lot of time at Grafenwohr, the brigade's gunnery range. Previous to this, half the men in 4-7 had no unit gunnery experience to their credit; 1–7 was better prepared but not quite war ready. Several sessions at Grafenwohr changed that. "We just jumped on that Bradley and shot," one platoon sergeant recalled. "Our soldiers were bussed to Graf where they fell in on the Bradleys of a sister battalion already there for training," Lieutenant Colonel Smith explained. "They ran all the ranges for us and provided all vehicle support while our crews conducted gunnery training. Our soldiers also requalified on their basic weapon, anti-tank weapons, and our infantry squads went down the Squad Assault Course. I consider it to have been very important." They became quite proficient with their 25mm chain guns, their coaxial machine guns, and their small arms. When they were done shooting, they relaxed, drank some beer, played cards, and generally enjoyed one another's company at a nearby recreation area known as the "Cottonbaler Lounge."

Mental preparation, as evidenced by Captain Sutherland's experience with his nonchalant men, was almost as important as technical preparation. Jamie Narramore, a twenty-seven-year-old staff sergeant who exemplified the resurgence of the post-Vietnam NCO corps, counseled each soldier in his platoon. Narramore and his immediate superior, Lieutenant Doug Morse, commander of the 1st Platoon, Charlie Company, 1–7, sat down together and talked with every man in the outfit: "Doug Morse and I brought in every single soldier, one at a time, and counseled him on where he was going, what he was gonna be doing, and what was expected of him." The counseling sessions worked very well. Sergeant Narramore was blown away by the sense of resolve he saw in the men of the 1st Platoon. "The glow in their eyes I'll never forget. You could see it. They were hungry . . . and it was beautiful. I would ask the soldiers, 'Are you ready . . . to do what we gotta do?' They would reply, 'Yes, I am. Let's go do it!' I was so confident when I left. The only hard thing was leaving your family."

Narramore had a wife and two children. He had spent his entire adult life in the Army after graduating from high school in Rio Linda, California, in 1981. Narramore's stepfather was in the Air Force, so the military was a family tradition for young Jamie. By 1990, Narramore had nine solid years of service under his belt, including three years as a drill sergeant and one year as an underranked platoon sergeant (he was a staff sergeant, or E-6, while most platoon sergeants held the rank of sergeant first class or E-7). Narramore was the epitome of the experienced, professional noncommissioned officer, the kind who made the U.S. Army work and fight so well in the coming war. Like so many other sergeants, he dedicated himself body and soul to the Army. Only family intruded on his profession. His wife worried about him, but she knew that he had trained his entire life for this opportunity. "She knew what my mission was and she supported me . . . but it was really tough on the kids."[19]

In the middle of December the Cottonbalers bade their vehicles goodbye. Wheeled vehicles traveled to German ports by road convoys. Snowy, icy roads presented some problems, but the convoys arrived safely. Tracked vehicles were loaded onto trains that took them to the ports. Between December 23 and January 10 the soldiers, loaded down with duffel bags and personal weapons, boarded planes that took them to Al Jubayl in Saudi Arabia.

Sergeant Narramore's platoon left the day after Christmas. He and his men lucked out. They rode in a DC-10, a far more comfortable mode of transportation than the C-130 and C-141 air force transports that conveyed the rest of Charlie Company. When the DC-10 landed and the men got off the plane, the cold of the Saudi Arabian winter stunned many of them. "We froze our butts off when we got there," Narramore said. "When we got there it was pitch-dark and we were on the tarmac and the wind was howling." They had been told to stow their cold-weather gear, so they shivered for hours in summer uniforms. "We had to stand there till daylight and it was cold. I hadn't been that cold in a long time."[20]

A bus took them to a tent city north of Al Jubayl. The military name of their new home was the Initial Staging Area, but the men called it the Desert Inn or the Dewdrop Inn. Here the men of 1–7 and 4-7 waited for their vehicles. Several days passed and then several more. Still the vehicles had not arrived. The Cottonbalers waited over two weeks for them. "This led to some ill feelings on the part of many soldiers for having been taken away from their families earlier than necessary," Lieutenant Colonel Smith recalled. He aptly classified this minor snafu as yet another example of the Army's "hurry up and wait syndrome." He wisely kept his troops busy with "discipline, personal hygiene, and training at the individual/crew/squad/platoon level. Units . . . made every effort to begin the acclimatization process through vigorous physical training activities. Daily meetings were conducted to outline responsibilities in the camp for security, police and other details. Information on the arrival of our equipment and intelligence updates on the Iraqis was also disseminated."[21]

In early January, with their combat vehicles safely unloaded, desert painted, and prepared, the Cottonbalers of the 1st Armored Division left the Desert Inn for Tactical Assembly Area Thompson, some 370 kilometers away, south of Al Qaysumah, with orders to watch for an Iraqi attack.

Instead of waiting around for enough Heavy Equipment Transporters (HETs) to move their tracked vehicles, the Cottonbalers simply rolled along the Tapline road, a two-lane highway that paralleled the Iraqi border. They made it to TAA Thompson in two days.

First Lieutenant Craig McClure, the executive officer of 1–7's Headquarters (HHC) Company, helped set up the battalion's area at Thompson. "I was one of the first ones out there and I actually staked out all of Headquarters Company's area out there. When the rest of the vehicles came in, they occupied the positions that me and the advance party had staked out for them." McClure was a twenty-five-year-old ROTC graduate of Bowling Green State University. The son of a high school history teacher, McClure fell in love with the idea of joining the Army and becoming an infantryman. He knew he was a leader—he had found that out during his time as an all-state offensive guard on his high school football team—so he wanted to be an officer. That career path took him through four years of college on an ROTC scholarship. When he graduated, he went straight to active duty, along with the usual bevy of training schools—jump school, Ranger school, and Bradley school. He was so determined to finish Ranger school with his training class that he ignored a back injury he sustained during the incredibly stressful, physically challenging Ranger training. During a rappelling exercise he fell several feet, right onto his back. He lay still for several moments groaning in pain before getting up and getting back to work. The back bothered him thereafter, and for good reason—he broke a vertebra but did not find out until several years later.

Lieutenant McClure's job now was to implement the orders of his boss, Captain Sutherland. That meant overseeing the entire combat logistical apparatus of the battalion. McClure had to make sure that everyone had enough ammunition, fuel, food, water, or anything else that might be needed. His role was similar to that of Lieutenant Huffines, the support platoon leader in 3-7, but on a bit larger scale. "We had responsibility for the vast majority of wheeled vehicles in the battalion . . . somewhere in the neighborhood . . . of ninety and one hundred wheeled vehicles . . . and we also had forty or fifty tracked vehicles. My main job was supervisor of all the maintenance operations for the company. All the mechanics fell under our supervision . . . in the neighborhood of fifty or sixty mechanics and all their associated toolboxes. We had millions and millions of dollars' worth of tools." Thus his job was "primarily the maintenance operations as well as physically running the logistics operations when we were out in the field. The support platoon leader ran the supplies back and forth, but I was the overall coordinator between the company and our support battalion . . . to make sure that all of our requests for logistical support were being met." McClure was a hands-on leader, though. When the war began, he alternated moving the vital supplies or "logistical packages" (LOGPACs) with his support platoon leader, Lieutenant Ken Romaine, so that each of them could catch a bit of sleep.

At TAA Thompson the Cottonbalers constructed crude shelters and latrines for themselves. "We were living in tents . . . smalls and mediums. We had our porta-shitters, the cardboard, plywood little hutch that . . . we put in the sawed-off fifty-five-gallon drums with kerosene . . . and diesel fuel in them. That's what we used to defecate in and then we had what we called piss tubes. We cut . . . water bottles off and stuck them together and put them in the ground and that's what we urinated in. We also built showers . . . out of plywood with the tanks on top. Of course it was ice-cold water." McClure had no love for such cold showers. "My record was thirty-five days without a shower."[22]

The soldiers of 1–7 and 4-7 spent about a month at TAA Thompson. Tankers from the 4th Battalion of the 66th Armored Regiment joined them. The commanders melded together the tanks and infantry into the most advantageous tactical formation and drilled their soldiers constantly in the wasteland of the Saudi desert. The weather deteriorated. "It was very cold and very rainy," Lieutenant Colonel Smith remembered. "Temperatures would fall below freezing at night, freezing the water in the water trailers. Vehicles moving across the rain-soaked sand turned the previously smooth surface into rutted quagmires. When the first vehicles arrived in the TAA, the surface of the desert was in pristine condition. Wheeled vehicles could drive at high speeds safely over its smooth surface. Movement during the rains caused deep trenches and ruts to appear. Coupled with digging of trash pits and blackout conditions at night, traveling from one unit to the other for meetings became a slow and somewhat hazardous undertaking. More than one person spent the night with his HMMWV [High Mobility Multipurpose Wheeled Vehicle, generally called a Humvee] nosed down in a trash pit."[23]

Such climate-related complaints by the comparative newcomers of 1–7 and 4-7 would probably have provoked rueful laughter from their regimental brothers of 2-7 and 3-7 who had endured the tribulations of the Saudi desert since August. By January, they had survived a melancholy Christmas and had been training for months, all the while battling homesickness. They were deployed farther to the west, in a similar assembly area, preparing for war but waiting to see how the tense showdown with Saddam would play out. On January 12 in anticipation of a possible Iraqi chemical strike, the 24th Division Cottonbalers went to MOPP-2, which meant constantly wearing the protective boots and suits of their chemical garb but not the mask. "We started wearing our Chemical Protective Overgarments . . . permanently," Lieutenant Huffines wrote that day to Caroline, "which is no real fun and a 'pain in the butt' but I guess it's for the better." One positive was that the itchy garments provided "an extra layer of warmth. We've also increased our security posture somewhat. Right now we're all wondering what Saddam's surprise is."

In fact, he had no surprise. The United States had succeeded in persuading the UN Security Council to authorize the use of force against Iraq if Saddam did not withdraw by January 16. Frenetic diplomatic negotiations took place as the fateful day approached, but nothing changed. The coalition wanted Iraq out of Kuwait, and Saddam would not budge. If that did not change, and quickly, war would soon begin. Nothing changed. Accordingly, in the early-morning hours of January 17 the coalition began the campaign to eject Iraq from Kuwait (called Operation Desert Storm). The first phase of this campaign mostly entailed the use of airpower to soften up Saddam's armed forces for a later coalition ground offensive.

In forward-deployed combat units like the Cottonbalers, very little changed when the air war began. They were already training intensely; they had already implemented heightened security measures; they were not going anywhere until the brass decided that the aerial campaign had diminished Iraq's ground forces enough to ensure the success of a ground war. Mostly, the ground pounders of the 7th Infantry watched in awe as the planes streaked overhead, bound for unseen targets beyond the horizon.

On the first night of the air war, Huffines watched the planes. "Planes constantly overhead," he wrote to Caroline. "A squadron of B52s with fighter escort just flew overhead to the cheers of all in the perimeter. Looks good so far. Go Air Force! My prayers are for our pilots and their families. I don't envy them and I hope St. Michael is with them. Noise of planes is constantly overhead. I don't think anyone but the military really know the lethality of the American Military. We are ready and willing to do all, anything to make this over faster . . . "[24]

When the air war began, Captain Averna's Charlie Company found itself in the rear. It was their turn to pull guard duty for their ultimate parent unit, the XVIII Airborne Corps, at its main depot about sixty miles behind the forward positions. Averna and his men spent much of the night weathering a nasty, persistent *shamal*. Sandy winds howled outside their tents. All of a sudden he heard an announcement over the base's loudspeaker to the effect that the "Desert Storm had begun." He exchanged quizzical looks with his sergeants. The *shamal* had been going on for hours. Why did some knucklehead feel compelled to announce over the loudspeaker that it had just begun? The Charlie Company Cottonbalers had no idea that the term "Desert Storm" meant that the long anticipated war had finally begun. However, they began to realize something was up when they received orders to leave the corps depot and return to their positions. By the time they returned to 2-7, they figured out what was going on: "Right on our side of the border you could see . . . the big KC-135 tankers flying big ovals and refueling airplanes. We watched that for a while."[25]

No one knew exactly how much time would pass before the ground troops would be needed. Infantrymen like the Cottonbalers had little choice but to shelve the natural excitement they felt over the imminent possibility of combat and continue with their tedious routine of intense preparation. They did practically everything grunts could do to prepare for war: live fire exercises, navigation exercises (the desert was featureless), refuel rehearsals, formation training, movement to contact scenarios, obstacle breaching rehearsals, full-up corps rehearsals, bunker assaults, field maintenance, and battalion-sized night movements. Days went by and then weeks and still the air war continued unabated. Once more, the ground soldiers grew antsy. They badly wanted to get on with the war, get it over with, and go home.

In the meantime, their senior leaders had prepared an elaborate ground offensive plan that hinged on deception. Saddam Hussein's forces were deployed in depth along the Kuwaiti-Saudi border and the Kuwaiti-Iraqi border and for about fifty to seventy-five miles along the Iraqi-Saudi border. Since the aim of this coalition's war effort was to eject Iraqi forces from Kuwait, the logical place for any ground offensive was straight into Kuwait. Knowing this, the Iraqis constructed strong defensive networks of tanks, barbed wire, berms, minefields, flaming trenches, and mobile forces in depth along the Kuwait-Saudi border.

In actuality, these enemy soldiers were deployed exactly where General Schwarzkopf wanted them. His grand plan called not for a big push into Kuwait but for a "left hook" flanking attack into Iraq and then eastward into Kuwait, behind the main Iraqi defenses. To that end, he unleashed an ingenious deception plan designed to make the Iraqis believe that the U.S. Marine Corps would launch an amphibious invasion of Kuwait's east coast even as the main coalition ground forces plunged into Kuwait from the south ("hey diddle, diddle, straight up the middle," his staff officers called that approach).

In reality, Schwarzkopf's main assault forces—the military equivalent of a powerful cocked fist—were deployed mostly along the Iraqi-Saudi border. This cocked fist was the 3rd Army, under Lieutenant General John Yeosock. Yeosock's 3rd Army was further subdivided into two corps-level concentrations. In the extreme west he placed the XVIII Airborne Corps, consisting of his most mobile units: the 101st Airborne Division, the 82nd Airborne Division, the 6th French Light Armored Division, the 3rd Armored Cavalry Regiment and the 24th Infantry Division (Mechanized), containing 2-7 and 3-7. The mission of this corps, under the command of Lieutenant General Gary Luck, was to provide flank security for the neighboring corps to the east. The soldiers of the XVIII Airborne were to move swiftly north into Iraq, capture key airfields and phase lines, then turn east toward northern Kuwait and southern Iraq.

To their right, General Franks's VII Corps, containing most of the coalition's armored might (as well as the 1–7 and 4-7 Cottonbalers), drew the main mission of destroying the Iraqi capacity to resist. This meant plunging into Iraq, advancing north and then east into Kuwait, outflanking the enemy forces, with the ultimate intention of destroying the much-ballyhooed Republican Guard divisions, Saddam's best-trained, best-equipped, toughest troops. From the perspective of the 7th Infantry, then, the unit experienced the broad sweep of the 3rd Army's ground war: the XVIII Airborne Corps's flank security attacks in the west and the VII Corps's sucker punch in the east.[26]

TWO WEEKS INTO FEBRUARY, THE Cottonbalers, along with thousands of their 3rd Army comrades, waited in forward assembly area positions for the word to attack. On February 14, carrying out their part of the deception plan, the 1st Armored Division Cottonbalers, along with their accompanying tank support, surreptitiously rolled 150 kilometers west to Forward Assembly Area Garcia, a mere 20 kilometers south of the Iraqi border. They pulled off this difficult move in two short days, even though a terrible *shamal* wreaked havoc on the newly erected tents and turned the area into a muddy morass that the troops sardonically called "Lake Garcia." The Cottonbalers of the 24th Division were hunkered down about seventy or eighty miles to the west, in a camp called Tactical Assembly Area Great.

One of those Cottonbalers, Sergeant Michael St. Peter of Delta Company 2-7, sat down in the moist sand to write a letter to Cottonbaler veterans of World War II, Korea, and Vietnam. His words encapsulated the feelings of so many of the men in the 7th on the eve of the ground war. "Now we are hoping to close another chapter of Cottonbalers history. All of us are hoping for peace. But if the call of duty comes down to fight, the 7th Inf. Rgt. will be leading the way for the rest of the divisions, kicking—and taking names. I would be lying if I told you we are not afraid. All of us are scared, but ready to fight. We all know we stand a good chance of dying if this does break out, but we are proud to be a part of the Cottonbalers. And if it takes dying to win this battle and to keep America at peace, then, by God, we'll die. '*Volens et Potens*.' Willing and Able. Cottonbalers, by God."[27]

Sergeant St. Peter's sacrificial rhetoric notwithstanding, none of the infantrymen of the 7th had any desire to die. They knew it could happen, but they also knew that if they did their job properly, it probably wouldn't. Most of them sensed how ready—even "overprepared" in Captain Averna's view—they were for a fight. They knew they were tough; they knew they were very good; they knew they enjoyed every advantage of firepower and support. Everyone had been briefed on the plan, ranging from the role of their platoon to the role of the whole coalition army. Most felt a great sense of confidence. "We just wanted to get going with it," Lieutenant McClure said. "There was some uncertainty. But we had every confidence in the world that we were fully ready to do the job that we were expected to do. We couldn't have been any more prepared. There was no doubt in anyone's mind that . . . there was nothing further that we could do to prepare ourselves. We just needed to go ahead and do it." Most men felt anxious rather than fearful.[28]

Some units, like Alpha Company 2-7, received last-minute replacements in anticipation of impending casualties. One of those replacements was Private Kurt Dabb, a wide-eyed eighteen-year-old kid from Iron Mountain, Michigan. Dabb badly wanted to go to war. He had actually lobbied for a chance to serve in the Gulf rather than sit out the war guarding ammunition at Fort Hood, Texas. Sometime in early February, his orders came through and he flew to Dahrain.

He joined his unit at its forward assembly area, right as these six months' veterans of the Saudi desert were making final preparations to cross the Iraqi border. The company first sergeant assigned Dabb to a platoon. He took a look at his bleak surroundings, heard from his new comrades that they were only miles away from Iraq, and realized the consequences of the choice he had made. Basically, it sank in for him that he was right on the cusp of war. "It was very unnerving, scary, lonely." Luckily for him, the veterans treated him very well. "They were actually really cool. I don't know if it was the fact that I was a fresh face and they . . . now had someone who could tell them what it was like back in the World. I bonded really quickly with everybody. It wasn't like I was led around by the hand or anything. They showed me where everything was; they gave me a new rifle." They told him that most of what he had brought with him—two duffel bags full of stuff—would be useless. "We had this big bonfire . . . burning government equipment." Private Dabb wisely listened to everything the veterans told him and did exactly what they said to do. In a matter of a day or so, Dabb blended right in with his new unit, just in time for war.[29]

Now senior leaders began to show up at the assembly areas, a sure sign that the ground attack (G-Day) was imminent. Colonel Riley, the Phantom Brigade commander, circulated extensively among his battalion commanders and the soldiers who would do the fighting. "As it became apparent that G-Day was approaching, I felt the need to go out and do a couple things. One was to look them in the eye and assess where they were. And second, to pass to them some of my own beliefs about organizations and about personal response to unknown and dangerous situations. And, to some extent, to reassure them they were up to the task." Riley knew what he was talking about. As a young lieutenant, he had led soldiers in combat in Vietnam. "My fear was I would see a lot of uncertainty, bordering on fear." To his relief, he saw nothing of the kind.[30]

He gave his officers a rousing speech that fired them up for the task ahead. "One of the most moving and inspiring speeches I have ever heard," Lieutenant Colonel Smith opined. "Its essence was that our men were ready and that it was time for quiet competence to come to the fore. Aggressive, 'killer' units survived with the fewest casualties. He expressed his confidence that 1–7 was a killer unit and that it was prepared to lead the 1st Armored Division to war."

A few days later, on February 23, General Franks himself visited the soldiers of 1–7. Similar to Colonel Riley, Franks wanted to look into the faces of the young men he would send into battle. The only way for a senior commander to truly assess the readiness of his soldiers is to look into their eyes, talk with them, and listen to them. Franks, another Vietnam veteran, and one who had lost part of one leg to a mine, understood this lesson quite well. Just before sunset, the general arrived at the brigade headquarters. He sat in on a brigade meeting and then expressed his desire to meet with a forward-deployed infantry company. Lieutenant Colonel Smith led him on a tour of Charlie Company. Franks "walked along the front line of soldiers talking to platoons, shaking hands, and having his picture taken."[31]

He stopped and chatted for a long time with the 1st Platoon—Lieutenant Morse and Sergeant Narramore's bunch—conveying a message similar to what Riley had communicated a few days before. What happened next is the stuff of Gulf War legend. As General Franks chatted with the 1st Platoon soldiers ("Raiders," they called themselves), he seemed to connect with them on a basic level, like a father with his sons. He loved being around troops, and it showed; the men could tell he was in his element. They felt so comfortable that one of them, an outgoing, say-what-comes-to-mind private first class, blurted out, "General Franks, would you like to hear our song, sir?"

Lieutenant Colonel Smith and the Charlie Company commander, Captain Tracy Cleaver, practically froze in their tracks. "Oh no. What the hell is this?" they both thought.

Lieutenant Morse had composed this bawdy song as the platoon's anthem. "It was our motivational song. When the going got tough, someone would start humming," Narramore said. Narramore and Morse hesitated for an awkward moment while the general urged them to sing the song; it wasn't exactly G-rated.

Just then, somebody started humming. "As infantrymen you don't hold back very much," Staff Sergeant Narramore explained.

The soldiers glanced at each other and, a second later, launched into the song. "We're a bunch of bastards, scum of the earth, filth of creation, gone from bad to motherfuckin' sonofabitchin'! We're known in every whorehouse, drink, smoke, and screw. We're the men of the Raider platoon . . . so fuck you!"

A second passed and all eyes fixed on General Franks. He blinked in surprise but cracked up. "Good song! You guys keep that to yourself, but that's a good song."

Franks was a fine leader. He understood that although the song was pretty vulgar, it stemmed from good morale and esprit de corps. In a crazy way, he knew it meant his men were ready for combat. "He saw the motivation that we had," Narramore said. Franks autographed one of the Raider platoon's Bradleys and posed for a group picture with the men of the platoon. Years later, the general still had the picture hanging in a place of honor on his office wall. "I think he left the brigade feeling . . . as I did, that things were pretty healthy and ready to go," Colonel Riley later said.

Smith was relieved that the general reacted well to the song. He watched Franks sign the Bradley, pose for the photo, shake more hands, and then leave. "He seemed genuinely moved as he departed. He could sense their confidence, but knew the dangers that lay ahead."[32]

THOSE DANGERS BEGAN THE NEXT day, February 24, when the ground attack plan went into motion. The first Allied troops, members of the French division, in addition to the 101st and 82nd Airborne, went into motion to secure the extreme left flank during the early-morning hours of the twenty-fourth. They had so much success that Schwarzkopf stepped up the timetable for the entire offensive, provoking a kind of ripple effect throughout both the XVIII Airborne Corps and Franks's VII Corps.

The planners had scheduled both the 24th Division and the 1st Armored to attack the following day, but Schwarzkopf's acceleration order changed that schedule. The 24th Division received orders to move out by noon on February 24 even as the VII Corps staff sounded out its units, including 1st Armored, about the possibility of going early. As it turned out, the 2-7 and 3-7 Cottonbalers of the 24th Division began their attack at about noon, while the two battalions attached to 1st Armored moved out about four hours later.

So the Victory Division Cottonbalers had the distinction of being the first 7th infantrymen officially into Iraq. Actually, they had already begun border crossings in the days leading up to the offensive. The 2nd Battalion, in particular, had carried out several border incursions, primarily reconnaissance missions. The men of 2-7 were deployed in the vicinity of an abandoned Saudi town called Nisab, After the Iraq invasion, the few Saudis who lived in Nisab deserted it. Then, for a while, a small detachment of Iraqi soldiers garrisoned the place, but they too left, probably in reaction to the arrival of the Americans.

The Cottonbalers had scouted the town in mid-February, found it deserted, and then turned their attention to an Iraqi outpost visible just across the border. Given Schwarzkopf's hopes for deception, security was of paramount importance. Commanders wanted to make sure that American dispositions and intentions would remain secret. That meant assessing the whereabouts of any nearby enemy soldiers and finding out whether they had any inkling of what lay ahead.

On February 14, Bravo Company, under the command of Captain Todd Sherrill, had crossed the border to have a look at the outpost. They encountered two border berms, roughly ten feet wide, eight feet high, and fifteen feet apart. Bravo's armored vehicles had no trouble negotiating their way around the berms. Sherrill had set up his Bradleys in an overwatch position, while his infantrymen dismounted, trooped forward, and set up ambush positions near the outpost. They watched and waited for any sign of activity, poised to blow away anyone who moved, but nothing happened. Two nights later, artillery sent a couple of rounds into the place. The shells damaged the building but did not destroy it. Still, nothing moved. If Iraqi soldiers were there, they were quite disciplined. The place seemed to be deserted, but no one knew for sure.

The battalion commander, Lieutenant Colonel Chuck Ware, wanted to find out for sure. Back in December, Ware had received the unenviable task of replacing a popular commanding officer, Lieutenant Colonel Arnie Canada, in command of 2-7, in a possible theater of war. The whole thing was a bit odd. It was true that battalion commands rotated on a two-year basis and Canada's time expired in December, but those rules were generally for peacetime, not wartime. Of course, the unit was not yet at war in early December, so technically the rotation should have taken place, but in the 7th Infantry there were many instances of officers remaining in command past their rotation time during Desert Shield and Desert Storm. Rick Averna, for example, had been in command of Charlie for almost two years, a long time for a company commander. No one gave the slightest thought to rotating him because it would not have made any sense. He knew his soldiers better than anyone else; he had trained them, and he was the man to lead them—end of story. "Why didn't the same commonsense approach apply to Colonel Canada?" many Cottonbalers wondered. No one knew the answer. Rumors flew that the division commander, Major General Barry McCaffrey, wanted to get rid of Canada in favor of Ware, his division's inspector general. When Canada's rotation came up, so the story went, McCaffrey seized on this technicality to get rid of him.

None of this could be substantiated. McCaffrey was well within his rights if he wanted to relieve Canada or simply carry out the usual rotation policy, but there was little question that Canada's exit was a bit odd, even somewhat risky for a unit about to go into combat. The men respected and trusted Lieutenant Colonel Canada. They did not know what to make of Ware. He had precious little time to get to know his battalion inside and out, the way a commander who leads his troops in war should, ideally, know his soldiers. He seemed competent but gruff and detached. By and large, the Cottonbalers of 2-7, particularly the junior officers, did not think highly of Ware. They found him to be too excitable on the radio, too preoccupied with trivial matters, too heavy-handed, too lacking in command presence. Sometimes, among themselves, they even called him "Colonel Night-Ware." Perhaps they never gave him a fair shot; perhaps they did. "He would have had difficulty no matter what, because he was the new guy," Captain Averna said.[33]

Ware's alleged lack of leadership aside, his order to recon the outpost made perfect sense. The Americans had to know for sure if enemy soldiers were observing them from the outpost. The job of finding out went, naturally, to the scout platoon, led by twenty-six-year-old First Lieutenant Kirk Allen, a Norwich University graduate who had been leading soldiers at the small-unit infantry level for almost three years. Colonel Canada had chosen Allen, a native of New Jersey, to command the scout platoon because he knew that Lieutenant Allen was one of his best young leaders. As with the support platoons, only the very best lieutenants were considered for this job of leading the scouts.

The scout platoon consisted of six Humvees and two Bradleys. Their job was to function as the eyes and ears of the entire battalion. They operated in extreme danger, in no-man's-land between enemy forces and their own somewhere behind them. They could be shot at by either side (sometimes the greatest peril for them in this war was American, not Iraqi, fire). Chances were very good that if they encountered the enemy, he would outgun them. The scout's job was to screen, gather intelligence, report information, and lead, not necessarily to fight. The soldiers who composed the scout platoon usually scored higher than the rest of the infantry on army intelligence tests. Plus, they were better trained. As scout platoon leader, Allen was similar to Bill Strobridge. Allen and Strobridge had much in common—military aptitude, independence, courage, calm resolve—and Allen would have found much to discuss with Strobridge.

Of course, in the early-morning hours of the seventeenth when he and his scouts had investigated the outpost, he had no time for such ruminations (though he probably would have found them interesting). For two days and nights, he and his men had sat under cover and watched the building. They were dirty, sandy, smelly, and tired. He and his men had taken photographs of the building, but later, under the watchful snouts of several Bradleys, they crossed the border and approached the building on foot. "We . . . dismounted, and cleared the building," Lieutenant Allen recalled. "It was only two floors. It was a brick-type building, two rooms on the bottom floor and two rooms on the top floor." They found nothing, but that did not mean their adrenaline wasn't pumping when they entered the outpost. "Your heart rate is up, the tension is up, but there was nothing there. It was the middle of the night. We had [night-vision] goggles on. We had thermals on our Bradleys." Lieutenant Allen worried a bit that enemy soldiers could hide behind the outpost's far walls. This would shield them from the thermal sights of the Bradleys. His scouts checked out the wall. Nothing was there. Only a few rabbits showed up on the Bradley's thermal sights. Allen grabbed the Iraqi flag and got his people out of there.

A few days before G-Day they went back across the border, where they took up concealed reconnaissance positions in the lonely desert, somewhere between 2-7 and 3-7.[34]

That's where they were when the order came for the main forces to cross the border at noon on the twenty-fourth. The forward assembly areas teemed with activity: soldiers running to and fro, vehicles revving up, commanders shouting orders, basically a scene of organized chaos. In some instances, word of the accelerated attack plan filtered down haphazardly to the soldiers. Lieutenant Huffines was standing near his Humvee, brushing his teeth, when he noticed a lot of activity on the other side of the perimeter. He wondered what was going on, so he got in his Humvee and drove over to the battalion S–4, or logistics officer (a man Huffines liked but did not particularly respect), to find out. "I walked up to the S4 and asked what was going on. He said, 'Didn't someone tell you? We're attacking. We have to cross the [border] berms by noon.' " Huffines stared at him in disbelief. "Sir, when were you going to tell me this?" The S–4 had no good answer. Huffines turned and noticed his company commander, Captain Perry, a man apparently prone to concise, dramatic sentences. Perry looked at Huffines and said, "Al, I'll see you on the other side." Huffines was still a bit peeved that he had not been informed of the attack order. "I told the S4 I should have been informed immediately and he said he had sent a runner around. I told him that was unsatisfactory. I saluted and went to alert my soldiers."[35]

Not far away, at Alpha Company 3-7's bivouac, Corporal Crochet was settling down on the front trip vane of his Bradley for a little nap when he heard the order to move out. Immediately, he snapped awake and prepared to go. He and the other men changed into fresh MOPP suits. MOPP suits diminished in effectiveness the more a soldier wore them, so with war imminent, officers issued orders to don fresh suits. The driver fired up the Bradley, Crochet jumped into his spot in the turret, the infantry soldiers crammed into the back, the ramp went up, and off they went. Engine noise from dozens of vehicles roared through the air.

Crochet watched as combat engineers led the way across the line of departure. "My platoon provided . . . cover support for the engineers to come and bulldoze the barriers . . . over the breach. At that point, my vision became very limited, because I was looking down the [gun] barrel." The bulldozers smashed the barriers (also called berms) into bits. Crochet could see tanks drive through the breach and fan out on the other side. "There was no one there. We were out in the middle of the worst part of the desert." Like an unstoppable tidal wave overwhelming a seawall, the accumulated combat might of the Cottonbalers, along with the entire 24th Division, poured through such breaches all along the line of departure.

Hundreds of vehicles drove forward, mostly in combat wedge formation (almost like an inverted V shape). In the process they kicked up huge quantities of sand and dust. The weather—windy, cloudy, and cold—only added to the jumble. Crochet's platoon was at the right edge of the battalion, on the flank. An hour went by, then another and another. Nothing and no one was out here, just rocky, flat, open desert. Corporal Crochet happened to glance to his left, and as he did, he saw something quite stirring. "I remember looking around . . . through my periscope . . . and just . . . as far as I could see . . . nothing but U.S. military hardware—tanks, Bradleys, artillery, MLRS [rocket-firing artillery], towed vehicles, a lot of . . . medics." Crochet stared at the spectacle with a sense of wonder and invincibility. "What could possibly stop them?" he wondered.[36]

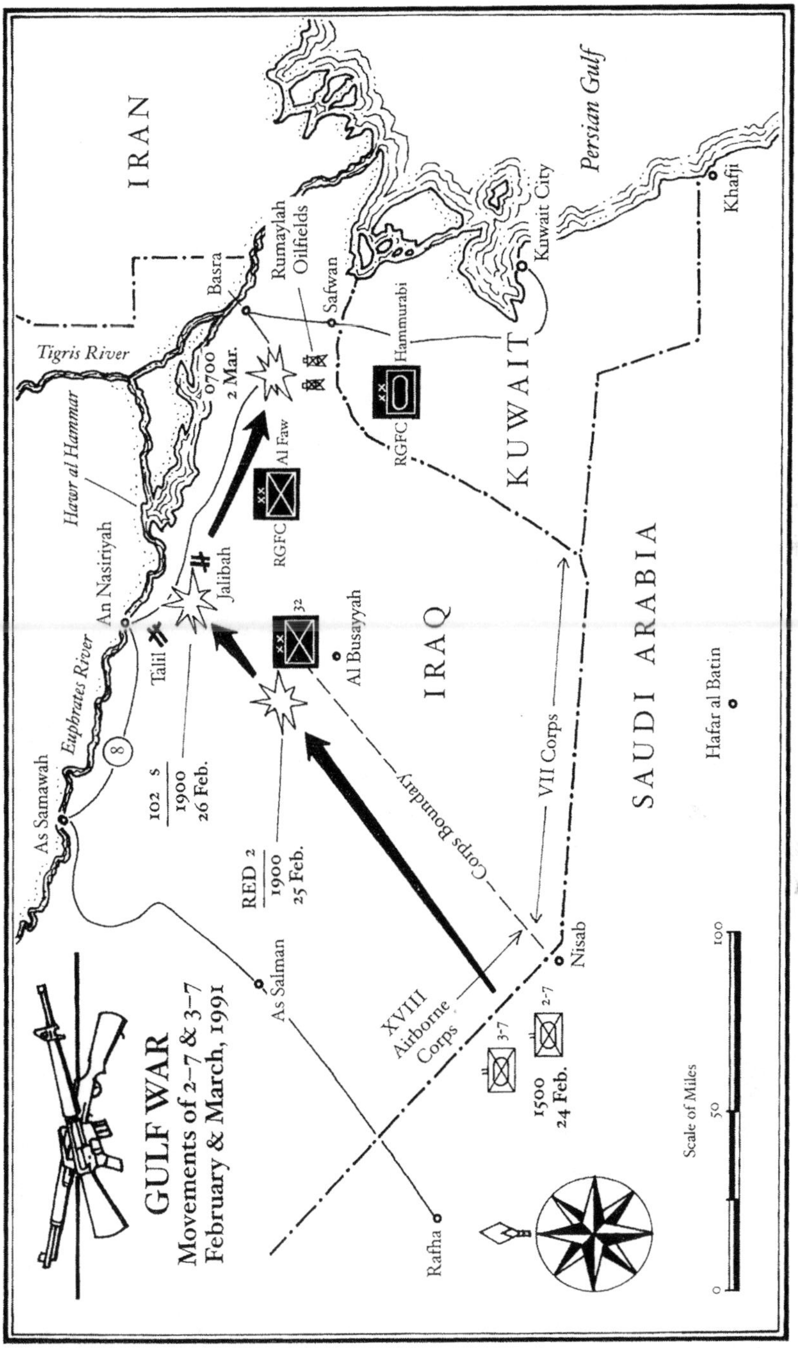
GULF WAR
Movements of 2–7 & 3–7
February & March, 1991
IRAN
IRAQ
KUWAIT
SAUDI ARABIA
Persian Gulf
Tigris River
Euphrates River
Hawr al Hammar
As Samawah
An Nasiriyah
Talil
Jalibah
Basra
Rumaylah Oilfields
Safwan
Kuwait City
Khafji
Al Busayyah
As Salman
Rafha
Nisab
Hafar al Batin
Hammurabi
RGFC
Al Faw
RGFC
32
8
0700
2 Mar.
102 s
1900
26 Feb.
RED 2
1900
25 Feb.
1500
24 Feb.
3-7
2-7
XVIII Airborne Corps
VII Corps
Corps Boundary
Scale of Miles
0
50
100

A few miles away, the scene was much the same for Captain Averna's Charlie Company 2-7. A sense of supreme confidence oozed through the captain and his men on this G-day, partially because they had carried out four cross-border missions in the previous week. "Two were reconnaissance; one was a company-sized ambush patrol. Then, on the twenty-third . . . our company did what was called a reconnaissance in force just to clear an area. But . . . our company met with no enemy contact. "These missions eliminated any remaining jitters the Charlie Company soldiers might have had. "We . . . gained some confidence in our ability to at least do something even though we didn't have anybody shoot at us."

Like Crochet, Averna's men watched engineers demolish berms. With that task completed, the infantry rumbled across the border, in box formation with Delta on the left, Bravo on the right, and Charlie just behind them, fighting heavy winds all the way. "When we crossed, the wind was so strong and the dust and everything was so thick in that storm. You couldn't see beyond . . . hundred meters." Captain Averna actually welcomed the sandstorm because he figured it would provide nice concealment for his unit.[37]

The storm did present problems, though. Charlie Company went straight through abandoned Nisab and into Iraq. Averna's 3rd Platoon leader, Second Lieutenant Mike Tschanz, tried to keep his platoon's vehicles in sight, an extremely difficult task in the sandstorm. Tschanz was a workout and fitness nut who had once worked at Gold's Gym but joined the Army for adventure. He made it through Officer Candidate School, and now he found himself in the middle of the biggest American mechanized offensive since World War II. "As we crossed into Irac [*sic*] through the town of Nisab the winds grew in intensity as I struggled to maintain contact with the tracks to my front. I felt a sense of excitement and dread as it dawned on me that this wasn't another one of those countless false alarms. I wondered if we were ready, but I wasn't worried. I knew I would be ok. I felt a strong inner peace with God and managed to completely put my trust in him. The terrain got extremely rocky as visibility continued to decrease, soon I could no longer see the tracks to my front."

Lieutenant Tschanz's heart sank. He and his platoon had lost visual contact with the rest of the company and its tank support. "I called the CO and reported the situation as I did my best to find them in the cold blowing wind and dust. After about 45 minutes we finally regained contact and continued our movement to the North."

As the experiences of Lieutenant Tschanz indicated, the main challenge at this point was keeping the formation together. "This routine task became extremely difficult due to the driving winds and sand whirling about the desert," wrote First Lieutenant Robert Jones, the commander of the First Platoon. "The soft sand of central Saudi Arabia had now been replaced by the rocky terrain of Iraq. This terrain would take its toll on wheeled vehicles [mostly flat tires], but my BFV's [Bradley Fighting Vehicles] were able to traverse the land with little problem." Lieutenant Jones wisely ordered his platoon's vehicles to close to within fifty meters of one another, so they could keep one another in sight. " A break in contact could have been disastrous. The platoon continued on for almost 48 hours straight with stops only for fuel."

In those first couple days, they plunged deep into Iraq, straight toward the Euphrates River valley, with barely any opposition. "We were now close to 100 miles inside of Iraq," Averna's executive officer, First Lieutenant Leon Grube, wrote. The soldiers huddled inside their turrets or compartments to stay warm, tried to keep visual contact with other Americans, and fought sleep. The contours of the desert bounced them around their vehicles in an endless series of kidney-stabbing lurches. They munched on MREs or goodies from home and washed the food down with bottled water. Bradley commanders hankered for fresh air untainted by sand grains or engine exhaust. One of the few design flaws of this wonderful machine was that it blew its exhaust straight at the commander's section of the turret right into the commander's face. Consequently, many of the commanders coughed and spat their way through Desert Storm. The soldiers dealt with such discomforts with their usual discipline. They knew that things could be much worse. The offensive was going well, and everyone was alive—the rest could take care of itself in its own good time.[38]

SOMEWHERE BEYOND THE 24TH DIVISION Cottonbalers' eastern horizon, the infantrymen of 1–7 and 4-7 also plunged into Iraq on G-Day. They jumped off about four hours later, at roughly 1600 hours on the twenty-fourth of February, right in the middle of the same sandstorm their brothers to the west experienced. Each battalion consisted of approximately six hundred vehicles of all types—Bradleys, Abrams, M113s, Humvees, self-propelled artillery and MLRS vehicles, trucks, bulldozers, M88 recovery vehicles, mortar platforms, basically the entire array of American mechanized firepower. As Sergeant Narramore's Charlie Company 1–7 crossed the border, Captain Cleaver's voice resounded in their headsets: "Gentlemen, put your 3rd ID patch on the other side. We're now at war." Since they were now in combat, they were entitled to wear their divisional patches on the right shoulder.[39]

Lieutenant Colonel Smith's 1–7 led the way for the Phantom Brigade. Smith estimated that visibility was at about one hundred meters. "Once across the border into Iraq, the terrain became rough and unexploded ammunition [mostly U.S. cluster bombs] was being encountered by some units. No casualties were suffered . . . and movement continued steadily until after dark."

During a short lull in the early-morning hours of the twenty-fifth, Romaine's support platoon refueled them. In the meantime, General Griffith ordered the Phantom Brigade to carry out an attack the next day on elements of the Iraqi 26th Infantry Division, who were believed to be dug in with tanks and bunkers, defending the route to Al Busayyah, a division objective.

On its axis of attack the brigade swung west and then north. Once again, the desert was alive with vehicles of every description, a windy maw of modern mechanized warfare. The Americans rolled, bumped, and shimmied much of the day. Sheets of rain moistened the wind. Late in the afternoon, around 1700, the scout platoon of 4-7 found the enemy. Utilizing their thermal sights, the scouts picked up two Iraqi BMP armored personnel carriers in the distance. The Bradley's 25mm chain gun was capable of firing armor-piercing or high-explosive rounds. The former worked well on "hard" targets like APCs; the latter were better for "soft" targets like trucks or people. The 4-7 scouts opened fire with both. One of the BMPs exploded. Flames shot from its turret.

The other one disappeared into one of the many depressions in this rocky, ravine-dotted portion of the desert. The Americans furiously scanned the desert with their thermal (heat-seeking) sights. All of a sudden, the BMP popped up about six hundred meters away. The scouts wrinkled their brows in confusion at an odd sight. In the driving rain, an Iraqi soldier was sitting on top of the BMP. "What in the world is this guy doing?" the Cottonbalers wondered. Then it hit them. The Soviet-made night-vision devices on the BMP did not work in the rain. The Americans opened fire on the BMP. The first round hit the unfortunate Iraqi soldier right in the head. In the colorful words of one historian, the enemy soldier's "brains were a green spray on the thermals." The Cottonbalers watched in horrified fascination as the brains "blew up and out as his body flipped over the side like a duck on a rail at a shooting gallery."

An armor-piercing round went right through the BMP. The vehicle halted; five figures came out the back, looked around, and got back in. Another round hit the BMP. This time, four figures got out, dragging two bodies that they dumped into the desert. Then they actually got back into their vehicle! The scouts could not believe their eyes. "This is like, 'how many clowns can get out of the car at the circus,'" one American exclaimed. Seconds later, several rounds penetrated the fuel tank of the enemy APC, turning it into a funeral pyre.[40]

The scouts veered to the right and made way for the rest of the brigade to unleash a massive amount of firepower on anything that betrayed heat in their thermal sights. From the turret of his Bradley, within a sea of 1–7 vehicles, Lieutenant Colonel Smith called in artillery and mortar fire on the targets. The rounds shrieked overhead and into the enemy positions, exploding with a terrifying ferocity. Smith heard a loud "whopping" sound overhead. He glanced up, saw American helicopters directly overhead, and frowned. It was very dangerous for them to fly overhead when artillery rounds were in the air. A stray round could hit one of the choppers, but luckily nothing of the kind happened.

Smith's men, meanwhile, shot up a handful of enemy vehicles. Sergeant Narramore's wingman—Bradleys operated in pairs, just like fighter planes—spotted a target hiding behind a berm. "He started firing at it. Then there was a short round from a mortar." The mortar round exploded harmlessly. Narramore never knew if his wingman hit his target.

In this first engagement the men were a bit jumpy, a bit too excited. Captain Sutherland, about half a mile to the rear, watched them fire at many of the same targets. "It was the first time the battalion had been in a firefight, and you could tell. There were some communications problems,

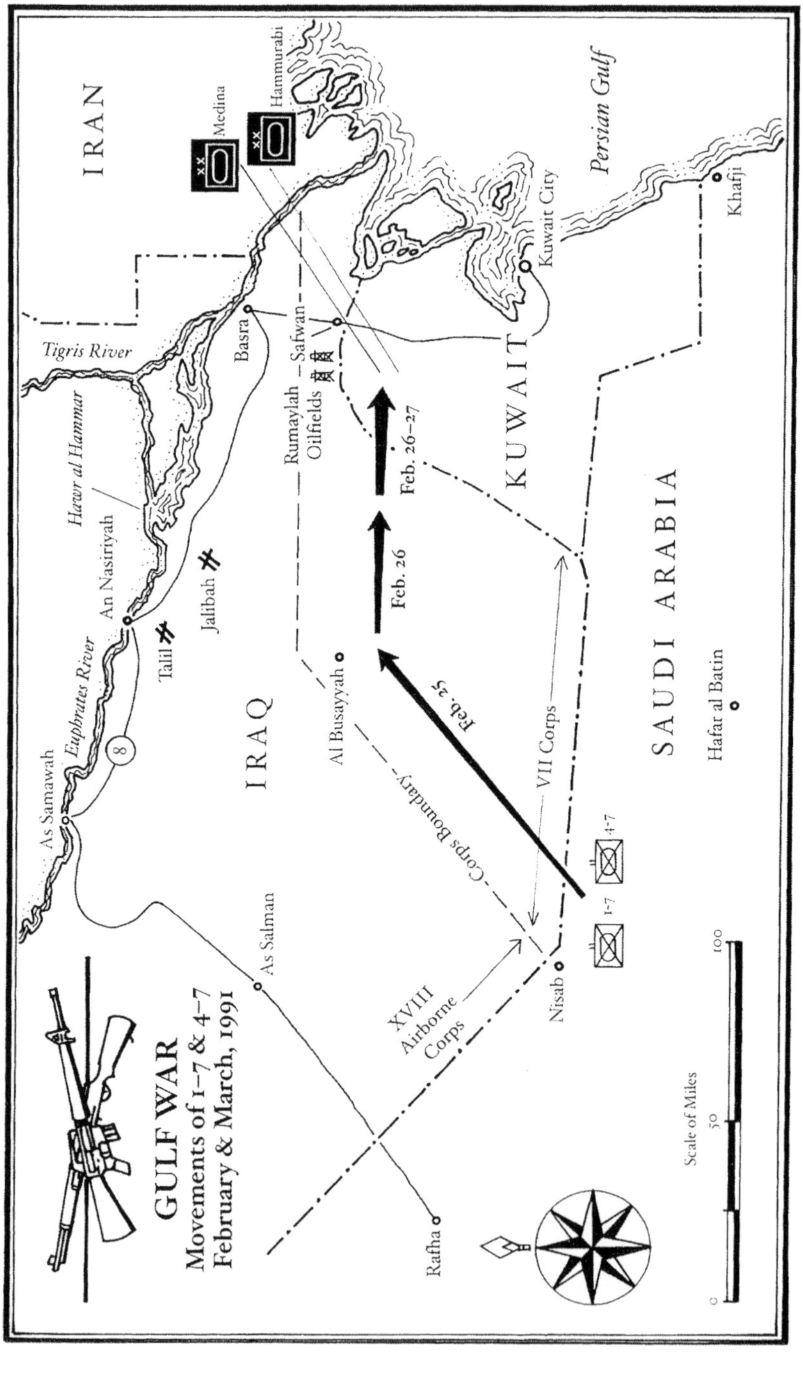
GULF WAR
Movements of 1–7 & 4–7
February & March, 1991
IRAN
IRAQ
KUWAIT
SAUDI ARABIA
Persian Gulf
Kuwait City
Khafji
Medina
Hammurabi
Basra
Safwan
Rumaylah
Oilfields
Tigris River
Hawr al Hammar
An Nasiriyah
Jalibah
Talil
Euphrates River
As Samawah
8
Al Busayyah
Feb. 26–27
Feb. 26
Feb. 25
VII Corps
Corps Boundary
Hafar al Batin
As Salman
XVIII
Airborne
Corps
Nisab
1-7
4-7
Rafha
Scale of Miles
0
50
100

people getting confused and yelling on radio, but it worked out. I think they killed this one BTR [an APC] about 48 times." They shot so many times at this hapless BTR that Smith deadpanned on the radio, "You probably don't have to shoot at it anymore. It looks pretty dead."

Within moments the Iraqis surrendered. Lieutenant Colonel Pat Egan's 4-7 snagged 229 prisoners (and a three-legged dog), while 1–7 took 70 prisoners of war. Lieutenant McClure, who had been insanely busy shuttling supplies since the war began, took a moment to study the enemy soldiers. "These poor guys . . . had just been stuck out there and probably had no idea what was going on anyhow. These were the conscripts. These were the cannon fodder that Saddam had set out by the berms. They didn't put up much of a fight." Colonel Riley also made sure to get a good look at the EPWs (Enemy Prisoners of War). He wanted to know exactly what kind of shape the Iraqis were in. "They weren't of a mood to defend. They were hungry, they were thirsty, they were pitiful." The Americans gave them water, medical care, and MREs. Later on, small groups of military police, who found themselves in great demand because of the large numbers of surrendering enemy troops in this war, showed up and directed the EPWs to the rear.[41]

The brigade rumbled on in the darkness before halting at about 2030. Refueling trucks from support platoons descended on the area. Combat vehicles took their turns driving over to the trucks and taking on fuel. Soldiers catnapped or snacked on MREs.

Hours later, they saw artillery lighting up the night. American howitzer and MLRS ordnance screamed at Al Busayyah in the distance. The spectacle was both beautiful and terrifying. The explosions, mixed with gusts of sandy wind and occasional sheets of rain, almost sounded muffled, but the ground rumbled.

In the morning, as the sun rose, they moved out again, this time with orders to converge on Al Busayyah, an Iraqi supply center. The Phantom Brigade received the assignment of protecting the northwest flank of the main attack. Intelligence believed that this would take them straight into the guns of an Iraqi commando brigade. The battalions formed a wedge with the armor in the lead. The tanks acted as makeshift mine disposal vehicles, since their heavy armored plate could easily withstand the explosions of the stray ordnance and mines in the desert.

Late in the morning the brigade ran into an enemy bunker complex. "We suppressed some bunkers and destroyed some abandoned equipment and supplies but otherwise encountered no organized opposition," Lieutenant Colonel Smith later wrote.

The original plan had called for him to halt his forces for a twenty-four- to thirty-six-hour rest at this point, but the offensive was way ahead of schedule, going better than anyone had anticipated. The main mission now for the 1st Armored Division, and thus its two battalions of Cottonbalers, was to destroy the Republican Guard. Apparently they were attempting to leave Kuwait and retreat back home. So the whole 1st Armored Division turned ninety degrees due east and continued its attack, running into soldiers from the Tawalkana Republican Guards Division on the afternoon of the twenty-sixth.[42]

In 1–7's wedge, Staff Sergeant Narramore watched as an enemy BMP materialized dead ahead. Everyone else apparently spotted it too, because the entire Raider platoon opened up on the BMP. The enemy soldiers in the BMP quickly raised a white flag. "We stopped hitting him, but he was smoking by the time we went by him." Soon there were other targets. "There were some antiaircraft guns up there and there was a berm. The 2nd Platoon sergeant . . . picked up a spot in a bunker, an antenna was what he called it, so we all started hitting it."

The antenna could have been from an Iraqi artillery observer, because incoming artillery started coming in. Narramore and the other Cottonbalers heard Colonel Riley over the radio. "Button up! Incoming!" A tremor of fear shot through the ranks. If one of those rounds scored a direct hit on a Bradley, the results would not be pretty. "Hatches go slamming down," Narramore remembered. He even thought he saw Lieutenant Morse's wingman get hit. "It looked like he got hit directly, because a big puff of smoke went right through his Bradley. Then all of a sudden I could see his Bradley backing out of there. Not too far from my Bradley one of them hit and I could hear the 'ting' off my Bradley hatch. I looked over at my gunner and his eyes were just huge." Captain Cleaver ordered them to back up out of range of the enemy artillery. "Shortly after that our artillery knocked it out." After that a bulldozer caved in the bunker with the antenna.

All of a sudden Lieutenant Morse spotted a T-72, the main battle Iraqi tank. "I got it!" Morse screamed. His Bradley launched a TOW missile. Narramore scanned the area and saw the T-72. "The next thing I heard was a whoosh from the TOW round. It goes out . . . and I'm watching it." The TOW ran straight and true, right into the enemy tank. "It was a big fireball. It knocked the turret off. Then, myself and my gunner got a truck and we took him out with AP [armor-piercing rounds] . . . and some . . . stationary antiaircraft guns too."

American jets also provided support. Two A-10 Warthogs and eight F-16 Falcons descended on Iraqi vehicles and an ammunition dump, wreaking havoc with their bombs and missiles. They scored a direct hit on the ammo dump, releasing immense waves of concussion. "You could see the explosion. When the sound got to you, it curled you up in your Bradleys. It hurt you so bad because of the force of the blast. I was just afraid the things might come our way." More than anything, Staff Sergeant Narramore was glad the jets were on his side. Even in his turret, while wearing his BDUs, flak vest, and MOPP suit, he still continued to feel concussions from secondary explosions as ammo cooked off.

He shook his head in wonder and stole a glance at his charcoal-stained arms. The MOPP suit had stained every inch of exposed skin a dingy black color. The same was true for all of his men; naturally this showed up more easily on the white soldiers, but he could tell that everyone's skin—black, white, Hispanic, whatever—was stained when he looked at his crewmen and his infantrymen in the back. In a way, that was appropriate. The pervasive MOPP suit grit served as a kind of metaphor for the blurring of racial and class distinctions among these modern infantrymen in combat. They were all Cottonbalers—combat infantrymen —and, out here in this godforsaken Iraqi desert, that was all that really mattered.[43]

That night they stopped in the midst of an Iraqi training and supply area around Al Busayyah that had been cluster bombed repeatedly by the U.S. Air Force. The area was so perilous that Sergeant Narramore would not even let his men leave their Bradleys. The men could see munitions all over the place. "[They] were everywhere. I couldn't even drop the ramp all the way. I dropped it halfway for the entire platoon so the guys could stand on the back and do their thing. I didn't even want to get them on the ground." The soldiers stood on the rear ramps of their Bradleys to relieve themselves. When the unit moved out several hours later, the tanks led the way, since their thick armor could absorb the fragments from the inevitable explosions without any damage at all. The Bradleys simply followed them in a straight line, but not without a few dicey moments "as tracked vehicles would set off explosions and fragments would careen wildly off the sides of adjacent vehicles," Lieutenant Colonel Smith wrote. No one got hurt.[44]

AFTER A DAY AND A half of advancing unopposed, the 24th Division Cottonbalers finally encountered some enemy soldiers around 1900 on the twenty-fifth. Lieutenant Allen's scout platoon had been advancing anywhere between five and ten kilometers ahead of the main force, trying to keep contact between 2-7 and 3-7, at the point of a brigade wedge bearing northeast. "My mission was to maintain contact with elements of Task Force 3-7." Allen, sitting in the passenger seat of a Humvee, wasn't worried about getting too far ahead of his battalion "because I was right there next to 3-7 Infantry." He kept his vehicles fueled by employing jerricans to constantly refuel his Humvees and Bradleys any time they stopped. The men gave their empty cans to Allen's wingman, who at times went to the rear, filled them up, and brought them back to disseminate among the platoon. The system worked well. Allen's outfit never ran out of fuel.

As the sun dipped below the western horizon on the twenty-fifth, the scout platoon was approaching Objective Red 2, Abu Ghar, an old mining town some two hundred kilometers inside Iraq. As usual, the wind was howling and sheets of rain spattered their vehicles. All of a sudden they saw some heat signatures in their thermals. "We called for fire." Through their thermal sights they glimpsed the green silhouettes of several Iraqi soldiers hit by the incoming fire: "The weather was turning really bad at that point." So bad, in fact, that it began to mess with the thermals. "Darkness, mist, and sand kicked up." Allen's men could not see with any certainty beyond a hundred meters, but they knew that Iraqi soldiers were close by. "We saw them walking. They didn't know we were there. They just kept walking." Allen maneuvered his Humvees in such a way as to surround the enemy soldiers. He felt that they could hear the engine noise from his two Bradleys but not his Humvees. "So we came up and turned on our headlights and they surrendered." They took between fifteen and twenty-two prisoners, questioned them, and gave them medical care. One of the prisoners told them, in English, about a nearby sleeping quarters large enough to hold two companies of soldiers. The scouts checked it out and found three more Iraqis willing to surrender.[45]

Lieutenant Allen's scout platoon had now demonstrated that the route to Objective Red 2 was clear, so several companies of Cottonbalers surged forward, in the process capturing more prisoners as well as the objective itself. Major Stenson's assistant operations officer interrogated many of the disheveled-looking prisoners. They were a composite group of soldiers and airmen who had been hurriedly thrown together and flung eastward in a vain attempt to slow the sledgehammer advance of the XVIII Airborne Corps. Stenson eyed them with more than a little pity. "Cold, hungry, some without shoes, with very few weapons and less ammunition, and little leadership, this element of the Iraqi 31st Infantry Division was certainly not a formidable force. Many were afraid they would be killed and a large number deserted three days before we arrived." The Cottonbalers set up a temporary EPW compound for them, in addition to providing some food and medical care.[46]

The next morning 2-7 and 3-7 set their sights on a new objective, called BP (Battle Position) 102, an intersection astride a main north-south road called Highway 8—the main line of communication between Baghdad and Kuwait. The Cottonbalers were supposed to secure this intersection, remain in place, and destroy anything that moved on the road. The high command knew that the Iraqis were leaving Kuwait as quickly as their legs, or vehicles, could carry them. Now the generals wanted to make sure that the nerve center of the Iraqi Army, the Republican Guard, did not escape to fight again another day. If the Cottonbalers could make it to BP 102, they would cut off a major avenue of retreat for the Republican Guard. "In short, we were closing the back door," Lieutenant Huffines summed up succinctly.[47]

After spending much of the morning rounding up more prisoners, the Cottonbalers pushed off at noon. The weather had gone from bad to worse. Howling winds, sometimes as much as 50 miles per hour, whipped sand everywhere. Cold rain pounded down in furious waves.

The formations closed to within meters of one another; the danger of getting lost was worse than the danger of collisions. Some of the confusion would have been alleviated with the dissemination of Global Positioning Satellite (GPS) devices, but they were not yet available in large enough quantities. Only Lieutenant Allen, his battalion commander, and one other officer had a GPS.

Late in the afternoon the storm modified a bit and visibility improved. The soldiers could see BP 102 in the distance. Just then, enemy mortar and artillery fire began to fall all around the American vehicles. At the leading edge of the American wedge, Lieutenant Allen's scouts were among the first to come under fire. "We received a lot of indirect fire, but it wasn't effective fire as we were coming up on the objective," Lieutenant Allen recalled. "At that point, scout platoon moved on-line, faced to the west, and began firing, and this is all heading into darkness." Allen could hear the chatter sound of his two Bradley's 25mm chain guns. He could not tell if his men hit anyone, but the Iraqi artillery crews who had dug their D-30 guns along the highway began to jump onto trucks and leave.

Immediately Allen's platoon drove to the abandoned guns. They hopped out of their Humvees and set about wrecking the enemy artillery. "We put thermite grenades in the D-30 batteries, into the actual guns, to destroy them as they were sitting there." Allen was just about to destroy one of the guns with a thermite grenade when he noticed something: "I . . . looked at the gun. The breech was open and there was a round in it and that's where I left it because I wasn't going to put a thermite inside a loaded gun. I didn't know what to do with it." He left it for the engineers.[48]

Even as Lieutenant Allen's scouts chased away enemy artillerymen, Captain Averna's Charlie Company assaulted east, right at the highway intersection. The sun had just about set. Enemy troops were dug into rocky trenches west of the highway. Averna ordered his Bradleys forward to close with the enemy and destroy them—a mission as old as the infantry itself "We cleared the trenches. The enemy was pretty well dug in. For me, that night was eerie, a lot of confusion. We were clearing stuff on the ground. We were on a flat plain and hit a dug-in battalion . . . with 57mm . . . ack-ack guns that were dug in as antitank weapons, but they had no night capability."

The enemy opened fire with everything they had—AA guns, machine guns, rifles, and grenades. In response, the Cottonbalers, at first, remained at a distance, hosing down the trenches and bunkers with their Bradleys. The high-explosive rounds from the chain guns splintered rocks, ripped into enemy bodies, and streaked through the night. Smaller caliber rounds from coaxial machine guns laced into the enemy positions. Tracers flew everywhere on both sides.

The Americans blasted anything that moved on their thermal sights. In the confusion, Captain Averna hollered orders over the radio, trying to manage the battle. In spite of the chaos, the Americans coordinated their firepower quite well. The longer the Bradleys shot up the trenches and bunkers, the more the enemy fire slackened. "We would move as close as we could to the bunker, then [the men] would dismount . . . get in there, and take it out, and we could pretty much suppress [the enemy] with 25mm as we were moving towards it, with infantry remaining protected in the back. You could almost drive over the trench line . . . and get into the trench line . . . without actually having to go against the fire man-to-man; the Bradleys would suppress them as we were closing on them. Once they got in the trench line, the soldiers had to take the enemy out or they'd surrender."[49]

Ever so steadily, the Bradleys, in this manner, began to close with the enemy. They got close enough to disgorge the dismounts who had been cooped up in their cramped rear compartments. Captain Averna himself dismounted so that he could have a good look at what was going on. Bradley commanders gave the order to lower ramps. No sooner did each ramp slam into position, kicking up sand and dust, than the infantry squads raced out of their Bradleys, straight into the enemy positions. These dismounted infantrymen performed exactly as they were taught. They moved in fire teams, emerging from their vehicles on either side, covering one another, moving on the flanks of enemy bunkers, hosing them down with automatic rifle fire or pitching grenades into them before assaulting them. Lieutenant Jones, the 1st Platoon leader, watched his dismounts overwhelm the enemy. "The platoon fired and maneuvered on the enemy. We soon overran the enemy. Three were dead, four wounded and the rest gave up. We quickly searched the POWs and destroyed their weapons and pointed them to the rear."[50]

This was war the old-fashioned way—close-up, nasty, smelly, dirty, tragic—so similar to what many generations of Cottonbalers had experienced. Captain Averna's troops came face-to-face with the ugly realities of war. "This was the first time everybody saw . . . what happens with that kind of situation . . . dead enemy soldiers, wounded enemy soldiers. Medics got a lot of good training, unfortunately." They saw that enemy blood was just as red as American blood. They found dead men with wallets containing pictures of wives and children. They smelled the sickly sweet stench of fresh blood, the new decay of fresh death. Averna lost two men wounded in this night engagement near BP 102, one of whom had been mistakenly hit by American grenade fragments. Both soldiers recovered. One of them even refused evacuation.[51]

Charlie Company cleared out the bunker complex, mounted up, and resumed the advance on nearby BP 102. Lieutenant Grube, from the perspective of his Bradley, watched as a column of enemy vehicles came into sight. "As we approached, we could see many unsuspecting Iraqi vehicles with their headlights on moving on the road. Soon we were given permission to fire and it wasn't long until there were flames instead of headlights. Once we reached the road we turned east keeping our left flank along the road with the entire company on line. As we moved, we destroyed howitzers and ammunition, and cleared bunkers of artillery positions. We moved like this . . . until 0500."

The battle had turned into a free-for-all, with the Americans shooting up anything that offered even a semblance of resistance. The Cottonbalers enjoyed every advantage possible—technology, firepower, leadership, training, tactical positioning, supplies—but this was still combat and that meant it was tough, dangerous, exhausting work. Lieutenant James "Mitch" Howell, Averna's 2nd Platoon leader, had once been an enlisted man himself, before going to college on an ROTC scholarship. He and his soldiers spent much of the night shooting up vehicles and clearing bunkers. "We started to pick up several hot spots in our thermals. These were vehicles of some sort. My platoon was firing on several dug in vehicles. Then came the order from [Captain Averna] to dismount and clear some bunkers. Capt Averna's track pulled up to mine and we dismounted. The bunkers were destroyed and started to have sympathetic detonations. We remounted. The next hour or so we kept on line and shot hot spots to our front." As Lieutenant Grube indicated, the fight lasted much of the night. At one point, Howell glanced to the north and saw "tracers from 3-7 Inf flying to our front left."[52]

In fact, Jensen's 3-7 was also in the thick of the fight. His men had swung north, to the left of 2-7, and pushed for the highway in the same sandstorm that harassed 2-7. The sand particles masqueraded as hot spots on thermal sights, meaning the Cottonbalers were essentially blind. At nightfall, random artillery fire started dropping around the 3-7 vehicles. "The artillery fire was not impressive and apparently unobserved," First Lieutenant Huffines commented. "The rounds fell in no specific order and were not being massed or bracketed. If they were the FO [forward observer] needed retraining . . . badly." Of course, the experience of being under any artillery fire was unnerving and dangerous, even inaccurate fire like this, especially for Huffines, who had only the thin skin of his Humvee to protect him, his driver, and the gunner on his Humvee's mark 19 grenade launcher. "All the armored vehicles around me . . . closed [their] hatches while I and my wheeled vehicles were left to hope the thin shells of our 'cars and trucks' could somehow defeat the 152MM rounds."[53]

In the darkness, Corporal Crochet's Alpha Company came under the same inaccurate fire. He buttoned up his Bradley and confidently expected American counterbattery artillery to take out the enemy guns. In the months leading up to the war, he had met many artillery soldiers who assured him that the moment enemy guns opened fire, they would be detected and eliminated. The artillery soldiers raved about their radar and tracking ability; enemy guns would be taken out in seconds. But, in this case, the supporting artillery was probably out of range, so the enemy fire continued. Crochet didn't care about any of that. He only knew that the artillerymen had promised him immediate assistance and had not delivered, so he seethed with frustrated anger. "I wish I had an artillery guy here right now," he thought. "I'd punch him!" Within a few minutes, the fire finally slackened. No one was hurt and the armor of the Bradleys easily withstood the shrapnel, which Crochet and the other infantrymen could hear clanking off their machine.

Corporal Crochet's Bradley negotiated some hilly terrain and, almost at the same time, he heard reports on the radio that Iraqi troops had been spotted. Then he saw something in his thermal. "I couldn't identify what it was and my BC [Bradley commander] couldn't see what it was either. So, I kept switching between my thermal sights and my day sights . . . and then I finally realized that it was a group of Iraqis laying down. By this time, they were pretty close. They were probably one hundred meters or so away." A few seconds passed as Crochet and his commander positively identified that the prone figures were indeed enemy soldiers.

The commander, Sergeant Dean, excitedly hollered at Crochet, "Bust 'em! Bust 'em! Bust 'em!"

Corporal Crochet hesitated a moment. He didn't understand what his commander meant. He glanced at Dean. "Fire?"

Dean glanced back. "Yeah, fire," he replied quickly.

Crochet pulled the trigger. "I fired a couple of rounds and it threw up a lot of dirt and then he called for a cease-fire and then we kept moving." The Iraqis never even shot back: "To this day, I don't know if I hit anything. I'm assuming I probably did, but I don't know for sure. We didn't get out to check."

Alpha Company kept moving toward Highway 8. They rolled past Iraqi supply trucks. Here and there small groups of Iraqi POWs drifted around the area. The battalion cooks began policing them up, sometimes encountering a few who picked up their weapons when the combat formations rumbled past. As his Bradley bounced and rumbled, Crochet decided to sight his gun. He blew up an abandoned enemy truck to make sure his gun was zeroed in properly. A little later, he spotted the highway. A truck full of enemy troops was rolling along unimpeded. Crochet wondered why he had not been given an order to open fire. Just then, an A-10 swooped down and blew the enemy truck apart. The Bradleys crossed the road and fanned out into fighting positions. As they did, the corporal glimpsed an enemy soldier cowering in a nearby ditch. "The only part I could see was a head with a helmet." Soon he got a better look: "There was a soldier in this ditch in a fetal position, hiding." Crochet and Sergeant Dean decided to live and let live. They let the enemy soldier go.

Throughout the night, a few enemy vehicles stumbled into the area. One of them, an enemy troop truck, came into Crochet's field of fire. "I fired high-explosive rounds at it. In the simulator when you fire into a soft-skin vehicle like that, hit it five times, it explodes. This one didn't. I remember it was just kind of strange." He kept pressing the trigger and finally destroyed the truck. "The back end just exploded and it folded into the ditch. Then, twelve people jumped out of it. I started to swing the barrel back around to engage them, but [Dean] said to cease fire. I'm glad he did, because they weren't a threat to anyone. They jumped out and just took off in the opposite direction of where we were."[54]

A kilometer or so away, Private Kurt Dabb's Alpha 2-7 was fighting this battle with the benefit of quite a security blanket, namely, several companies of M1 Abrams tanks. Alpha 2-7 had been cross-attached to the brigade's tank battalion. They approached the road, warily searching for targets in a landscape already littered with wrecked, burning equipment. At this moment, which for him was the culmination of a lifetime of anticipation about war, the tanks opened up on something. "At that point it was like, 'Wow, the shit's really hit the fan.' You could see off in the distance stuff getting blown up." His Bradley crewmen opened up on unseen targets. The whole fight lasted only a few minutes before the Cottonbalers and their armored partners cut the road.

Private Dabb's unit received orders to guard the road. Dabb and the other dismounts left their Bradleys and set up positions along roadside berms. The Bradley crews stayed in the vehicles and overwatched. Plain and simple, anything that drove down the road was to be killed. Several minutes elapsed. All of a sudden, the Bradley gunners opened fire. A vehicle was driving on the road heading directly for the company positions. The 25mm rounds smashed it to pieces. Private Dabb and several other infantrymen approached the vehicle to investigate. "It happened to be a . . . civilian milk truck. There was a dad who was driving, the mom, and two little kids. They were all expired. That was . . . a . . . shock." Dabb glumly surveyed the remains of this little family and thought, "Wow, ten seconds ago these people were alive, and now they're dead." He felt bad, but he knew that the dead civilians had no business being here. No one else felt especially good about this, but they knew they had only followed orders in opening fire. The men wondered why the strange vehicle had materialized when and where it did, but they soon put it out of their minds and went back to their positions.[55]

The two battalions of 24th Division Cottonbalers moved swiftly and effectively that night, crushing all significant Iraqi resistance in front of

BP 102, but inevitably some armed Iraqi troops got bypassed. Due to his capacity as support platoon leader, Lieutenant Huffines's fuelers had been riding around all night refueling combat vehicles. He had not slept a minute since the war began. All night long on the twenty-sixth, a line from the movie *Battle of the Bulge* kept flashing in his mind—Petrol is blood." Huffines knew that if he failed to keep the Bradleys and Abrams adequately supplied with fuel, his entire battalion's advance could grind to a halt. "I'd get very jealous of my fuel." Even so, he did try to take in his surroundings as much as possible. At one point, Huffines noticed a bunch of dead enemy bodies and decided to dismount from his Humvee and check them out. He had never seen a KIA before. "I got out and walked up to the bodies. These men were still warm. They were in a small group. They were pretty chewed up. Our medics had already been there and had covered the dead men's faces with empty sandbags. I walked up and pulled the bag off one's head and looked into his eyes." The eyes were open and staring back at him. "It was pretty grisly. The rounds had just chewed him from south to north. I looked at him for a few seconds; then we moved on. I was enough of an historian to know that some people freaked out at the sight of blood or bodies. I wanted to be able to control my emotions whenever I encountered KIAs and this seemed the best time." Huffines got into his Humvee and they went back to work.

Later he caught one of his crewmen, a former drug dealer from Seattle, looting one of the bodies. "He didn't have a lick of sense to him, but he was funny . . . always good for a laugh." Huffines stopped him. "I am not having an Iraqi soul chase me through nine levels of hell just so you can get a free watch. Get back on the Humvee. We're not looting any bodies." The gunner complained, but he obeyed.

Not long after this incident, Major Stenson, from 2-7, showed up and helped himself to some of Huffines's fuel. The lieutenant was not pleased, but Jensen ordered him to comply. Moreover, he told Huffines that 2-7 was low on fuel and needed a refill to stay in the fight for BP 102 farther to the south. Huffines was to take two of his vehicles, follow Stenson, and refuel a company from 2-7. In essence, this meant that Lieutenant Huffines had to do the 2-7 support platoon leader's job for him. Naturally, Huffines was none too thrilled with this assignment, but combat was combat and orders were orders.

As a good leader, Huffines knew that he should go with the two fuelers to the 2-7 company himself. He did so and weathered some enemy mortar fire in the process. "With the darkness you could see the hundreds of tiny red-hot metal bits flying outward from the center. It looked like a rocket fired on the 4th of July, only these were but meters from me and my vehicles." After fifteen minutes of this they accomplished the refuel and started back, but Huffines, stewing a bit, had made a mistake. He did not consult a map. Instead, he figured that he and his men would follow their own tracks back to their own battalion. Even with night-vision goggles, this didn't work. They got lost.

The last thing he wanted to do was approach the battalion unannounced in the middle of a fight. That was a friendly fire incident waiting to happen. He could see fire and explosions in a 360-degree panorama around him. He radioed for help but got nowhere, so he kept going. Seconds later, his Humvee crashed into a ditch they "could not see, being we were all wearing NODs [Night Observation Devices] and had no depth perception." Huffines crawled out of the vehicle and surveyed the damage. The Humvee was caught in the ditch on the driver's side. The lieutenant felt enormous anger welling up in his chest. The accumulated stress, danger, and sleeplessness, combined with this ridiculous mission, sent him over the edge. "I pitched a royal fit. I threw my helmet. I just started cussing . . . for about five minutes straight." At the end of the tantrum he settled down a bit and remembered where he was and what his responsibilities were. He looked at his men and "noticed the looks on their faces. I was the officer, I was supposed to protect them and get them home. They were all staring at me with huge eyes and worried looks. I gathered my emotions." One of the fuel vehicles had a winch, and they quickly extracted the Humvee.

Huffines got back on the radio to the battalion and pleaded for them to shoot a star cluster so that he would know which direction to head. After hemming and hawing, they finally did so. The support platoon soldiers made a beeline for the cluster—Huffines in the lead—also taking care to inform the battalion exactly which direction they expected to approach them. Huffines breathed a sigh of relief and removed his night-vision goggles to improve his depth perception. "We drove. The entire battlefield up to this point was a sea of fire, like something out of Dante's. Burned and burning vehicles, bodies, screams and isolated gunfire saturated our senses." Suddenly they entered a strangely pristine area. The lieutenant glanced to his right and saw, about three meters away, "an intact trench line filled with Iraqi soldiers looking back at me. At the same time my gunner . . . spotted them as well. He yelped . . . 'OhJeesoo, ohJeesoo!' "

A second passed as the three shocked Americans decided what to do. The driver looked at Huffines questioningly. The lieutenant knew he could not get into a firefight with these people. He understood that, infantry or not, his job at this moment was to fuel, not to fight. "Drive, motherfucker, drive!" Huffines yelled. The driver floored the gas pedal. As he did, Huffines could see motion out of his peripheral vision. "The Iraqis . . . were scrambling and running at us from out of the trenches." Huffines's Humvee left them in the dust, as did his fuelers. The lieutenant never knew whether these bypassed Iraqis were trying to surrender, trying to capture him, looking for a fight, or what. He and his men made sure not to hang around long enough to find out. They made it safely back to the battalion.[56]

BY MORNING ON THE TWENTY-SEVENTH, the 2-7 and 3-7 Cottonbalers had effectively "closed the back door," securing complete control of their section of Highway 8. That route of escape was now closed to the Iraqis. In addition, 2-7 and 3-7 spent much of the twenty-seventh pushing farther east, against very light resistance, to within sixty kilometers of Basra, a sizable Iraqi city. As they did this, the 1st Armored Division Cottonbalers finally found their quarry—the Republican Guard. The Cottonbalers had already crushed elements of two Republican Guard divisions, Tawalkana and Adnan, respectively. Now, from midday on the twenty-seventh until the early-morning hours of the twenty-eighth, the massed fury of the 1st Armored Division was unleashed on the Medina Division, the most armor heavy of all Republican Guard outfits. Medina was dug in along a ridge—the Americans called it "Medina Ridge"—just to the northwest of Kuwait.

Medina had drawn the mission of protecting thousands of Iraqi soldiers streaming out of Kuwait, just east of the ridge. The Americans unleashed a devastating blend of supporting firepower on them, including Apache helicopters, air force fighter-bombers, MLRS rockets, and eighteen hundred rounds of 155mm artillery ammo. Griffith positioned his tanks in front, at the vanguard of all three of his brigades. Then, late in the morning on the twenty-seventh, he lined up all three of those brigades, placing the Phantom Brigade in the middle, and attacked. The 2nd Brigade, to the north, dealt with the brunt of the Medina Division, but the Phantom Brigade, and its two battalions of Cottonbalers, found plenty to keep them busy.[57]

At first the Cottonbalers fought remnants of the Tawalkana and Adnan divisions. These Iraqi soldiers were effecting a retreat in the direction of Medina Ridge. In the three days of war, Lieutenant Colonel Smith and his 1–7 Cottonbalers had slept very little. They were tired, hungry, and filthy with MOPP suit detritus and sweat. There would be plenty of time later to worry about such things. Right now, Smith knew that the campaign was reaching its climax. He systematically directed his companies through the Republican Guard infantrymen like a scythe through wheat. "We tried to maximize our firepower and superior range to reduce the risk to our soldiers. The fighting was intense at times with the concussions from exploding enemy vehicles and ammunition rattling the battlefield. The weather was very heavily overcast, windy, and rainy. The fires and explosions cast a red glow as they reflected off the clouds. I recall thinking that I was looking into the gates of Hell as the violence and destruction took place."

The battalion paused a few hours to police up prisoners and realign their battle formations. Then, at 1130, they plunged into the Medina Division. "Once again the fighting was intense with lots of enemy targets that appeared to be attempting to flee north while some appeared to be defending to our front." In front of Smith's infantry, American armor destroyed enemy tank after enemy tank. The Bradleys shot some TOW missiles at enemy tanks but spent more time concentrating on killing BMPs, trucks, and a few stray infantry who seemed belligerent. Explosions, fires, and concussion rocked the desert landscape. The noise was thunderous, massive, all consuming.[58]

The fight lasted well into the night. For the combat soldiers in the Abrams and Bradleys, adrenaline repelled exhaustion. Lieutenant McClure, in the course of his duties as HHC executive officer, got a chance to watch the battle unfold. He found some high ground with an almost panoramic view, got out of his Humvee, and stood transfixed, taking in the whole awful but somehow stirring sight. "When our M1 tanks would fire, I could see the concussion . . . and then a couple of seconds later, I would see an explosion of a huge yellow orange fireball . . . which used to be an Iraqi tank. I was impressed." The Iraqis tried to fight back, but they were outgunned and outranged. Their tank rounds typically fell one thousand meters short of their targets. Their vehicles did not have the optical sights or night vision common to the Americans. All they could do was shoot at whatever they thought might be a target and hope for the best. In almost all cases, they missed while, seconds later, an American shell ripped through their compartment. McClure could see this happening. "Everything in it was incinerated, the turret blown off; all the fuel and ammunition on board explodes."[59]

Unable to score with their tanks or infantry, the Iraqis threw whatever artillery they could at the Americans. Some of it fell in 1–7's area. Lieutenant Colonel Smith saw the enemy shells exploding outside of his Bradley, near his task force. "Two separate heavy concentrations landed just behind the task force and then landed directly to our front. I was convinced that the enemy was trying to adjust fire onto the task force. I ordered the task force to back up 100 meters. No sooner had this been done than heavy artillery landed on our previous positions. I felt that I was playing a cat and mouse [game] with the enemy observers as we moved several times while pouring fire into . . . enemy bunkers to our front and counterbattery fires were conducted by the artillery. Eventually the enemy fire came to a halt. Three soldiers in my combat trains had been wounded and five vehicles damaged or destroyed by the enemy artillery. Artillery channels reported that between 4 and 6 enemy artillery battalions had been involved in the engagement."

Close to midnight, Colonel Riley ordered 1–7 to pull back in favor of 4–66 Armor. In about eight hours of fighting, the Cottonbalers of Smith's battalion had destroyed seventeen tanks, eighteen BMPs, and twenty-one other vehicles. They also took forty-six prisoners. Smith's men got some badly needed sleep, but soon rumors of a cease-fire swept through the unit. President Bush knew that the aims of the coalition had been fulfilled. Saddam's troops had been decisively kicked out of Kuwait. The president did not want any more bloodshed (on either side) than was absolutely necessary, and he did not want to take the risk that the fragile coalition of Arab and Western nations might fall apart. At first, Smith heard that the cease-fire would take effect somewhere around 0400, but then that was changed to 0800. In the meantime, General Schwarzkopf ordered his commanders to keep attacking, with every weapon at their disposal. He hoped to destroy as much of the combat power of the Iraqi Army as possible before the shooting stopped.

Near dawn, American units opened up with a massive artillery barrage in all sectors. Once again, the incredible lethality of American firepower was on display. The MLRS rockets streaking through the air looked particularly impressive. The pounding went on for forty-five minutes. Smoke and fire were everywhere. Some grunts wondered how anything could live under the weight of all that fire. When the artillery lifted at 0615, the Cottonbalers of the 1st Armored Division carried out one last attack on the Medina Division. "The task force hit the line of departure right on time and was almost immediately in contact," Smith recalled. "We continued to move forward as a part of the brigade, engaging the enemy at long range and driving through the exploding ammunition and burned vehicles as we went. At . . . 0750 the word was passed that a cease fire would go into effect at 0800 hrs. The task force destroyed 6 T-72 tanks, 6 BMP, 11 other vehicles and took 62 prisoners during the last engagement."[60]

Then, with almost strange alacrity, the guns fell silent. Lieutenant McClure heard the silence descend over the area. He had first heard about the cease-fire over the radio when Captain Sutherland ordered Lieutenant Romaine, his support platoon leader, to take the blackout tape off his vehicle's headlights. McClure was mildly surprised at the cease-fire because the Republican Guard had not been completely destroyed, but he understood. "We didn't have any beef about it. We said, 'OK, fine. I guess the powers that be have decided we've done what we need to do. Then, so be it.' I can't second-guess anybody for that."[61] Colonel Riley was absolutely thrilled. "I had an indescribable feeling of elation. We had done it, done it successfully, with far less casualties than anybody anticipated."[62]

Even with the cease-fire in effect, the Cottonbalers of the 1st Armored Division had dangerous work to do. When the fighting stopped, they found themselves right on top of an extensive bunker complex that was peppered with booby traps and unexploded ordnance—a lot of it buried deep in the sand—from coalition air strikes. A young medic in 1–7 stepped on one of the cluster bombs and had his leg blown off. Cottonbaler medics saved his life.

Staff Sergeant Narramore and his men had made it through the Medina Ridge battle only to be given the tedious, dangerous assignment of clearing the bunkers. Narramore had not slept at all during the four days of war, nor had he washed. He munched on a chicken and rice MRE, splashed liberally with Tabasco sauce, and then went to work. The Raiders found bunches of brand-new AK-47 rifles, still packed in grease, along with many other weapons. That was the pleasant side. One of Narramore's men found something much more gruesome: "He found a leg . . . blood, guts too, stuff that had been hit by, I guess, B-52s. There was no one around." Narramore saw plenty of booby-trapped bunkers. "Once you saw a wire, you stayed back." Engineers were combing the area. "They were constantly blowing stuff up." The Raiders had to destroy most everything; only a few bayonets and berets survived to become souvenirs.

WORD OF THE CEASE-FIRE ALSO reached the 24th Division Cottonbalers quickly. They were hunkered down in defensive positions along Highway 8, preparing to attack in the direction of Basra when the news filtered down to them. Corporal Crochet had caught some much-needed sleep during the night. For once he slept on the ground, right beside his Bradley. Bleary-eyed but a bit refreshed, he mounted his turret in the morning and waited to move out on the day's attack. "Then there was a delay. We waited . . . and waited. We noticed the division artillery rolling forward. We saw . . . Apaches flying by. It seemed like the entire division passed us over. We were just sitting there waiting." Wondering what was going on, Crochet flipped on a shortwave radio his family had sent him and heard about the cease-fire. "We were happy. It was just the best thing that we could possibly hear at that point." They exchanged high fives and spent much of the day waiting for orders to move.[63]

Lieutenant Huffines was shaving when he heard about the cease-fire over the BBC. Not long after hearing the good news, he penned an excited letter to Caroline. "No wounded or casualties in the battalion so far.

Have seen many horrible things. Dead Iraqis everywhere. 25MM does terrible things to people. War is incredible. I have never been so scared and exhilarated at the same time. We heard President Bush this morning and we know we have won. The American Army is lethal. I never dreamed it would be this destructive. This is an incredible, powerful feeling." Always the historian, he could not resist adding a postscript. "We are the greatest military force ever." He pledged to come home soon.[64]

Private Kurt Dabb's company had just started their day in a defensive security position when they heard the great news. "While some were eating and others taking care of personal hygiene, a message came over the radio. 'The war is at a cease-fire,' the DJ said, with a very blithe and sanguine voice. It was amazing. Everyone was jumping around, huddled around this radio. It was rather exciting." Not long after hearing about the cease-fire, they heard they would be the first unit to go home. "The whole company of men [most of whom had been there for six months] was jumping around, screaming, and hollering like school children outside at recess."[65] For Dabb's Alpha 2-7 and also the Cottonbalers of 3-7, the fighting was over.

THE SAME COULD NOT BE said of the rest of 2-7. Ironically enough, their, biggest fight was still ahead of them. After bunker-clearing duty on the day of the cease-fire, the four other companies of 2-7, Bravo, Charlie, Delta, and Echo, took up blocking positions near Highway 8, right in the middle of the massive Rumaylah oil fields, on March 1 and 2.

At this point, there was still a significant amount of confusion on the battlefield. The cease-fire was, technically, only a suspension of offensive operations. Before it went into effect, the Americans passed along a slew of conditions that had to be met for the shooting to stop. Originally one of those conditions was that the Iraqis had to leave all equipment in place and simply move north on foot—a difficult stipulation to enforce without some big fights, but one that arose from the fear that unscathed Republican Guard tanks might live to fight again another day. Realizing the difficulty of enforcing such a "no equipment" order, the White House let the matter drop. They preferred that any intact Iraqi units stay in place until the cease-fire was formalized but implicitly accepted the inevitability that Iraqi forces would in this chaotic, fluid situation continue to retreat north. Of course, this could only happen in the few avenues of retreat still open to them, most of which were overwatched by American forces. Bush made one thing very clear, though: if American forces were fired upon, they could return fire.[66]

For many of those Americans in the danger zone, very little changed in the immediate forty-eight hours after the cease-fire. Skirmishes broke out here and there; U.S. and Iraqi artillery sometimes exchanged shots. Confusion reigned about where and when the Iraqis were supposed to be moving, along with whether they were supposed to be moving with their heavy equipment. "I'm not sure if the chain of command did a very good job of telling us exactly what was going on, but that's beside the point," Captain Averna said. As far as he and many others in the Rumaylah positions were concerned, they were still in the middle of a hostile situation. These Cottonbalers were sitting astride a major thoroughfare, including a bridge across the Euphrates, the Iraqis had to use to get from Kuwait back to Iraq. Averna outlined the mind-set and the rules of engagement as the 2-7 soldiers understood them: "If you see an enemy armored combat vehicle moving . . . you need to take action to protect yourself. You need to try to get him to surrender, but if it fires on you, you can treat it as an enemy force. Basically, whatever you need to do to protect yourself." Averna and many other commanders believed that the Iraqis were supposed to leave their equipment behind. "They were supposed to stop in position. No combat vehicles were supposed to move. They were supposed to move all their soldiers . . . and then leave combat equipment behind so it could be destroyed and they wouldn't have the advantage of taking it back."

Confusion notwithstanding, the bottom line was that the 2-7 Cottonbalers were willing to allow the Iraqis in their area to move north *peaceably*, even with their equipment, especially if their tanks traversed their turrets harmlessly to the rear. If the Iraqis demonstrated any hostile intent or opened fire, then the situation changed; the Cottonbalers would treat them as an enemy force to be destroyed, the only right and proper thing to do. The safety of American soldiers had to come first. Even the slightest hint of hostile intent, even a stray shot or two of hostile fire, could not be tolerated if it threatened the life of even one American soldier. This was Averna's mind-set and that of his fellow commanders as well.[67]

On the evening of March 1–2, Lieutenant Allen's scouts took up positions east of Highway 8, near another highway, this one paralleling a railroad in the oil complex. Both the highway and the railroad eventually spanned the river, just to the north. Shortly after dusk on the first, Allen's men rolled into position near a Russian-built pipe factory complex. They captured some equipment and eight prisoners. Allen's men warily picked around the complex, finding a Russian flag and some unopened Russian mail. For the rest of the night, they took up observation positions near the complex. A few kilometers to the east, on the highway that spanned the Euphrates, they saw a commotion. "We saw a lot of movement from the south to the north, Iraqi units moving back on HETs" on and off the road. "We reported that so early the next morning, we were repositioning a task force in defense" in case the Iraqis decided to turn west and move toward the 2-7 positions in the oil complex. Allen and the other 2-7 officers were mainly concerned with an Iraqi westward movement, not a northerly evacuation across the river. "If they're going to the north, hey, fine. They're not supposed to be going anywhere right now. They're supposed to be sitting still." But unless they moved west, presenting a threat to 2-7, they would be left alone. Early in the morning, just before the sun rose, Allen's scouts moved south, to the extreme right flank of the 2-7 companies. The lieutenant and his men watched tensely as more and more Iraqi vehicles—tanks, trucks, APCs, HETs, artillery moved north on the highway.[68]

Meanwhile, in reaction to Allen's reports, three companies from 2-7, Delta, Charlie, and Echo, had moved farther east, almost perpendicular to the highway. Their mission was to assess Iraqi intentions, watch them closely, and be prepared to defend themselves if the Iraqis demonstrated any hostile intent. For the first time in days, the weather was clear, greatly enhancing visibility. At 0630, as the sun rose in their faces, the soldiers of Delta Company squinted at the sight before them. They could see as many as fifteen T-72s and twenty BMPs moving north on the road. Fifteen minutes later, Lieutenant Colonel Ware ordered three companies forward for a better look. He and his commanders were quite worried about their position in relation to this large Iraqi force. If the Iraqis swung to the west, they could possibly envelop the three forward-deployed companies, in addition to the scouts.

The situation grew more tense by the moment. On the right (southern) flank, Captain Averna fanned out his vehicles west of the road on which the Iraqis continued to roll. Averna did not like this situation at all. To his left, much of his tank support, specifically six out of fourteen tanks from Bravo Company, 4-64 Armor, had gotten bogged down in a subkah, a desert marsh. The six tanks sat helplessly mired in the soft, muddy sand waiting for M88 recovery vehicles to pull them out. They could shoot, but they could not maneuver. On the radio, Averna could hear Ware, whose personal vehicle had gotten stuck, frantically trying to arrange for extraction. To the left of the tanks, those Bradleys of Delta Company 2-7 that had not become stuck in the subkah sat in overwatch positions, watching the column, counting the vehicles, fighting the sun. Averna looked to his right and saw that his company was deployed adjacent to the railroad, which, in this area, was built on a turret-high berm. That meant the captain could not see much of anything on the other side of the railroad. He knew that Allen's scouts were deployed in screening positions somewhere on the other side of the railroad but couldn't see them. If the Iraqis made a wrong move, Lieutenant Allen and his thin-skinned vehicles could be in deep trouble.

Dead ahead, some two thousand meters away, Averna could clearly see the extensive Iraqi column, dozens of tanks, BMPs, artillery, and other combat vehicles, on the road: "Its formations were organized and they had deployed a security zone with a rear guard." Captain Averna believed that this movement was in direct violation of the cease-fire: "Such actions were to be considered hostile, but no action was to be initiated against such forces unless they initiated it first."

For about fifteen to thirty minutes, the Americans watched this in frustration. Some of the commanders asked Ware for permission to engage. He denied them permission. They could only engage if fired upon first. Just in case a fight broke out, Captain Averna ordered his FSO (Fire Support Officer) to prepare a fire mission. The FSO called his batteries and requested, if necessary, that the road and the intersection where the road crossed the railway be shelled.

Averna spotted a large opening in the railroad embankment. He knew that his flank on the other side of the railroad was quite vulnerable. If the Iraqis happened to send some tanks or BMPs into that area, they could close to within close range of his company, right on their flanks, thus negating the long-range advantage enjoyed by his Bradleys. He had no desire to mix it up with T-72s or BMPs at close range. So he sent his 3rd Platoon, under First Lieutenant Tschanz, the fitness guru, through the railroad opening to explore the other side of the embankment.

The 3rd Platoon Bradleys rumbled gingerly through the opening. As they began to spread out on the other side of the railroad, they came face-to-face with dug-in Iraqi troops, along with a BMP. A long moment passed as Lieutenant Tschanz tried to assess their intentions. "Suddenly . . . enemy dismounts with an RPG, [and] mortars fired at us . . . but missed." Even though the opening volley had missed, Tschanz knew he and his men were in danger. Still, he was disciplined enough to radio Captain Averna for permission to open fire.

Back on the other side of the embankment, Averna strained to hear his lieutenant's transmission. Averna heard something about the enemy opening fire, but not much else. Out of the corner of his eye, he saw something move. "I observed a white smoke signature [from an RPG shot] forward of my 3d Platoon position. The round fell short." Again Tschanz's voice crackled over the radio. "[He] reported that the RPG team was preparing to reengage." Averna radioed Ware and asked him for permission to shoot but still didn't get it (the battalion commanding officer was busy trying to receive permission to engage from General McCaffrey at division headquarters).

Averna saw that the Iraqis had opened fire again on his 3rd Platoon. Once again, Lieutenant Tschanz's transmissions were garbled. The captain did not have anywhere near as much information as he wanted—how many Iraqis were over there, what weapons they had, if they were reinforced —but he had seen enough. His men were in danger, the enemy had shot twice at them, and the rules of engagement clearly allowed for him to fire back. He could not have lived with himself if his hesitation cost the lives of any Charlie Company soldiers. He told Ware about the enemy fire and then gave 3rd Platoon orders to open fire (assuming they could hear him). Frustrated by his lack of information and the fact that he had lost communication with the 3rd Platoon (usually called the fog of war), he decided to go over to the 3rd Platoon to find out about the situation for himself. "Unable to cross the embankment in my Bradley I dismount and move approximately 150 meters to 3rd Platoon under 60mm Mortar fire now falling around the platoon," Averna wrote in a present-tense description.

Averna ran to the 3rd Platoon as fast as he could. He could hear the mortar rounds exploding uncomfortably close. He reached Tschanz's Bradley and asked him for a report. Like Averna, he had lost radio contact with his men. But, the two officers could see the dug-in enemy in the distance, even as more mortar rounds slammed into the ground around them. Averna sprinted to the next track, "home" to a dismounted infantry squad commanded by Staff Sergeant J. Harris. The captain climbed onto the turret of this Bradley, found Harris, and gave him an order: "Hey, look, Sergeant. You need to engage. Move forward and capture that position!" The sergeant nodded. "Yes, sir!"

The rear ramp of the Bradley lowered, and Harris's men sprung into action. Three 25mm chain guns from various Bradleys chattered in support. They raked the enemy position, suppressing them almost completely, paving the way for Harris's squad to assault the position. They did so with incredible speed and efficiency. Almost in the blink of an eye, Harris's men shot up the trench, overran it, and captured eight Iraqis. Harris's men found several RPGs, a 60mm recoilless rifle, and two mortars.

Seconds later, the dug-in BMP fired a Sagger missile, the Soviet equivalent of a TOW. The captain took cover and watched the Sagger. "I could see a thick white puff of smoke . . . when it came off the rail. It looked like the space shuttle from the back of it, a big white plume and red ball." His heart raced as he watched the Sagger streak wildly in the air. To his immense relief, it exploded well behind his 3rd Platoon vehicles. Tschanz's men answered with 25mm armor-piercing fire. Their rounds punctured the thin armor of the BMP and blew the enemy APC up. Harris's troops then surged forward and secured the entire area around the burning BMP.

Averna congratulated his men on a job well done and went back to his Bradley. He no sooner got himself situated in the turret when the radio came alive with contact reports. Possibly as many as twenty to thirty T-72s and BMPs were maneuvering off the road, some of them bearing down on Tschanz's 3rd Platoon, some on the north side of the railroad embankment threatening Lieutenant Jones's 1st Platoon, in addition to the entire flank position of Charlie Company. Some of the enemy tanks were even rolling immediately parallel to the rail line, but the BMPs skirted around it. Averna grabbed his binoculars and studied them for a few moments. The enemy vehicles opened fire. He quickly gave orders to engage all of them.

At this point, the battle got much bigger. McCaffrey's headquarters had ordered many of the division's nearby assets into battle. This meant that American tanks and helicopters soon converged on the area. As they did, Charlie Company fought for its life. Missiles—TOW and Sagger—flew everywhere. Tank barrels belched. Chain guns poured forth a lethal blend of firepower. A thunderous crescendo of explosions shook the whole area. Lieutenant Jones and his 1st Platoon fired at any target they saw. "We were in a fight. I informed my platoon all sectors were clear for fire. My vehicle let a TOW missile fly and it met the flank of a T72. The tank seemed to bend and collapse in a fireball." Jones's men, along with Lieutenant Howell's, immediately adjacent to him, remained stationary in their vehicles, picking off tanks with their TOW missiles. They scored eight kills on ten advancing enemy tanks.

Lieutenant Tschanz saw a terrifying array of enemy hardware no more than a couple thousand meters in front of his position, immediately west of the highway. "My CO told me to engage the tanks on my front and side. The order came down to engage everything on the road, which we did, destroying tanks, BMP's, trucks, artillery pieces etc. and then we were told to move forward." His platoon destroyed seven BMPs in a matter of a few minutes.

The rounds from the enemy tanks fell short of the American tracks. The enemy's Soviet-made T-55s and T-72s did not have enough range to score any hits on the Americans. American artillery, probably called in by Averna's FSO, began crashing into the area. At first, a round fell short, almost right into the Charlie positions, but successive rounds fell where they were supposed to—right on top of the Iraqis. Some of the enemy tank crews halted or abandoned their vehicles.

Within half an hour, the enemy attack had clearly been broken up. Ware ordered Averna to capture the railroad/highway intersection from which many of the enemy tanks came. Averna left his 3rd Platoon in place to provide fire support and ordered his other two platoons forward. "We assaulted forward and took the intersection that the Iraqis were coming from and captured six more BMPs and a few more tanks that were not destroyed but were abandoned by the crew." Averna ordered his men to dismount and secure the area. They took eighteen more prisoners who were more than eager to surrender. The 3rd Platoon then rolled forward, capturing several abandoned BMPs and T-72s. "We held that position until about 1030, the rest of the enemy withdrew and began to move north. Then 4/64 armor moved through us" in pursuit of enemy forces. The Charlie Company Cottonbalers had destroyed about forty enemy tanks, trucks, and BMPs, all belonging to the Hammurabi Division, the one major Republican Guard outfit the coalition had not previously been able to locate. Eleven years later, the company received a Valorous Unit Award Citation for its actions at Rumaylah.

The 7th Infantry's involvement in the Rumaylah fighting had ended, but other 24th Division units, mainly armor and helicopters, spent much of the day destroying the rest of this brigade from the Hammurabi Division. It was one of the most one-sided battles in American military history. The Americans suffered no casualties even as they destroyed 187 enemy armored vehicles, 37 artillery pieces, and 400 wheeled vehicles, in addition to killing, wounding, or capturing hundreds of enemy soldiers. The carnage was immense, powerfully odorous, almost mind-blowing—flaming tanks, burning trucks, burning flesh, burning hair, all the detritus of modern war.

Private Dabb was not involved in the fighting, but he later witnessed its results: "It was total carnage, everywhere. There were APCs, tanks with turrets blown off, civilian cars, bodies everywhere." He could smell the rot of death and destruction. "There was a very overwhelming smell . . . oil, rubber, gas, incendiary grenades . . . a horrible, horrible stench." The young private walked over to a destroyed BMP and opened its rear door to have a look inside. "There were six burnt Iraqis sitting back there just like we did in ours with their weapons between their legs, and their helmets on and here they were just burnt to a crisp." Dabb looked at them for a few moments, then shut the door and moved on.[69] First Lieutenant Grube also studied the aftermath of the battle. "The road to our front was covered with flaming hulks. The famed Hamarabi [*sic*] Division of Iraq's invincible Republican Guards, had been decimated."[70]

Indeed they had, to the point where some wondered if perhaps too much force, too much firepower, had been employed against a beaten enemy. Even within the 24th Division some soldiers debated whether the response to the Iraqi provocation had been excessive. Postwar criticism eventually centered around General McCaffrey, especially when the Army's inspector general received, in August 1991, a letter, possibly written by someone on the general's staff, alleging that he was guilty of a war crime. The letter claimed that he had deliberately provoked and ordered the slaughter of the Hammurabi Division to feed his own glory. McCaffrey was a highly-decorated officer. He had led troops in combat in Vietnam and been severely wounded and was one of the Army's most distinguished commanders. These were serious charges. The Army conducted an investigation and found no evidence to substantiate them. The mass destruction at Rumaylah may have been excessive, but that was war, not a war crime. Probably the most compelling piece of evidence in McCaffrey's defense was the indisputable fact that the Iraqis had opened fire first (and second) on Captain Averna's men. "My troops on the ground were under attack," McCaffrey later explained. "My sole focus was the safety of my soldiers." The matter seemed to be closed.

However, several years later, in May 2000, journalist Seymour Hersh (known for his articles about the My Lai massacre) published an accusatory article against McCaffrey in *The New Yorker*. A veritable hatchet job, Hersh's piece alleged not just that McCaffrey had indeed been guilty of war crimes at Rumaylah but also that soldiers in his division had been guilty of killing prisoners of war. The Army in the 1990s had repeatedly investigated the latter charge, stemming from an incident involving Lieutenant Allen's scout platoon on February 27. The scouts captured about two hundred prisoners, many of whom were wounded and riding in a hospital bus on Highway 8. The Americans gave them food, water, and whatever medical attention they could. They also stripped the Iraqis of their weapons, piled them up, and prepared them for demolition.

Allen then received orders to move out immediately. After he and his men remounted their vehicles and started to move out, they heard firing to their rear. An unidentified Bradley unit (possibly from 2-7 Infantry) had suddenly appeared and was shooting its weapons at something or someone. Three of Allen's men, Specialists John Brasfield, James Manchester (both scouts), and Edward Walker (an attached engineer), thought they saw the Bradleys firing at the prisoners. "We could see the prisoners moving and scattering, but I didn't see any fall down," Lieutenant Allen said. "I believe honestly in my heart that they did not fire at those prisoners. There was no need to hose down a large group. They were not a threat." He and his men did not have much of a vantage point. They were craning their necks backward in their Humvees as they drove away in the desert dust. In truth, they could not tell for sure just what the mysterious unit was firing at, perhaps abandoned vehicles the scouts had not destroyed, perhaps not.

Walker felt that the killing power of the Bradleys was so extensive that they could not have helped killing many of the prisoners. He felt strongly that the incident should be investigated. As mentioned, the Army carried out many such investigations. "Follow-on forces found prisoners . . . but no bodies," Allen explained. The investigators never found any evidence of any bodies or any deliberate shooting of prisoners. Instead, follow-on units, according to the investigators, found plenty of live prisoners. Hersh's story relied mainly on accounts from Allen, Brasfield, Manchester, and Walker. Allen, in particular, believed Hersh pulled many of his quotes, and those of others, out of context. "The story . . . got shot down right away." Armed with a bevy of facts, McCaffrey went on television to defend himself. As Allen indicated, the story pretty much went nowhere.

So what really happened at Highway 8 that day? The whole truth will probably never be known. The repeated investigations, the poor vantage point of the scouts, and the lack of any concrete physical evidence point clearly toward the conclusion that no deliberate killings took place. Most likely there was plenty of gray area. The Bradleys might have heard explosions from the demolished Iraqi weapons and opened fire in that direction. They might have opened fire at nearby abandoned vehicles. They might even have shot at the prisoners for a short time until they realized that they were harmless. But they almost certainly did not hose down two hundred Iraqi prisoners of war with deliberate malice.[71]

Hersh's accusations against McCaffrey were also, in the final analysis, quite weak. Most of Hersh's "evidence" consisted of circumstantial quotes assassinating the general's character, questioning the morality of the Rumaylah turkey shoot, or painting the Hammurabi soldiers as innocent lambs being led to a slaughter. In actuality, as the accounts of Averna and his men made quite clear (Hersh did not describe the experiences of Charlie Company in any detail), American soldiers were clearly fired upon by an enemy who was violating the terms of the cease-fire. Averna's Charlie Company responded to this threat with force. McCaffrey's division then responded to it with overwhelming force. That was absolutely proper and appropriate in time of war, even with a tenuous cease-fire in place.

Like many generals, McCaffrey may very well have wanted eternal glory for himself, but as his words indicated, the welfare of his soldiers was at the forefront of his mind on March 2, 1991 at Rumaylah. Once the shooting began, his primary duty was to eliminate the threat with the least possible damage to his own forces. If he had failed to use all the weapons at his disposal and American soldiers had died because of it, he quite rightly would have been condemned (maybe even court-martialed). If an entire Iraqi brigade of Republican Guards had to be roasted to prevent that from happening, then such were the terrible fortunes of war.

Only one aspect of McCaffrey's performance can be fairly criticized. He could have chosen to keep his troops in place along Highway 8, but the day before Rumaylah he ordered them to push east, thus intersecting the causeway where the climactic battle took place. This put them on a collision course with the Hammurabi Division. Obviously, the whole battle could have been avoided had McCaffrey's troops not been in the area. However, maybe it wasn't such a bad thing that Saddam Hussein was deprived of a unit that would have enhanced the postwar rebuilding of his shattered army.

Of course, all of this is hindsight, the great privilege of the journalist or historian, but like many other luxuries, hindsight is something that is denied to soldiers in combat. "Analysts and historians often have the luxury of days, months or years of research and have access to a large volume of information across a wide spectrum of resources and levels of command," Averna wrote years after Rumaylah. "Their picture is broad with the ability to see simultaneously related events either enhanced by eyewitness accounts or clouded by interviews with participants far from the actual event. And so with this hindsight the event is placed in a historical perspective. What they fail to comprehend is that decisions on the battlefield are made with immediate information at hand often raw, outdated and requiring quick action to rectify the situation. Indecision is met with unacceptable results."

Not surprisingly, Averna felt that the Hersh article did not express the truth of what happened at Rumaylah or, for that matter, the truth about General McCaffrey. "I thought it was unjust and unfair, having been there and having seen what happened . . . I don't know how somebody who wasn't there can say . . . 'You did wrong.' Had it happened the other way and we let them take out five, six, seven or eight Bradleys and let them kill or wound 20 or 30 soldiers and do nothing, how would that have gone? To have them kill or wound Americans within at least 12 hours of the next day, the 3rd of March, when they actually signed the [official cease-fire] agreement would have just been awful. I probably could not have lived with myself." Averna held no special grudge against the Iraqis and took no pleasure in seeing them die in the battle. But he had absolutely no regrets about his actions, or McCaffrey's, that day. The captain brought every one of his soldiers home, and that superseded everything else in importance. "As far as I was concerned, that was success for me."[72]

In the final judgment, the Cottonbalers of 2-7 did their job at Rumaylah. They fought a battle on behalf of one another and their country; they won that battle decisively and overwhelmingly. In the long run, that was all that mattered to them.

THE 24TH DIVISION COTTONBALERS HAD been in Southwest Asia the longest, so they got to go home first. McCaffrey made sure of it. Within a few days of the end of the war, his troops were on their way back to Saudi Arabia, where they cleaned up their equipment—not to mention themselves—and prepared to deploy home. The drive back to Saudi took the better part of a day on a four-lane highway, but it was like a joyride. Corporal Crochet never forgot the feeling of euphoria that gripped him as he sat in the gunner's seat of his Bradley on that wonderful day. "I think that's one of the . . . happiest moments of my life. Even the birth of my son, getting married . . . they don't compare to the feeling that I had when we were all lined up . . . going in the same direction, on a highway filled bumper to bumper with military hardware. [It] was the best feeling that I've ever had in my life. I remember driving through little towns and people cheering and celebrating."

Some of the people they saw were too hungry to cheer. They stood by the road begging for food. One of Crochet's sergeants slipped them a case of MREs. The sergeant, a gruff type, was embarrassed when the other soldiers noticed his altruistic act. "He made a bravado-type joke. He said, 'I'll bet they're not going to turn down that pork,'" a reference to the fact that MREs sometimes contained pork and Muslims were forbidden to eat pig products. Crochet and the other men laughed, but they knew the sergeant made the joke "to cover up his soft spot."

Once they got back to their base in Saudi Arabia, the men blew off steam with an endless series of poker and crap games. "I don't know what it was. Maybe it was just the joy of being alive and having all this money that we hadn't spent for the last four months . . . but everybody was gambling." Upon reflection, Crochet thought that maybe the gambling fellowship came from the fact that now the men could park their vehicles near one another. During the long months in the desert, security demanded that vehicles be spaced far apart, negating socializing, at least to some extent. "We really didn't have the opportunity to get together in such large numbers."[73]

The Cottonbalers loaded their combat vehicles onto HETs that took them to ports. The men stayed in Khobar Towers until it was time to fly home. These freedom flights were, of course, a wonderful experience for the soldiers. Most of the flights were on American commercial airlines. The civilian flight crews treated the returning soldiers like kings. Lieutenant Huffines flew home on Tower Air. The attendants showed a video of Tower Air employees thanking the soldiers for what they had done. Huffines was flabbergasted. He had thought of his service in Desert Storm as just a job like any other. He never dreamed that people would thank him for serving. "I had never considered it like that. To me, it was like a . . . giant NTC rotation. I guess I thought of it as if I was a fireman who had just put out a fire out in your house. I was doing that because

I wanted to do it. I was kind of appreciative, in a perverse way, of being able to participate. The video just really impacted me." After seeing the video, he knew that his job was not like any other. He knew that he had been part of something special. He felt grateful to the civilians for taking the time and effort to thank him.

One of the flight attendants had taped various *Saturday Night Live* skits. She rolled the tape for the soldiers. These men had been in a media vacuum for months. Giddy with excitement over going home, grateful to be alive, loving life in general, they roared at "Wayne's World" and the other skits. "It was so funny. We were dying. I mean, the whole plane was rocking with laughter."

The plane landed at Hunter Army Airfield, about forty-five minutes from Fort Stewart. Crowds of people were waiting at the tarmac to welcome the soldiers home. This was so much different from what had happened twenty years before, during the Vietnam War, when returning soldiers were spat on, shouted at, shunned, ignored, or, in the best-case scenario, welcomed only by family, but always against the backdrop of controversy over the war. The Gulf War had served as a sort of catharsis for many Americans, a latter-day attempt to exorcise the demons of Vietnam. In the immortal words of General Colin Powell, "The American people had fallen in love with their military." Consequently, returning soldiers came home to joyful, welcoming crowds of grateful people.

Realizing this, commanders usually made sure that their Vietnam veterans got off each plane first, so that they could experience the loudest cheers. Lieutenant Huffines watched these proud soldiers—the men who had helped rebuild the Army—line up at the front door of the plane. "There was a huge crowd out there waiting for us." The Vietnam veterans began filing off the plane and the crowd went wild. "It felt so wonderful to see that. They had never gotten anything like that. It was an incredible, incredible thing."

The adoring crowds at Hunter Airfield were only the beginning of the postwar welcome. Most of the soldiers' families were waiting at Fort Stewart. The Cottonbalers boarded buses that took them down Interstate 95 to Fort Stewart. Huffines could barely contain his excitement as "the busses pulled up on the far side of Cottrell Field; the stands were full of people. A quick formation, then forward march to the division band's music. The crowd was incredible." The formation halted in front of the stands and then was dismissed. In a spontaneous spasm of joy, the soldiers and their families converged on each other. It did not take long for the young lieutenant to find his wife, Caroline. "Amongst the hundreds assembled, I found my wife wearing a dark blue dress with polka dots. She was holding a sign in the shape of a Hershey's Kiss that read in white letters: 'Kisses here for 1LT Huffines.'"[74]

Not far away, Rick Averna and his wife, Elaine, were reunited after more than seven months apart. He had been looking through the crowd, unable to find her. "She found me and it was pretty emotional. We both cried." He hugged Elaine and little Nathan too. Rick and Elaine were so happy to see each other that they could hardly find the words to speak.[75]

Crochet, the Cajun kid from Baton Rouge, reveled in the simple sight of trees. Where he came from, trees were everywhere. For months, in the treeless desert, he had felt awkward, like something very important was missing. At Fort Stewart, he stared at the Georgia pines in almost childlike fascination. His family could not make it to Georgia that day (the homecoming came about with too short notice for many of those who did not live near Fort Stewart to make it there in time), so instead he basked in the adulation of the crowd. "There were these crowds of people cheering with signs . . . or there were banners hung, welcoming us home." The young corporal resolved to never forget this beautiful moment when the American people welcomed their soldiers with open arms.[76]

The Cottonbalers of the 1st Armored Division spent several more weeks in Southwest Asia before returning to their base in Germany. Compared with their regimental brothers in the 24th Division, they were relative newcomers to the theater, so it was only proper that they stick around for a while and take care of postwar duties. They spent their days policing up the battlefield, standing guard at checkpoints, maintaining their equipment, dealing with refugees streaming out of southern Iraq, and watching the internal fighting (uprisings against Saddam's government) going on in nearby Basra. This tore their hearts out. They knew that Saddam's troops were obliterating Iraqis who wanted to rid their country of this bloodthirsty, malicious dictator. Naturally, the Americans wanted to intervene, destroy the rest of Saddam's army, and get rid of him, but under the terms of the peace agreement, they could not. The American mission had been to eject Iraq from Kuwait, not change the internal power structure of Iraq. American policy makers certainly hoped that Saddam would fall from power, but they knew that the Arab members of their coalition would not tolerate any kind of direct American attempt to get rid of him. All of this, of course, portended serious consequences for the future.

For now the Cottonbalers merely dealt with the human tragedy unfolding each day, treating the symptoms instead of the disease. "Our soldiers lived up to all expectations," Lieutenant Colonel Smith asserted. "They showed great respect for the women, children, and elderly. Their compassion for these people was genuine and appreciated by most of the refugees that passed through the checkpoints."[77]

Finally the Cottonbalers went back to Saudi Arabia (breathing oil well smoke all the way), sent their vehicles to ports, and boarded civilian planes back to Frankfurt, Germany, arriving there on May 1, 1991. Their reunion with friends and families was just as joyous, just as emotional, as the reunion had been for the 2-7 and 3-7 Cottonbalers a few weeks before. The Army had bused the soldiers' families to Frankfurt to welcome the soldiers. The families waited behind a line of tape for the soldiers to get off their planes. Staff Sergeant Narramore could not wait to see his wife, his son, and his little girl. Narramore had done his duty in Desert Storm well. He had brought all his soldiers home unscathed. On the plane ride to Germany, he had received the privilege of riding up front with Lieutenant Colonel Smith and the other officers. The sergeant was elated but restless.

When he filed off the plane, he waited impatiently in formation while the assistant division commander of the 3rd Infantry Division made a congratulatory speech to the men of 1–7 and 4-7. "He got about halfway through and . . . Colonel Riley's wife broke the tape and that was it. He didn't even get to finish talking." The families stampeded the field in a spontaneous surge of ecstasy. Narramore quickly found his family in the maw of jubilant people. He took a second to look at his daughter. "She was holding an American flag and so was my son." Narramore could not hold back tears. He hugged his wife and children for what seemed like minutes.

Later, back at Aschaffenburg, he saw that the families had prepared a nice surprise for the returning soldiers. "All the wives had made the beds for the troops, and had candy on the beds, and had a couple trash cans of beer. We were off . . . seven days. It was fantastic. I've deployed twice since then, and that was the best homecoming I've ever had. I definitely appreciated all that" the American people did to welcome him home.

For the 7th Infantry, the Persian Gulf War was now just the newest chapter in a long, storied history. The Cottonbalers who fought that war were now veterans. In the years to come, their lives took many twists and turns. Jamie Narramore stayed in the Army ten more years, made first sergeant, and then retired, after a twenty-year career, to the Fort Chaffee area in Arkansas. Craig McClure stayed in the Army for a few more years and even commanded a light infantry company in the 101st Airborne Division, but he soured on the Army of the 1990s, whose size and readiness were being cut back by politicians even as its deployments were doubled. He married a Polish national whom he met in Germany right before he went off to Desert Storm. They started a family, and McClure left the Army in 2000, electing instead to pursue a doctoral degree in political science at Miami University in Ohio. Kurt Dabb served the rest of his enlistment, then went home to attend Northern Michigan University, with the help of the GI Bill. He earned a degree in criminology, joined the Michigan National Guard as an MP sergeant, but then left the Army for good, got married, and found a job in Arizona as a parole officer. Bryan Crochet also served the rest of his enlistment and went to college, partially using the money he earned in the Army. He graduated from Southeastern Louisiana University and decided to go to graduate school at Mississippi State University. Crochet had inherited some of his father's artistic ability and put it to use in pursuit of a master of fine arts degree, concentrating on computer and graphic art. He also married and fathered a son.

Some of the Gulf War Cottonbalers stayed in the Army well into the twenty-first century. Kirk Allen commanded troops in Somalia, Haiti, and eventually as a lieutenant colonel in Iraq. Single during the Gulf War, he actually met his wife because of the war. "My mother had put a picture of me in the local paper back home. It ended up that different people wrote to me. One of the girls that wrote to me I continued to write, and after I came back, I met and we ended up getting married. I actually met her when I got back to New Jersey, when my parents threw . . . a welcome home party at the VFW. I'm married and I have three daughters now."

Alan Huffines also had three daughters with his wife. In the years after the war, the Texan won promotion to lieutenant colonel and earned an active-duty job preparing his state's National Guard for combat readiness (many National Guard units were not combat ready when needed during the Gulf War). He also changed combat branches, from infantry to cavalry, in the process subjecting himself to quite a bit of ribbing from his infantry friends. Huffines's love of history motivated him to write and publish two books, including an excellent history of the Alamo siege and battle.

Rick Averna commanded troops many more times after the Gulf War. He even returned to his beloved 7th Infantry, serving a two-year stint from 1996 to 1998 as the executive officer of 3-7 at Fort Stewart. Like Huffines, Averna got picked for a job preparing National Guard troops for war. In Averna's case, he went to Oklahoma, where he took command of a National Guard infantry battalion. Promoted to lieutenant colonel, he had served in the Army over twenty-five years by 2006. By then he and Elaine had given Nathan two siblings.[78]

All of these men were part of the most prepared, professional army in the history of American warfare. Truly, the Army had come full circle, from a demoralized, disintegrating mess to a mighty weapon of war. Confident, powerful, and overwhelming, the U.S. Army in the Gulf War was perhaps the best in the history of the Republic. It was the product of years of technological research, years of anguish, years of soul-searching, years of professional evolution, years of hard lessons learned on the battlefields of the twentieth century. It achieved a total military victory over a well-armed foe at the cost of seventy-nine ground combat deaths, many of which were caused by friendly fire. Rarely, if ever, has one side prevailed over the other so totally and bloodlessly in modern warfare. It happened, partially, because the Iraqis foolishly chose to engage in the exact kind of war the Army was designed to fight.

The 7th Infantry and its performance constituted a fair reflection of the U.S. Army in Desert Storm. The four battalions of the 7th accomplished every mission given to them, without losing even one soldier killed, an unprecedented feat in the history of the regiment and one that will most likely never be equaled in any sizable conflict. The Cottonbalers had helped restore the U.S. Army to greatness. They had won an important victory for the stability of the world's oil supply and its international economy. Even more important than that, every commander in the 7th Infantry—from squad leader, to platoon leader, to company commander, to battalion commander—could hold his head high and make the statement, "I brought every one of my soldiers home."

In that sense, there has never been, and probably never will be, any greater victory in the history of the 7th Infantry Regiment.

Korea. Soldiers from C Company give covering fire to advancing troops in May 1951. *(National Archives)*

Cottonbalers ascend a ridge in Korea. Notice the truncated trees, indicative of a pre-attack artillery bombardment. *(U.S. Army Military History Institute)*

The fight for Hill 717–Iron Triangle, 1951. This hill was one of many where the Cottonbalers fought in Korea. *(USAMHI)*

Mines were a constant hazard on the hills and trails of Korea. In this photo, men from the pioneer platoon probe for mines during Operation Doughnut, July 1951. *(National Archives)*

Exhausted, grimy Cottonbalers from I Company eat C rations in the summer of 1951. *(National Archives)*

A 3rd Battalion machine-gun crew provides supporting fire with a .30 caliber Browning air-cooled gun, the standard light machine gun for the U.S. Army in both World War II and Korea. *(National Archives)*

7th Infantry machine gunners watch as a Chinese-occupied ridge is bombarded with mortar and artillery rounds. *(National Archives)*

Interrogation of a Chinese prisoner at Hill 717. A South Korean officer pumps this enemy soldier for information while L Company officers and enlisted men watch. The Cottonbalers found that most Chinese soldiers, when captured, were willing to talk. *(National Archives)*

An integrated Cottonbaler recon patrol questions an elderly woman near Chorwon. By the summer of 1951the racial integration of the U.S. Army was well under way, beginning a new era in the regiment's history. *(National Archives)*

The Battle Patrol, spring 1952. Although lightly armed, the men are wearing brand-new armored flak vests. *(National Archives)*

The cold Korean winter. Sergeant Robert Demarco and Corporal Robert Skaaden attempt to thaw out their .50 caliber machine gun after a snowfall. The 7th Infantry spent three winters in Korea. It was not unusual for temperatures to dip twenty degrees below zero. *(National Archives)*

Corporal Jerry Crump earned the Medal of Honor for falling on a grenade near Hill 284 in September 1951. Incredibly, Crump survived his wounds. He is one of twenty-eight Cottonbalers to earn the nation's highest military decoration. *(USAMHI)*

An anonymous, but very typical, Cottonbaler in Vietnam receives a new decoration to go with the coveted Combat Infantry Badge he already wears over his left breast. The writing on his helmet camouflage cover sums up all he holds dear: “Frances, my love; Oklahoma, my home; April, my month” to rotate home. *(National Archives)*

Vietnam. From 1966 to 1970 the 7th Infantry operated as part of the 199th Light Infantry Brigade, mainly in the area around Saigon. Here PFC Meryl Hokel of Alpha Company, 3rd Battalion, watches Vietnamese boat traffic. *(National Archives)*

Lieutenant Colonel William Hartman, commanding officer of 3rd Battalion, 7th Infantry, in Vietnam, 1966–1967. Notice the star between the oak leaves of the colonel’s Combat Infantry Badge, over his left breast, indicating that he had already seen battle in two wars before Vietnam. *(National Archives)*

A big part of the job in Vietnam was finding out information on the whereabouts of the Viet Cong. In this scene PFC Noel Lerley of E Company, 3rd Battalion, speaks to children in a village southwest of Saigon during a cordon and search operation. Lerley is assisted by a pair of ARVN soldiers. Notice the radio strapped to Lerley's back, marking his status as an RTO (radio telephone operator). Also he has scrawled a message on his helmet's camouflage cover, a common practice among Cottonbalers in Vietnam. *(National Archives)*

Saigon, Tet Offensive, 1968. The Cottonbalers fought in Cholon, a western suburb of the city and helped to decimate an entire VC regiment. *(National Archives)*

Officers from E Company, 3rd Battalion, check their maps during the fight for Cholon, February 10, 1968. *(National Archives)*

The Phu Tho Racetrack, an ideal landing zone for helicopters and thus vital to the 7th Infantry in the fight for Cholon. This racetrack changed hands several times during the Saigon fighting. At one point the Cottonbalers traded shots with VC who were in the concrete seating areas visible in the background. *(National Archives)*

Cottonbalers move away from Phu Tho Racetrack in anticipation of setting up a night defensive position. The soldier in the foreground is carrying on of his most valuable possessions—his insect repellent—in his helmet band. *(National Archives)*

A Cottonbaler M60 machine gunner with ammo belts crisscrossing his shoulders. Affectionately known as "the Pig" for the way it voraciously ate ammunition, the M60 was a lethal, durable gun capable of firing over five hundred rounds per minute. *(National Archives)*

Two Cottonbaler grunts on patrol near the Pineapple Plantation, southwest of Saigon in 1969. The 7th Infantry's area of operations consisted of swamps, marshes, rice paddies, and, of course, jungles too. *(National Archives)*

Huey UH-D1 helicopters were workhorse, all-purpose vehicles and standard transportation for Cottonbalers in Vietnam. Here a group of Hueys takes off from the Phu Tho Racetrack in February 1968. *(National Archives)*

First Lieutenant Craig McClure standing outside his Humvee during Desert Storm. Notice the difference in equipment from the Vietnam era. By the time of the Persian Gulf War, American soldiers were equipped with later-generation M16s along with coal-scuttle style Kevlar helmets. *(Craig McClure)*

Captain Rick Averna, commander of C/2-7, standing outside his tent in the fall of 1990. Averna's soldiers spent many lonely months waiting for the word to invade Kuwait. *(Rick Averna)*

Captain Averna and his command group with the regimental colors in the Saudi desert. *Front row, left to right:* Second Lieutenant Bob Jones, 1st platoon leader; Second Lieutenant Mike Scott, fire support officer; First Lieutenant James "Mitch" Howell, 2nd platoon leader; Second Lieutenant Mike Tschanz, 3rd platoon leader. *Back row, left to right*: Averna, First Sergeant Brunn, First Lieutenant Leon Grube, executive officer. *(Rick Averna)*

Cottonbalers rest and regroup outside their Bradley Fighting Vehicles during the Gulf War. From the late 1980s onward, the Bradley afforded 7th Infantrymen a powerful platform for supporting fire and reliable transportation. *(Rick Averna)*

The remnants of a catastrophic kill. This was all that was left of a Republican Guard T-55 following its fight with 1st Armored Division Cottonbalers, near Medina Ridge. As was typical, the turret of the tank blew off and flipped over when it was hit by a TOW missile or an M1 Abrams 120 millimeter round. *(Craig McLure)*

Soldiers of the C/2-7 assemble around a Bradley in the fall of 1990. Captain Rick Averna is visible in the middle of the picture, helmetless, standing next to the regimental colors. *(Rick Averna)*

The aftermath at Rumaylah, March 2, 1991. Republican Guard tanks from the Hammurabi Division burn fiercely after being hit. The Americans destroyed hundreds of vehicles; they killed, wounded and captured hundreds of Iraqi soldiers in one of the most one-sided battles in U.S. history. In the postwar era this slaughter was to become controversial, but there is no question that the Iraqis fired first at Captain Averna's C/2-7. *(Rick Averna)*

Captain Chris Carter *(left)* and his executive officer, First Lieutenant Eric Hooper. These two officers led Attack Company, 3-7, into Iraq in 2003. *(Chris Carter)*

Sergeant Paul Ingram *(standing at far left)* poses with his rifle squad next to an Abrams main battle tank. These Cottonbalers were the very embodiment of the excellence of American infantry circa 2003 —well equipped, heavily armed, and well trained. *(Paul Ingram)*

Bradleys and other vehicles from Attack Company, 3-7, roll into Iraq during the early stages of the Iraq War, March 2003. *(Paul Ingram)*

Cottonbaler "dismounts" packed into the back of their Bradley. The rear of a Bradley could fit five or six of these soldiers, but with no leg room or comfort of any kind. *(2-7 Infantry)*

Major Kevin Cooney, executive officer of 2-7, talks on the phone inside the Tactical Operations Center (TOC) during the early days of the invasion of Iraq. *(2-7 Infantry)*

Lieutenant Colonel Scott Rutter *(seated with the phone to his right ear)* speaks with one of his company commanders, somewhere in southern Iraq. *(2-7 Infantry)*

Vehicles from the 7th Infantry roll over the Escarpment, just outside Najaf. *(2-7 Infantry)*

Three Cotton-balers stand guard over prisoners taken at the Escarp-ment. *(2-7 Infantry)*

A typical mud hut at Objective Raiders. Even the most diminutive Cottonbaler had trouble getting inside them. They had to be cleared out one by one. *(2-7 Infantry)*

Detritus left over from the car bombing of March 29, 2003. This suicide bombing killed four members of Rage (Alpha) Company, 2-7. *(Bradley McNish)*

Objective Peach, the bridge over the Euphrates River. *(2-7 Infantry)*

A glimpse of the fighting at Baghdad International Airport. On April 4, 2003, the 7th Infantry engaged in a bitter fight there with elements of the Republican Guard. In this photo, dismounts clear an area while their Bradley covers them. *(2-7 Infantry)*

Mounted patrol in Baghdad. In Iraq the biggest challenge was not overrunning the country and toppling Saddam Hussein; it was the aftermath. The invasion led to the rise of a ruthless, persistent insurgency. In the summer of 2003 and again in 2005–2006, the 7th Infantry matched wits with the insurgents. The goal was to secure a democratic, terror-free Iraq. *(2-7 Infantry)*

The remains of one of the T-72s destroyed by a 7th Infantry Javelin team during the airport fight on April 4, 2003. The ensuing fire was so intense that it caused the bogey wheels of the tank to disintegrate into a molten puddle. *(2-7 Infantry)*

Dismounted patrol circa 2003. *(2-7 Infantry)*

Cottonbalers in Iraq. Soldiers of 3rd Platoon, Attack Company, 3-7 Infantry, pose around a Bradley Fighting Vehicle. Some of these men served three tours in the Iraq War. *(Reon Brown)*

CHAPTER 4

The Post-9/11 War on Terror

Kosovo and the Beginning of the Iraq War

TO THIS GENERATION OF COTTONBALERS, 9/11 was what Pearl Harbor or Fort Sumter had been to earlier generations. It was a jarring event, a world-changing event, a rallying cry for service and sacrifice. A country that had slumbered through much of the late twentieth century content to all but ignore the rise of Islamic terrorism now awoke to the unpleasant reality that murderous fanatics could bring bloodshed to American soil and could do so with shocking ease. The post-cold war, post-Gulf War "peace dividend" that Americans had talked so much about in the early 1990s was nothing more than a distant, pleasant memory now. The events of 9/11 ushered in a new struggle for Americans, this time against small but deadly groups of dedicated, disguised, multinational, extranational, well-funded, zealously committed, humorless, hateful, ruthless men intent on killing Americans in any way possible, all in the name of God. For the better part of three decades the United States had usually avoided employing a military response to Islamic terrorism, even when terrorists attacked New York City's World Trade Center in 1993 and the USS Cole in the fall of 2000. However, in the wake of 9/11, as thousands of Americans lay dead in the ruins of that same World Trade Center and even the Pentagon itself, President George W. Bush and his administration opted for a military response and a military solution to global terrorism. This shift in policy led to a war in Afghanistan in the fall of 2001. It also eventually led to another war with Saddam Hussein's Iraq. As in 1991, the 7th Infantry would play a major role in the fight against Saddam.[1]

WHEN 9/11 HAPPENED, THE COTTONBALERS were in Kosovo on a peacekeeping mission. In the spring of 2001, the soldiers of 3-7 had deployed to that troubled land to protect Albanian Kosovars from their traditional Serb enemies. For officers like Captain David Gardner, this peacekeeping mission, and the possibility of terrorist attacks on American interests anywhere, required constant vigilance. Day after day in 2001 he and his men patrolled the towns and countryside of Kosovo. On a typical patrol he studied his surroundings with a keen, practiced eye. One day he watched his Cottonbaler soldiers file down a rain-slicked street in an anonymous town somewhere in Kosovo. The soldiers were shorn of their overwatching Bradleys. Clad in Kevlar helmets, flak vests, and BDUs, spread out in patrol formation, they trooped smoothly down the street, M16 rifles and SAWs at the ready, eyes roving, always on the watch for trouble. Like most modern-day Cottonbalers, these soldiers were superbly trained and led.

The people here were very friendly, but that did not matter all that much. The tragic ethnic violence that had brought the 7th Infantry to this Balkan trouble spot could break out again at any moment of any day. A certain amount of tension permeated every patrol, every mission, every weapons search, every checkpoint, every reconnaissance sweep. Any moment could bring violence and more bloodshed. Any wrong move by an American soldier could set off more fighting between local Albanian Kosovar guerrillas and neighboring Serbians. Any casualties among these Cottonbaler peacekeepers might also spark furious political debate at home about the wisdom of placing American troops in such jeopardy in a place that few Americans had ever heard of, a place that seemed, to some, to lie outside the vital interests of the United States, especially with a war on terrorism to fight.

With more than a touch of pride, Gardner watched his soldiers carry out their patrol. Then he climbed back into his Humvee to go have a look at another patrol, in another small town. Even as the Cottonbalers were fighting many of the key battles of the Gulf War, Gardner had been enduring his plebe year at West Point. He graduated in 1994, completed airborne and air assault training, the infantry officer's course, Ranger school, and Pathfinder school too. In the 1990s, as a young lieutenant, Gardner served for three years as a small-unit leader in the 82nd

Airborne Division. In December 2000 he joined the Cottonbalers as the commanding officer of A (now called "Attack") Company, 3-7 Infantry. This was the same unit in which Bryan Crochet once served as a Bradley gunner, the same unit Roland Merson once shepherded through the paddies and jungles of South Vietnam.

Now, as America geared up for a protracted war against terrorism, Captain Gardner led a new generation of A Company Cottonbalers on this twenty-first-century mission of peacekeeping. He made sure to keep his Attack Company soldiers fresh. They worked eight straight days and then enjoyed four days off at the regiment's base, Camp Montieth, a nice post with a PX, movie theater, gym, televisions, VCRs, phones, a recreation center, beds, and, of course, showers. Platoons rotated various mission assignments. He made sure that squads focused on training, even when carrying out patrols: "A squad may focus on training night movement while on patrol. It keeps their mind sharp."

The captain knew that the ultimate enemy was complacency. He constantly harped on this problem. His unit was earmarked to serve a six-month rotation here. Inevitably, over the span of that time, soldiers grew tired, bored, and disaffected. Their minds wandered; they thought of home, beer, food, women, camp, and whatever else captured their fancy. Gardner knew that they could not afford the luxury of such thoughts while out on patrol. Kosovo seemed peaceful now, but it could be very, very dangerous. Like any good officer, the captain knew to rely on his sergeants to implement what he wanted from his soldiers: "Like all things Army, the single best way is an NCO in their ass daily; supervising, correcting, listening, caring."[2]

In a way, this mission was similar to the one carried out by Cottonbalers on America's far frontiers in the nineteenth century. They secured borders, watched out for trouble among the local population, and tried to keep rival tribes from killing one another. But that's where the similarity ended. Nineteenth-century Cottonbalers usually viewed Native Americans as a dangerous, potential enemy; if need be, they fought them. Here in Kosovo, the greatest enemy was the failure of peace. Peace was their goal, their hope, their guarantee to the people of this troubled land. Any violence, even a small firefight, represented the failure of peace. The entire mission of the 7th Infantry in Kosovo boiled down to the notion that on-site strength could motivate people to put aside centuries of hatred in favor of living together peacefully. Thus the Cottonbalers represented a kind of bluff—the threat of force in pursuit of, ironically enough, peace.

For the soldiers this challenging mission required vigilance, restraint, and, above all things, professional discipline. Professional discipline meant focusing on the mission at hand, staying alert, working as a team, turning a blind eye to potential provocation, and treating people with dignity, even people with whom the Americans had little in common. Gardner's men, and the rest of 3-7 Infantry, passed the difficult six-month test Kosovo posed. They confiscated weapons, supervised movement of forces, prevented banditry, sealed borders, and, most important of all, kept the peace. In November 2001 the men of 3-7 rotated home to Fort Stewart and began their preparations for a much more demanding mission—the invasion of Iraq.

BY THIS TIME, THERE WERE only two battalions of Cottonbalers left. The downsizing of the Army in the middle 1990s had led to the deactivation of 1–7 and 4-7. The two battalions that had served with the 24th Infantry Division (Mechanized) in the Gulf War, 2-7 and 3-7, remained at Fort Stewart. The 24th Division was deactivated; the 3rd Division came home from Germany to a new home at Fort Stewart and, in so doing, absorbed both 2-7 and 3-7 in to its 1st Brigade.

For a time in the 1990s, downsizing and cuts in defense led to some morale, readiness, and substance abuse problems in the Army that had achieved such heights in the Gulf War, but these problems paled in comparison to the near disasters of the 1970s. By the middle of 2002, when the Cottonbalers were actively preparing for an imminent war with Iraq, the quality of the all-volunteer soldiery was as good as ever. Over 90 percent held high school diplomas (many of those who did not have diplomas were high schoolers enrolled in special pre-enlistment training programs) and almost none scored in the lowest range on the Armed Forces Qualification Test, while a whopping 70 percent scored in the highest range on the test. Of course they had to be bright and motivated to handle the dizzying array of weapons and responsibilities of modern combat infantrymen. "There's so many smart guys you meet in the infantry," a rifle squad leader in 3-7 asserted. "I'm a physics major in college and there's guys that were smarter than me that I served with in the infantry." Every man in his squad had an IQ of 120 or higher, and this was not atypical. "The stereotype of the infantry being the dumb guys is not true. There's a lot of smarter guys that really are there because that's what they wanna do. They wanna be the real deal."

Their social backgrounds and reasons for joining the Army were quite similar to those of the all-volunteer force that fought the Gulf War. They came from all over America, "everyone from country-western to punk rock," as one Cottonbaler put it; they were white, black, Latino, and Asian. "They were all races, creeds, and colors. I don't really think there's a typical soldier," one officer said. They joined to get money for college, provide for young families, because they had nowhere else to go, or out of a sense of service. The lowest-ranking enlisted men were generally between the ages of nineteen and twenty-two, the senior noncoms were in their thirties, and the junior officers were mostly between the ages of twenty-four and thirty.

The Army of this era offered more than one hundred military occupation specialties, most of them noncombat, so there were plenty of other options for the soldiers besides infantry. This meant that most of those who ended up in the infantry wanted to be there. Their motivations for becoming infantrymen varied—perhaps out of a sense of service, maybe to be at the center of the action, to prove something to themselves, or even, in the simple words of one young soldier, "to seek adventure, see the world, and blow stuff up."

Some were idealistic. After 9/11 the 7th Infantry was infused with more idealists than at any other time since World War II. "We had an influx of these studs that just wanted to join because of September 11th," Lieutenant Stephen Gleason, the scout platoon leader of 2-7, said. He cited the example of his driver, Private First Class Donovan Camelin, a married man and father in his late twenties who, before 9/11, had never even thought of enlisting in the Army. "He had no inclination to join the Army until that happened. He performed superbly." Young men like Camelin were outraged by the terrorist attacks on their country and wanted to do something to make sure nothing like them ever happened again. Similar to Camelin, they would never have joined the Army if not for 9/11. In 2002 and 2003 these newcomers mixed with the Cottonbalers who had joined for such a blend of other reasons and together they became a lethal fighting force.[3]

IN THE FALL OF 2002, the questions was where that lethal fighting force would be employed in the struggle against terrorism. Neither battalion of the 7th Infantry played any role in the war in Afghanistan. This was no surprise, since mechanized infantry was not ideal for the mountainous terrain of that country. Clearly, the 7th Infantry would not be sent there. North Korea was a possibility. President Bush had mentioned North Korea in his famous "axis of evil" speech, and with the nuclear capability of that country a reality, there was some tension along the troubled DMZ. Mechanized task forces like 2-7 and 3-7 would be greatly needed in a prospective war with the North Koreans, but the policy makers, for obvious reasons, preferred diplomacy to war with North Korea.

Then there was Iraq. Another named member of Bush's axis of evil, Saddam Hussein's Iraq continued, in spite of its catastrophic defeat in 1991, to be a serious impediment to stability in the Middle East. The Bush administration suspected Saddam of harboring and aiding terrorists. For years the dictator had been flouting UN resolutions and shooting at British and American planes over the no-fly zones of northern and southern Iraq (even though Hussein had agreed to those no-fly zones in exchange for peace in March 1991). During the Clinton years and then in the Bush administration, American policy makers fretted over their belief that Saddam possessed weapons of mass destruction. Presidents Clinton and Bush both believed that Iraq possessed such weapons, especially when Saddam turned away UN weapons inspectors. In the post-9/11 era Bush felt that Saddam was too dangerous to tolerate. What if he coordinated with terrorists on a WMD strike at the United States? Such a possibility was too terrible to imagine and must, in Bush's view, be prevented at all costs. He felt that the United States could no longer afford to simply wait and react to threats; instead it must preempt them. Thus began a standoff between a fledgling American-led coalition (consisting primarily of the United States, Britain, Italy, and Poland, with the notable absence of France, Russia, and Germany) and Iraq. The coalition wanted Saddam to prove to UN weapons inspectors that he had no

WMD and would fully cooperate with the agreements he had made in 1991. Weapons inspectors did visit Iraq, but Saddam continued to obfuscate and hinder their efforts. At best his cooperation was lukewarm. The standoff lasted for the better part of 2002 and part of 2003.

During this time, the Cottonbalers intensively prepared for war with Iraq. Most of them understood that in the near future they would go to Kuwait, either as a show of force or for a real war. The first unit to deploy overseas was none other than Attack Company 3-7. For a complicated blend of administrative and tactical reasons, the company was attached to the 2nd Brigade (unlike the rest of 2-7 and 3-7, which remained with 1st Brigade). In November 2002 the 2nd Brigade deployed to Kuwait. Thus the Cottonbalers of Attack 3-7 were the first 7th infantrymen to go overseas. Captain Gardner was no longer the company commander. He had rotated over to command of the battalion's headquarters company. The new commander of Attack was Captain Chris Carter, a thirty-one-year-old native of Watkinsville, Georgia. An avid hunter, fisherman, and football fan, Carter had graduated from the University of Georgia in 1995 and earned a commission through ROTC. If ever there was a kindred spirit to Roland Merson, Carter was it. Like Merson, Carter was a natural leader who, from an early age, dreamed of being a combat infantryman. "I grew up the typical southern guy infatuated with the military and serving the country. I wouldn't have it any other way but to be in the infantry. I think that the whole infantry thing gets under your skin and you just can't let it go. Everything that's in the military supports the guy with the rifle."

Upon graduation, Carter went through the usual army training for young infantry officers—basic course, airborne, and Ranger schools. For a time, he served in the 82nd Airborne Division. In 2002 he took command of Attack, a job he was literally born to do. In no time he won the respect and admiration of his noncommissioned officers (he and his first sergeant, Cedric Burns, were practically joined at the hip) and his soldiers. "Captain Carter was probably the best CO I had," Sergeant Paul Ingram, a squad leader, said. Carter's greatest strengths were his intuitive understanding of tactics and terrain and his down-to-earth, plain-spoken integrity. "He knew how to employ firepower in a way that was amazing—simple plans that were very creative and got the job done,"

Carter's executive officer, First Lieutenant Eric Hooper, a fellow Georgian, said. Hooper, a West Pointer who was to become Carter's closest friend in combat, admired his commanding officer's "uncompromising integrity. I would never in any event question anything [he] ever told me as not true . . . or embellished. The men not only respected him for what his talents were and his knowledge, but they loved him because they knew he was their leader. They were proud of him. He was very plainspoken." Carter had the knack of being able to comfortably hang around with soldiers without coddling them. Ingram admired these qualities: "He was a straight shooter. I always trusted him. I definitely think the men appreciated him as a leader. They were confident in him." More than anything else, Carter understood that command of the company wasn't about winning glory for himself; it was about taking care of his soldiers and accomplishing missions. He knew that any credit for success belonged to his men, not himself

Carter's soldiers traveled to Kuwait by plane and immediately went to Camp New York, a 2nd Brigade base camp staging area in the Kuwaiti desert. There were three such camps, each named for a state affected by 9/11—Camp New York, Camp New Jersey, and Camp Pennsylvania. The camps were built to accommodate battalion-sized units but now needed to be expanded to house brigades. Two days before Thanksgiving, when Carter's soldiers got to Camp New York, they found themselves in the middle of a mess. "We got there at nine o'clock at night," Hooper recalled. "It was pitch-dark. At that point they'd just put up barely enough tents for us. The tents had nothing in them. There was no electricity. We couldn't see anything." The sergeants passed out chem lights and told the men to find a tent and crash for the night. In the morning, they began the hard work of settling in. They found some wood lying around and used it to build furniture (later they found out the wood belonged to an engineer unit). They set up electricity, makeshift showers, and training areas. Camp New York was crowded, but it was now home. The camp consisted of rows of tents, Porta Potties, a PX, a mess tent, a morale tent, a makeshift gymnasium tent, and plenty of soldiers.

In this austere, isolated environment, they could easily concentrate on training and readiness. For several weeks during the holiday season in 2002, Attack Company trained in the desert. "The company normally got up and did platoon PT [physical training]," Carter remembered. "Then if we didn't have responsibility for some type of security detail or the normal stuff that comes with administrative life, we would focus on a lot of individual drills and training, anywhere from room clearing to reflexive fire, stuff like that." On the one hand, the men hated to be away from home during Thanksgiving and Christmas; this kind of thing was horrible for family life. On the other hand, the weeks of desert isolation brought the company together like nothing else could. Day after day they rehearsed for battle, trained for any contingency, prepared their combat vehicles (which they had drawn from pre-positioned stocks), and got to know one another intimately. "I really think that was the key to the success of our company," Hooper believed. "Everyone became closer. We rehearsed our battle drills. We moved beyond simply knowing how to react in combat to knowing how each other reacted and what each other would think. You knew exactly how much one person would give or take. We were so familiar with one another."

Naturally there were flare-ups and scuffles, but these were minor problems. Carter's soldiers were developing a tight camaraderie. Sergeant Ingram noticed it during the long days of training. He and the other soldiers had the opportunity to prepare for urban combat in a mock city. The Army called this kind of combat MOUT—Military Operations on Urbanized Terrain. Mechanized infantry soldiers rarely prepared for this kind of battle, but the Cottonbalers knew they would end up fighting in Iraqi cities. As Ingram and the other men learned the intricacies of city fighting, he marveled at the teamwork they were building in this detached environment: "There's no drugs out there; there's no clubs out there; there's no people's wives out there getting screwed. There's just work and everybody hanging out together, so a lot of stupid pressures that cause rifts weren't there. I think a lot of the smaller units . . . came together a lot better from being out there together."[4]

CHRISTMAS CAME AND WENT AND still the standoff with Saddam continued. The United States was attempting, unsuccessfully, to get a UN resolution passed authorizing the use of force against Iraq if Saddam continued to flout the many previous UN resolutions requiring him to allow inspections. Neither side appeared ready to budge.

Even as Attack Company toiled in the desert, the rest of the 7th Infantry stood ready for deployment. To those in the know, the question was not if the remainder of the 7th Infantry would be sent to Kuwait but when. Between Christmas and New Year's, when most of the soldiers were on leave, the news broke that the remainder of the 3rd Division would soon be deployed to Kuwait. Most of the soldiers found this out by accident while watching CNN or Fox News. For a few days, many wondered if they should return to Fort Stewart immediately, but there was no need. The deployments would begin on January 13, affording these Cottonbalers one last chance to enjoy their families and some semblance of peace.

Soldiers got their personal affairs, equipment, and weapons in order, bade good-bye to their weeping families, and boarded planes at Hunter Army Airfield. Most of the men flew out in the middle of the night. In the departure area, Red Cross volunteers handed out goody bags to the troops before they boarded their air force transports. The volunteers were mostly senior citizens, "blue-haired ladies" who could just as easily have been mistaken for somebody's grandmother. Whenever the men asked them why they were doing this they said, "We enjoy our way of life, and you are protecting it." The young Cottonbalers were touched and impressed with this kind gesture. First Lieutenant Mark Schenck, a twenty-five-year-old West Point-trained battalion liaison officer, picked up his goody bag and prepared to board his plane. As he did so, he and his group walked through a gaggle of fifteen more volunteers. "At 3 AM in the rain they formed a cordon and waved little American flags and cheered as groups of 10 filed from the building to the plane. Absolute patriots." Schenck had "no questions why I was deploying after such a simple gesture from 15 folks." The hundreds of other deploying soldiers felt the same way. The volunteers brightened an otherwise dreary, rainy night in which men tended toward the morose after leaving their loved ones behind.[5]

IN THE NEXT TEN DAYS, the men of both 2-7 and 3-7 experienced the dizzying process of flying to Kuwait, getting acclimated, drawing and maintaining new vehicles and equipment, and convoying to Camp

Pennsylvania, the 1st Brigade's base camp, located in the middle of the Kuwaiti desert less than twenty miles from Iraq. Camp Pennsylvania was the westernmost 3rd Division base camp, and it was basically a tent city. It featured two mess tents, a gymnasium, a morale, welfare, and recreation tent, a chapel, dwelling tents, some showers, and a PX trailer. For security reasons, soldiers had to forfeit their cell phones. Several weeks into the deployment, signals people installed an AT&T World Wide phone bank and even some limited Internet access. Previous to this some soldiers traveled to Camp New York to use the phones. In either case, the service was not very reliable. Lieutenant Gleason sometimes woke up in the middle of the night in order to have any chance of calling his wife, Meg. "You had, like, one phone trailer and, like, six phones and . . . the line was always three hours long at least." Even then there was no guarantee of getting through. "It was really a pain in the butt because it took like twenty-five minutes for you to get through to anyone," Specialist David Faulknor, a machine gunner in Bravo Company 2-7, recalled. "They would go out on you, and then you had to go to the back of the line and wait about three hours." Some men had phone cards that allowed them to talk for up to an hour, but usually conversations were very brief for soldiers like Specialist Joseph Blum, a Bradley gunner in Bravo Company 3-7. "When you get on the phone, you talk like maybe . . . ten or fifteen minutes at the max."

The phones were a mixed blessing. They were just as likely to lower morale as raise it. Staff Sergeant Bradley McNish, a Bradley commander, had been a Marine artilleryman in the Gulf War. In those days his unit had no communications with home. "We didn't have none of that and you maintained your focus." But in Camp Pennsylvania in 2003, thanks to the phones, sergeants like McNish constantly had to deal with the possibility that their soldiers might receive bad news from home. "The morale phones were a problem . . . because they were finding out about stuff happening . . . with their wives. We started getting issues with rumors and a lot of garbage happening back here and it started affecting people." Some soldiers worried incessantly that their wives or girlfriends were not being faithful. The phones provided a firsthand source of rumors, innuendos, and awkward, accusatory conversations. There was no more helpless feeling for a young soldier than the realization that his marriage or relationship was crumbling and he was stuck thousands of miles from home, with no power to do anything about it.

Conversely the phones could and sometimes did enhance morale, especially for those with strong, stable relationships. Private First Class Shawn Swears, a college-educated Bradley driver in 3-7, relished the opportunity to talk with his young family. "I felt pretty good when I talked to my wife and my kids. No matter how long it was . . . it was great for me." The same was true for Lieutenant Gleason. His nocturnal phone calls to Meg always made him feel better. "She was strong as an oak. She was the hero to me. Every time I called her she was very positive. She never complained. She always picked me up. So I didn't have to worry about her. I had to worry about my job. A lot of my soldiers' wives . . . were cheatin' on 'em and giving 'em a bunch of crap about being over there and 'when are you coming home?' She stayed very positive. It really helped me a lot."[6]

Like the phones, the PX trailer was there to enhance morale, but its value was questionable at best. The forty-foot-long trailer featured junk food, CDs, DVDs, greeting cards, soda, tobacco, and a few other amenities. But as with everything else at Camp Pennsylvania, there were long lines to get in. "If you weren't there early in the morning there'd be nothing left," Specialist Douglas Kautzman, a Bradley driver in Alpha 2-7, said. One day Kautzman waited hours to get into the trailer only to find that everything desirable had been picked over, leaving only worthless magazines for him. "There were backpacking magazines. That's what every soldier wants," he said sarcastically. Sergeant Adrian Newcom, a fire team leader in Kautzman's unit, wanted to send a Valentine's Day card home, but he had to settle for anything he could find. "I ended up with a card that had a big monkey on the front of it. It wasn't even a Valentine's Day card [but] I sent it home. That was all I had." For entertainment and relaxation the men read, watched satellite television, played cards, listened to music on their MP-3 players, or watched movies (such as *Band of Brothers*) on laptops or portable DVD players.[7]

At Camp Pennsylvania, the troops ate two hot meals a day: breakfast and dinner. Breakfast consisted of scrambled eggs, bacon, sausages, sauteed potatoes, oatmeal, chipped beef, and cereal. Dinners varied, although hot dogs and hamburgers were consistent staples. "The chow tents were badly sagging enormous cloth tents desperately attempting to collapse at the corners," Schenck later wrote. "The tents were up a small hill from Task Force 2-7 and always a hub of activity during breakfast and dinner. Times for meals constantly changed, and arriving at the door a minute late equated to no food, regardless of how much time was invested in waiting in line. Each tent had two service sides. One side was hamburgers, hotdogs and fries. The other a rotating menu line. The employees in those tents were all third country nationals, over watched by army personnel. After the food line there were several options for beverages. Soda, and eventually even ice for the soda, milk, water and some juices were all available. Folding tables and white plastic chairs provided ample seating."

There were two types of showers. Shower shacks, the first type, were trailers with ten showers and eight sinks. They had hot water but were quite crowded and not all that clean. The second type of shower was improvised at best—outdoor plywood stalls with water tanks bolted to their roofs. They had sinks too, but not hot water. Sand was of course ubiquitous, especially with the frequent *shamals* that rocked the camp, so the sinks were often full of gritty, grainy, wet sand. The water was "absolutely frigid," in the memory of one soldier. In spite of these drawbacks, some men did use the plywood showers, if for no other reason than to avoid waiting in a long line.

The ever present lines stemmed from one unhappy fact of life at Camp Pennsylvania—it was terribly overcrowded. The camp was designed to hold a battalion of seven hundred men; instead, it was home to a whole brigade numbering more than forty-five hundred souls. By far the worst aspect of the camp was its sanitation. Pennsylvania had no sewage system. This meant that soldiers had to relieve themselves in blue Porta Potties (or Johnny-on-the-spots), and at first there were not enough of these to meet the demand. Task Force 2-7, for instance, initially had only seven Porta Potties for seven hundred soldiers. After a few days of this, the battalion had twenty, which represented an improvement but hardly a surplus. Each company had its own Johnny-on-the-spots. The Kuwaitis hired foreigners, mostly Indians, Pakistanis, and Egyptians, to clean and service these stinking temporary toilets. They did not come anywhere near often enough. As a result, the whole area around the Porta Potties was engulfed with a nauseating stench. "The shitters would always fill up to . . . overflow," Specialist Jonathan Beck, a Bradley gunner, recalled, "and the people that would come clean 'em were always late. So sometimes you had to walk a mile to somebody else's porta potties. That was the worst part about it for me."

To make matters worse, many soldiers dealt with serious bouts of diarrhea during the early days of their time at Pennsylvania. One officer dismissed the diarrhea outbreak as "a result of stomachs getting used to the daily diet," but Sergeant McNish was not so sure. "We started getting a lot of problems with diarrhea and vomiting. One of my squad leaders and numerous people in my platoon and throughout the company and the battalion came down sick, so that they had to get IV's and had to be monitored at the aid station. I don't know if it was the food or the way the [foreign nationals] were handling the food or if it was the porta potties." The diarrhea and nausea problems ran their course, but for those soldiers who were affected it was a miserable time.[8]

The inadequate sanitary facilities, combined with the monotonous nature of daily life at Camp Pennsylvania, inevitably produced some strange behavior in some of the soldiers. Within a few days of arrival at the camp, a "mad crapper" began to plague 2-7. This odd individual defecated in the showers and smeared feces on the floor, toilet seats, and walls of the Porta Potties. He even relieved himself on an "unlucky vehicle hatch." Each day he would leave his disgusting calling card, sometimes even going so far as to write feces-smeared messages such as "2-7 rules" or "This place sucks" on walls. Actually, he had begun his bizarre work before the deployment back at Fort Stewart. He had left turds on the floor of an outhouse at Stewart, and in the estimation of Sergeant McNish, "he thought he'd bring that to Kuwait."

The commander of 2-7, Lieutenant Colonel Scott Rutter, a veteran infantryman who had led soldiers in combat as a company commander in the Gulf War, was determined to put a stop to the mad crapper. Rutter ordered guards posted on the showers and circulated rumors that he had summoned the Criminal Investigation Division to perform a DNA test on the wayward excrement.

In the meantime, NCOs like First Sergeant Robert Wilson of Bravo Company attempted to ferret out the culprit. Wilson was the classic example of an individual who finds a home in the Army and thrives in spite of adversity earlier in life. In high school, back in Watertown, New York, he had fallen in with the wrong crowd, doing drugs, going nowhere. Before he knew it he had an illegitimate child and a stockpile of problems. In an attempt to start a new life and get out of town, Wilson joined the Air Force, but they found out he had lied about his fatherhood status and dumped him. The Army was waiting with open arms. Wilson joined the Army, loved it, served in the Gulf War with the 15th Infantry as a Bradley commander, and, in the 1990s, spent several years with the Cottonbalers. In 2002 he ascended to the highly respected status of first sergeant.

First Sergeant Wilson did not think much of Lieutenant Colonel Rutter's DNA rumors. "He threatened all kinds of stuff—the crazy old man—but everybody knew there was nothing you were gonna do. You gonna find out who it is and then . . . send him to war? Make him eat MREs all day long? There's nothing you can do to the guy. It was funny." Wilson preferred deductive reasoning to threats. The more he analyzed the mad crapper's patterns, the more Wilson came to realize the culprit came from his company. "The mad crapper never struck in my latrines. Right then, it hit me. I think it's one of my guys 'cos no guy wants to go out and clean up his own crap. He was going over there striking near Headquarters Company, striking near the showers, stuff like that." By observing the soldiers and checking rosters of who had been near the outhouse at Stewart and was still with the company, Wilson soon figured out the identity of the mad crapper. Wilson and the other NCOs, including Sergeant McNish, concurred on the identity. The combination of this detective work and the colonel's threats ended the mad crapper's rampage. Everyone in Bravo knew who it was, but they let the weird incident pass in exchange for an end to the madness (they told me the man's name, but I believe there is no sense in publicly embarrassing him).[9]

BY LATE FEBRUARY, LIFE AT Camp Pennsylvania had settled into a routine of sorts. Units used the camp as a base while spending much time in the desert training. They did live fire drills, reflexive fire drills, PT, MOUT training, formation training, and a myriad of other things to sharpen themselves for the possibility of war. The training chased away boredom and enhanced morale, but the soldiers were nonetheless getting antsy for something to happen. "It was pretty boring for the most part," Specialist Michael Smith, a rifleman in Charlie Company 2-7, said. "You trained for the first few hours [of the day]. You watched movies in the evening times. People played cards. There wasn't much to do. The showers kind of sucked. It was just really dull."[10]

While most of the soldiers held no love in their hearts for Camp Pennsylvania—when asked what he thought of it, one soldier responded succinctly; "In one word—SUCKS"—it was much better than what was to come. In early March the Cottonbalers left Pennsylvania to make room for the newly arrived 101st Air Assault Division. The men of the 7th Infantry were now in the middle of the desert, just a few miles from the Iraqi border. "Limited phone access turned into none, showers evolved into wet wipes, and tents protecting us from the stinging sand storms were all left behind," Lieutenant Schenck wrote. The men now lived in their vehicles, small pup tents, or even holes. They ate MREs and T-rats. They had makeshift plywood latrines, but the waste had to be disposed of, and that meant shit-burning detail for the lowest-ranking enlisted soldiers. Each day they poured diesel fuel into cut-down fifty-gallon drums and set the contents afire. The noxious smell would waft over the entire camp area and would have been readily familiar to any Cottonbaler Vietnam veteran.[11]

THE TRAINING, PREPARATION, AND ANTICIPATION continued. The troops received brand-new MOPP suits and real ammunition (as opposed to the training ammo they used at Fort Stewart). They practiced the berm-breaching techniques they would use if ordered to cross the border. War seemed imminent. The soldiers could sense it, especially when their commanders started to make speeches. In 3-7's assembly area, the commanding officer, Lieutenant Colonel Jack Kammerer, called many of his soldiers together early one morning and spoke to them as honestly as he could: "Listen up. It's getting closer and closer. We are trained and ready. Who thinks we are not trained and ready? Anybody?" No one moved. "We gotta assume we're going north. We wear the American flag on our right shoulders for a reason. We represent the Army and our country." The colonel, with sunglasses shading his eyes, paced in a circle as he spoke. "A lot of people back in the States love you guys. They are proud of you guys. They understand and respect the sacrifices you are making here. Why will we fight? For freedom. We'll fight for what's right, for our country and for our friends and our families and a lot of people. And for each other. I owe it to you guys to bring you guys back. You guys are my friends. You guys are my soldiers. I've got all the confidence in the world in you guys."[12]

Even as Kammerer and other officers made "eve of war" addresses, the Bush administration made it clear that Saddam's time was running out. The Americans had not succeeded in persuading the UN Security Council to authorize the use of force against Iraq. France and Russia remained adamantly opposed. Despairing of his quest for UN permission, Bush mulled over the possibility of attacking Saddam without the United Nations' stamp of approval. Following many weeks of tension, Bush announced on March 17 that Saddam and his sons had forty-eight hours to leave Iraq; otherwise the coalition would invade his country and remove him from power. "He sounded like John Wayne. You got forty-eight hours to get out of town," Sergeant Duane McKenny, a medic in Charlie 3-7, said as he listened to Bush's speech on a small battery-powered radio. Sergeant Ronald Palmer, listening right next to McKenny, agreed. "He's John Wayne, with a bunch of crazy Army guys and Marines like us to do his job. He said pretty much what I expected him to say."

Most of the Cottonbalers did not hear the speech, since it was made in the middle of the night, Kuwaiti time. But as McKenny and Palmer indicated, the ultimatum fit their mood perfectly. The vast majority of the soldiers wanted to cross the border and go to war. Many had trained long and hard for something like this. "You train, train, train for years . . . and you finally get a chance to do it. You're ready to go to the big game," one officer said. "It sucks that . . . you have to leave your family . . . but that's just the shit you gotta do." Some compared it to a major athletic contest like the Super Bowl. "It was like the big game," a Bradley commander said. "You go out there and [train] and you wanna go do the real thing." Some wanted to go out of idealism. "I felt we were ready and I felt we were justified," Lieutenant Gleason said. Sergeant Ingram also thought that Saddam Hussein had burned all of his bridges. "The idea of America backing down . . . would have repulsed me."

While most all of the Cottonbalers believed in the justice of their cause, their main hope was that war would break the monotony of so many weeks of waiting. "After they make you sit for so long in one place," Sergeant Newcom explained, "and you're just staring at sand forever, you're like, 'I don't care where I go. I just wanna get out of here, man.' "The prevailing sentiment was that "the ticket home was in Baghdad," as one soldier put it. In other words, the sooner they invaded Iraq, took Baghdad, and toppled Saddam, the sooner they could go home. This mind-set reflected the lack of American planning for a post-Saddam Iraq, but it was how the soldiers thought in 2003. The men were apprehensive about the dangers of war, but they were quite confident in their training, their weapons, and their leadership. More than anything else, they wanted to go home, and the path to home seemed to go through Iraq.[13]

No sooner had Bush finished his speech than the Cottonbalers received orders to move to Attack Position Dawson, a jump-off point a few miles from the Iraqi border. Now things were getting very serious. Most understood that they would soon be at war. At Dawson there was little to do but make final preparations, worry about Scud or chemical attacks, and wait for the word to go. Even now engineers and Kuwaiti breaching teams were in the process of breaking down the border fences and building modified roads over tank ditches and through berms. Commanders lined up vehicles in the formations they wanted. The combat vehicles were poised and waiting in pre-positioned breach lanes on the Kuwaiti side of the border. The sight of all these Bradleys, tanks, and other tracks was awesome. Like a pack of tan monsters, they stretched for mile after mile all the way to the horizon. The whole 3rd Infantry Division was in place, like a coiled spring or a taut sprinter waiting in his blocks.

The barren desert was windy, and sand blew everywhere, even into the keyboards of laptop computers that staff officers were using as they sat in the tents that functioned as their Tactical Operations Center (TOC—pronounced "tock"). The officers dusted off their computers with paintbrushes.

All over Attack Position Dawson, Cottonbalers clustered in or around their vehicles and contemplated what lay ahead. At the sandy patch of bleak desert where Alpha 2-7 was waiting for orders, one infantry squad stood outside of their Bradley and debated what music they should play when they rolled across the border. The nickname of this company was "Rage." But the music Sergeant John Harper had in mind was anything but warlike. Harper, the squad leader, turned on his CD player. A mellow R & B tune crept out of the speakers. "Are you kidding me?" Private Scott Morgando blurted. "That's, like, making-baby music, not crossing-the-border music." The song faded into the background as the men argued the merits of various musical selections. One soldier wanted something patriotic. Another wanted to hear Tupac. "What about Julio Iglesias?" Harper joked. The men continued their inconclusive debate. They could not decide what to play.

Not far away, Specialist Jennings Roberts III, the driver for Lieutenant Colonel Rutter, was sitting in a Humvee and writing poetry. The twenty-six-year-old Roberts wanted to be a teacher when he got out of the Army. In idle times like this, something compelled him to write poetry. He scratched and scribbled until he got this poem down the way he wanted it.

Adrenaline flows, anxiety flushed.
Questions answered, rumors hushed.
The day of reckoning is finally here,
a day some covet, a day some fear.
Tonight we rest, tomorrow we soar
on the wings of a nation ready for war.
In defense of freedom and all that is right,
we are willing and able and ready to fight!
Cottonbalers by God!

Roberts showed the poem to Michael Corkery, an embedded reporter from *The Providence Journal*, and the correspondent was kind enough to publish it in one of his articles.[14]

Near the leading edge of 2-7's long column, Lieutenant Gleason watched his men make their final preparations. Some were cleaning weapons or checking over their Humvees. Others were smoking, chatting, or reading. As scout platoon leader, Gleason had ten Humvees under his command. Half of them were equipped with .50-caliber machine guns; the other half, with Mark 19 grenade launchers. Half of them were uparmored; the other half, including Gleason's personal vehicle, were thin-skinned. A devout Catholic, the twenty-five-year-old West Pointer had made his peace with God a few days before at a desert Mass. "I prayed real hard. I was like, 'All right, this is it. It's out of my hands. It's now in your hands. If I go, I go, and I'll go to a better place. If not, that's your decision.' " Now, as the Philadelphia native waited for the word to go into action, his thoughts centered on his men, not himself. "I was more worried about my guys than my own self." Would he lead them well enough? Would he find the bravery and the skill to be the kind of commander they deserved? What if, God forbid, he did something that got someone killed? Like so many other young leaders in the 7th Infantry, these were his greatest concerns.

The scouts were not scheduled to be in the lead when the task force crossed the border. This was a job for heavier formations such as the rifle companies or engineers. But Gleason knew that after that he and his men would log plenty of time as the lead element. He was the latest Cottonbaler incarnation in the lineage of scouts that included Bill Strobridge and Kirk Allen. There was a remarkable similarity among these men. They were all young, bright, curious, courageous, observant, and adventurous. Gleason had never even heard of the other two, but he was about to join their unique reconnaissance fraternity.[15]

THE FOURTY-EIGHT HOUR ULTIMATUM PASSED rather quickly. Saddam and his sons remained firmly in place. With his ultimatum unheeded, Bush now had no choice but to strike. The war began with bombing raids on Baghdad. Acting on intelligence regarding Saddam Hussein's whereabouts, Bush ordered air strikes on Hussein's suspected hideout in hopes of toppling the regime and winning a quick, bloodless victory. The raids did no damage to Saddam. The ground troops would have to roll.

All day long on March 20, the news of the air strikes drifted among the Cottonbalers. Anyone who still doubted that they would go to war had now changed his mind. There were numerous Scud and chemical weapons alerts. Other than that, the waiting game continued, but everybody knew the order to cross the border would come very soon. In Charlie 3-7's lane, soldiers tried to pass the time and stay focused. Their vehicles were lined up in three long columns. Each column was about fifty yards away from the next one. The men played cards and dominoes and read Tom Clancy books. One man perused a copy of *Penthouse*. A small group passed a football around. On the side of one Humvee someone had painted "We're baaack" in a veiled reference to the Gulf War. Beneath the veneer of this normal scene was great anticipation and nervousness. "It isn't training no more," one soldier said. The company commander, Captain Will Neubauer, agreed. "This is no longer a game. The show is on." Neubauer, a former enlisted man who had worked his way up through the ranks, sat and thought about two things-his company's mission and the promise he had made to the families back at Fort Stewart that he would bring all of his soldiers home alive. "We're really going now and I made a promise," he thought. "How am I gonna keep that promise?"

The Army being the Army, strange things began to happen that only added to the headaches of the commanders. A few miles away from Neubauer's Charlie 3-7, in the 2nd Brigade sector, the soldiers of Attack Company 3-7 ate a final meal of T-ration spaghetti and meatballs. It was about 1800 now. The order to go had to come soon. Lieutenant Eric Hooper had just finished his dinner when he noticed several trucks pull up to his column. Several soldiers hopped off the trucks and reported to his Bradley. They were brand-new replacements—augmentees, in army parlance—arriving on the eve of the invasion. The newbies did not have ammo for their rifles, proper body armor, or much of anything else, yet Lieutenant Hooper, as the executive officer, had to figure out what to do with them. "We had no plan as to how to move these soldiers. Our Bradleys were maxed out, so I had to find a place to put 'em. You don't want to stick 'em in a rifle squad that had trained together now for six months and mess up the chemistry." Hooper spoke with First Sergeant Burns, and the latter found creative ways to equip and situate them. Most of the new men rode as extras in the wheeled vehicles. A couple rode in Captain Carter's Bradley as veritable deadweight.[16]

In the early-evening hours, the shooting finally began. Unseen artillery units began shooting MLRS at Iraqi border patrol stations. The excitement among the soldiers immediately jumped to a fever pitch. Some men whooped and cheered as they watched the rockets streak overhead. "The first night . . . when the artillery started shooting across the border at some of those check points . . . there was a level of excitement like 'Let's go and do it!'" one officer remembered. Some of the younger men could hardly contain themselves. In Bravo 2-7's area, First Sergeant Wilson was lying on top of his M113 enjoying a cup of coffee and a cigarette, alternately napping while listening to the rockets overhead: "My driver keeps tapping me on the shoulder saying, 'Look, First Sergeant, they're shooting!'"

The experienced thirty-five-year-old first sergeant was unimpressed. "Okay, guy, get some sleep. We're about to go to war here." The way Wilson figured it, they should get as much sleep as possible now because in the days ahead they wouldn't get much, if any. The young driver could not wind down, though. He kept oohing and aahing over the MLRS strikes. "You just couldn't talk anything into him," Wilson sighed.

Even some of the experienced men were quite agitated to see the shooting start. In Alpha (Rage) 2-7's area, Sergeant Nicholas Driggers and several other men were playing a game of improvised baseball when the shooting started. Driggers was a twenty-two-year-old Bradley gunner from Las Vegas. He and the other men had set up T-ration trays as bases. Bats consisted of gas masks ("pro masks"), and the ball was a big roll of tape. In spite of their limited equipment, the soldiers carried on with their game and were having a great time. "The first sergeant [Benjamin Moore] came by and started talking to us." Moore, knowing that combat was imminent, wanted to make sure that each soldier understood his responsibilities. "Okay, you guys, when you go across the border, don't be scared now. Don't be running away." All at once the MLRS streaked overhead. Driggers and the other "ballplayers" craned their necks and watched in awe. One of them looked in Moore's direction. "What's that, First Sergeant? First Sergeant?" Moore was nowhere to be found. At the first sound of the MLRS he had taken off in excitement in order to make sure everyone knew that the war had really begun. This struck Driggers and the others as funny, and they had a good laugh.[17]

THE ARTILLERY PREPARATION LASTED ONLY a few minutes, and then it was time for the infantry and armor to roll. In the declining hours of March 20 and the early hours of March 21, combat elements of the 3rd Division began crossing the border. The 3rd Brigade went through first, followed by the other two brigades. With the exception of Chris

Carter's Attack Company 3-7, every Cottonbaler formation was with the 1st Brigade. The Gulf War had proven the lethality of combined-arms doctrine in modern war. Tanks needed infantry support and vice versa. Thus some of the Cottonbaler rifle companies were cross-attached to armored battalions. This was the case for both Charlie 2-7 and Bravo 3-7. Both of these companies were assigned to the 3rd Battalion, 69th Armor. In return this armored battalion gave one of its companies, Bravo Tank, to 2-7. At an even lower level, it was not unusual for company commanders to cross-attach platoons with their armored or infantry brethren. For instance, Alpha 2-7 (Rage) lent one of its Bradley platoons to Bravo Tank 3-69 while Bravo Tank 3-69 gave one of its tank platoons to Alpha 2-7. No longer did the Cottonbalers fight as one regimental entity. This had been the case since the Vietnam era, but by the Iraq War the order of battle setup was even more complicated. The Cottonbalers now fought in dispersed company-or platoon-sized groups, as part of combined-arms (infantry, armor, engineers, signals, ADA, etc.) battalions or "task forces."

All through the night and into the early-daylight hours on March 21, Cottonbaler formations, in tandem with their armored partners, poured across the border. The first Cottonbalers to cross were from Charlie Company 2-7 (nicknamed "Charlie Rock"). They crossed at around 2100 on the evening of March 20. The commander of this company was Captain Todd Kelly, a personable, articulate West Point graduate who vaguely resembled Kirk Rueter, the former major-league baseball pitcher. Kelly had once played guard on the academy basketball team. In the preinvasion briefings, he had been repeatedly told to expect hundreds of capitulating Iraqis. Intelligence seemed to believe that there would be little, if any, opposition to the invasion. While they were correct that many Iraqis would soon welcome the invaders, their optimistic forecast of little opposition would not stand up in time. Now, as Charlie Company prepared to roll, Kelly spoke to his soldiers over the company net, explaining, in the recollection of one of his men "what a mass capitulation would be. It was like a twenty-minute talk about what a mass surrender looked like." Within half an hour of this lecture, they rolled: "We were the spearhead . . . the very front."

They rolled through the border berms and sped north. As they did so, thick clouds of dust and sand clung to their vehicles. The night was moonless. The dust, in combination with the darkness, made it difficult for Bradley crewmen to see, in spite of their sophisticated thermal and night-vision sights. The drivers struggled to keep their Bradleys in the designated breaching lane. A heavy metal song called "Bodies" by Drowning Pool blared over the loudspeaker of one of the company's Humvees.

Somewhere in the middle of Charlie Rock's formation, standing in the turret of the command Bradley, Captain Kelly ("TK" to his fellow officers) was getting frustrated at the suffocating dust. "I can't see shit out here!" he snapped. As if on cue, American artillery rounds exploded somewhere up ahead, lighting up the night like heat lightning. "Is that bright enough for you, sir?" someone asked Kelly over the radio. The captain could only chuckle and nod his head. Tonight Kelly's men had three objectives-two border guard posts some six miles across the berm and a suspected command post that was located deeper into Iraq. Even now the artillery was battering the first two objectives.

Charlie Rock rolled up to the first guard post. In the back of one Bradley, Sergeant Curtis Kelly (no relation to the captain) was listening to the excited voices of the Bradley crewmen over the company net. Kelly was a twenty-five-year-old fire team leader from Warsaw, Missouri. He had joined the Army less than two years before, out of a desire to serve his country. Like all of the dismounted infantrymen, he saw very little from the back of his crowded Bradley. In order to hear what the crewmen were saying, he was wearing a Combat Vehicle Crewmember Protective Helmet, usually just called a CVC. This was his only real link to the outside world, and he was lucky to have it. Only his team leader status afforded him the opportunity to listen in on the CVC. His men could only sit and wait for orders.

Outside artillery rumbled. Kelly kept hearing the crewmen say the artillery was not hitting the guard post. Who knew what could be out there? Kelly and the others were shrouded in ignorance, but the reports of inaccurate artillery fire did not bode well. "Man, we're gonna get across the berm twenty feet and then fuckin' die as soon as we cross over the border," Sergeant Kelly thought. The order came to dismount. The ramp of the Bradley went down. Kelly and his fire team plunged into the darkness. Bradleys were firing their 25mm guns at the dilapidated

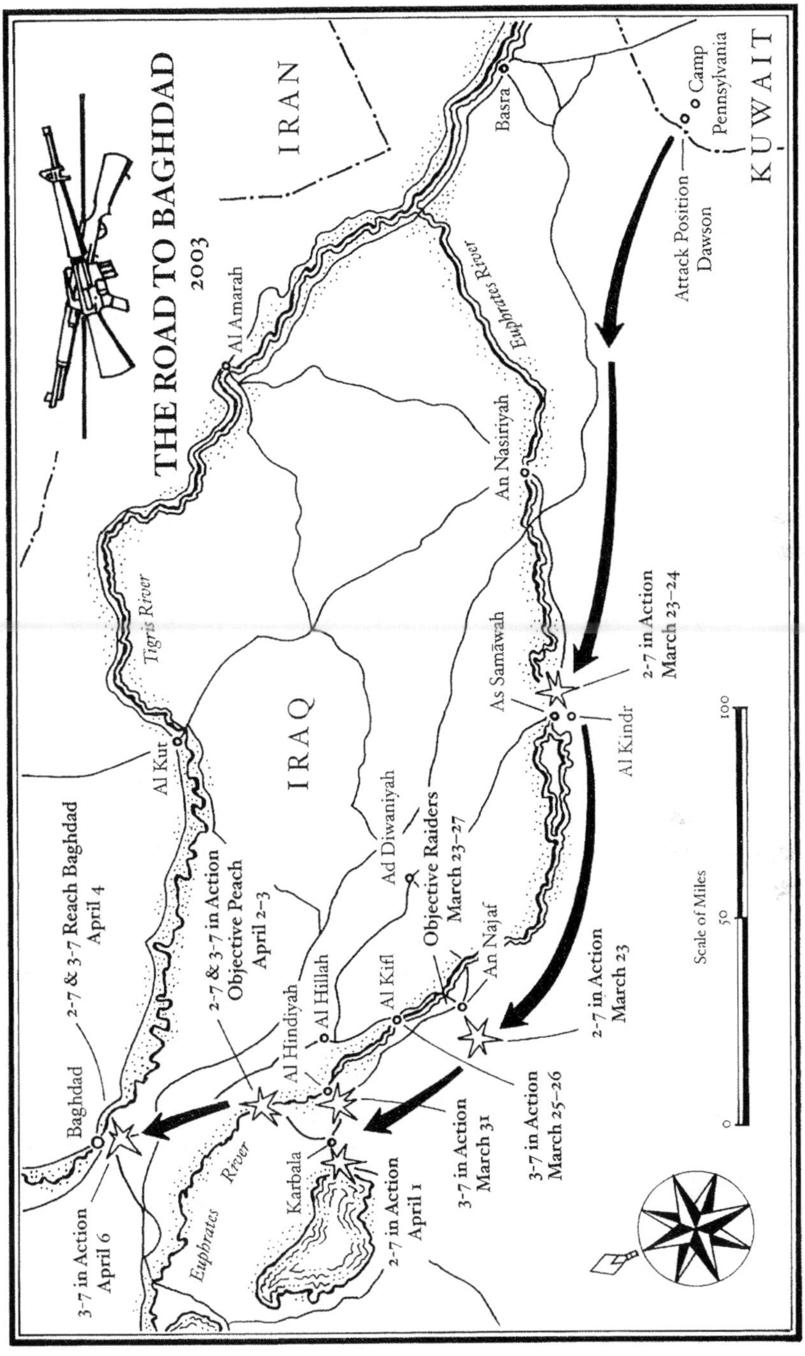
THE ROAD TO BAGHDAD
2003
IRAN
IRAQ
KUWAIT
Basra
Camp Pennsylvania
Attack Position Dawson
Al Amarah
Euphrates River
Tigris River
An Nasiriyah
As Samāwah
Al Kindr
2-7 in Action March 23–24
Al Kut
Ad Diwaniyah
Objective Raiders March 23–27
An Najaf
2-7 in Action March 23
Al Kifl
Al Hillah
Al Hindiyah
2-7 & 3-7 in Action Objective Peach April 2–3
2-7 & 3-7 Reach Baghdad April 4
Baghdad
3-7 in Action April 6
Karbala
Euphrates River
2-7 in Action April 1
3-7 in Action March 31
3-7 in Action March 25–26
Scale of Miles
0
50
100

guard shacks. Within seconds, Kelly and the other dismounts realized, with relief, that the post was deserted. Contrary to the radio reports, the artillery had demolished much of this place. If there had been any Iraqis here, they were long gone now.

The story was the same at the second objective. They got to the third objective, the command post, as Captain Kelly called it. Most of the men thought of it as a compound. The place consisted of a series of sheet-metal buildings. The experience of clearing the first two objectives had eased some of the nervousness in the men. They had now shot some live rounds and done their jobs. No one was hurt. Things were going smoothly. They were within a couple thousand meters of the compound. Staff Sergeant Andrew Sorenson was standing in the commander's hatch of his Bradley, scanning the area with his thermal sights, looking for threats. Immediately to his left, his gunner, Private First Class Nathan Bennett, was laying down some suppressive fire on the buildings. All of a sudden, Sorenson heard the booming sound of an Abrams unleashing a main gun round. One of the tankers had found a target: "It was a great shot. It was a Suburban. It was like 2,000 meters away and it was going about forty miles an hour. His gunner tagged and bagged that thing with a HEAT [High Explosive Anti-Tank] round. We saw the whole ass-end of the SUV just kind of disappear."

Captain Kelly also had a good view of the Cottonbalers' first catastrophic kill in this war. "It was very eerie. It didn't hit the engine, so the lights remained on although the truck was destroyed and there were three KIAs . . . Iraqi guards." Once the captain was satisfied that there were no more enemy vehicles in the area, he ordered his infantrymen to dismount and clear the buildings. They piled out of their vehicles and quickly organized into fire teams. Each fire team covered the other as it bounded forward. Behind them, they knew the Bradleys and tanks were there providing security, like sentinels in the chilly night.

Rifleman Michael Smith's squad made it to the buildings. "They were all padlocked. We had to clear all those. They gave us shotguns but they gave us no rounds for the shotguns so we couldn't breach the fuckin' doors. So we just shot the padlocks off with M16's or SAW's." This was definitely not standard procedure, because the bullets from those weapons were likely to ricochet and inadvertently hit someone. But at this point the infantry soldiers had little other choice. In any event, no one got hurt and the buildings were empty.

With the compound secured, the soldiers of Charlie Rock now turned their attention to dealing with the remains of the three dead Iraqis in the wrecked SUV. "We were responsible for the care of . . . any type of casualty or enemy KIA," Captain Kelly said. The vehicle was so mangled that it took the Americans about half an hour to pry open the door and remove whatever was left of the dead Iraqis. Specialist Smith got a glimpse of the remains: "They were pretty fucked up." The soldiers put them into body bags and tried to identify them. They found a tremendous amount of money in the Iraqis' wallets. The whole thing was quite sobering to young men not acquainted with violent death. "Training is good, but there is never anything that can prepare you for that first sight of . . . destruction or loss of human life," Captain Kelly said. "It was quite sobering . . . but probably good because the angst and butterflies . . . and nervousness were now gone." When they were done with the bodies, Kelly's people mounted up and pressed on. They ended up at Jalabah Airfield, an airstrip the coalition needed for supply reasons. Charlie Company waited there while engineers cleared ordnance, some of which dated back to the Gulf War.[18]

In the meantime, hundreds of other Cottonbalers were spending their first hours in Iraq. Bravo Company led the way for 2-7 across the border. Along with a supporting unit of engineers, they breached the barbed-wire, fences, and berms at the border, cleared a lane through any potential obstacles, and paved the way for the whole battalion. The men were jumpy, nervous, and scared. For most, this was their first time in combat. They had prepared months, even years, for this night. The brigade reconnaissance team had reported the presence of enemy tanks somewhere up ahead. They claimed they had been fired upon by a T-72. There were also reports floating around the net that an American helicopter had been shot down. Artillery had pulverized the company's first objective, a border observation post. The column kept rolling.

In the gunner's seat of one Bradley, Specialist Jonathan Beck scanned the dark horizon, looking for hot spots that might betray the presence of the reported enemy tanks. All at once, he picked up the chilling sight of dozens of tank turrets. He had never seen battle before and he was nervous as hell. Most of the tanks showed up as cold on his thermals, meaning they were unoccupied, but one was different. “I saw one and it looked hot, so I told my BC [Bradley commander]” and requested permission to shoot. Many other gunners were doing the same.

The request went up the chain of command. In his M113, First Sergeant Wilson shook his head when he heard talk of shooting at the enemy tanks. Wilson knew they were old hulks left over from the Gulf War. The reports of the brigade reconnaissance team notwithstanding, Wilson knew that there were no active enemy tanks out there, just an armored graveyard. He got on the net: “Hey, look, we’re inside the graveyard; don’t worry about it.” Back at the battalion TOC, Major Kevin Cooney, the executive officer, had the same opinion. “I don’t know if that’s a live Iraqi tank or a camel blowing hot air,” he said.

In spite of the reservations of Cooney and Wilson, Bravo’s commanding officer, Captain Stephen Szymanski, gave the order to open fire at any hulk that yielded a heat signature. The captain agreed with Wilson and Cooney that the tanks were unoccupied but wanted to appease the brigade reconnaissance team and give his men a chance to open fire for the first time. The hulks were only five hundred meters away, so he knew his men could not miss them.

Beck took aim and fired. “I shot it and nothing happened of course ‘cos it was dead. I wanted to shoot at every one that I saw but they wouldn’t let me because of the ammo. We didn’t know when we’d get resupplied.” Gunners like Beck hit their targets, and the company moved on. There were no Iraqis in the tanks. Most were rusty old T-55s left over from the Gulf War.

Bravo (nicknamed Bushmaster) roared through the armored graveyard and made it to Holding Area Able, an assembly point from which the battalion could continue its advance after sunrise on March 21. As his company waited for the rest of the task force to catch up and the first rays of sunlight peeked over the eastern horizon, First Sergeant Wilson sat in his M113 and, for the first time in several days, thought about the gravity of the situation. There had been no real opposition yet, but that would change and he knew it. During the Gulf War he had been a young man, a Bradley commander with responsibility for nine lives (his two crewmen plus seven dismounts in the back). Now that seemed like small potatoes. As first sergeant, he was responsible now for the welfare and safety of more than fifteen times that many men. He shook his head and thought, "Oh my God, what am I doing? I'm that delinquent . . . that eighteen-year-old . . . drug dealer, doing drugs and stuff, and now I'm gonna try to bring these hundred and fifty guys home. I hope to God I can bring 'em all home alive."[19]

Even as Wilson contemplated his life-and-death responsibilities, the sun was rising on the first full day of the ground war. All along the carefully breached lanes that stabbed across the border, Cottonbaler vehicles drove north. At many of the border berms, patriotism was on display as engineers or MPs stood atop the berms and waved American flags at the infantrymen. At the western edges of the 3rd Division assault, Captain Chris Carter was in the same patriotic mood. He played a country tune over his company's net as they crossed the border. "It was probably right around the time the sun was coming up. I played Toby Keith's . . . 'Courtesy of the Red, White and Blue.'" They were in column formation, rolling north against no opposition. So far the operation was going well.[20]

The columns, containing thousands of vehicles, drove north, deeper into Iraq. As they did so, they made their first contact with Bedouins. Major Rod Coffey, the operations officer, or S-3, of 2-7, was with one of the lead units when they saw their first Bedouins. "There they were, in little shanty villages. A camel caravan . . . just crossed right through us. We waved and they waved." It was quite a clash of cultures—Americans riding in ultramodern, powerful weapons of war commingling with shepherds who, if not for their pickup trucks, might just as well have been living in biblical times. The two sides were friendly to each other, but they kept a respectful distance.

Special Psychological Operations teams were eager to do their jobs after months of training. The Bedouins were their first subjects. The Cottonbalers' Psy-Ops team rode around in a Humvee with a loudspeaker attached. These men had prepared a series of Arabic tapes with instructions for the local population. Most conveyed the basic message that the Americans did not wish to hurt anyone. Their quarrel was not with the population, only the regime or anyone who endangered the lives of U.S. soldiers. The Psy-Ops team broadcast these messages "imploring the Bedouin shepherds to stay in their tents and out of the way of the advancing troops," one observer recalled.

At one point, the team drove up to a Bedouin family and popped a new CD into their player. They had intended to play a soothing message about how the Americans were here to protect them, but the Bedouins fearfully shot their hands up in a gesture of surrender. "That's the wrong tape," Sergeant Souika Vongsvirates told his team. This tape was telling the Bedouins to surrender or the Americans would shoot them. Vongsvirates stopped the CD and put the proper one in and the mood of the Bedouins changed. "This is so embarrassing," one of his men said. The Americans felt so bad about this that they dismounted, walked over to the Bedouins, and offered them Juicy Fruit gum and an Arabic leaflet explaining that the soldiers meant them no harm.[21]

There were humorous incidents too. Sergeant Driggers's Bradley was rolling past a group of Bedouins when he noticed a man riding atop a camel. "One of these herders was sitting cross-legged on this camel and he was just beating this camel, like, to death. All at once, the sonofabitch just fell off it. I was . . . laughing my ass off." Other men saw it too and they roared with laughter. "I've never laughed so hard in my life," one of them said.

With the invasion now almost a day old, it was apparent that the Iraqis were not going to defend their desert borders. The Americans, facing almost no opposition, simply rolled north, stopping every so often to refuel, and headed for Highway 8, the first serious road that could take them into the interior of the country. By nightfall on March 21 they had already covered eighty miles. With so little opposition to worry about and to maximize speed, the order came down to turn on vehicle lights. "As far as you could see, all the way across the horizon . . . it looked like five or six freeways worth of . . . vehicles coming," Driggers remembered. "It was pretty awesome." The lights reminded Captain Carter of rush hour in Atlanta. Major Coffey watched the lights with awe. He knew he was looking at a once-in-a-lifetime scene. He told his crewmen to take a look at the incredible sight. "Hey . . . turn around and look at this." For many moments, they stared at the enormous convoys. "It was like a huge, powerful, massive snake, but several of them, all these white lights, all throughout this nighttime desert scene, reaching up toward Baghdad. Thousands of vehicles were all within sight, all with their headlights on." Coffey was a graduate of Carnegie-Mellon University. He had once thought about becoming an actor and even a priest before deciding on Officer Candidate School and a military career. He was thoughtful, cerebral, a very well-read scholar of military history. Tonight he knew that his eyes beheld something unique in the annals of warfare. He thought of Saddam Hussein's regime, so impotent and unable to defend its own borders, and, for the briefest of moments, almost pitied them. "These guys have no idea what's coming at 'em," he thought.[22] Of course, the same was true of the Americans too.

The convoys rolled on through the night. The greatest problem was keeping the task forces together. Vehicles were breaking down or getting stuck in the sand. Wheeled vehicles-trucks, Humvees, and the like—in particular had problems, especially the heavy trucks and tractor-trailers of the Patriot batteries. The Patriots were supposed to defend the convoys from Scud attacks, but aside, from a few launches, the Scuds had been pretty quiet. Confusion, traffic, and breakdowns multiplied as the hours wore on. For instance, in 2-7 the Patriot batteries became so bogged down that Lieutenant Colonel Rutter had to leave them behind, under the charge of his executive officer, Major Cooney, while the task force kept going. Cooney, with the assistance of some of Lieutenant Gleason's scouts, spent the better part of a day and a half getting the Patriot vehicles unstuck and herding them to a rendezvous with the swiftly moving combat formations of 2-7. The officers in the 2-7 TOC dubbed the ragged column "Cooney's Carnival" and the name stuck. In all, Cooney's Carnival contained 241 vehicles.[23]

Meanwhile, the Cottonbalers simply continued to drive through the desert. Everyone was fighting exhaustion now. Many of the commanders had hardly slept since before the invasion. "Out of the first thirty-six to forty-eight hours," Captain Carter said, "those who were in leadership up in the turrets or driving maybe got four hours of sleep." Carter himself had not slept at all. He knew he was tired, but his adrenaline kept flowing, perhaps because of his considerable responsibilities.

Some Bradley gunners and drivers were lucky enough to have backups riding in their tracks. They swapped out with their understudies and caught a few hours of sleep in the back of the track, but many crewmen were not so fortunate. At the vanguard of Rage 2-7, Specialist Kautzman, like many other drivers, remained in his seat, trying to keep his eyes focused on the track in front of him. But his eyes were so heavy with sleep, he kept nodding off "I slept for most of the drive. I was driving but . . . I was just so tired. It was like, 'Kautzman! Wake up!'" Each time his gunner or commander hollered at Kautzman, he woke with a start, only to nod off again at some point later. In Bravo 2-7's convoy, Specialist Beck sat uncomfortably in his gunner's seat and tried to focus on scanning for possible threats. "We couldn't sleep that whole time because . . . the lives of the guys back there [the dismounts] depended on us." After a while, he began experiencing hallucinations. "One of our squad leaders . . . had to come up and relieve me." Several miles away, Private First Class Swears, a Bradley driver in Bravo 3-7,was not just tired. He was sweaty and thirsty, and several times in the course of this desert movement he had had to pee. He knew he could not stop the convoy to answer the call of nature, so he had to improvise a way to relieve himself. "I'd have to kind of stand up a little bit because of the way the seat was. I'd just lift my body up to stand on one foot . . . while I had one foot still down on the gas. I was hunched down . . . looking through the periscope. I'd open up a [empty] water bottle and piss right in it." This worked, but it was awkward and, with the constant bouncing and bucking of the Bradley, somewhat messy. Swears also had to be careful to keep the urine-filled bottle away from his water bottles. With no ice or refrigeration in Bradley, one bottle was as warm as the other.

With no way to brew coffee while on the move, some crewmen opened up the contents of MRE coffee packets and simply ate the coffee powder. Others nibbled on crackers or energy bars or talked to stay awake. "I was just talking trash the whole time," Sergeant McNish recalled. "Me and my driver and my gunner sometimes would sing and scream in the turret just to stay awake." McNish and his crew caught a few short catnaps in their turret, but that was about it. Some vehicle commanders, like Staff Sergeant Steven Collier, a thirty-year-old Bradley commander from Norton, Virginia, stayed awake because of the nauseating exhaust fumes that kept blowing in their faces. "I don't know who put that exhaust underneath the Bradelys the commander's face, but that thing sucks. The fumes get bad sometimes."[24]

The dismounts, packed into the backs of the crowded Bradleys, by far had it the worst. Although they could catch some sleep here and there, their circumstances were generally far too uncomfortable for any sort of sustained rest or relaxation. They were packed together, usually six or seven, fully equipped, in a space the size of the rear of a family minivan. Some Bradleys even carried eight men. The unluckiest man sat miserably in what was called the "hellhole," a little emergency space on the left side of the track, right behind the driver. For many hours at a time, the men were wedged in among ammo, water bottles, boxes, extra weapons, and a dizzying array of other items. The Bradleys stank of dirty socks, body odor, and foul exhalations. The soldiers sat with their weapons pointed downward, safeties on, grenades taped securely in place, dozing or waiting for the order to dismount. Basically, it was a claustrophobic's worst nightmare. "You didn't have …leg room," Specialist David Youngson, a SAW gunner in Bravo 2-7, said. "When everybody got comfortable and you found enough leg room, after awhile you'd want to move your legs but you wouldn't be able to because there wouldn't be no room." In many Bradleys men got angry with each other for invasions of personal space. "Soldiers started to get annoyed with other soldiers 'cos one soldier is leaning his head down too far in a soldier's personal space," a squad leader recalled. Sometimes men would nod off, inadvertently let go of their weapons, and awake to hear them plinking against someone else. The chagrined sleeper would then endure a round of barbs.

The whole experience was disorienting, strange, like being trapped in a tin can. The men had periscopes, but they offered only a limited view of the outside world. The Bradleys at times bucked, rolled, and shimmied. Conversation was limited because of the engine noise of the armored monsters. "You can't hear each other," Sergeant Raul "Rudy" Belloc, a fire team leader (and the same man discussed in the Introduction), explained. "You'd just be quiet. The person right next to you . . . is probably the only person you could talk to 'cos it's just so loud in there. It's hot, dark, whatever you can think of." The stuffy heat of the Bradleys, combined with the MOPP suits, BDUs, armored vests, and Kevlars the men were wearing, meant that they had to constantly drink warm bottled water to stay hydrated. For many this meant having to relieve themselves in the crowded confines of their surroundings. "I just went in water bottles," Sergeant Newcom of Rage recalled. Other more adventurous troopers urinated out of the troop hatch at the rear of the Bradley. Woe to the occasional soldier who had a bowel movement under such circumstances. Some did their business in empty MRE boxes and threw the contents out of the troop hatch in the back. A few used the troop hatch itself as a moving toilet. "You'd have some kind of 550 cord and they'd latch it to your vest or . . . maybe just hold you, while you use the bathroom, shut the door and that's it," Sergeant Belloc said.

The hours wore on and on and still the Americans kept rolling. The miserable dismounts were yearning for refuel stops so they could get out and stretch their numbed limbs. "You couldn't even feel the bottom of your ass," one man said. When the convoys did stop to refuel, the Bradley drivers lowered their ramps and the infantrymen poured out and breathed fresh air for the first time in many hours. When Bravo 3-7 stopped for its refuel, First Sergeant Fraziar Harris, an experienced infantry soldier, watched the dismounts swarm out of their Bradleys and felt great sympathy for them: "We had guys riding in the back . . . for eight, nine, ten hours at a time. They were trying to eat, maybe catch some sleep, use the bathroom. They were laying . . . on the ground. I didn't say anything to 'em 'cos I've been there. After that long a period of time, you have to let them get some rest, stretch out a little bit 'cos you're all cramped up. We just kept moving and moving and moving."[25] The road to Baghdad seemed wide open.

MOST OF THE REFUEL STOPS lasted anywhere from thirty to sixty minutes. Then the vehicles got moving again. The three brigades of the 3rd Division made it to Highway 8 and followed it to the northwest, in the general direction of As Samāwah and Baghdad. The invasion was two days old now, and for the Cottonbalers there had been almost no opposition. They were more than one hundred miles into Iraq. Parts of Highway 8 were paved, so the better road quality allowed the Americans to move faster than before. While rolling in sand they had averaged about 10 miles per hour, but now they were moving two or three times as fast.

Late in the afternoon on March 22, Lieutenant Colonel Rutter's 2-7 was in the lead, rumbling north on Highway 8. The road went from four lanes down to two. The task force was moving in column formation up the road. The scouts were in the lead, followed by Alpha Company, the tanks, and Bravo. At the leading edge of the scouts, Lieutenant Gleason was sitting in the passenger seat of his Humvee. He and his men were a couple miles in front of the rest of the battalion. Gleason's vehicle was second in the column, right behind his senior scout. As Gleason sat there, he was doing a balancing act of sorts. He was manipulating two hand mikes, one to talk to his platoon, the other to talk to the battalion. On his lap he had a notebook he was using to jot down spot reports. He was navigating with the help of a wonderful new piece of equipment called an FBCB2. The FBCB2 was a small computer that was connected to a satellite transmission system. The screen, resting to his left where a radio mount would have been, showed a series of icons on a map. The maps did not show all the necessary details of the terrain ahead but were still quite good. Each icon on the map represented a vehicle in the task force. "It was awesome. It was a great piece of equipment. As long as I had a good signal and my GPS was working, it was virtually impossible to get lost. [Also] we completely mitigated fratricide." Gleason could thus see, in real time, where his platoon and nearly every other unit in the task force were. Through the computer he could send e-mails or instant messages to other commanders and noncommissioned officers. In the rifle companies, every platoon leader, the executive officer, and even some of the platoon sergeants had FBCB2s. In the scouts, Gleason and his second in command, Sergeant First Class Terry Mulligan, were equipped with FBCB2s.

Gleason was looking back and forth from the computer screen to his notebook and, at the same time, listening for any contact reports from his men. Afternoon shadows were creeping across the road, hinting at an impending sunset. Gleason glanced out of his window and noticed that they were now driving through a populated area. As he and his amazed men watched, Iraqis came out of their homes and began to line the road like a parade route. Most were waving and cheering. Some had blank stares. A few glowered. Children were the least inhibited. Some of them ran alongside the Humvees, begging for food, gum, candy, or even cigarettes. A few Americans tossed MREs at them. Gleason and his scouts were pleased at the reaction of these Iraqis to their presence but still wary. The crowd was getting bigger by the minute. Anyone could take a potshot with an RPG or an AK-47 rifle. The scouts waved, smiled, and kept rolling. They were now at the fringes of a town called Al Kindr.

In a Humvee immediately behind Gleason's, Sergeant Zachariah Farrell was standing at his Mark 19, scanning for threats. He pressed his face against a fantastic piece of equipment called an L-RASS (Long-Range Advanced Scout Surveillance system) whose thermal optics allowed him to see and identify targets anywhere between four and twenty kilometers in the distance. Farrell was bright-eyed, enthusiastic, and sharp. He could see hundreds of people waving and smiling at him, but he knew that danger could lurk anywhere. All it took was one person with a weapon and the wrong disposition. Farrell scanned the area with his L-RASS and saw something that made his heart practically skip a beat. "Sergeant Gaines," he said to his section leader, who was sitting in the passenger seat of the Humvee, "there's a BRDM up there." A BRDM was a Soviet-made combat vehicle with a gun that could blow away a Humvee. Sergeant Gaines was surprised to hear that there was one in Al Kindr. "Really, where?" he asked Farrell. The young sergeant started to point in the proper direction.

At that exact moment, Gleason and his crewmen saw the BRDM. It was rusty and nasty and generally did not look combat worthy. "That looks kinda odd," Gleason thought. The thought had no sooner passed through his mind when he heard a loud cracking sound and saw a bright flash. "A shot came across my hood . . . an RPG, like five feet over my hood." He saw the RPG out of the corner of his eye and watched it whiz past his Humvee. Gleason was pleased to see that Private First Class Camelin did not hesitate a moment. "We immediately took evasive action. We got off to the side of the road . . . behind this . . . mud hut." Gleason's legs were shaking uncontrollably. He kept thinking, "Oh my God, I was almost killed."

The radio was alive with reports of the RPG. Gleason was not sure if the shot had come from the BRDM or a dismounted crew. All of the scout vehicles were off the road, taking shelter in ditches or behind cover. The gunners scanned the area in an effort to see the RPG team, but with no luck. The BRDM was on the move now, heading back into Al Kindr. Hearing the radio reports, Lieutenant Colonel Rutter ordered Rage Company forward. The Bradleys and tanks of this unit got to Al Kindr in no time and peeled off into combat formations covering either side of the road. Some of the Bradleys rumbled toward Al Kindr's buildings, in the direction where the shooting had come from. In so doing, they churned through muddy fields that bordered the road. Many of the people had scattered at the sight of the RPG. The sound of vehicle engines filled the air as tracks and Humvees maneuvered for positioning on and off the road.

At one intersection, Major Coffey was in position alongside several M1s from Bravo Tank. The tankers had just found a flipped-over white SUV with "TV" stenciled on the doors. The SUV was abandoned, but its windshield wipers were still at work. Taking in this sight, Coffey was wondering, "OK, what should I be doing now?" He decided to send out his security team to see what was in a nearby gas station building. The team consisted of two surplus riflemen. No one was in the gas station, but the men found spent casings and a warm teapot. They continued searching behind the building and quickly discovered two armed Iraqis who wanted to surrender. "They had found two . . . very, very frightened [Regular Army] types," Coffey recalled. The two men were wearing green uniforms: "They surrendered and they were processed."

The frightened POWs gestured at another building, indicating that there were more Iraqis hiding in there. Sure enough, the Americans captured eight more green-clad, scared enemy soldiers. Elsewhere in Al Kindr, Captain Rob Smith, commander of Rage Company, now had his vehicles in position to cordon off the town. Some of Smith's men had dismounted to deal with more prisoners and also some weapons caches. Specialist Brian Butler, a rifleman, charged out of his Bradley with the rest of his fire team and, in a matter of moments, dealt with prisoners. "We found four Iraqis with mortar rounds. They had changed out of their uniforms. We took 'em into custody and found all their mortars." The prisoners hardly looked imposing, "They were crying and scared," Lieutenant Gleason recalled.

The sun had set now. No one knew where the BRDM had gone. While Lieutenant Colonel Rutter and his key commanders decided what to do next, the Cottonbalers waited in their Bradleys and scanned the area with their thermal sights. The shooting had long since died down, and people were now milling around everywhere. Some of them seemed to have weapons, but the Americans could not be completely sure. In one Bradley that was overwatching the company support vehicles (usually called the company trains) and the aid station, Lieutenant Ed Cuevas was looking through his thermals. He and his gunner, Sergeant Ken Gainey, saw all sorts of people roaming around, picking up weapons. Cuevas was the executive officer of Rage. A native of Saint Charles, Missouri, Cuevas had once been a long-haired kid with an earring, a goatee, a party-boy attitude, and rotten study habits. He flunked out of college several times. When his parents refused to pay for any more college, he decided to join the Army Reserves as a way to fund his schooling at the University of Missouri. At that point, he straightened up and got serious. He excelled as a soldier, got involved in ROTC, and eventually graduated with an infantry commission.

Now Cuevas and many other soldiers in Rage Company were wondering if they were allowed to shoot at the human shapes that were wandering, armed, out there in the night. "We were trying to gain . . . support from everyone . . . so we don't want to just be lighting up everyone that we see. We're trying to win the hearts and minds of the people so that they'll overthrow Saddam and be friendly to us. There was a lot of confusion." The unit, really was still in a peacekeeping mode. As Cuevas indicated, this stemmed from the political objectives of the invasion, but it also was a hangover from the Kosovo experience. For now, the Americans chose to live and let live.

Out of necessity this soon changed. In an effort to disorient the Americans, the Iraqi fighters in Al Kindr cut power to the town. In one eerie instant, the lights went out, bathing the whole area in an inky darkness. This was a foolish move by the enemy, though, because it only enhanced, rather than diminished, the considerable American advantages. Throughout the entire campaign in 2003, the opposition had little concept of just how well the Americans could see in the darkness with their night-vision equipment and thermals.

Tonight the Americans gaped in amazement as several Iraqi fighters, with RPGs and rifles strapped to their backs, began low-crawling toward the scouts and leading Bradleys of Rage. Sergeant Farrell, peering into his L-RASS, could clearly see these brave enemy stalwarts. In the Humvee right next to Farrell's, Sergeant Jeffrey Davis could also see them through his thermals. Davis was Lieutenant Gleason's .50-caliber machine gunner. The Iraqis were crawling and then taking shelter behind small berms. Davis and Farrell asked for permission to engage them. Several minutes passed as the commanders sorted out whether the rules permitted them to open fire or not. Rutter, tiring of the hesitation he was sensing in his men, ended the debate. In a firm and steady voice, he told the scouts to engage.

Standing at his .50-cal, Sergeant Davis opened fire at the shapes in his thermals: "The first guy that popped over the berm—I was firing .50 cal at him—you could see his body parts just fly off of him. I could see his arm just pop right off. I saw this through my thermals."

Once unleashed, the American firepower grew to a frightening climax as other scouts and nearby Bradleys joined in the fray. The 25mm guns of the Bradley completely shot away one of the berms the enemy had been hiding behind. Davis's bullets then shredded them. By the time the shooting died down, eight enemy soldiers were dead and several more were wounded. The survivors waved frantically, at once asking for help and surrendering. Still some Americans kept firing. "Stop shooting!" Lieutenant Gleason hollered into his mike. In seconds, the firing petered out. Dismounts policed up the surviving Iraqis and took them to the medics, and the fighting ended. As they did so, the sickening reality of war began to sink into Gleason's psyche. "Man, we just killed people," he thought. Deep down, he knew it had been necessary for the survival of his men, but that made it no less repugnant and troubling. "It really hit me hard. I joined the infantry and I always knew it in the back of my mind, but I just never thought I was gonna kill somebody." In a few moments, the lieutenant forced such thoughts from his mind. He had a platoon to lead. The moral ambiguities and waste of war could be dealt with later. For now, he knew he had to focus on his job. He successfully did so.

After this firefight, Rutter decided to leave Rage Company and the medics in place to keep the road around Al Kindr secured, while the rest of the battalion pressed on to refuel and secure As Samāwah. The brigade reconnaissance team had run into an ambush there, and two soldiers had been wounded. They were going to be medevaced. Rutter did not want to leave his battalion in place as a target for any remaining enemy at Al Kindr. He knew his job was to keep up the momentum of the advance. Rutter put his tank company and himself in the lead and the bulk of 2-7 took off on Highway 8. Captain Smith's Rage Company remained behind at Al Kindr. "We were supposed to be relieved in place by a unit from the

3rd Brigade. Basically my company was left . . . there to secure that part of the road."

Hour after hour passed and still the 3rd Brigade did not show up. Smith and his men spent a wary, uncomfortable night waiting for relief, wondering if the Iraqis might be planning another attack. "It was really tense," Lieutenant Cuevas remembered. "We didn't know if they were . . . organizing behind the walls [of the city]. We didn't go inside the city. We . . . went in the fields around the sides. Are they all of a sudden gonna rise up with, like, eight million RPGs on the top of the walls and light up the place or what? We had no idea." Several American units passed by Rage's vehicles and headed for As Samāwah, but none of them relieved the Cottonbalers: "There was units flying by . . . passing us. It was just kind of weird." To make matters worse, Cuevas and the other Rage Company men could clearly see the Iraqis moving weapons back into the city, but since they were not presenting a direct threat to the Americans, the GIs were not allowed to engage them. For now, the GIs could only wait and hope for the best.[26]

IN THE MEANTIME, THE REST of 2-7 was snaking its way north up highway 8 toward As Samāwah. As planned, the convoy stopped to refuel. As the ungainly fuel tankers topped off the thirsty tanks of many Bradleys, Abrams, Humvees, and other combat vehicles, Rutter and Coffey agreed upon a plan. They knew that the brigade reconnaissance team had been ambushed at an overpass immediately west of the city. Realizing that they now had two batteries of 155mm self-propelled guns (Paladins) available, they decided to shell the overpass, dash through it, and continue on until they found the turnoff to Highway 28. This road would allow them to skirt around the city and keep advancing north. Throughout this campaign, the 3rd Division's job was to act as a veritable cavalry. Their job was to move with lightning speed, capture terrain, bypass cities or strongpoints, and keep up the momentum for the drive on Baghdad. Other units could clean up any bypassed resistance later. All of this reflected the overt political goal of toppling Saddam's regime, but little sense of what would follow. For Rutter and Coffey, it meant avoiding a full-scale battle in the urban jungle of As Samāwah. Such a fight would slow the advance and risk unnecessary casualties.

At 2300 the convoy resumed its advance, and soon it was within sight of the enemy occupied overpass. A platoon from Bravo Tank was in the lead, followed by Rutter, the scouts, and several fire support Bradleys. These Bradleys contained forward observation teams for artillery and close air support. In one of those Bradleys, First Lieutenant R. Lee Simmons was maneuvering for a good look at the overpass. Simmons came from Hendersonville, Tennessee, a town outside of Nashville. He had always wanted to be in the Army because he had had so many relatives serve in previous American wars. After high school, he had enrolled in the ROTC program at East Tennessee State University and graduated with an artillery commission in 2000.

He and his forward observation team were attached to Bravo Tank. Simmons's team consisted of four soldiers—Simmons; his assistant, Sergeant Berger, who sat in the gunner's slot of the Bradley; his radioman, who sat in the back; and a private who did the driving. Simmons, of course, stood in the commander's hatch. He was a pretty laid-back officer, with an easy manner and a hypnotic southern drawl. His men called him "sir," but mostly there was very little rank distinction among his team. Back at Fort Stewart, Simmons and Sergeant Berger would often eat lunch together or play video games at Berger's apartment.

Now, in the darkness outside of As Samāwah, the driver rolled the Bradley to a stop several hundred meters from the overpass. Lieutenant Simmons peered through his thermals and was fairly sure that he saw a squad of enemy infantry in prepared positions on the overpass, but he figured that another pair of eyes might be useful. He called Lieutenant Gleason, who was looking at the overpass through his NODs. "We both agreed that that's where the target was," Simmons said, "so we called up a fire mission on it." Simmons got on his radio and called the battalion fire support team: "Able 3–0 X-ray, this is Knight 3–0, fire mission, over." He passed along the grid number where he estimated the overpass to be. All up and down the chain of artillery command, several voices confirmed the grid numbers, the target, and the certainty that there were no friendly units in the target area. "Able 3–0 X-ray, this is Knight 3–0, enemy on an overpass. Fire for effect, over," Simmons said. In his CVC, the voice on the radio confirmed his request. A moment later Lieutenant Simmons heard the rounds screaming in. They were devastating, right on target. In a matter of seconds, the rounds savaged the Iraqis, blowing several men into bits and driving any survivors into a hasty retreat.[27]

The task force resumed its advance, rolling underneath the overpass. They were supposed to make a left turn somewhere just beyond the overpass. On the maps, the left turn seemed to be a major road, but the map was wrong. The crew of the lead tank became very confused when the reality in front of them did not coincide with their maps. The actual left turn was nothing more than a dirt road that looked like a dead end. Thinking that this could not possibly be the turn, the tank crew bypassed it. In so doing, they unknowingly led the convoy straight into the city.

At first all was peaceful. The tank crews saw that there were more buildings and walls around them, but they did not yet know they were lost. One tank crew spotted an empty pickup truck with some sort of anti-aircraft gun mounted on it. They requested permission to shoot and soon got it. Sergeant Driggers's Bradley was in a guard position back at the overpass. He heard Rutter grant permission to fire and thought, "Oh, cool, I want to see this." Since the sergeant's Bradley was on top of the overpass, he had a good view of the tank as it shot at the pickup truck. "I scanned over there and saw him blow the shit out of it. There was fire everywhere." As he watched the pyrotechnics, he noticed that the tanks kept moving, deeper into the city.

At this very instant, dozens of Iraqi fighters opened fire on the tanks. No doubt the enemy soldiers had heard the pickup truck get blown up. Armed mainly with machine guns, AK-47s, and RPGs, they fired from buildings, alleyways, and even the streets themselves. Driggers's eyes widened as he watched this through his thermals. "They just came out of the woodwork. There were RPGs flying. I mean, it was crazy." Lieutenant Simmons was immediately behind the lead platoon of tanks. He quickly shut the commander's hatch of his Bradley and buttoned himself in. In his mind, the act of shooting the pickup truck had been like "kicking the hornet's nest." Everywhere he looked there were Iraqis running around. "We were all in a big column. Dudes started coming out and running around us."

Basically, this was exactly the kind of situation Rutter had wanted to avoid. He now had a column of tanks and other vehicles stuck inside the confines of a city, where they were vulnerable to an enemy who could shoot at them from the cover of buildings or walls. Those who were shooting at the Americans were doing so from the close range of fifty to two hundred meters. To make matters worse, there were now hundreds of people prowling around the streets of As Samāwah. Some were armed. Many were not. Rutter kept thinking of the movie *Black Hawk Down*. As in the movie, he felt that the enemy was trying to lure the Americans into a populated area so that they could use civilians as shields and force the Americans to kill friend and foe alike.

Rutter got on the net and ordered the commander of Bravo Tank, Captain Jimmy Lee, to back his tanks up and get the hell out of there, but this was easier said than done. The road was tight, not to mention that there were buildings and people all around. As at Al Kindr, the Americans did not wish to use their fire power indiscriminately. Lee kept asking for permission to engage. At first Lieutenant Colonel Rutter did not want his men to return fire, partially for fear of killing many innocent people in the growing crowds but also because he thought there might be friendly reconnaissance elements in the city. He soon understood that there was little choice. They could shoot back or do nothing and put themselves in serious danger (in any event, Rutter's staff soon told him that there were no friendly units in As Samāwah). With Rutter's blessing, they returned fire, mostly with coaxial or .50-caliber machine guns, at enemy muzzle flashes or RPG signatures, but tried as hard as they could to avoid shooting innocent bystanders (a policy the 7th Infantry continued during its entire time in Iraq). "The ensuing machine gun fire from the monstrous tanks slammed into the armed crowds quickly clearing much of the crowd," one officer recalled, "all scrambling and seeking out shelter from the vicious barrage of overwhelming fire." The bullets scythed through anyone who was unfortunate enough to be in their path, whether they meant the Americans harm or not.

Enemy soldiers were still shooting back with everything they had. Major Coffey, from the vantage point of his Bradley outside of As Samāwah, watched in amazement as tracers and RPGs streaked through the night. "There were a lot of RPGs shot right near the fire support officer's track, right around all of . . . Bravo Tank's vehicles, the colonel's Bradley itself." Lieutenant Gleason was even closer to the shooting. His Humvee was twenty or thirty feet behind the lead tank platoon. As he observed through his NODs, the enemy continued to target the lead tanks. "They were getting hit by RPG after RPG on the front slope. The colonel's Bradley got hit by an RPG too." Gleason knew that his Humvees were very vulnerable to the RPG fire, but at the moment, he was more worried about his commanding officer and his armored comrades. "Oh my God, this is crazy! Holy shit, the colonel's gonna die," he thought.

Much of the fire was coming from a two-story concrete building straight ahead. Gleason could see about twenty muzzle flashes from the upper story. The enormous tanks were trying to maneuver around, partly in an effort to evade fire and partly in hopes of turning around and exiting As Samāwah. They were bumping into buildings. Gleason was terrified that they would lose sight of his little Humvee and crush him. All at once, several of the tanks shot main gun rounds into the building where Gleason had seen muzzle flashes. The destruction was total and immense. The building exploded and collapsed. "We . . . watched over 30 bodies come flying out the windows," Captain Lee, the armored commander, recalled. Pieces of concrete flew everywhere. There was no more shooting from the building.

Slowly but surely, Captain Lee, following careful directions from Lieutenant Colonel Rutter, began to get his tanks turned around and headed out of As Samāwah. As they did so, they continued to battle groups of Iraqis who were still taking shots with RPGs or small arms. One of Lee's tankers identified a target and unleashed his 120mm main gun. Lieutenant Gleason's Humvee was trailing along only a few feet behind the tank as it fired. The noise and concussion from the shot were overwhelming. "[It] just rocked your world," Private First Class Camelin said. Standing at his gunner's station, Sergeant Davis felt like he had been knocked out by a sucker punch. "The force of the tank just threw me down . . . through the turret to the floor of the Humvee. My ears were ringing. My NOD's were out." Gleason, knocked out by concussion, awoke to find both Davis and Camelin on top of him. The three men were lucky they hadn't been killed by the concussion of the main gun. The shot was so earsplitting and so overwhelming that the lieutenant at first thought their Humvee had been hit by an artillery shell or an RPG. Like Davis, his ears were ringing badly. Gleason was fuming. When he realized he and his men were OK, he got on the radio to Captain Lee. "You need to tell your tanks to hold their fire until we're clear out of there!" Lee called back, "Sorry."

The convoy was now close to being out of the city. The shooting was dying down. Still, the Americans, through thermals or NODs, could see small groups of Iraqis with weapons running around or popping their heads up from behind walls to take shots. Lieutenant Simmons was right behind Captain Lee. Simmons and Sergeant Berger spun their turret to the left and noticed several men with rifles climbing aboard a truck some hundred meters away. Berger fired several rounds at the truck with his coax, but the gun jammed. "Hey, switch it to 25," Lieutenant Simmons commanded. The 25mm fire blended with some .50-caliber fire from one of Lee's tanks. "I can still see it in slow motion," Simmons recalled. "I can see their tires coming apart and one of the guys in the back get hit. So we turned the 25 on it and fired 25 HE [High Explosive] . . . right at the engine block and pretty much stopped it. The guys went to bail out. Right as a guy was getting out of the passenger side making his way around the front, Sergeant Berger squeezed off a round and nailed him, blew him back into the car. It was . . . so surreal to actually turn that thing on a human. I remember the adrenaline was really going." No sooner did Simmons's track stop shooting when he remembered that today was his one-year wedding anniversary. "My anniversary will always be memorable, but for more reasons than the obvious."

The destroyed truck was now a flaming funeral pyre. By coincidence it was close to the turnoff for Highway 28, so the Americans used it as a landmark to navigate their way out of As Samāwah. By the early-morning hours of March 23, Rutter's 2-7 was safely out of As Samāwah and rolling northwest on Highway 28. The highway was little more than a small desert road running parallel to a buried pipeline, but it was exactly what Rutter wanted—an open area over which his task force could move quickly. Rutter's men had killed 150 Iraqis-some of whom may well have been noncombatants—while incurring no losses of their own. The armor of a Bradley or an Abrams could generally withstand a direct hit from an RPG, and this was good because if it could not, then there would certainly have been many American casualties at As Samāwah.

Rutter put Lieutenant Gleason and the scouts in the lead. All night long and part of the next day on March 23, the task force drove unmolested for its next major objective—the Najaf escarpment.[28]

AS THEY DID SO, CAPTAIN Smith's Rage Company was still at Al Kindr, many miles behind Rutter and the rest of 2-7. As the sun rose on March 23, Smith began to understand that no relief was coming. Every American vehicle he saw simply whizzed by and headed north toward As Samāwah. The task force was so far away now that he had lost radio contact with them. Smith called Lieutenant Cuevas: "Hey, have you looked at your computer? You should check it out. Look where the rest of the task force is." Cuevas had spent much of the night pulling guard duty for his track. When the captain called, Cuevas had just woken up after a couple hours of much-needed sleep. Cuevas punched up his FBCB2 and looked at the screen through wide eyes. The blue icons of 2-7 were way north on the map. "Holy cow! We are so far behind. What are we gonna do?"

"I don't know," Smith replied.

Cuevas asked if any relief had arrived and Smith told him no one had shown up. "What do you think we should do about that?" Lieutenant Cuevas asked.

"I say we wait for about another hour and if nobody comes by, we leave."

"Sounds good to me. We need to catch up with the rest of our group."

Sure enough, the hour passed and no one came. This was a classic judgment call situation for a junior officer. Technically Smith's orders were to remain in place. However, he knew that every minute he stayed here his parent unit got farther away, even as his company continued to be an inviting target for any remaining opposition. Should he stay here and follow orders strictly to the letter, or should he risk the unknown, abandon his post, and go north? He decided the latter was the best option, and it was the right call.

At 0900 Rage Company moved out. The movement north turned out to be a real odyssey. Hundreds of American vehicles jammed the road. The original route through As Samāwah had been closed off because of the accidental fight that had taken place there during the night. Through a combination of bluff, bluster, resourcefulness, and luck, Rage negotiated its way around and past the dizzying array of vehicles. First Sergeant Moore begged, borrowed, and stole whatever fuel he could lay his hands on. He got a break when he found an errant National Guard fueler that kept Rage Company's thirsty fuel tanks full enough to keep going. "It was a day and a half of driving and getting stuck," Cuevas recalled. "So many units were moving up and we're trying to barge ahead." It was like trying to drive through rush-hour traffic in an American city. "It was a huge clusterfuck of vehicles . . . a massive traffic jam," Staff Sergeant Thomas Ziegelmann, Captain Smith's gunner, said. "Meanwhile we look on our computer screens and see battalion just haulin' ass and we're . . . getting left behind." Cuevas coined this crazy odyssey "The Miracle Mile." Smith was sending e-mails to Coffey and Rutter, but they still had no radio communication. For now, Rage remained on its own, isolated from the rest of 2-7.[29]

THE OTHER ELEMENTS OF 2-7 could not afford to pause and wait for Rage because the 3rd Division had orders to take the Najaf escarpment as soon as possible. The Iraqis were off-balance, on the run, disorganized, so why not keep them that way?

The escarpment was a unique terrain feature. It was 150 feet high, a sandy, rocky cliff that was bisected by Highway 28. As the road slashed through the escarpment, it became very steep, rising to a 12 percent grade. Beyond the escarpment was a plateau. So this embankment was a natural ambush point. Anyone dug into the escarpment, on either side of the road, had a perfect view and excellent fields of fire on vehicles attempting to climb the escarpment. Nor was there any way to flank it. The only way over the escarpment was straight up Highway 28, right into the guns of any enemy who wished to defend it.

At first glance, this seemed an unlikely attacking point for the ambush-conscious Americans, but that, after all, was the point of attacking it. The enemy would probably expect the Americans to stick to the main roads like Highway 9 and avoid natural choke points like the escarpment, so the plan was to cross them up. Plus, Highway 9 led right into Najaf, one of the holiest cities of Shiite Islam. If the Americans did not want to get into an urban fight in As Samāwah, they certainly did not want to do so in Najaf. The city was home to the golden-domed tomb of Ali ibn Abi

Talib, the son-in-law of the great prophet Muhammad, founder of Islam. In 661 A.D., Ali had been stabbed to death by rival caliphs while praying at a nearby mosque. His remains, sacred to all Shiites, had been buried in the shrine for thirteen centuries. For a Shiite Muslim, Najaf was second only to Mecca in terms of holy significance. Every year thousands of families paid large sums of money to have deceased relatives buried in the environs of Ali's tomb. Najaf was a trading center, but its biggest business was religion, particularly the brand of Shiite Islam common to Saddam's opponents. The last thing the Americans wished to do was get involved in a destructive battle for this holy place, thus risking the alienation of the very people who were most likely to want Saddam and his Sunni elite gone.[30]

So on March 23, the Cottonbalers had orders to secure the escarpment. The plan was for 3-69 to go first, take the escarpment, bear east, and protect that flank while 2-7 followed, roared over the escarpment, and fanned out to the west. The unit leading the whole attack was none other than Captain Todd Kelly's Charlie 2-7. They were well suited for this kind of battle. "We had prepared for a similar mission . . . at NTC," in the fall of 2002, Captain Kelly said. "At that time NTC set up a . . . causeway where we fought basically down a two-lane road for several kilometers into a fortified position. It was very similar to our fight going into the escarpment." Kelly deployed three platoons in the following manner: In the lead he placed a mixed platoon of two tanks and two Bradleys. Right behind them was a full platoon of Bradleys followed by another mixed platoon. Charlie Company was in a roadbound column. The ground around the road was marshy, with wet, glutinous sand. There was no artillery support because this attack had come together so quickly and the guns could not keep up. There was some close air support from A-10s. Kelly could see them flying east to west, raking over enemy foxholes on the escarpment. When Kelly's troops were about three thousand meters from the escarpment, they began to see signs of the enemy. There were fighting holes, dug-in ADA guns, and some trucks too.

The Iraqis opened fire with mortars, ADA, and small arms. The Cottonbalers deployed into fighting formations and began to return fire. In one of the lead Bradleys, Staff Sergeant Andrew Sorenson and his gunner, Private First Class Nathan Bennett, identified a quad-barreled anti-aircraft gun mounted on a pickup truck. "As soon as we get within range of the TOW, go ahead and tell me. We'll stop and raise the TOW and light it up," Sorenson said.

Moments later, the TOW box was raised and Bennett was ready to shoot. "All I could see was the barrel sticking up over a berm. I just kept lasing it, and as soon as we got within range of it . . . I shot." The TOW missile whooshed out of the box. Bennett kept it right on target. On and on it flew for several thousand meters, locking right onto the truck. In one sonic moment, it hit the truck. "It blew the truck up. It was just like a movie explosion, something you'd see in a movie. It was just unreal. As soon as it hit, there was just a big fireball. That's all you could see. Then we started pushing forward."

When they got within range for the 25mm gun, Bennett opened up. Standing right next to him, in the commander's slot, Sorenson noticed a puff of smoke from the escarpment: "It looked like an antitank missile signature, so we popped our turret smoke and backed up." As they did so, a tank and a Bradley got stuck in the sand. Kelly's mechanics, Donald Gimlin, Dennis Buse, and Michael Gilmour, drove up and attempted to extract the vehicles, all under fire. Sergeant Sorenson, unaware that the artillery was out of range, requested, through his lieutenant, a fire mission on the spot where they had seen the puff of smoke. They waited for what seemed like an eternity and still no artillery.

At this same time, Captain Kelly was hollering into his radio, telling them to get moving up the escarpment. The captain knew that constant motion and suppression were the keys to taking this position. He also knew that the Iraqis had not shot an antitank missile at Sorenson's track. However, Sorenson could not hear the captain. His radio was only good for speaking to his platoon, not the whole company. Sorenson never did hear Kelly. On his own, he decided to go forward. The remaining unstuck tank and another Bradley in his platoon went with him. Together they rumbled on the dusty road and began the ascent. Behind them, more American vehicles warily trod forward. They were all under mortar, RPG, and small-arms fire. In return, the GIs were shooting back with their 25's.

Sorenson and his tank buddy were now in the middle of the escarpment. Iraqi fire was coming from either flank. The Americans were keeping up a steady volume of fire, but then a dreaded glitch happened. In a few horrible instants, the other Bradley's gun malfunctioned and Sorenson's turret got stuck. Sorenson had never felt so hopeless and frightened in his life. The Iraqis knew right where he was. How long would it take them to fire an antitank missile or some sort of antiaircraft round that would slash through the armor of his Bradley and waste everyone? He could not escape the fatalistic thought that they were all about to die. The other Bradley commander felt the same way. That being the case, there was no sense in keeping the dismounts cooped up. Maybe they could get out of the vehicles and somehow survive. As Sorenson frantically labored to get his turret working again, he told his driver to lower the ramp and he shouted into his CVC, "Dismount!"

In the back of Sorenson's Bradley, Sergeant Curtis Kelly, the Missouri kid, had been listening to Sorenson's running conversation with the other Bradley commander but had little idea what was going on. When the order to dismount came, Sergeant Kelly and his team scrambled out of the Bradley as fast as they could. In the first moment outside of the Bradley, he saw that there were foxholes on either side of the road. He also saw that there was no cover or concealment anywhere for his guys. "There was just no place for us to go, so we kind of used the Bradleys for cover for a minute while we got everybody together." This was hardly standard procedure. Usually a fire team would spread out in a choreographed tactical formation on either side of the Bradley. In this case, though, Kelly was doing the exact right thing. He had no idea of the enemy's strength or location or even what his mission was supposed to be, so it made sense for him to keep everyone under cover while he assessed what to do. He heard the crackle of small-arms fire and mortar rounds exploding. He could hear the popping sounds of 25mm guns coming from farther down the escarpment. That must be the rest of the company.

Kelly's soldiers were in the process of exiting the Bradley and getting situated behind the cover of the vehicle. The Missourian peeked around the edge of the Bradley for a look at the right side of the escarpment. In the nearest foxhole, he saw a man waving a white flag. "All right, these guys are gonna give up," he thought. The thought had no sooner passed through his mind when the same man took aim and fired his AK-47, all the while with his white flag tied to the end of it. Kelly ducked back behind the Bradley and saw rounds impacting in the dirt a few feet away. He turned to his fire team. "I don't give a fuck if you're ready—let's go!"

In a flurry they moved as they had been trained, in short rushes, laying down suppressive fire, closing on the enemy foxholes. Sergeant Kelly himself took aim with his M16 and squeezed off a shot that he was sure hit the flag waver in the arm. In what seemed like seconds but was probably minutes, Kelly and his people were among the enemy foxholes. "They had foxholes every ten or fifteen feet all along the escarpment." The men chucked grenades into the holes, then assaulted them with careful three- or five-shot bursts. The sergeant was vaguely aware that, at some point, Sorenson's Bradley and the other one were back on-line, providing supporting fire. Their 25mm guns spat out rounds at the area beyond the dismounts, kicking up rocks and dust, smashing into the flesh of any Iraqis who were unlucky enough to be in their way.

The rest of Kelly's squad, under the direction of the squad leader Staff Sergeant Patrick Taylor, was also working over the foxholes near Sergeant Kelly's team. On the other side of the road, more dismounted infantrymen from other squads were doing the same thing. Captain Kelly, from the vantage point of his Bradley in the middle of the column as it ascended the escarpment, could see his infantrymen fighting at close quarters. "Basically the Bradleys came up . . . provided some overwatch . . . and suppressive fire. Someone would suppress [the foxhole]; they would go up and use a hand grenade and clear the bunker."

The assault was over in twenty minutes. In clearing a whole nest of foxholes, Sergeant Kelly's team alone had killed three enemy soldiers and captured fifteen others. "It was pretty intense but we cleared it like it was training. We did it right. It worked."

The combat vehicles drove over the escarpment and onto the plateau. The dismounts dealt with prisoners. Sergeant Kelly's team caught a high-ranking officer. "He kept telling us to kill him there because he didn't want to go through the torture that Saddam was gonna put him through." The Americans tried to calm him down, but to no avail. "Kill me now!" he begged. "Saddam will kill me, pull off my toes!"

Kelly and the others, as typical Americans, could not comprehend such fear of a dictator. The more the man carried on, the more annoyed they got. "He was saying all kinds of weird shit. We just gave him a bottle of water and told him to shut up." The infantry soldiers ran down a few more Iraqis who were trying to escape in civilian clothes, cuffed them, and put them in an improvised holding area with their countrymen. Some of the POW s were scared to death. They dropped to their knees and shouted, "Mistah, mistah, don't shoot!" They had been told that the Americans would kill them, but the GIs quickly disabused them of those notions. They gave them water and some MREs and even conversed with those who could speak English.

On the plateau beyond the escarpment, the Bradleys and tanks of Charlie 2-7 found more targets. Iraqi militia fighters were coming out of Najaf, mostly in trucks, trying to prevent the Americans from keeping control of the escarpment. Bennett, the gunner, watched as three trucks, with mounted antiaircraft guns, drove toward his group of Bradleys. "There was two of 'em that came up together and the other one was trailing behind. Before they could even turn around we were hitting 'em . . . with AP and then the tanks were hitting 'em with main rounds. I remember the LT's tank hit one of 'em."

These trucks were easy targets, but other enemy fighters were better hidden. The Bradleys and tanks were moving at a fast clip, gaining ground, shooting at whatever looked dangerous. However, moving this fast made it more difficult to spot targets and shoot accurately. Bennett and Sorenson were fixated on what appeared to be enemy fighters getting in and out of trucks near a small shack. Bennett was buttoned up in his gunner's seat. Sorenson was standing in his turret, partly exposed. All of a sudden, Sorenson's peripheral vision picked up something streaking toward him from the left. "What the fuck is that?" he wondered. He soon got an answer. An RPG was sailing through the air, right at him! "It was so close to me . . . that my boom mike picked it up. [The sound] went over the intercom system." The rocket sailed past, missing his head by about a foot. Immediately Bennett and the two tanks traversed left and saw that the RPG shot had come from a complex of buildings and berms on the left. They sprayed the place with everything in their arsenal, blasting the buildings and wiping out the berms.

Gradually the Cottonbalers ran out of targets. "Everything was secure escarpment-wise by 1500 or 1600," Captain Kelly asserted. The area around the escarpment was littered with dead enemy, burning trucks, and even a few stuck American vehicles. Along line of vehicles from 3-69 and 2-7 began streaming over the escarpment. The Americans were through this daunting terrain feature and beyond, but the area was still under intermittent mortar and artillery fire. Indeed, two Charlie Company men got shrapnel wounds, but they were minor. Mostly the enemy fire was inaccurate albeit unnerving.

To newly hardened combat soldiers like Sergeant Kelly, it was nothing more than background noise. When the Bradleys charged onto the plateau, he and the other dismounts had been told they would come back to pick them up. As they waited for the rides to return, they placed guards on the prisoners and settled down to rest. "We just picked out a trench line . . . started drinking some water and talking about the little firefight we just got into. Artillery rounds started coming in. Everybody had their K-Pots off, rounds were hitting over there, and we were just sitting laughing at all these people [rear-echelon types] running around. I saw a major drop his weapon and start running."

The major ran two hundred meters and plopped into the trench with Kelly's fire team. "This is the second time today," he wailed. The officer was a National Guard doctor. The infantry soldiers had no sympathy for him. "He started crying and we just sat there laughing at him. It was hilarious." Shortly after that, the Bradleys came back, picked up their dismounts, and resumed the advance north.[31]

All afternoon and evening, American vehicles poured over the escarpment. In 2-7 the scouts were in the lead. Such was the confusion of the moment that some of them thought they were at the spear point of the whole division, attacking a fortified position by themselves. They rolled to the peak of the escarpment only to discover a myriad of American vehicles all over the place. The scouts were mostly relieved and a little disappointed. They drove past burnt-out vehicles that Charlie Company had destroyed. Inside were the remains of Iraqi soldiers. Lieutenant Gleason got his first close-up look at dead bodies. "They were just crispy critters. You could see their white teeth, but they were just charred. You can't even tell they're human beings really. The vehicles were completely burned out." Standing right behind Gleason, in the gunner's turret of the Humvee, Sergeant Davis saw the truck that Bennett's TOW had destroyed during the early stages of the fight for the escarpment. "You could smell the bodies in this truck burning. They had pointed their gun tube down the road. The truck was on fire. You could see three dudes sitting in the cab of it, all shrunken and burning up."

The scouts and Bravo Company fanned out to the west and came upon a fenced-in complex. Gleason's Humvees got out of the way while Bravo's Bradleys plowed through the fences and into the complex. It consisted of roughly twenty warehouse buildings that contained all manner of weapons. The garrison of about a hundred soldiers surrendered quickly. To the north was another complex with bunkers. Some suspected it of being a WMD site. Bravo Company also quickly seized this complex against almost no opposition. At times they took some mortar fire, but mostly the seizure of the whole compound was unopposed.

Some Iraqis, instead of surrendering, tried to take off into the night. Such was the level of American restraint at this point that instead of shooting them in the back, the Americans would usually try to chase them down. Naturally many got away. Captain Lee, the armor commander, grew so tired of this tedious process that he called Major Coffey and asked in exasperation, "Can't I just kill them?"

When Coffey heard this question, his face fell. "Jeez, if I tell this guy to do so, men are immediately going to die who might otherwise live," he thought. To this point, the Iraqis had performed like incompetent bumblers. They really had not posed much of a threat to the Americans, creating a sense of invincibility among the Cottonbalers. Coffey even felt a little bit sorry for the Iraqis.

"Well, no, let's still try to capture them," Coffey ordered Lee. The major found it very troubling that, at that moment, he had the power of life and death. He turned to Sergeant Kenneth Stephens, his gunner. "I didn't like that."

"Yeah, I know. I could tell by your face," Stephens replied.

In a matter of a few days, Coffey would have no such compunctions.

The Bravo Company men spent the better part of the evening clearing out empty bunkers, confiscating weapons, and escorting prisoners to a battalion collection point. "We spent all night just running these guys back and forth," Specialist Beck recalled. "We would pick some up, drop them off, pick some up, drop them off. "Most of the prisoners had no desire to fight for Saddam. They were scared and hungry.[32]

IN A MERE FOUR DAYS the Cottonbalers, and much of the 3rd Division, had traveled more than two hundred miles. The Marne soldiers had gotten into some fights, bypassed some resistance, and mostly rolled north against little opposition, but they could not keep up this pace. The deeper into Iraq they got, the more daunting it was to supply them. The Americans were having trouble keeping main supply routes open and getting necessary matériel forward to leading units like the 7th Infantry. Enemy fighters were ambushing some supply convoys (the most notorious example being the bushwack of several trucks from Private Jessica Lynch's 507th Maintenance Company at An Nasiriyah). This ambush problem was a vexing one that would eventually plague the American war in Iraq.

More than enemy action, though, the main challenges now were distance, terrain, and climate. Wheeled vehicles were not holding up well in the desert, and as mentioned, lead combat units were far away from supply depots. Combat officers like Coffey were not impressed with the performance of their logistical colleagues in forward and division support units: "We were kind of disappointed in some of our logistical leadership. They should have done better. We were not happy with a lot of the logistical world. At times there was very much a lack of push and drive, it seemed to me. "It got so bad that 2-7's support platoon had to go back to a division depot to pick up supplies: "It's not their job to do that. They're doing that because someone else had failed to do their job."

These failures on the part of the divisional support staff made the job of Captain Scott Knight, 2-7's S–4, much tougher. Major Coffey, frustrated with the supply issues, would say to Knight, "Goddamn, Scott, I thought I was in the American Army, not the Albanian Army."

"Oh, sir, they're all fucked up back there," Knight would reply. There was little that Captain Knight could do. At some point, the rear-echelon types had to push supplies forward to combat units, not vice versa.

Among the soldiers of 2-7 and 3-7, the supply problems meant that they did not have enough water or MREs. Soldiers were making do with one or two bottles of water and a couple of MREs per day. They were getting ammo, but replacement parts for vehicles were nonexistent. The brigade commander, Colonel Will Grimsley, had little choice but to halt their operations while all of this got sorted out.

Thus, as the sun rose on March 24, the TOC and other lead elements of 2-7 settled down in a cluster of onion fields known on their maps as Objective Raiders. Crude mud homes, reminiscent of Native American adobe dwellings, bordered the onion fields. The horizon, fringed with dust and rocks, hinted at the nearby desert. Planners had randomly named this place after the Oakland Raiders. Here the Cottonbalers from both 2-7 and 3-7 now established blocking positions between Highways 28 and 9, north of Najaf, regulating movement to and from the city. Objective Raiders and its environs would be home to the Cottonbalers for most of the next week.

Even with proper supplies, it would have been difficult to keep going. "Everyone was completely drained and exhausted from the previous seventy-two hours of contact and movement," a 2-7 officer recalled. Throughout the day on March 24, Cottonbaler units converged on Objective Raiders and, grateful for a much-needed respite, set up in weary perimeters. This included Captain Smith's Rage Company, which had finally finished its Miracle Mile odyssey and linked back up with the rest of 2-7. Smith felt this was a defining moment for his company: "That gave the unit a lot of pride in themselves, that we could do something like that. That really built the will and strength of this company." When Captain Smith walked into the 2-7 TOC, Major Cooney and Captain Sam Donnelly, the assistant S–3, greeted him with hugs, like a long-lost brother. "For some reason they thought we were just goners. Everyone was so happy and excited to see us."[33]

The giddiness soon wore off In one of the onion fields a small group of Iraqi fighters carefully crawled to within rifle range of the unwitting Americans. One of the Iraqis found a target, aimed, and pulled the trigger. The single shot pierced the silence. Less than a second later the bullet tore into Specialist Gregory Sanders, a tank crewman from Bravo 3-69 who was standing atop his Abrams, adjusting some items. The round struck just under his helmet, right in his neck, where the cerebellum meets the spine. Sanders collapsed and died in a matter of seconds.

It took a few minutes for the men in the surrounding tracks to realize what had just happened. Sanders's crewmates rushed to him, but it was too late. He was gone. In the other Bradleys and tanks the word spread like electricity through a wire. There was a sniper. Someone was down. A few hundred meters from Sanders's tank, Specialist Brian Butler was sitting inside a Rage Company Bradley. When he heard the shot and realized that a sniper had hit Sanders, Butler blinked in stunned, fearful surprise. Mere seconds before the shot, he had been standing atop his Bradley taking footage with his video camera. What an ideal target he must have been! "Jeez, I was just standing on top of the Bradley," he thought, "and the other guy gets shot." Like so many other survivors of combat, he could only wonder why he had been lucky enough to live.

Where moments before the perimeter had been the very picture of idyllic relaxation, now it was a scene of consternation and activity. The Americans, sprung to full alertness now, were vigorously searching for the whereabouts of the sniper. All sorts of conflicting, confusing reports clogged the radio waves. Lieutenant Gleason was sitting in his Humvee, some four hundred meters from Sanders, listening to the excited voices on the net. The lieutenant told Sergeant Gaines to scan in the general direction where the shot seemed to have come from. Gaines's Humvee was right next to Gleason's, but he had the best view of the suspected location of the sniper. Standing behind Gaines, Sergeant Farrell, the Mark 19 gunner, scanned with his L-RASS. At first he saw nothing. Then, ever so slowly, there seemed to be movement. He looked closer. Yes, there was definitely some sort of movement out there. "I saw some hot bodies in this onion field. This was, like, two hundred meters in front of us. I saw three guys . . . crawling in rows." The men had weapons strapped to their backs. Farrell excitedly reported this to Gaines, who dutifully told Gleason. The lieutenant called Colonel Rutter and promptly got permission to fire.

Farrell unloaded three quick rounds from his Mark 19. The neighboring tracks, spotting where the Mark 19s had landed, lit up the surrounding terrain. Sergeant Farrell pumped round after round out there until he had gone through his entire box of thirty-two Mark 19 grenades. When he looked through the L-RASS again, the Iraqis seemed to be gone. Had they gotten away? Just what in hell was going on?

While Farrell was shooting at the suspected enemy sniper team, Captain Smith ordered his Bradleys to cordon off the area and his dismounts to get out and search the mud huts. The dismounts painstakingly went through the little huts. Most had entrances that were little more than two feet high. Sergeant Charles Johnson, a blond-haired fire team leader, was a short guy, probably no more than five feet five or six, but even he had a difficult time getting through the doorways of these huts. "When you've got all your gear on, you just can't hardly get up in there. You've gotta go, like, sideways to get . . . in there." The soldiers found a few discarded Iraqi Army uniforms along with some chickens and dogs, but no people.

Undoubtedly there had been people in there only a few minutes before, but they had scattered. Sergeant Driggers, the Bradley gunner, was stationed in his vehicle, right outside one house, protecting Sergeant Johnson and other dismounts as they searched one hut. All at once, Driggers saw people emerge from the adjacent hut. "These five guys just jetted out of the house, jumped in their trucks and [took off]." Driggers asked for permission to engage, but the men were gone before he could get approval. Was one of these men the sniper? We will never know.

When Captain Smith was sure there was nobody inside the huts, he ordered the Bradleys to level them. There was no more shooting now for the simple reason that there was nothing to shoot at. Rifle squads swept through the area where Farrell had seen the men crawling. They found no intact bodies—only parts of bodies. "All they found was pieces of hands and fingers and arms and legs and feet . . . catastrophic kills," Sergeant Davis, Gleason's gunner, said. This was consistent with the way that Mark 19 rounds would kill or maim. They had a kill radius of five meters, and their deadly fragments, combined with .50-caliber fire, were certainly capable of shredding people into tiny pieces. Did Farrell kill the sniper? Again we will never know.

Medics dealt with the body of Gregory Sanders. They laid it between a couple of tracks and carefully cataloged his personal effects. Master Sergeant Winston Kelly was a mechanic, not a medic, but he had once served in 3-69 and he knew Sanders. Kelly walked over to pay his last respects: "That's my first experience with seeing someone that I knew . . .

dead. I took a good look at him. He looked like he was sleeping until I looked and saw his . . . skull just wide open."

Sanders was the first man to lose his life in combat with 2-7 since the Korean War, a period of fifty years. The Americans, riding around in their powerful armored vehicles, had, to this point, felt invincible. The low casualties suffered in the Gulf War against the Iraqis only enhanced that sense of immortality. Since no one, from Rutter on down, was old enough to have experienced Vietnam, there was no institutional memory that ground wars could be costly. Instead, there was a naive expectation that wars could be fought without American soldiers getting killed. The death of Sanders was a wake-up call that Americans could and did get killed in war. He was nineteen and left behind a young widow and daughter.[34]

The day after the sniper killed Sanders, a powerful sandstorm hit central Iraq. The storm played hell with everything. Supply convoys had even more problems than before. Only vehicles equipped with FBCB2s could find their way around. Staff officers in the TOC had to use a vacuum to clean their maps of sand. Walking anywhere was an exercise in futility. Swirling, dusty grains of sand whipped around like tiny razors. Anyone standing outside with exposed skin soon regretted it, as the sand lashed against faces, arms, and necks. Cleaning weapons was a sheer impossibility. The minute a man cleaned one part, it was already inundated with sand before he even finished cleaning the next part. The sand was so thick that men got lost if they strayed more than a few yards from their vehicles.

Most of the troops simply hunkered down, in vehicles or any other kind of shelter, and tried to wait the storm out. The whole experience was disorientating, strange, like being in another world. "You felt like you were on Mars," one rifleman said. The swirling sand, combined with rain and the low clouds that obscured the sun, bathed everything in an eerie orange-reddish glow. Captain Carter said it was like being cooped up in "a small closet . . . [with] a red bulb . . . in there and . . . a whole bunch of sand around you." Sergeant Vongsvirates, the leader of the Psy-Ops team, slept in his Humvee during the storm. After several hours of fitful sleep, he discovered that he was covered with sand. He looked in the mirror and recoiled. He had so much mud, grime, and sand streaked over his face that he looked forty years older.

Like Sergeant Vongsvirates, Lieutenant Gleason mostly stayed in his Humvee. The sand was so overwhelming, so engulfing, that Gleason, Camelin, and Davis could hardly see outside. All they could hear was the whipping sound of millions of grains of sand colliding with their Humvee. When the sun set and the storm continued, the darkness was overwhelming. They could not see their hands in front of their faces. At one point, Gleason grabbed Camelin by the shoulder and joked, "Hey, man, are we dead?"

Camelin chuckled, shook his head, and said, "Oh no, sir, this is crazy."

Gleason certainly agreed. He and his men could do little about it, though. "It was very strange. I mean, you had sand in every orifice of your body. It got into all your equipment and we had to clean out our engines. Our weapons were just clogged with sand."

As bad as the storm was, it did allow the men to catch up on some rest while logistical officers figured out how to resupply them and commanders mulled over their next moves. Knowing that the Iraqis were probably hindered by the storm even more than the Americans (with all their sophisticated equipment), units generally engaged in only bare minimum security. Mostly they stayed put, existed, and waited.[35]

However, to the south, where the storm was not as bad, two companies from 3-7 did pull missions. Captain Will Neubauer's Charlie 3-7 repeatedly assaulted a Fedayeen ADA complex that many officers felt was responsible for continued mortar and artillery fire on U.S. troops as they moved over the escarpment. The Fedayeen were militiamen of sorts. Most were loyal to Saddam and the Baath Party. They wore a mixture of civilian and military clothing and generally functioned as light infantry. Neubauer's company killed several Fedayeen, captured several more, and had some very close calls. The captain himself came close to dying more than once. In the first attack, an RPG hit his Bradley. "It just hit in front of the vehicle and destroyed our MREs and water. Nothing happened to the vehicle itself, not even a scorch mark." He and his crew never found the RPG crew.

The next time they assaulted the compound, it was unoccupied but still under artillery fire. A round hit the captain's Bradley on the back sprocket: "It looked like my whole Bradley went up on fire. The smoke coming off my Bradley was pitch-black. I lost all electronics; my communication devices all went down. My halon bottles exploded. Right behind me was my battalion commander [Lieutenant Colonel Kammerer] and he kinda decided I was out of it and started turning around and running back with my company, pulling back." While the commanding officer fled, First Sergeant Edwin Garcia pushed forward with the first-aid track to save his captain. He found that Neubauer was not "out of it." Amazingly, he and his crew were unhurt. Luckily, they were not carrying any dismounts in their track.

With Neubauer OK, his men set about clearing the compound. They found a series of fighting caves and blew them in with grenades. They also found weapons and ammo. Engineers wired all of it up and blew it in place. As Neubauer supervised, he thought of how lucky his unit had been to emerge from this unscathed. He kept thinking of his promise to bring everyone home alive. He now wondered, and even doubted a little bit, if he could do so.

The soldiers of Charlie 3-7 were not pleased with their colonel. Privately, they—and many other 3-7 combat soldiers—considered Lieutenant Colonel Kammerer as a nice guy, but a coward. He rode around buttoned up in his track. The way the soldiers saw it, when Neubauer was hit, Kammerer seemed more than ready to abandon him to save his own skin. Perhaps these were just perceptions and a bit unfair, but where soldiers were concerned, perceptions of leadership were reality. If combat soldiers thought an officer was cowardly or inadequate, then he might as well have been, for he would be worthless in their eyes. Kammerer's standing in 3-7 was not high. Conversely, the soldiers of 2-7, save for some of the NCOs, admired and respected Lieutenant Colonel Rutter, whose courage and commitment were beyond question.[36]

AS NEUBAUER'S CHARLIE 3-7 CLEANED out the Fedayeen complex, Bravo 3-7 drew the mission of securing a bridge over the Euphrates River in the town of Al Kifl. Their purpose was not to forge a permanent crossing of the river; instead, they were supposed to deny the bridge to the enemy and establish blocking positions. Basically, they were supposed to hold the eastern flank for their immediate parent unit, Task Force 3-69 and the whole 1st Brigade.

On March 25 the company lined up in column formation and drove east to Al Kifl. When they were within sight of the town, they began to take mortar and rifle fire from enemy soldiers who were in holes along the road and in hidden positions within the town. "We had multiple RPG's hitting us at the front of the column," Captain Dave Benton, commander of Bravo 3-7, remembered. The Americans kept moving, returned fire at the holes, and began scanning for the mortar positions. The 60mm mortar rounds were exploding uncomfortably close to Staff Sergeant Steven Collier's Bradley. Collier, the Virginia native, was scanning everywhere. All at once, he and his gunner saw a man who was tied into a tree. "I don't know if he was their FO or what, but, sure enough, he was up in the trees." They blew him away. The man's body hung limply from the ropes he had been using to tie himself to the tree.

The Americans quickly pushed into the town and up to the bridge. Some of the Bradley commanders were disgorging their infantrymen to deal with whatever mortar positions remained in the town. At one position near the bridge, Sergeant Rudy Belloc and his small group of infantrymen were assaulting an enemy mortar pit. "The Bradleys had seen it while they were driving clown [on overwatch]. The Bradleys lit it up with HE [High Explosive]." The crew was behind a concrete blocker and they were in no mood to fight: "On the other side of the slab they had mortar rounds in a big old box. Well, the HE round hit the box, so it was on fire. As we were trying to get the EPW's away from that spot, the mortar rounds started shooting up and exploding. Stuff was blowing up everywhere." They hustled the prisoners out of there immediately.

First Sergeant Fraziar Harris was in his 113 at the rear of the column, outside of the town with the company trains. This was right where he was supposed to be, but he was not happy. He was listening to the company net, hearing contact report after contact report. He yearned to be up front with his guys. He turned to his driver. "You know what? I'm not staying back here."

They drove to the bridge and took in the chaotic scene of the company in combat, and Harris's chest swelled with pride. "I saw vehicles supporting infantry on the ground, infantry clearing buildings, taking prisoners, happening simultaneously on either side of the road. I would say it was picture perfect. There was a guy dropping mortars on us. [Somebody] shot some HE rounds over there and . . . blew that guy's butt off. I had the utmost confidence in the company."

An officer saw Harris and was worried about the first sergeant's safety. "You shouldn't be up here now. It's not safe."

"I've got nothing to worry about," Harris confidently replied.

Not far away, the two lead tanks rolled right over the bridge, to the east side of the Euphrates. Other vehicles were following. The Iraqis, mostly Fedayeen types, attempted to blow up the bridge with preset demolition charges. They did something wrong, because instead of collapsing into the water and carrying the American vehicles with it, the bridge was still intact, albeit damaged. Captain Benton believed that one of his tank lieutenants had killed the enemy officer responsible for detonating the bridge.

Whatever the reason for the failed detonation, the battalion commander, Lieutenant Colonel Ernest (Rock) Marcone, ordered every vehicle off the bridge. One by one the Bradleys and tanks backed off the bridge. When it came time for Specialist Swears to back up his Bradley, he relied on spoken directions from his vehicle commander, since there was no rearview mirror in his driver's slot. The college-educated Swears had joined the Army a year before for two reasons: to repay his college loans and to get some payback for the terrorist attacks on his home state of New York. He could never have imagined how close he was about to come to dying.

At the vocal cue of his commander, Swears backed up and hit the gas pedal. The commander stopped talking, so Swears assumed he was going in the right direction. "His intercom with me got disconnected." Hearing nothing from his commander and having no clue that the intercom was out, Swears kept backing up. After a few seconds of this, something—he didn't know what—made him hit the brakes. Up in the turret, his commander was screaming at him to stop, but he could not hear him over the engine noise. Swears happened to glance to his left and what he saw made his blood run cold. "I was dangling . . . probably close to three quarters off the bridge. It was about a hundred foot drop. The dismounts in the back were yelling 'Stop! Stop! Stop!' This was all going on while we were still receiving incoming fire."

Swears could hardly believe the heavy Bradley had not fallen into the river, drowning everyone inside. The thing was teetering precariously over the side of the bridge. It seemed like anything, even the wind, could blow them over. In the Bradley right behind Swears, his wingman, Specialist Brandon Moore, watched, horror-stricken, as all of this developed. Swears's Bradley seemed almost suspended in air. Moore drove his Bradley over to Swears, hopped out, hooked up a towing cable, got back into his driver's seat, and tugged him off the bridge. "I thought they were gonna fall off," Moore said. "I wouldn't have wanted to be on there."

When all the vehicles were finally off the bridge, Marcone pondered what to do about the two stranded tanks. He ordered a group of infantrymen to go to the bridge and make sure it had no more explosives. They did so. For a time he explored the idea of sending infantry across on canoes, but he discarded the idea. Eventually he himself crossed the bridge on foot—even though it was covered with the bodies of dead enemy fighters—and made contact with his tankers. Engineers repaired the bridge and Marcone then crossed it with his own tank. In his wake, Lieutenant Brad Castro and his platoon of Bradleys got across and pulled security on the town's main thoroughfare.

In the meantime, the rest of Bravo 3-7 secured positions in the town, along a northerly road that paralleled the river. About this time, the sandstorm came to Al Kifl, limiting everyone's visibility, turning this into a protracted, close-in fight. The sand swirled around the Americans in brownish-orange clouds. Bradleys took up positions covering the road and the bridge. Dismounts holed up in buildings or behind Bradleys, spitting sand out of their mouths and keeping an eye out for the enemy.

Afternoon turned into evening. The Fedayeen wanted the bridge back. They began a series of furious counterattacks. They drove up in pickup trucks and attempted to drop off infantry soldiers to infiltrate the American positions. The storm was so bad now that the Bradley and Abrams crews were lucky to see four hundred meters away, even with their thermals and night-vision devices. "They were coming down the road," Sergeant Collier said. "They had their . . . headlights on. We couldn't see 'em in the thermals but my driver was picking 'em up in his night sights. He could see the two little dots where they had their headlights on. We'd have to wait 'til the gunner could see 'em. Then we'd shoot 'em."

Not far from Collier's Bradley, Specialist Joseph Blum engaged a steady stream of enemy fighters who were driving toward the Americans in trucks, hoping to get within RPG range: "It was just nonstop firing . . . for two or three hours. You would see two buildings. You'd be shooting at guys in between buildings. They'd drop. Then you'd see another guy peek out, look around and try running. You'd just shoot him." Other Fedayeen actually tried hiding behind bushes in the erroneous belief that the Americans could not see them. Blum shook his head, fixed them with the laser-guided system on his gun, and opened fire. "Can they be any dumber?" he wondered. Lieutenant Castro, whose platoon on the other side of the bridge was dealing with the same kind of head-on attacks, ascribed the enemy tactics to fanaticism. "They weren't afraid to jump in the car and go meet Allah in a few seconds."

As Castro indicated, most of the enemy fighters got killed or wounded before they ever got out of their trucks. However, a few successfully exited their vehicles and slithered, with the help of the sandstorm, through the urban terrain and into the midst of the Cottonbalers. The night was tense with sand blowing everywhere, mortars exploding, and the sound of shooting echoing among the buildings.

Staff Sergeant Collier's Bradley was in an alleyway. There were no dismounts in the back. They were all outside, hunkered down in buildings or behind whatever cover they could find. He and his crewmen were scanning for targets, trying as gamely as they could to see through the sandy maw. Suddenly they heard an explosion on the side of their track. Somehow an enemy RPG team had gotten close enough to shoot and hit them: "It went through the side skirt and right into the track. We drove forward." By driving forward he was hoping to find and outflank the RPG crew. Collier's driver and his gunner were buttoned up inside the track, but not Collier. He was standing partly exposed in his commander's cupola. The sergeant was scanning around, looking for trouble spots. All at once he saw a flash come from the doorway of a nearby building. Before he could even react, an RPG streaked through the night and headed straight for his turret.

Sergeant Rudy Belloc was on the ground, a few meters away, watching the horrifying scene unfold. He could hear the airy whistling sound of the RPG as it sailed toward Collier. Belloc felt completely powerless. "[It] hit probably ten inches from where his head was and then it bounced off the track and hit against the wall of a building." Collier only saw a flash and heard an explosion. Instinctively he ducked down inside the Bradley. For several awful moments, Belloc thought the RPG had taken Collier's head off. Then, ever so tentatively, the Virginian peeked out of his commander's hatch. Belloc breathed a huge sigh of relief. In his estimation, only one foot of space, along with some pretty darned good armor, had stood between Collier and decapitating death.

Now that the shock of this close call had faded, Collier's gunner, Belloc, and the other dismounts fired everything they had at the Iraqi RPG team. The Iraqis ran as fast as they could and attempted to take cover behind a destroyed truck. The combination of 25mm, machine-gun, grenade, and rifle fire turned them into mush.

The fight at Al Kift lasted all night. The enemy kept up a steady volume of inaccurate fire. "Through the night, we were . . . engaging enemies trying to probe our defense line and test our thermal imaging system," Lieutenant Castro recalled. "We even had guys crawling with packs of dogs to see if they could find out where we were."

The Americans did not want to waste ammo. Already they were running low on high-explosive ammo and First Sergeant Harris was worried that this fight would continue with no resupply. Not until morning was he able to start bringing in more ammo and water. Meanwhile, Sergeant Belloc's fire team—and many others around Al Kifl—spent the night and much of the next morning returning fire whenever they saw targets. "I don't think they were knowing what they were shooting at. They were just letting them go. The machine guns, what they were shooting at . . . you could see 'em walking it. You'd see 'em hit the . . . road or hit the street beside the building where we were at or hit the Bradley. You could hear it clinking off the Bradley. There were a lot of close calls, but God was with us and nothing happened to us."

By late morning on March 26, most of the Fedayeen counterattackers had been killed or driven off. The carnage around the town was sobering and disgusting. "The next day we had . . . a pile of cars out in front of our positions," Collier said. "There was probably a pile of ten cars . . . there." Dismembered enemy bodies were lying everywhere.

Late in the day, with the sandstorm still raging, another unit relieved Bravo 3-7. The Cottonbalers were exhausted, filthy, thirsty, and hungry. They loaded aboard their Bradleys and left Al Kifl. In all, the fight had lasted thirty-six hours. The troops of Bravo 3-7 had more than done their job. Not only had they held the brigade flank, but they had also denied a vital bridge to the Fedayeen and inflicted terrible damage upon them. First Sergeant Harris estimated enemy losses at twenty to thirty vehicles and over two hundred men. The Americans took no casualties.[37]

BACK AT OBJECTIVE RAIDERS, RUTTER'S 2-7 continued to man roadblocks along Highway 9. In the wake of the sandstorm, 2-7 lost another soldier, but this time it was to accident, not enemy fire. The locals in this area drew their water from centuries-old wells that burrowed as deep as sixty feet into the earth. The wells were difficult to spot. One night, a Bradley from Rage Company, while returning from a patrol, fell right into a well. The Bradley was commanded by First Lieutenant Mike Gruber. He suffered broken bones but was lucky to survive, because the forward motion of the tumbling Bradley hurled everyone and everything toward his turret and the front of the vehicle in general. The soldiers inside were piled on top of one another. One of them, Sergeant Roderic Solomon, got hit in the back of the head by an equipment box, which crushed his skull. By the time medics and other soldiers got to the scene and extracted Solomon and the others from the Bradley, he was fading. The medics desperately tried to save Solomon, but he died at the scene. In total, six soldiers were wounded. Several, such as Staff Sergeant Jon Dixon, had to be medevaced—the Cottonbalers were highly agitated that it took nearly three hours for the medevac helicopter to arrive. The accident caused permanent paralysis for the unfortunate Dixon. The others eventually recovered, but the trauma of the terrible accident never left them.[38]

In the wake of the accident, the Cottonbalers kept up their daily routine of manning roadblocks, conducting patrols, dealing with the local people, and, every now and then, engaging in small firefights with ragged groups of enemy fighters. The Americans were getting sick and tired of Objective Raiders or "the sheep shit place," as one soldier called it. Supplies were now getting to them and men were catching up on sleep, but they were tired of sitting in this weird locale. Most soldiers were antsy to keep pushing for Baghdad. After all, they thought that was the ticket back to the States. In the minds of the men, capturing Baghdad meant victory and home. Besides, why keep hanging around here as stationary targets, sitting ducks really?

On Saturday, March 29, the troops awoke to another day of this onerous routine. Out on Highway 9, the men of 3rd Platoon, Rage Company, were pulling roadblock duty in the late-morning hours. For several days, the Americans had been regulating all traffic in and out of Najaf. The Cottonbalers knew that Fedayeen and Iraqi Army troops were moving in and out of the city, hauling or stashing weapons, hoping to ambush the Americans. The GIs also were on the alert for the possibility that Saddam would launch a counterattack from the north.

The roadblock consisted of a burnt-out truck that was sprawled across the road, barbed wire, sandbags, fighting holes, Bradleys, and several dismounted infantrymen. There was also a sign in Arabic warning the Iraqis of the checkpoint. Since the majority of the local population could not read or write, Psy-Ops teams had been busy broadcasting to the people, telling them to stay inside, away from the roadblock, and generally out of the way. All approaching vehicles were to stop when they got to the roadblock. If they didn't, the Americans fired warning shots. If they kept coming, the troops shot their tires or engines out and were authorized to use deadly force. This had happened a few times (largely with white pickup trucks full of Fedayeen fighters), but most of the Iraqis complied with instructions. They stopped, had their vehicles searched, and were either turned away to the north or allowed to pass. Sometimes orange and white taxicabs pulled up to the checkpoint and disgorged Iraqi men who wished to surrender. This morning the soldiers were simply doing what they had been doing for the last few days—scanning for trouble, halting cars, searching people and vehicles, while always maintaining a two-foot buffer zone between themselves and their subject. Today there were more cars and people than usual, but it was Saturday after all.

Eight hundred meters north of the roadblock, Lieutenant Gleason and some of his scouts were nestled in among some small huts beside the road. Their job was to maintain an observation post and warn Rage Company of any developing problems. Gleason's men were exhausted. They had not had much sleep lately. Nothing much was going on up here and the lieutenant knew his men needed some rest, so he called Rutter and received permission to withdraw. They left, drove back to their assembly area, and settled in for some much-needed sleep.

At the roadblock the Americans were searching a bus whose driver had complied with the order to halt. Lieutenant Simmons, the forward observer, was nearby, talking to Lieutenant Russ Porter, one of his artillery colleagues. The two men knew each other from back at Fort Stewart and were good friends. Like nearly everybody else, they were sick and tired of Objective Raiders. The sniper, the accident, technical problems with their radios, and just tension in general had all taken their toll. They spoke for about ten minutes and then, almost as if they could read each other's minds, both said, "This place is evil," at the exact same instant. They blinked in surprise, nervously laughed, and went their separate ways.

About fifty meters away, Sergeant Adrian Newcom was also on the ground talking to a buddy. Newcom had not seen Private First Class Diego Rincon in several days. Rincon's 3rd Platoon was attached to Bravo Tank, so the rest of Rage Company had hardly gotten to see them since the war started. Today 3rd Platoon, nicknamed the Outlaws, had taken over the roadblock from Newcom's 1st Platoon.

Newcom smiled. "What's been goin' on?"

"Oh, nothing," Rincon replied. "How about you?"

"Yeah, man, yesterday they fired, like, twenty RPGs at us!"

Rincon's eyes widened. "Really?!"

Newcom chuckled. "Naw, I'm kiddin' man. It's been pretty quiet, boring." They shook hands and Newcom went on his way. "See you soon," he said over his shoulder.

At almost the same time, Specialist Butler was settling into a foxhole alongside the roadblock. There were three holes here, each containing one or two men. Butler's squad leader loomed over them. "Hey, guys, be prepared. We think we're gonna go up there and . . . start checking cars."

He went away for a few moments and then came back. "No, Sergeant Urquart's squad is gonna take over."

Butler felt relief. He was watching all the people milling around the bus as American soldiers searched them. "Man, look at all those people walking around," he thought. "God, this is way too many people out here. I don't like this." He was content to stay in the foxhole, rather than risk his skin up there, dealing with people.

At the roadblock itself, a man limped away from the bus crowd and sat down on a curb. The four American soldiers who were working the roadblock, including Private First Class Rincon, searched the man. He was clean. He pantomimed that he had hurt his ankle and needed to get off his feet. Minutes later, a taxi approached the roadblock, slowly passed the warning sign, and braked to a stop. The Americans had seen this car several times this morning. Each time it had come near their position and turned around. That wasn't exactly unusual, but it was different enough to warrant further investigation. "I'm here to pick up that injured man," the driver said in English. The fire team, led by Sergeant Eugene Williams, surrounded the taxi and told the driver to get out. He did so; the Cottonbalers searched him and found no weapons. "Open the doors of your car," Sergeant Williams said.

A couple dozen meters away, Sergeant Driggers was sitting in the gunner's seat of his Bradley, observing the whole scene. "Man, these guys just want to give up, Sergeant Driggers," his driver said. Several yards from Driggers, Specialist Kyle Hartley, a rifleman, was sitting in a foxhole, watching Williams and company conduct their search. One by one, the Iraqi cabdriver opened the car doors as the Americans stood a couple feet away, their weapons trained on him. As Hartley watched, Specialist Michael Curtin, while covering the back of the cab, gestured at the Iraqi to open the trunk. The cabdriver calmly opened the trunk. "All of a sudden, all I saw was just a flash," Hartley said. An enormous explosion, emanating from the trunk, blew everything and everyone around it apart. The concussion was overwhelming. "The next thing I know, no one is there, just the frame [of the car]. I looked up and saw parts of the car flying over me. I was . . . in total shock." The explosion of the car bomb was so powerful it blew Sergeant Driggers's glasses off. Another man had been standing on the ramp of his Bradley. The blast blew him off. Neither Driggers nor the other man was hurt.

Sergeant Newcom was a couple hundred meters away. He heard the enormous boom of the explosion, turned around, and said, "What in the world was that?" Lieutenant Cuevas was fifty yards away from the blast, reading in the back of his Bradley, with his troop door open, when he heard the explosion: "There was this sound like the end of the world. It was a huge . . . BOOM! The Bradley just shook." To Cuevas it felt like a heavy wind was rocking his Bradley: "All this dust just . . . rushed inside . . . in the troop door . . . all this smoke and dust and stuff."

In another Bradley just down the road from the immense explosion, Specialist Kautzman was resting in his driver's seat when he heard the blast. He and his commander had no idea what had just happened. "Holy shit, man, did you see that? That tank just blew up that car?" Kautzman's commander said. "What are you talking about? I didn't hear a gun go off," Kautzman replied.

"Wait a minute: something's not right," the commander said. He told Kautzman to find the gunner and get him inside immediately. The awful realization of the car bomb sank home to them.

In Specialist Butler's foxhole, the young rifleman was staring at the remnants of the cab: "All I saw was black smoke and all this stuff, I couldn't tell what it was. Next thing you know, all this debris started falling down right there in the holes and everywhere we were at."

Butler's sergeant hollered, "What was that? Were our guys up there?"

Butler by now understood the grim reality. "That was a car bomb."

Just ahead, on the road, he could see the remains of Sergeant Williams: "I could see the BDU's right there in the middle of the street."

Williams's squad leader, Sergeant Chad Urquart, was up on the road now. At the sound of the explosion he had leaped out of his foxhole and hustled to the scene. It was more awful than anything he could imagine. His men were blown to bits. Three had been killed instantly. Another was in his death throes, gasping for air. He died before Urquart could do anything. Urquart felt a deep sense of sadness, shock, and anger. These men were his responsibility, but more than that, they were his brothers, "the most important people in my life." Whatever remained of the four dead

Americans and the two Iraqis was literally scattered in pieces throughout the vicinity of the blast site. There was a huge crater in the road. A plume of dusty black smoke rose from the scene, like some kind of macabre guidepost.

Many Cottonbalers, upon hearing the explosion, originally thought they were under artillery fire, but by now they all understood what had happened. Their first inclination was to give in to grief and anger, but their training steadied them. Almost immediately groups of soldiers re-established the roadblock and pulled security. Bradley crews repositioned their vehicles to cover the road and the men on the ground. Officers and noncoms hurried around, giving men things to do so that they would not dwell on the horror around them.

Lieutenant Cuevas left his Bradley and ran to the blast site. He was amazed at how calm and focused the soldiers were. He saw something lying on the ground and realized it was the remains of one of the American soldiers. "There . . . was no blood, but I think the concussion killed him. There was no parts blown off or anything." Cuevas saw Lieutenant Brian Johnson. "How many we got down? I gotta call the [medevac] bird," he said to Johnson. The other lieutenant replied that there were four men down but made no mention that they were all dead. Thinking that they might instead be wounded, Cuevas ran back to his track, got on the radio, and called for a medevac. He made a conscious effort to calm himself before he spoke on the radio, but it was no use. His voice was choppy and strained, difficult to understand. Lieutenant Schenck, listening on the other end, could barely understand Cuevas. Cuevas thought he was talking very clearly. He was so frustrated now that he threw his hand mike against the wall of his Bradley.

For several minutes this vexing bout of miscommunication went on, until Lieutenant Johnson showed up. "Dude . . . they're all dead," he said to Cuevas. "We don't need a bird." Cuevas felt like he had been kicked in the gut. He keyed his mike: "Cancel the bird. They're all dead."

Two kilometers to the south, at the TOC, Cuevas's words struck like a thunderbolt. In the confusing moments after the bomb went off, there had been all sorts of conflicting, agitated reports. But it was official now. Four American soldiers from Rage Company were dead. Captain Smith was in the TOC, listening to the whole thing. At first he had heard the four soldiers were from Jimmy Lee's Bravo Tank. Now Smith knew the horrible truth. Four of his own men were not going home alive.

On the exterior, Smith was often brash, tough, and gruff, "half Patton, half pirate," in the estimation of one of his officers. But Smith was also a deeply honest, caring man, an infantryman's infantryman who knew his soldiers intimately. He was more likely to hang out with them, dip snuff, and shoot the breeze than order them to keep their hair short. He cared little for military niceties like saluting or protocol. Like Chris Carter, Rob Smith was a man you took at face value. What you saw was what you got. A Cleveland native, Smith had joined the Army Reserves for college money during Desert Storm. He had served with a local medical unit, loved the Army, and eventually got an infantry commission through ROTC. His wife was now pregnant with their second child and scheduled to deliver any day. He hated being away from her at this time, missing the whole pregnancy. His family meant everything to him. But so did his soldiers and the idea of serving his nation. Like many Cottonbalers of the early twenty-first century all-volunteer Army, he was deeply committed to the idea of defending American ideals and principles. "What keeps me doing this—I always go back to our founding fathers, at the sacrifice they were making for the greater good. It's not always about the money and it's not always about the glory. It's about doing the right thing basically for the greater good. I truly believe in that."

Two days earlier, when Smith had lost soldiers in the well accident, he had wanted to quit, go home, forget about this awful place. He had cried for two hours. But when he finished crying, he put the accident behind him, knowing that his soldiers needed him. Now, in the wake of the car bombing, they needed him even more. Smith strode out of the TOC and got into his Bradley. He had to go to the scene, talk to his guys, make them understand that they had to hang together now, keep fighting, and honor their comrades by doing their jobs well. Smith and his crew made the short drive to the site. When they got there, Captain Smith dismounted, surveyed the nightmarish scene, and circulated among his men. "We've . . . got to keep our heads in the game," he said. "We can't let their deaths go . . . unhonored. Keep it together. Keep it cool." His presence helped the men cope with what had just happened. To Smith and the rest of Rage Company, the war had just become personal. Terrorists had just killed four members of the family in one of the most horrible ways imaginable. The men of Rage would continue to operate with the discipline that had been so ingrained in them, but they were now hardened, suspicious, and even angry. They knew now that everyone had the potential to be an enemy. "It made us live up to our name—Rage," Staff Sergeant Ziegelmann said.

The NCOs made sure that a cleanup effort began immediately. Groups of soldiers began searching the area, some on their hands and knees, looking for body parts. Nothing would be left behind. Every body part and piece of equipment would be accounted for. Specialist Butler's sergeant rounded up Butler and several other men for this grisly job. "Hey, guys . . . we've gotta go . . . get these guys out of the road," he said. Butler climbed out of his foxhole and immediately came upon the remains of Sergeant Williams. He had seen what was left of Williams land right next to his hole, and he now stood over the body. Butler and another man helped carry Williams to the medics' track. They found the largest remaining parts of the other three men, wrapped them in ponchos, and hauled them to the track. One man had been reduced to a torso, and only his body armor held that together. "All you saw was this [torso], no arms, no legs, nothing, just a chest. It was just kind of black, charcoaled." Lieutenant Cuevas was hauling one body that kept breaking apart. "I had to . . . pick up the middle . . . before they brought . . . a body bag and stretcher . . . so that we could put the stuff [body parts] on there. It was gross, but . . . surreal, like not really happening."

Unfortunately, it was all too real. At the medics' track, Butler was hoisting a poncho inside. "I remember just putting my hands on—I don't know who it was because he was covered up—I put my hands underneath and it was gooey. It was nasty." Another soldier reached down with one hand, picked up some charred, poncho-wrapped remains, and put them in the track. Butler realized that this was all that was left of his friend Specialist Curtin, the soldier who had been standing behind the Iraqi when he opened the trunk. Butler was devastated. Curtin was a good friend. For Butler, seeing him like this was almost too much to take.

It was also tough on the medics, even experienced men like Sergeant First Class Robert Davis, a platoon sergeant who had served in the Gulf

War. He and his men worked closely with First Sergeant Moore of Rage Company to comb the area for any flesh or body parts. The dead men still had grenades on their armored vests, and for a time the medics were worried that the grenades might explode. Fortunately, they did not. Davis and the medics set up a screen around their track so that men would have trouble seeing the bodies. At one point, after they had gathered up most everything they could and stored it in the back of the track, Davis looked in there. "It was a shock to me." Davis had to take a few moments to compose himself. Another experienced man, Sergeant First Class Kevin Green, was standing nearby. As the NCO in charge of the company trains, his job was to account for the personal effects of the dead men, so that they could all be sent home with the remains. "You got to write everything down. It was a gruesome thing to do . . . go in and see if they've got ID cards, if they've got rings on, tags or any personal effects that'll stand out. I mean, from head to toe." As Green went about his difficult task, all he could think about was that he had played football with some of these guys. Now they were charred, blown up, disfigured. "It was kind of hard on me. I'll never forget that."

Within hours of the car bombing, Rutter visited the site and relayed the same message that Smith had communicated earlier—stick together, don't quit, focus on your job. Quivering with a barely concealed fury, the colonel talked to the soldiers, consoling them, keeping them sane. He changed the rules of engagement. Any vehicle approaching an American checkpoint had five seconds to comply with a halt order and turn around. If it did not, it got shot. Any white truck was fair game. One Cottonbaler remembered Rutter saying, "Whatever the fuck you see come at you, you kill!" The soldier was impressed. "I had never heard an officer talk like that. Usually they're a little more reserved."

Rutter knew that his soldiers would keep fighting, but he wanted his men to understand what this war was about. "The war became very personal to us. We were fighting evil. The Iraqi forces resorted to this tactic after realizing that there was no way to penetrate our forces or break our will to fight using conventional methods. They exploited our sincerity in allowing innocent Iraqi people a path to their homes."

Needless to say, the mood at the roadblock was very tense now. In the two days that followed the car bombing, the Americans shot several vehicles that violated their new rules of engagement. Tragically, they probably killed some innocent people, but in most cases those who died probably meant to do harm. There were numerous skirmishes as small groups of Iraqi fighters attacked the Americans or got caught moving around in pickup trucks.

From here on out, the Cottonbalers fought the war with a kind of controlled fury. "There was a steeliness that entered the unit after that car bomb," Major Coffey said. This was especially true for Rage, which came together even more than it had after its Miracle Mile experience. There were no reprisals, no indiscriminate shootings or anything of the kind. The soldiers remained disciplined and professional, but they were angry about what had happened. They felt like they had dealt with the Iraqis in good faith only to have that good faith repaid with treachery. They were now more jaded, wary, and cynical about the locals but still as committed to their cause as ever. They knew that most Iraqis did not represent a threat and were actually friendly, but they also understood that they had to constantly be on guard, and they resented this. Mostly they blamed the suicide bombing on Saddam Hussein and the evil nature of his regime. "Saddam Hussein may not call himself a terrorist," Major Cooney said, "but he is certainly using every trick in the terrorist handbook." Indeed, the regime in its official announcements praised the bombing and said it would be the first of many. They were absolutely correct.

In retrospect, the car bombing was a seminal moment in the history of the Iraq War. Rather than an isolated incident perpetrated by a couple of fanatics, suicide bombings became standard operating procedure for America's adversaries in this war. While the Hussein regime, in the short time it had left, did not employ the tactic again (one suspects out of impotence rather than any change in morality), the insurgency would do so with terrible impunity. The car bombing, then, was a harbinger of what was to come. It was an ominous precursor that the war was already transitioning from conventional to guerrilla, that it truly was a war against terrorists and all of their tactics, and that it would ultimately be about much more than simply toppling Saddam. The war would become a battle for the hearts and minds of the Iraqi people. In that sense, one can say that the four American soldiers who lost their lives at that Highway 9 roadblock were the first casualties of the insurgency. Their names were Sergeant Eugene Williams, Private First Class Diego Rincon, Specialist Michael Curtin, and Private Don Creighton.[39]

CHAPTER 5

The Iraq War

On to Baghdad and Beyond

THE COTTONBALERS COULD NOT WAIT to leave Objective raiders, and within three days of the car bombing, they got their wish. The next objective was the Karbala Gap. As at the escarpment, the Americans wished to fool the enemy about their intentions. The Karbala Gap was a narrow strip of road, wedged between Lake Razzaza on the left and the city of Karbala on the right. This was a choke point, the kind of constricted area that could negate the American advantages of maneuverability, firepower, and technology. If Saddam Hussein (or whoever was now running his regime) wished to launch a chemical attack, this would be the ideal place, since the Americans would be so constricted. Every fiber of logic seemed to argue against moving through the Karbala Gap, and that was exactly why American commanders chose to do so. Major General Buford Blount, the 3rd Division commander, set April I for the attack. His 1st Brigade, with 3-69 in the lead, would be first into the Gap. Before they rolled, however, Blount decided to play another trick on the Iraqis. Since he wanted them to believe that the main attack was coming east of Karbala, along the Euphrates, he ordered the 2nd Brigade to launch a feint at Hindiyah, a town located astride a major Euphrates River bridge.

The unit chosen to make this foray was Captain Chris Carter's Attack Company, 3-7, plus two tank companies for support. So far the war had been fairly quiet for Carter's people. They had had a few skirmishes, but they had not seen any major action. Now, on the morning of March 31, their mission was to roll into Hindiyah, seize two bridges over the Euphrates, and hold them while an armor company crossed the river and kept the enemy busy. Intelligence estimated that there could be as many as five thousand enemy fighters among the city's population of eighty thousand.

As the sun rose, they rolled out of their desert assembly area and headed for Hindiyah. Before long the terrain changed from desert to tropical. The road was flanked by date groves and some buildings. Most of the buildings were two or three stories high and painted yellow or green. Here and there, people were milling around with curious looks on their faces, but mostly all was quiet. First Lieutenant Eric Hooper, the company executive officer, was nervous and apprehensive. He had been uneasy ever since the previous evening when he and his buddy Carter had planned this mission. To Hooper, the mission was slightly ambitious. What was it his battalion commander, Lieutenant Colonel Philip "Flea" DeCamp, had said? He had called sending one understrength infantry company to seize two strategic bridges a "hell of a mission." That about said it.

As Hooper tried to concentrate on his duties, the column turned left and began to roll into Hindiyah itself. "All hell broke loose—RPGs flying, small arms. It was very chaotic. Everyone's reporting contact. I'm trying to decipher what to report. I'm in contact. I'm trying to shoot too. I go to fire my coax. My coax malfunctions." The young West Pointer knew that his track had an extra coax, so he crawled into the back and told his extra gunner to swap the guns.

Meanwhile, the orders were to engage and keep moving. The tanks shot up any military vehicle they saw. They also blasted trucks full of Fedayeen fighters clad in civilian clothes with checkered scarves over their faces. Nearly every Bradley in the column was shooting at something or someone. Several times, the Americans saw Fedayeen fighters using women or children as human shields. The Fedayeen would push them ahead as they moved around or pack them into trucks with them. Near the head of the column, in Captain Carter's Bradley, Sergeant Robert Compton, an extra gunner, was sitting in the back, looking through a periscope. "There's a guy to the left! I think he's got an RPG!" Compton shouted into the intercom.

"Where? Where?" Staff Sergeant Bryce Ivings, Carter's master gunner, asked.

Carter had already seen the man. "Scan left! Open fire!"

Ivings squeezed off several rounds, presumably killing the man with the RPG, but they couldn't be sure because they kept moving.

Not far away, a Fedayeen fighter let fly with another RPG. This one slammed into a Bradley that was commanded by flamboyant Staff Sergeant Thomas Slago, a man who had painted a bull's-eye on his CVC helmet. The RPG hit near the driver's compartment and filled the Bradley with acrid smoke, but the driver, Specialist Sciria, kept going.

The Americans would shoot and move. As they did so, they caught glimpses of the enemy attackers. "I remember seeing people run out of alleyways shooting," Lieutenant Hooper said, "people driving trucks with machine guns on top, toward us—shooting the trucks, the trucks blowing up, kind of careening out of control."

After several minutes of mobile fighting, Carter's Bradleys approached the main bridge. The tanks stationed themselves at key intersections around town and shot any vehicles that came toward them. Carter deployed his Bradleys in a half-moon formation along the bridge's western approaches. There was still some fire coming from the eastern side of the river and some of the surrounding buildings on the western, American-controlled side. Carter ordered his infantrymen to dismount and secure the buildings. They found no enemy troops, only a few scared civilians. The grunts spread out into positions that covered the road and the bridge. Some of the Bradley gunners shot up the roofs of the buildings just to be sure that no one snuck up on the dismounts from above.

An engineer track pulled up to the bridge. As the infantry and Bradleys covered them, engineers disgorged from the track and checked the bridge for explosives. They found wires, but they were harmless. Suddenly, there was motion on the bridge. Everyone looked up to see a dark blue car speeding over the bridge, heading straight for the Americans. An Abrams fired a main gun round and stopped the car in its tracks. The automobile blew up and caught fire. Oily smoke billowed from the carcass.

The Americans were also taking RPG, mortar, and small-arms fire from the other side of the river. The 2nd Brigade's commander, Colonel David Perkins, was on the scene, along with the division artillery officer. Perkins turned to the artilleryman, pointed to the opposite side of the river, and said, "Guys are shooting RPGs from across the river, in all those reeds. Let's put some artillery in there." In only a few minutes, several 155mm rounds screamed into a building on the opposite bank of the Euphrates. The enemy fire slackened, but it did not completely cease. Perkins knew that Attack Company's mission was to keep pushing across the river, but now he saw no point to that. Why risk crossing the river into a nest of enemy resistance and losing soldiers for no true purpose? The real point to this, after all, was not to seize the east bank of the Euphrates but to distract the Iraqis from the real effort at the Karhala Gap. Clearly, they were succeeding in that mission. So Perkins ordered Carter and the armored companies to stay in place and keep tying up the Iraqis.

The battle ebbed and flowed. Sergeant Ingram's squad was holed up in a building that overlooked the river. He and his men had earlier strung concertina wire around the half-moon position in an effort to discourage civilians from nearing the Americans. As they strung the wire, they came under mortar fire. For a time, they took refuge in their track, but now they were back on the outside, looking for targets on the east side of the river. One of his men set up his M240B, a new-generation machine gun that was now in service as a successor to the old M60. The 240 was heavy at twenty-five pounds, but it was fairly reliable and could shoot between six and eight hundred rounds to an effective range of about eight hundred meters. Ingram and his machine gunner could see figures running between buildings on the other side of the Euphrates. Now and again, the figures stopped, aimed an RPG, and fired.

The machine gunner squeezed off several rounds in response, and Ingram thought he saw them strike home. "I think we got one. We could see him fall. It was about three hundred meters across the river." Soon Ingram worked out a system with the supporting tankers and Bradley crews. Whenever his gunner spotted targets, he fired tracer rounds in that direction. The tankers and Bradley gunners watched the tracers and followed suit.

Just outside of Ingram's building, Lieutenant Hooper's Bradley was facing in the opposite direction from the river, effectively covering Captain Carter's back, since Carter's Bradley was pointed at the bridge. Hooper was scanning the area for targets. He examined the top of a building and saw what looked to be a sniper aiming his rifle right at him.

Before Hooper even had time to react, the company sniper, Specialist Chad Prindle, lying under cover in a nearby building, fired two shots that killed the enemy sniper and his buddy. Just for good measure, Hooper had his gunner, Specialist Gary Bipat, light up the roof of every surrounding structure so that the enemy "couldn't climb over the top and have a vantage point to shoot down at us."

No sooner was Lieutenant Hooper calming down from that close call than he saw several Fedayeen fighters trying to cross an alleyway fifty meters in front of his track. They were aiming their AKs and firing as they ran. Hooper hollered at Bipat, "You got him! Shoot!" Bipat fired his 25mm gun. As he did so, they both realized that the gun was set to fire armor-piercing rounds that were used to kill vehicles, not high-explosive or coaxial machine-gun rounds used for killing people. Hooper watched the results through his thermals. "He gets the first round off. It hits the guy. All I remember is that there was two of 'em, and it hit the guy and it looked like the guy evaporated into, like, a puddle. His form just kind of morphed. I don't know if it cut him in half or what it did, but he just was, like a puddle of shit. . .just a red blob. You could see his buddy just kind of grab his ears. I don't know if it was the sound of the AP or the static pressure or what. At that point I hit coax and he shot the other guy with coax."

After that things quieted down at Hooper's position, but there was still some desultory small-arms fire coming from the other side of the river. A couple of Carter's platoons were searching a police station and the local Baath Party headquarters. They found great quantities of weapons and ammo along with maps, plans, and even several prisoners who claimed to be Iraqi Army deserters.

Sergeant First Class Eric Wright, the platoon sergeant for 3rd Platoon, was keeping an eye on the bridge. Since the first minutes of the fight in Hindiya, he had noticed the inert form of a black-chador-clad woman lying on the bridge. She had been caught in the cross fire and Wright assumed she was dead. However, as he watched her now, he saw her moving, waving for help. He radioed this over the company net, but then the next time he looked, the woman was motionless again. Again the Americans assumed she was dead. Several minutes later, Sergeant Wright saw her move and noticed a pained look on her face. "Hey, she's waving again. The woman looks like she's in trouble. Should we do something?"

Captain Carter heard Wright's question and decided, right then, that he and his soldiers had to go get the woman off the bridge. The captain was an idealistic man to whom the words "justice," "honor," and "sacrifice" meant everything. He strongly believed in the rightness of this war in Iraq. He and his men had come here to rid this country of decades of oppression and tyranny. Carter believed that only by freeing others of such tyranny could the United States enjoy true security and peace. He knew nothing about this woman except that she needed help, and in his view, that was why he and his guys were in this hellhole—to help the local people. "To leave her out on that bridge would have gone against the grain of why we are here," he later said.

Carter cleared his rescue mission with Lieutenant Colonel DeCamp and then walked over to Wright and the 3rd Platoon. Actually the captain had been on the ground for much of this fight in Hindiyah. He believed that a commander could only learn so much in his turret. A good infantry officer eventually had to get on the ground to know what was happening and lead his soldiers. Carter asked Wright for two volunteers to go up on the bridge. "We've got to get her off that bridge," the Georgian said. Specialists Choice Kinchen and Joshua Butler (no relation to Brian Butler of Rage 2-7) stepped forward.

When they were ready, the three men trotted over to the captain's Bradley. As Carter's driver, Specialist Zachery Watkins, drove the vehicle forward, Carter and the other men advanced behind it. The Bradley came to a stop right at the foot of the bridge. With Carter in the lead, the three Cottonbalers hustled up to the first girders of the bridge and took cover. This span was two lanes, with an iron suspension frame, girders, and guard railings on either side. Carter looked around the girder and saw the woman a few feet away. There was no question that he would be the one to go to this woman. He could not ask his soldiers to face dangers he would not risk himself. His first worry was that she might be wired with explosives. He had heard about the car bombing, so he knew death could come at any time, even amid innocent-looking circumstances. Even if she was clean, it was dangerous to go out to her, since he would be exposed to any enemy fire that was coming from east of the river.

In spite of all this, he felt strangely at ease, almost serene. He was so calm that he caught himself thinking about the river below, "Wow, this is pretty cool. I wonder what kind of fish are down there?" Later, when he reflected on this moment, he wondered if perhaps his serenity came from the hand of God protecting him. He grabbed a smoke grenade, activated it, and tossed it around the girder. In one rush, he bolted over to the woman and knelt beside her. She was middle-aged, "maybe fifty, but she. . .looked a lot older than that." He could see the pain of her wound on her face. She pointed to her backside. Several feet behind Carter, Butler and Kinchen stood behind the girder, covering their captain. In sign language, Carter told her to roll over so he could examine her wounds and check for explosives. An awkward moment passed as she tried to understand what he wanted her to do, but then she rolled over. He gave her a bottle of water and patted her down. Small-arms rounds were zinging here and there, but Captain Carter could not hear them. He was too intent on helping the woman. He could readily see that she was not rigged up with anything. She was bleeding badly and crying. Her blood had seeped through her clothes and had stained her dusty spot along the guard railing. The captain saw that she had been shot through the buttocks and had an exit wound in her abdomen.

He scuttled back behind the cover of the girder and waved the medics forward. As they performed first aid and moved the wounded woman off the bridge, Carter and his two soldiers provided cover fire. Soon they got her to the medics' M113 and put her inside. They saved her life.

Within a couple hours of this rescue, Attack Company and its supporting tank companies left Hindiyah. Before they did so, they blew up the Baath Party headquarters and all of the weapons they had found. Tired, dirty, sweaty, grimy, and generally spent, the Cottonbalers of Attack Company made it back to their assembly area without further incident. They had accomplished their mission.

Back in Watkinsville, Georgia, that same morning, long before anyone in the United States knew anything about Carter's bridge-side rescue, his mother sat down to pray. As she spoke to God, a distinct feeling came over her. She had the clear and urgent sense that, sometime that day, Chris would be involved in a rescue effort and would save someone's life.[1]

WITH THE HINDIYA FEINT ACCOMPLISHED, Blount attacked the Karbala gap on the evening of April 1–2. A massive and impressive bombardment preceded the assault troops. Intelligence expected resistance from an old adversary—the Medina Division, in particular this unit's 14th Brigade. Air strikes battered every possible target, as did MLRS and artillery. Soldiers outfitted themselves in their special chemical protective gear ("I feel like a clown with these fucking boots on," one man said of his MOPP suit). In the darkness, many soldiers sat atop their tanks or Bradleys and watched the bombardment. Hour after hour it went on until finally the word came to roll.

Captain Todd Kelly's Charlie 2-7 led the way. The columns moved almost unopposed. Here and there a few infantry or vehicles put up some resistance, but they were no match for Charlie Company. "It was very important to get through that choke point," the captain recalled. "We hit it probably about daybreak." Overhead, Apache helicopters and A-10S hunted for targets. On the ground, the combat vehicles rolled from desert wasteland to muddy farmland that was honeycombed with irrigation canals. Kelly's outfit refueled and pushed on for Objective Peach, the planned Euphrates River crossing north of Al Musayyib.

As they did so, the bulk of Rutter's 2-7 poured through the Karbala Gap, protected the west flank of the advance, and then pushed north. They too encountered light resistance. Major Coffey had been thinking about this battle for many weeks. He had planned for every contingency. But, for the most part, the 14th Brigade was a no-show. They lobbed some mortars at 2-7. The bravest of the 14th's infantrymen remained in their holes and angled for RPG shots. Now and again, in some spots, a few armored vehicles or trucks put up some resistance. In the main, the Americans eliminated these stalwarts with alacrity. The vaunted Medina Division melted away. Most likely, many of these Iraqi soldiers deserted (maybe some knew what had happened to their predecessors in the Gulf War), retreated, or went underground to fight as insurgents. Others surrendered. The Americans suffered no casualties.

At Karbala, as elsewhere, the Americans were sometimes confused about what or whom to shoot at. Specialist Jonathan Beck, a Bradley gunner in Bravo 2-7, engaged at least one truck with enemy soldiers in it. But at one point, while under fire, he accidentally shot up a civilian truck, killing several innocent people. His platoon sergeant excoriated him, threatening a court-martial. "You gotta keep your eyes open and pay attention!" he screamed at Beck. The young gunner knew his sergeant was right but also knew that the environment around him was confusing and full of the possibility of death. Nothing ever came of the court-martial because the officers knew the shooting was an accident. Beck felt horrible about killing noncombatants and knew he would have to live with it the rest of his life. "It was my fault. I felt terrible, but. . .that shit happens. It's hard. . .when bullets are flying. I wasn't going to take a chance. . .and let them come close and. . .kill me. . .and all the guys ridin' in my track. It was just a mistake."[2]

By midafternoon on April 2, the 1st Brigade was through the Karbala Gap and strung out in positions all along the Euphrates. While 2-7 covered the western and southern flanks of the advance, lead elements from 3-69 were in the process of securing Objective Peach. After all the permutations, machinations, and obfuscations of the last several days, this was the place the 3rd Division would finally cross the famous Euphrates. Tankers from Alpha 3-69 were in the lead, while Charlie 2-7 trailed in support. Intelligence said that Objective Peach was a major six-lane bridge. Intelligence was wrong. When the Americans got within sight of the bridge, they saw that there were only two lanes, slightly separated from each other, creating in effect two small bridges. All of this was bordered by foliage, meaning that the Americans would have to approach it in column formation, instead of spread out in support by fire positions along the banks of the river.

Knowing the importance of this bridge, the Iraqis were defending it with a couple of mixed battalions of Fedayeen and Republican Guard troops. A few hundred meters from the bridge, American tanks and Bradleys opened up on any trucks or fighting positions they were able to spot through their thermals. The Iraqis responded with whatever they had. "Kill 'em in the holes!" Lieutenant Colonel Marcone commanded over the net. "I need you to kill all the infantry at the bridge!"

Tanks slammed 120mm rounds into trucks and cars. Overhead, an A-10 dived at an unseen target. A long burst from the plane's 30mm gun sounded "like a big fart" in the estimation of one soldier. Everywhere there were explosions as the Americans wasted Iraqi vehicles or fighting holes.

At the leading edge of the American column, Captain Kelly was dispersing his company into the marshy soil on either side of the road. His mission was to secure the west side of the Euphrates so that dismounted infantrymen could capture the bridge and cross the river while he supported them. Kelly felt almost disoriented by the rapid change in terrain and climate he and his men had experienced over the course of this stressful day. They had gone from the barren cool of the desert to the humid, stifling tropical rain forest feel of the Euphrates valley. The captain felt sweat running down his back. He saw that a couple of tanks were already stuck on the left. His recovery crews, under fire, were working to extract them. By and large, though, his vehicles were where he needed them to be. They were in position to cover the bridge, the river, and the far side.

To Kelly's right, his executive officer, Captain Mike Pecina, was supervising a group of soldiers with smoke generators. Their job was to release their smoke when the infantry crossed the river. Pecina was the opposite of a recruiting-poster soldier. Balding and a bit paunchy, he was not the gung ho career officer type. He had earned his commission through ROTC at Sam Houston State University, and now his main desire was to do his job, go home, and get out of the Army. "I've seen enough history, " he once said. "Now I want to go home and work on my golf"

Now Pecina saw a man approaching his vehicle. "Stop!" he shouted at the man.

"Say *kif*!" one of Pecina's crewmen advised.

Kif (pronounced "Kuf") is the Arabic word for "halt." Pecina hollered "*Kif*," but to no avail. The man walked right on by. In the next instant, Pecina saw a truck on the east side of the river, driving toward the bridge. "There's a vehicle coming! Open fire!" he shouted at his gunner, Corporal Timothy Smith. At first Smith shot high, but then he found the mark, destroying the truck within sight of the bridge.

Pecina was still scanning. He saw a white Nissan parked several hundred yards away, alongside the road. "Open fire on that truck," he told his gunner.

"I don't see any movement inside the vehicle," Smith replied.

"You have to shoot it."

Smith fired several high-explosive rounds at the truck and it blew up.

The enemy fire tapered off a bit now. Kelly's Cottonbalers, plus many tanks from the armor companies, were shooting anything that moved. The time had come to seize the bridge, but that might be quite difficult.

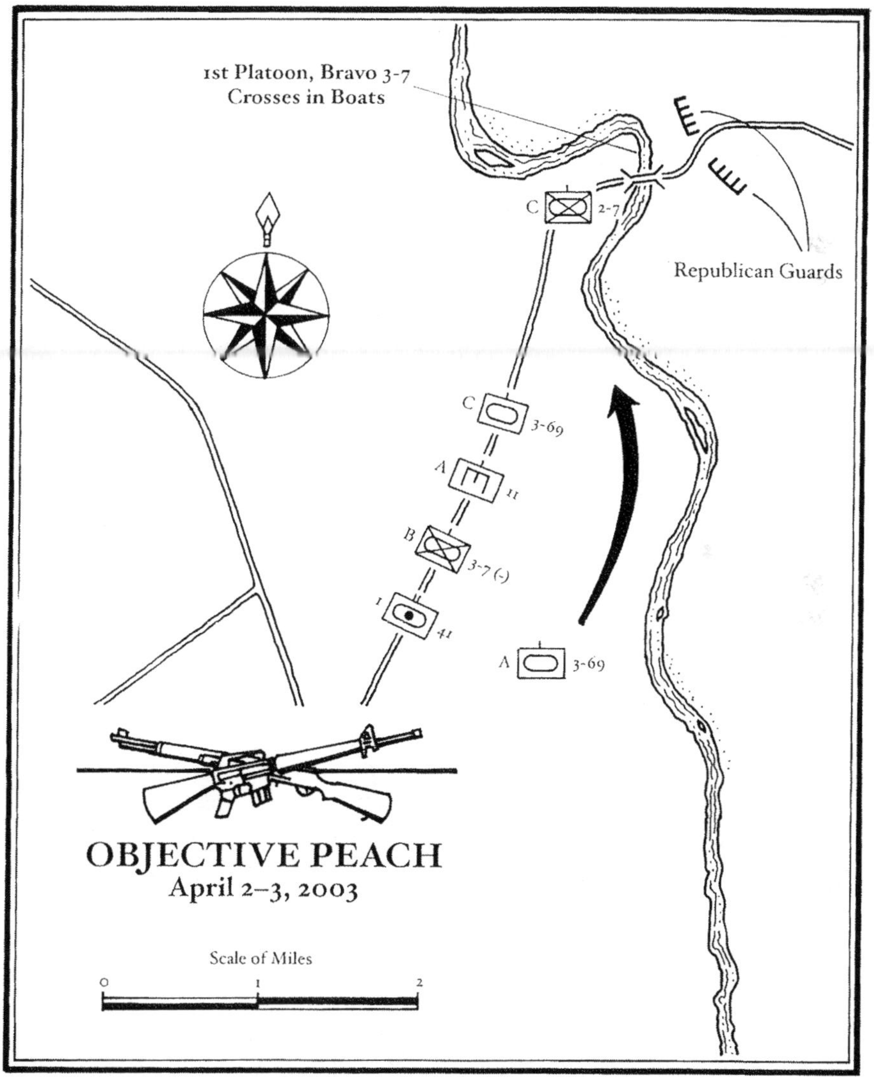

The Americans knew that the bridge had been damaged and might not hold the weight of their combat vehicles. Plus they were worried that if the vehicles rolled onto the thing, the Iraqis would blow it from under them. So there was only one way to take this bridge that made Objective Peach so important—dismounted infantry.

This was no easy proposition. The infantry could not simply charge onto the bridge. They would be just as vulnerable as the vehicles if the enemy detonated the bridge. Even if the enemy didn't blow it, any grunts on the bridge would be under the guns of every Iraqi on the east side of the river. There were several buildings on the other side, along with plenty of foliage, so the enemy had adequate cover. They were probably hurting from all the American firepower that had been poured in on them, but their small arms and mortars could still inflict much damage on dismounted infantry.

There was only one answer to the problem. A group of grunts and engineers had to hop aboard boats, ford the river, secure the bridge, and clear the way for all those powerful armored vehicles waiting on the west side. The United States possessed weapons of every destructive capability—nuclear missiles, cruise missiles, nuclear subs, supercarriers, destroyers, massive bombers, smart bombs, dumb bombs, helicopters, unmanned drones, self-propelled artillery pieces, tanks, and anything else that could be produced by the military-industrial complex that had so dominated the country since World War II. Yet the crossing of the Euphrates came down to a handful of ground pounders armed with rifles, machine guns, and handheld antitank weapons.

It just so happened that several infantry squads from Bravo 3-7 were trained for this mission. Before the war, they had actually trained with boats in a desert setting, all in anticipation that they may have to cross the Euphrates and capture a key bridge while under fire. Now these men manhandled their rubber boats off trucks and carried them all the way down to the west banks of the Euphrates.

As they did so, the Charlie Company soldiers watched them with absolute amazement. "They were getting stuck in the vegetation," Captain Kelly recalled. "They'd drag 'em through." Sergeant Sorenson almost had to rub his eyes to make sure he wasn't hallucinating. The sight of American soldiers dragging boats was too out of the ordinary, bordering on the bizarre. He could see that the job of hauling the boats was taking its toll on these guys. Groups of struggling men were spread out everywhere, trying to drag their boats to the river's edge. There were six boats, and each one was crammed with weapons and equipment. The Bravo 3-7 men stumbled along, exhausted, while Sorenson watched intently. The lead groups reached the river and gently lowered their boats into the water. Sorenson chuckled at the sight of them. "Yeah, it sucks for you," he thought, "but it's not me so it's funny."

A second later, he quit laughing when he saw tracer rounds zip from somewhere on the east side of the river and fly past the intrepid boatmen. Sorenson's track, and many others, began laying down suppressive fire on the opposite side.

At the riverbank, Staff Sergeant Robert Gasman and his squad from Bravo 3-7's 1st Platoon hit the dirt, kept their grip on their boats, and steadied them in the water. Gasman had been training for a moment like this for many years. A native of Yucaipa, California, the thirty-one-year-old squad leader had been in the Army since 1991. As a youngster out of high school he had taken some college classes but decided to join the Army because that was something he had always wanted to do. He had been in the 7th Infantry for almost five years now. He was serious, logical, and understated.

Gasman and the others splashed and thrashed around for a few moments while they got into their boats. Another sergeant was having trouble getting into the boat, so Gasman and one other soldier reached out and dragged him in. Plenty of fire was still coming from the other side. A lot of it seemed to be originating from one building that loomed over the east bank. The boats had no motors, so Gasman and his men had to paddle. They were very tired (and truthfully a bit ticked off) from the considerable exertion of carrying their little craft down here, but that was just too bad. The enemy did not care if they were tired, only that they were targets.

As quickly as the grunts could, they paddled into the Euphrates current. Each boat held between eight and ten men. Two soldiers rowed from the back and two from the front. "As we were trying to get. . . coordinated enough to row. . .across the river. . .we had guys that were watching this one building where we knew we were receiving fire," Gasman said.

Bullets were zipping uncomfortably close. Fire was coming from in front of and, strangely enough, behind them. Spent bullets splashed into the water, like oversize raindrops. A round hit their boat and it started losing air, but somehow it held together. The rowing and paddling of the men were not terribly efficient and the boats were quite vulnerable all alone in the middle of the river, but they made it across in a matter of minutes. Sergeant Gasman's squad was the first to make it to the other side. "Our boat ended up landing at a makeshift dock in front of the house that we were receiving fire from."

Captain Pecina's smoke generators were supposed to have obscured the whole area, but something must have gone wrong, because when Sergeant Gasman's squad got to the dock, they were in full view of the enemy that was shooting from the building in front of them. "We were supposed to have about fifty minutes of smoke," Lieutenant Kevin Caesar, the platoon leader, explained, "but we probably only got about ten minutes."

For Gasman and company, only an embankment offered any cover. "We dismounted from the boat and went up the side of the embankment and told the engineers that we wanted to see if they could call for smoke. Maybe about six feet in front of me, I started seeing a little green puff of smoke. They were shooting [M]203's from the other side of the bridge. A 203 smoke grenade does not offer a whole lot of concealment." Basically, these smoke grenades, shot from rifle-mounted M203 grenade launchers, were worthless. Rather than concealing the Cottonbalers, they merely served as markers, guiding the enemy fire to the Cottonbalers' position.

Sergeant Gasman knew that he had to keep his people moving. While the engineers began moving to the right, toward the bridge, he and his infantrymen maneuvered around for a good position to return fire on the enemy-held building. They were wading through muddy, marshy reeds. The humidity oozed over everything and everyone. Their boots were filthy and sticky with the stench of mud. They found a spot and shot at the building, and then a Bradley rumbled up to the west bank of the river and fired several high-explosive rounds into the building. The shooting died down.

The other boats, coming across the river in no particular order, had all landed now, and soldiers were spreading out everywhere. Even as the engineers were examining the two small bridge spans and finding them wired up with explosives, vehicles started crossing. The engineers worked as quickly as they could to remove the explosives. They cut the wires to one span. However, the Iraqis detonated the charge on the other span. It was not destroyed, but it was severely damaged, and the explosion put quite a scare into the men inside the Bradley that was crossing at the time. Sergeant Rudy Belloc's fire team was in that Bradley and it took him several minutes to calm his guys down from this near disaster.

On the east bank, the members of Gasman's squad, along with a few vehicles and some other dismounts, were fanning out on either side of the road: "We looked down the road and we could see a guy with a wheelbarrow and he had another guy . . . in the wheelbarrow and he was holding a white flag. We went up to the wheelbarrow . . . and searched him. He had been shot and most of his insides were hanging out of his back." They called their medic and evacuated the wounded civilian.

Now enemy fire started coming from at least two buildings adjacent to the road. Gasman's Javelin team came up, pointed their weapon at one of the buildings, and fired. The Javelin was a handheld, bazooka-like weapon. It fired a powerful and accurate missile that could destroy armor or punch through stone. In this case, the Javelin missile demolished the enemy-held building. Lieutenant Caesar exulted as he watched the building disintegrate. "When the Javelin hit the building, it was the sweetest thing I've seen in a long time." The Javelin effectively ended enemy resistance. "It ended up taking out three rooms and we had no problem from that building anymore," Gasman said.[3]

By 1700 the fighting at the bridge had died down. Charlie 2-7 remained in place to guard the bridge area and wait for the rest of the brigade to come up. Bravo 3-7 and two tank companies began pouring across the one-lane span that was still undamaged. They turned left and headed for Highway I, a main road that led to the airport and Baghdad itself. These smaller roads were confusing, though, and for a time the Americans had to sort out which way to go, but they soon pushed northeast to expand the bridgehead.

Captain Leroy "Dave" Benton was able to alleviate the confusion and get his Bravo 3-7 rolling on a narrow, single-lane raised road. He himself was in the lead. The road twisted and turned several times. At one of the turns, the captain came in contact with an enemy armored vehicle (probably a BMP or BRDM). His gunner destroyed the vehicle, but then his 25mm jammed. All at once, other Bradley crews behind the captain saw several more enemy vehicles camouflaged in the foliage beyond the road. One after the other, the Americans picked them off. The enemy APCs exploded and burned. The carcasses belched dark, oily smoke into the late-afternoon air.

The Americans were stationary, lined up in a single-file, linear column on this raised road. With the Iraqi vehicles destroyed, Benton's soldiers noticed that there was an extensive series of bunkers on the right side of the road. The road was raised, like a causeway, so it sloped down, almost like a sheer drop. The Iraqis had used this as a natural ambush point. They had dug their bunkers at ten-meter intervals, paralleling the road. Three to six men were hunkered down in each bunker. From here, they were popping up, taking RPG and rifle shots at eye level before diving back into their holes. The men in these bunkers were real soldiers from a Republican Guard reconnaissance company.

Bravo 3-7's fire support officer, Lieutenant Rasky, first reported the bunker system. "Enemy dismounts! RPG teams!" he roared over the company net. None of the Bradleys could get a shot at these enemy soldiers. They were too low and too close. The barrels of the Bradley's machine guns and 25's could not depress that low. Rasky grabbed his M4 Carbine and tried to shoot down at the enemy soldiers, but he was probably not doing much damage. Once again, as at the bridge, only dismounted infantry could deal with the bunkers.

Benton's executive officer, Captain Douglas, pulled his Bradley into position on the right side of the road. Douglas was in communication, via his CVC, with Sergeant Belloc, whose fire team was ensconced in the back of the track. Douglas said to Belloc several times, "Be ready to dismount. Bunkers on the right."

"All right, just let me know when we're gonna get out," Belloc responded each time.

As they readied themselves, Belloc and his team were tense, high on adrenaline. Belloc himself was frightened but ready. As described in the Introduction, he was a diminutive man from Phoenix, Arizona, who spoke with just a trace of the northeast in his accent. Three years earlier, he had left college to join the Army. He was twenty-seven, with a wife and kids back home. In the Army he had proven to be a brilliant shot with a rifle (hence his status as the company's sniper).

At last the ramp lowered and Douglas ordered them to dismount. In seconds they were out on the road, looking for the bunkers, taking shelter behind the Bradley. Belloc positioned his three men on the left side of the Bradley while he covered the right. The Bradley was slowly moving along the road. From his vantage point on the right side of the Bradley, the little sergeant could not see the enemy holes. They were somewhere below the slope of the road. Enemy small-arms fire was sweeping along the road. The only thing the grunts could do was shoot downward at the enemy. To do this they would have to expose themselves to the Iraqi soldiers who were shooting upward from their bunkers, most of which were five or six feet deep. Belloc understood that this would be dangerous, but he knew that if he did not do it, no one would.

His team members laid down a wall of SAW fire on where they thought the first bunkers were. Belloc unhooked a grenade from his flak vest, left the cover of the Bradley, activated the grenade, counted three seconds, and tossed it over the edge of the road. He heard an explosion. He rushed to the edge, pointed his M4 Carbine at a bunker below, and squeezed the trigger several times. His rounds struck home, finishing off several green-uniformed Iraqis who had been wounded by fragments from the grenade. Out of the corner of his eye, Belloc saw airborne jump wings pinned on the tunic of one of the corpses.

There was no time to linger. Sergeant Belloc grabbed another grenade and assaulted the next bunker and then the next. A few yards away from Belloc, Specialist Joseph Blum, who served as Captain Douglas's gunner, was in his slot, watching Belloc make his one-man attack on these bunkers: "[He] was walking up to the side of the road" and looking for the bunkers. "[He] couldn't see 'em, so he just went up to the edge of the road and he just started shooting down on top of the bunkers, right at the guys—'Boom! Boom! Boom!'" He'd come back, drop a hand grenade in."

For Belloc's men, it had only been a few minutes since they had dismounted, but it seemed like several hours. The heat was intense, almost overwhelming. The engine exhaust from all the Bradleys and tanks only added to the thick, steamy, languid air. Enemy soldiers were still pouring fire up and down the road. Their spent bullets clinked off vehicles, or snapped as they whizzed by. Each grunt was wearing BDUs, a MOPP suit, a Kevlar helmet, and body armor, along with various pieces of equipment. The men were all sweating profusely. The road seemed to wind into eternity. Who knew how many bunkers were down there? It seemed endless.

It did to Belloc as well, but he was very determined to clean out the enemy bunker system. Right now, as he focused his entire being on destroying the enemy bunkers, he was more frustrated than anything else. His grenades were supposed to cook off at five seconds, but they were lingering several more seconds before they exploded. In training he had specifically been taught to count to three and then throw, leaving only two seconds until the detonation. But as he worked his way along the road, he noticed there were several long seconds between his throw and the explosion. He was sure he was counting to three. He even contemplated counting to four seconds, but that, he felt, was just too risky. "I didn't want it to blow up in my hand."

Belloc crept up to a new bunker and tossed a grenade into it. As he waited for the explosion and kept his eyes focused on the bunker, he saw an especially brave Iraqi soldier catch his grenade and throw it right back at him. The thing was turning in the air and it looked as big as a softball. Sergeant Belloc knew it could explode at any second. He was a mild-mannered person who was quick to joke and smile. But right now, as the grenade soared toward him, he was filled with anger, almost a blinding rage. A lightning-quick thought flashed through his mind. "That grenade could take out my whole fire team!" The very idea that his own grenade could be turned against his team, killing or wounding his men, was so unthinkable, so horrible, that Belloc could hardly stand it. Everything he had done on behalf of his team, all the promises he had made to these men to look out for them, would be for naught. It would all be his fault, he thought. "That kind of pissed me off because I didn't want none of my soldiers . . . to get hurt."

In the next instant, he hurled himself backward and the grenade flew right by and landed on the road a few feet away. His men were perilously close to the grenade. "I pushed one on the ground, and I jumped onto the ground and I rolled underneath the . . . FIST'er's Bradley [a FIST is an artillery fire support team]." Not more than half a second later, he heard the grenade explode. "When it went off, you heard . . . the [shrapnel] hitting" the sides of the Bradley. Sergeant Belloc quickly got up and checked on his men. Fortunately, none of them were hurt. The sergeant was relieved, but he was still filled with white-hot anger that the Iraqis would have the temerity to turn his own grenade back on him. His face betrayed his rage. His normally jovial features were now tight, strained, with narrowing eyes and thin lips. The dirt and sweat that creased his young brow and cheeks only added to this war face.

Belloc had now reached the point of no return. This was a fight to the finish. He was in a kind of frenzy. He would kill all of these enemy soldiers or die trying. It was like a personal war. Everything came down to this face-to-face encounter with men who wanted to kill him and his team. It was combat at its most basic and primitive, the kind of fighting that had rarely occurred in the Gulf War but was more common in this war. Cottonbalers of the past, like Jerry Crump or Hiroshi Miyamura, would have understood exactly how Belloc felt at this moment. It was as if nothing else existed, only the fight.

Sergeant Belloc was getting ready to assault a new bunker when he saw a pickup truck a couple hundred meters away, driving toward the lead Bradley. The truck was crammed with enemy soldiers. Some were popping off inaccurate shots as their truck careened forward. Belloc hollered at the FIST'er track, "There's a truck! Engage it!" But the 25mm gun on the FIST'er track was jammed. No other American vehicle seemed to have a shot at the truck. Like any good sergeant, Belloc had prepared his team for something like this before they dismounted: "I made sure . . . that somebody took an AT-4 because I knew there was a lot of armor out there."

An AT-4 was a handheld antitank weapon. It was not as modern or deadly as a Javelin, but it was quite accurate within a two-hundred-meter range. It weighed fifteen pounds and shot a fin-stabilized warhead. Belloc slung his Carbine and grabbed his team's AT-4 off the back of one of his men. With amazing fluidity, given the gravity of the situation, Belloc aimed the AT-4 and fired. The warhead shot out of the tube, streaked through the air, and slammed into the truck, blowing it sky-high. The skeletal remnants rolled forward a few more feet but came to a fiery stop.

The soldiers inside were killed instantly or were rolling around on fire. Most likely, none of them survived. The concussion of the explosion engulfed the Americans, rumbling Captain Douglas's Bradley. Specialist Blum, who watched the whole thing through his gunner's sites, shook his head in admiration and said, "Damn!"

On the ground a few feet away, Sergeant Belloc was worried that he had not shot the AT-4 properly. Before squeezing the trigger, he had not glanced behind him to make sure his men were clear of the backblast. "I didn't clear the back, which I should have." One of his men had been pretty close, but nothing serious. "He told me it rocked him, but he was all right."

WITH THE TRUCK DISPOSED OF, Belloc got rid of the AT-4 and turned his attention, once again, to the bunkers. There was still plenty of fire coming from them. Clearly there were many more left to deal with. Two of his men were so exhausted and so dispirited by the prospect of going after more of these seemingly endless bunkers that they could not continue. Belloc told them to get back into Captain Douglas's Bradley.

Meanwhile, the sergeant resumed his one-man assault. With only two men covering him, he went after the next series of bunkers, pitching grenades, shooting downward, right into the faces of the Iraqis. "I must have used at least nine grenades." Captain Douglas tossed him whatever grenades he had. "I used the company's whole supply. There were a lot of holes, from the beginning of the road to the end of the road. After the explosion, I would have to go in there and clear it, because there was more bodies in there, so the grenade was not killing most of them. You'd see an arm blow up. I would go and check and the guy would still be alive . . . not the guy who got blown up, but the two or three guys under him." Belloc by now was a ruthless killing machine. He simply pointed his Carbine at these survivors, fired several aimed shots, and finished them off, man-to-man, face-to-face.

As he did this at one bunker, several Iraqi soldiers in the next bunker opened fire on him: "One round hit my radio, one just nicked my leg and the other went straight through my pro mask. It was close but I didn't even know [they] hit me at first."

Specialist Blum did. He was several yards away, watching the whole thing. He saw the enemy rounds walk along the road and into Belloc. "Sergeant Belloc got shot!" Blum screamed. He expected to see Belloc go down in a heap, but he just stood there, seemingly unaffected. One of the bullets appeared to go right up his back. Blum was thunderstruck by the sight of this. "How in the world could Belloc survive that?" he wondered. He expected the sergeant to collapse at any moment, yet he kept fighting.

Belloc had no idea how this looked to the other Americans or, indeed, how close he had just come to death. He only knew he had to keep going. No sooner had the Iraqis in that next hole shot at him than he killed them. His bullets tore into them with almost surgical precision. Belloc was out of frag grenades now. He used whatever he had, even a smoke grenade. He tossed it into one hole. The smoke gave him enough cover to jump down and shoot the hole's occupants. But now he was out of smoke grenades too. This fight had come down to one courageous man with a rifle against an enemy about twenty or thirty times his size.

Belloc kept going from bunker to bunker, firing his Carbine point-blank at the enemy. Many of them were paralyzed with fear or inertia. Some cowered in their holes as Belloc shot them. Others tried to shoot back, but somehow they missed the American sergeant. Belloc went through clip after clip of ammo, probably more than three hundred rounds in all. He attacked and attacked, like some kind of avenging angel, literally eyeball-to-eyeball with his victims. "I saw their faces. I saw every single one of them. Some of them acted like they were dead. They would shut their eyes and then they would open up to see if I passed them, but I would still be looking at 'em." Belloc shot them and moved on to the next hole. He was usually within a couple feet of them, close enough to see the expressions on their faces as they died. It was horrible but almost monotonous too. Finally, at last, there were no more holes to assault. "To me this felt like forever but . . . it was, like, fifteen or twenty minutes." He got back in his Bradley and only then did he notice that his leg was bleeding from the close call Blum had witnessed. The wound was just a scratch, nothing serious.

In that short fifteen or twenty minutes of combat—less time than it takes some people to shower or cut the yard—Belloc killed at least fifty enemy soldiers and negated any possible threat to the lives of his Bravo 3-7 comrades. It was combat at its crudest, most elemental level. It was personal, intimate even. Once again, as when the Cottonbalers had assaulted across the Euphrates just hours before Belloc's exploits, the entire outcome of a battle rested upon the shoulders of a few lonely infantrymen. Indeed, in this case, it could be argued that the outcome rested on the shoulders of one man. In just a few minutes, one motivated, brave, well-trained soldier destroyed an entrenched enemy force that outnumbered him fifty to one. Belloc's actions on that steamy April day in Iraq must go down as among the bravest and most heroic in the storied history of the 7th Infantry Regiment. Almost single-handedly he saved his unit from a certain RPG ambush that might have caused casualties. His actions also helped pave the way for the whole 3rd Division to exploit the river crossing and turn north to the airport. Belloc was a normal man, probably at heart a peaceful man. He took no pleasure in killing so many people. But on that day, he knew it had to be done. War puts men in such a position. What made him do it? To be sure, anger and aggression were factors. But overall, he did it for his buddies. He was protecting his fire team and, in a larger sense, his whole company. He got the Silver Star, but he probably deserved the Distinguished Service Cross or even the Medal of Honor.[4]

ONCE BRAVO 3-7 HAD CLEARED the bridghead east of Objective Peach, the better part of the whole 3rd Division began the process of crossing the river, turning north, and heading for the airport. The bridge and its environs were still under intermittent attack, but the Americans were now ready for their big push on Baghdad. At the bridge there was a tremendous bottleneck as hundreds of vehicles sought to cross. Stuck vehicles only added to the traffic problem. Terrain and the inevitable chaos of a mobile campaign were the greatest impediment to Baghdad for the Yanks, not Iraqi resistance. The lead elements of 2-7 were trying to get across the river, but there were innumerable delays. North of Al Musayyib, Rage Company had been waiting in a blocking position, protecting the flank of the 1st Brigade advance through the Karbala Gap. Accompanying armor from Bravo Tank got stuck in the marshy ground and Rage had to babysit them while crews worked to get them extracted.

As they did so, they came under RPG attack. They spent the night of April 2–3 fighting off these small attacks, most of which were minor. There was a close call, though. An RPG came close to taking Captain Smith's head off. Luckily, he was fine and his men captured the enemy crew.

Now, at dusk on April 3, Rage, Bravo Tank, and Bravo 2-7 all managed to get through the traffic jam and across the Euphrates. Major Coffey was everywhere, bullying support units to get out of the way. "I remember getting on top of vehicles. I was yelling at them to get off the road. We had to pass through first. It was the classic fight-for-the-road traffic-jam type of thing."[5]

As Coffey and Task Force 2-7 crossed the river, Charlie 2-7 and much of the rest of Task Force 3-69 took off north. Their job was to attack the airport from the southwest and take the actual runways. Saddam International Airport was located about ten miles west of downtown Baghdad. Captain Kelly's Charlie 2-7 rolled north on Highway 1, a road that curved west of the city itself. The journey was strange for these men. Hundreds of people greeted them as they rumbled into the western suburbs of the capital. Some of the people cheered and waved. A few frowned or stared in puzzlement. One man was wearing a Guinness T-shirt. Some of the Cottonbalers smiled, waved, and threw MREs to the crowds. Others, like Captain Pecina, were wary of an ambush. "It's making me nervous," he said. "I wonder if they always hang out outside like this."

He had reason to be worried. Not far from the friendly crowds, small but dedicated groups of enemy fighters began a series of ambushes along Highway I. The enemy had chosen to dig in and fight along the major roadways in and around Baghdad. These fighters were not just Iraqis. Many came from Syria or other Arab countries to fight in what they perceived to be a jihad against infidels.

Captain Kelly's vehicles were going about 20 or 30 miles per hour. From either side of the road, he could now hear the rattle of small-arms fire and whooshing sounds of RPGs: "We were encountering . . . dismounted ambush teams, RPGs . . . everything from RPGs, small arms . . . not a whole lot of tanks or anything, but a lot of ambushes and pockets of resistance."

The Americans responded with massive firepower. They spewed 25mm and Abrams-main-gun fire at the enemy positions. Sergeant

Sorenson's Bradley raked them over with killer fire, but he could not help admiring the courage of these outgunned enemy soldiers. "I have the utmost respect for [them] because they had mortars, RPG's, gun trucks, APC's. These guys were in foxholes. They'd pop up and shoot an RPG and in return, they'd take a main tank round or a twenty-five right into that foxhole. There was no surrender here. They were fighting to the death. It was extremely close range, just shit flying everywhere. It was two hundred, three hundred meters at the most."

An RPG came close to destroying a scout vehicle from an accompanying cavalry unit. This light reconnaissance unit, probably from 3-7 Cavalry, came to a halt and got mixed up with Charlie 2-7. After a short delay, they got moving again. The last thing the commanders wanted was to stop and present a stationary target. They knew that if they kept moving, their columns would be hard to hit and they would maximize their advantages of maneuver and firepower. Besides, the objective was the airport.

Near the front of the column, Private First Class Bennett, Sorenson's gunner, spotted several enemy vehicles in an ambush position on an overpass. "There was one BMP and there were . . . three full sized trucks. They had .50 cals mounted on the back. I got all three of them and hit the BMP. I wasn't expecting the HE to really do anything but it blew up." The BMP's turret flew off when Bennett's high-explosive round hit it.

As Bennett continued scanning, he saw dismounted enemy fighters all over the place. Some were running. Some were in foxholes. Some were shooting small arms at his track. Others were maneuvering for RPG shots. Bennett sprayed coax rounds everywhere. In the back of the Bradley, Sergeant Kelly, the fire team leader who had played such a big part in the capture of the escarpment, was listening to the battle on his CVC. Kelly and his guys were busy passing Bennett fresh boxes of coax ammunition. The gunner was going through rounds with lightning speed. Kelly was amazed at all the shooting he heard outside the track: "I'm hearing mortars coming in, an RPG fly by here and there." He kept hearing a distinct pinging sound. It was bullets hitting the track. "I'm lookin' out the periscope. You can't see shit 'cos there's vehicles on fire. So they're [Sorenson, Bennett, et al.] just haulin' ass through the smoke, not knowin' what's in front of 'em." There was so much smoke and dust that Bennett and many other gunners could hardly see anything, just hot spots.

Charlie 2-7 was nearing the exit road that would take them to the airport. Predictably, enemy fighters were dug into fighting positions all around the exit. They knew that the Americans wanted the airport and that they needed this exit to get there. In the command Bradley, Captain Kelly watched as his company poured a withering volume of firepower on the enemy holes and roadside ambush spots. "Literally it was like driving down the interstate and you come to the exit and there's your off-ramp going into the backside of the airport. We were actually fighting to get off the off-ramp against different pockets of resistance from guys mounted on trucks to dismounted RPGs . . . you name it. The Bradleys, the 25's, and the tanks did a devastating number on those guys."

They seized the exit and fought their way onto the airport road. The enemy fire died down, and things got fairly quiet. Kelly reorganized his unit and prepared to make the final push to the airport.

Back on Highway 1, in the vicinity of the exit, the enemy was battered but not finished. One problem with the policy of rolling right through them and not stopping to clear out resistance was that it left many enemy behind to attack the lightly armed supply and support convoys that followed the lead combat vehicles. Lieutenant Brett Gendron, a young West Point officer who was assigned to the S-1 section, was riding in a Humvee along Highway I. This support column had a few old M113s but little else in the way of armor. All at once, the enemy opened fire from both sides of the road. "I've never seen so many fucking vehicles . . . shooting at us from both sides. The deuce [-and-a-half truck] behind me took three RPG's. One came in through the tarp and ripped it off. Everything in the back of that . . . thing was peppered. One round hit the side of it." Like the heavier Bradley and tanks, the support column kept moving while returning fire with .50-cals and small arms. Fortunately for those riding in the truck behind Gendron, many of the RPGs did not explode. The ambush faded away, like a storm left behind in the rearview mirror.

Kelly's leading elements were no more than a kilometer from the airport. The night was pitch-black and they found it difficult to see where they were going. In the desert the men had gotten used to driving with

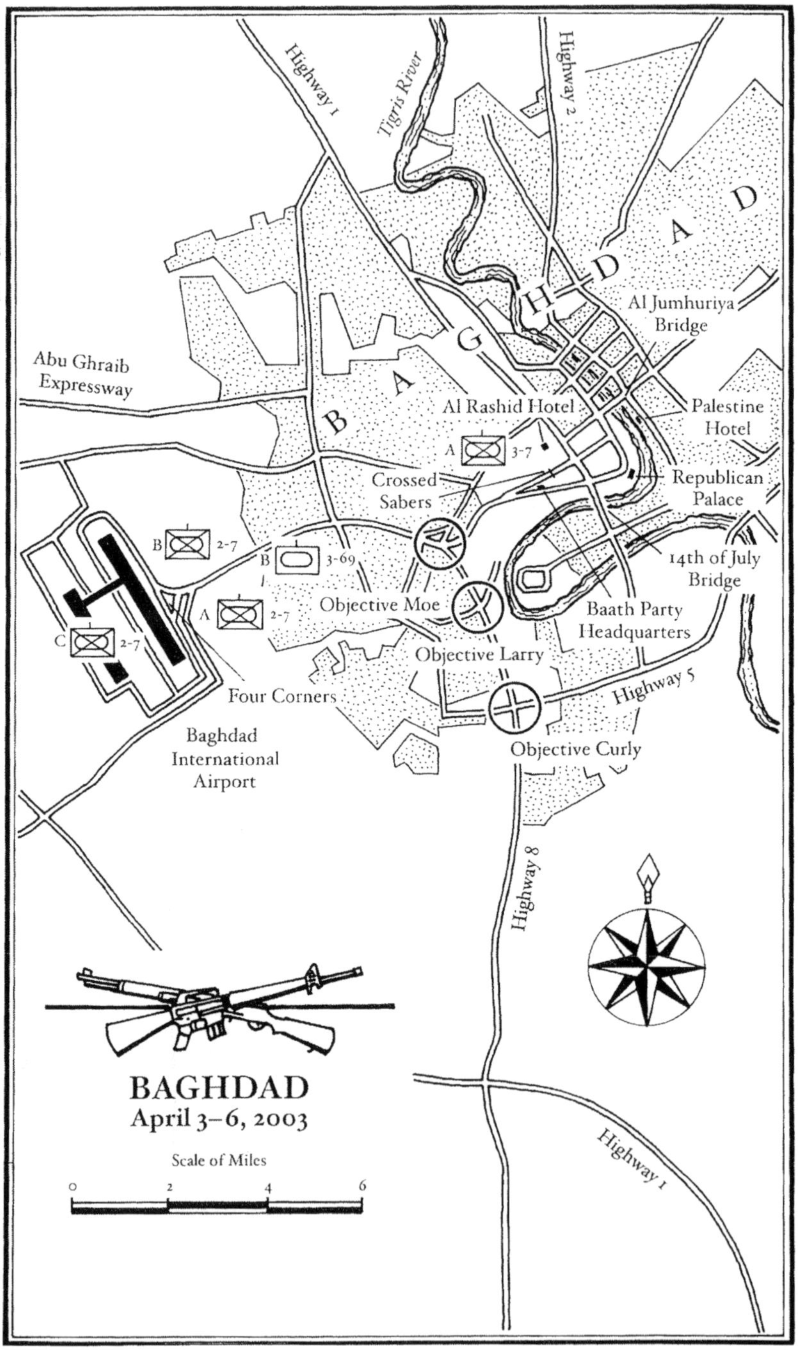
Highway 1
Tigris River
Highway 2
BAGHDAD
Al Jumhuriya Bridge
Abu Ghraib Expressway
Al Rashid Hotel
Palestine Hotel
A 3-7
Crossed Sabers
Republican Palace
B 2-7
B 3-69
14th of July Bridge
A 2-7
Objective Moe
Baath Party Headquarters
C 2-7
Objective Larry
Four Corners
Highway 5
Baghdad International Airport
Objective Curly
Highway 8
BAGHDAD
April 3–6, 2003
Scale of Miles
0 2 4 6
Highway 1

their lights on, but they couldn't do that here. Even with NODs, it was hard to see. Plus, there were walls everywhere. The Cottonbalers knew that there had to be an opening into the airport, but nobody could find it. The lead vehicles rolled to a stop in front of one wall. Captain Kelly was sure the airport was on the other side, so he ordered the tanks to shoot a hole through the wall. A tank fired two rounds to no avail. The second shot ignited a propane tank, causing a fire that lit up the night. By the flickering light of the propane fire, the captain could now see an unopposed gate that obviously led into the airport. His driver maneuvered his Bradley to the gate and punched through and into the airport. They had no idea what might be waiting for them. After a few awkward moments, other vehicles joined them, and together they drove onto the main runways of the airport against little opposition. Kelly's people shot up a couple airplanes on the tarmac until Lieutenant Colonel Marcone told them to knock it off. For the rest of the night, they remained in place, literally on the runways, waiting for other Cottonbalers to catch up with them.[6]

WHILE CAPTAIN KELLY'S MEN WERE breaking into Saddam International Airport, Lieutenant Colonel Rutter's Task Force 2-7 was experiencing the night movement from hell. The traffic jam they encountered during the Euphrates crossing had been bad enough, but once across they had navigation problems and eventually became enmeshed in a network of muddy canal roads. The terrain was a wafflelike cluster of irrigation canals and dirt roads. These roads were small and delicate, no more than six feet wide, hardly adequate for a mechanized task force. The sides of each Bradley and Abrams hung over the road as the vehicles gingerly drove on them. There were so many canals that the area was like one big maze. The Cottonbalers had studied satellite photos of these canals but had no idea what they were really like. The earlier passage of dozens of vehicles from 3-69 had weakened the canal roads significantly. On top of all this, Rutter's battalion was driving on them in pitch-darkness, making it that much harder for drivers to make their way.

At some point along this shaky route an unsupported bridge gave way, "Water flooded into these areas, making them all but impassable," one officer recalled. Parts of Bravo Company, the scouts, Major Coffey, and

Lieutenant Colonel Rutter had made it across the water before the bridge collapsed. However, Rutter now had at least half of his task force stranded west of the collapsed bridge.

First Sergeant Wilson's M113 was one of the stranded vehicles. He was truly enraged. Tonight his Bravo Company had finally been put in the lead of the task force. He and several other Bravo Company NCOs had been seething for days over the role Rutter had assigned them: "We weren't getting any of the good missions." Wilson believed his company was the best and yet it always seemed to be relegated to a supporting role. Rutter kept assigning the desirable missions to Rage Company, all the while telling Bravo that he needed them in reserve because they were his best outfit. "That's BS. Go tell that line to somebody else," Wilson thought.

So now, when Bravo finally did get to lead the way, the whole thing was unraveling. He knew he had to do something to save the situation. He had to find where the rest of the company was and identify a new route for the stuck task force. "Hold the company!" he radioed Captain Szymanski. "I'll find the lead."

The first sergeant told his driver to get moving. In no time, they got disoriented in the maze of canals. They turned on their headlights, but to no avail. All of a sudden, their M113 slipped off the road and onto its side in a sloppy, wet field. Wilson's .50-caliber machine gun swung around and conked him in the head, but he was more angry than hurt. Now he had gone and done it. Instead of being a hero, he was a goat. His vehicle was lying on its side, stuck in the maw. The medical track rushed over to him, but fortunately no one was hurt. Two Bravo Company Bradleys watched over Wilson's crew as they spent the whole night attempting to extract their APC from the mud.

Wilson's misadventure convinced Rutter that he had no choice but to improvise. He and the other vehicles that were already across the water—about one-quarter of his combat power—pushed for the airport immediately. The rest of the task force spent many hours arduously backing their vehicles off the road, since turning around was out of the question on this narrow isthmus. They eventually backed up, one by one, and found an alternate route to the airport.

So Rutter's Task Force 2-7 moved to the airport in staggered, disoriented groups. Most of them had made it by 0430 on April 4. The first vehicles made it a couple hours before that. Rutter's job was not necessarily to take the airfield itself. Instead he was supposed to set up a blocking position east of the airport, right on top of a Republican Guard complex. Here all the major highways came together in an intersection called Four Corners. Rutter's battalion was supposed to secure Four Corners, neutralize the Guard complex, and protect the east flank.

There had been a few firefights during the night, but mostly the area was quiet as the exhausted Cottonbalers pulled into position around Four Corners. The runways and hangars of the airport were somewhere up ahead, on the left but not visible because there was a fifteen-foot-high wall on the left side of the road. In front was the intersection with its spaghetti-like mishmash of overpasses and bridges. On the right, there was a patch of palm trees, and beyond that, the Republican Guard buildings. Rutter planned to push outward and secure the entire surrounding area around Four Corners.[7]

Some Cottonbalers posed for pictures beneath a sign that read: "Saddam International Airport," but most were too weary. They had been on the go for more than two straight days, and they were exhausted. Lieutenant Gleason, who had guided the first vehicles to the airport and then found a good spot for the TOC, settled into a deep slumber in the passenger's seat of his Humvee. Lieutenant Cuevas was equally tired. "It was horrible. We were fighting to stay awake. Guys were falling asleep standing up in their hatches." He dismounted and walked over to speak with his buddy Gleason but found him sound asleep with his radio mike cradled against his ear. Nearby, Sergeant Newcom was standing guard for his fire team while they caught some "rack," as the soldiers often referred to sleep. "I had a whole cargo pocket full of . . . coffee packets from MRE's. That's what I lived on, about four or five of them every hour or two. [The men] were laying in the street. I had to stand up to eat that coffee." After about an hour of this, the sun began to rise and Newcom, in spite of the coffee, could not stay awake. He woke his guys and told them to pull security. "I laid down on the concrete. I had my Kevlar under my head and my weapon was just laying there on my chest." In the growing daylight, one of his men ate an MRE, while another stood watch and chewed his fingernails.

Across the street, under an overpass, the TOC vehicles were in place and all was quiet. With the TOC now set up to his satisfaction, Major Cooney, the executive officer, finally had a chance to answer the call of nature. He picked out an unobtrusive place about twenty meters away, in some bushes, took off his MOPP suit and his helmet, lowered his pants, and went about his business. A few moments later, he heard the crack of a rifle. A bullet zinged several feet over his head. "Hey, sir, are you OK?" several men at the TOC yelled.

"Yeah, roger, I'm good," the major replied.

Cooney actually was not very concerned. He figured it was a stray sniper who wasn't much of a marksman. "No big concern. The next round lands in front of me. The next round goes a little closer to my head. I reached out and put my Kevlar on." Then things got more serious. "The next round lands, like, ten feet in front of me and ricochets over my head so I ducked down a little bit." A mortar round exploded somewhere overhead, knocking him onto the ground but not wounding him. Major Cooney grumbled to himself in exasperation. Couldn't they give him a moment's peace? Apparently not, because the fire was intensifying. He knew that he had to get out of here—fast.

He told his men at the TOC to lay down suppressive fire for him. They opened up on some foliage where they thought the AK fire was coming from. Cooney was still under fire. He had no time to get situated. "I grab my stuff and begin to run. My suspenders . . . were dragging behind me. I had managed to pick up this ten-foot-long date palm frond hanging from my suspenders. So I've got all my stuff in my two hands . . . put my flak jacket on . . . now I'm running back."

The enemy sniper shot at him again. Cooney was disheveled, but he was running for all he was worth. The Arkansan was damned if he was going to die this kind of ignominious death so close to Baghdad. He had been in the Army sixteen years. This was no way for a career officer to expire. "As I got up and started running . . . I identified a piece of cover." He saw some bushes and planned to jump over them and then behind his new cover. "Well, ladened with the ten-foot palm frond . . . hanging off me and all my gear . . . flapping around and my inability to jump . . . I jump over these bushes and my feet get caught. I just went . . . facedown into [a] mud puddle."

Not far away, Specialist John McNamara III, a Mark 19 gunner in Gleason's scout platoon, was pumping rounds at the Iraqi rifleman who was tormenting Cooney. Most of the other scouts were dismounted, taking cover and shooting back with their personal weapons, but he was at his gun. He saw the major trip and go facedown into the mud puddle. "All he's got on is his vest. He was dragging everything behind him, pants and MOPP bottoms around his ankles." In spite of himself, McNamara had to laugh. Cooney was, after all, a field grade officer, and it wasn't often that they looked so tousled and undignified.

Cooney actually felt the same way. He was a good-natured man, with an infectious laugh and a steady smile. Even though his life was in danger, he saw the inherent humor in this situation. Somehow he made it to the TOC and the shooting stopped. Cooney was filthy, out of kilter, and chagrined, but he was alive and that was the main thing. Of course, he took quite a bit of ribbing for his little "incident," but he understood it was all in good fun. "The image of his muddy smiling face . . . is a memory all those present will never forget," Lieutenant Schenck wrote.[8]

As it turned out, Cooney's close call was the beginning of a savage battle for the airport. While Charlie 2-7 and parts of 3-7 cleaned out the runways and hangars, Rutter's 2-7 found itself in a close-quarters, 360-degree fight with the Republican Guard. These Iraqi soldiers had slept through the night in their compound. When the sun rose, they awoke to find the Cottonbalers of 2-7 all around them and they attacked.

Basically, Bravo Company was north of the Four Corners intersection, Rage was south of it, and the TOC and various other units were at the intersection or nestled below an overpass, while Bravo Tank was east of the whole mess. By 0730 nearly every unit was in heavy contact.

On an overpass above the TOC, a FOX chemical detection vehicle was driving along, hoping to find a good position to test the area for the presence of chemical weapons. A hidden T-72 fired a round at the FOX. The shell skipped underneath the American vehicle and exploded harmlessly. The FOX team frantically backed their vehicle off the overpass. So now the Americans knew they were facing armor in addition to scores of dismounted infantry soldiers.

First Lieutenant Paul Mysliweic, a platoon leader in Bravo Company, ordered two of his Bradleys to ascend the overpass, find the enemy armor, and destroy it. The dismounts got out of the Bradleys, grabbed their Javelins, and trailed about one hundred meters behind.

In one of the Bradleys, Specialist Beck was intently scanning for the T-72. This was very serious business. He knew that this enemy tank had the capability to destroy his Bradley. Ever so cautiously, Beck's Bradley crept forward.

"Hey, Beck, scan left! Scan left!" Sergeant Root, the vehicle commander, ordered. He had just spotted the T-72.

Beck hit the slew button to scan left. At the same moment, he heard an awful high-pitched squealing sound. "A round hit us. It. . . knocked the shit out of the whole Bradley. It blew . . . a big assed cloud of fire in our faces." The blast blew Sergeant Root out of his turret and onto the front deck of the Bradley. The shell hit right behind Beck, bounced off the compartment where the dismounts would have been, and set off burning boots, rucksacks, T-shirts, and whatever else had been stored on the side racks. In the gunner's seat, Beck felt like he had been cold-cocked in the face. "I got knocked half unconscious. My driver was still good because the round hit right behind my seat. He threw it in reverse and backed down off the . . . overpass."

Specialist David Faulknor, a young machine gunner, ran up, grabbed Beck, pulled him off the Bradley, and took him to the aid station. Beck could hardly see where they were going. "I had all kinds of . . . shrapnel in my face.[The medics]kind of slapped some sense into me, flushed my eyes and shit." The aid station was close by, right below the overpass, near the TOC. Beck, Root, and the driver, Private First Class Gee, were very fortunate. None of them were seriously hurt, and they returned to action within a few minutes.

As they received medical attention, Faulknor and the other dismounts were up on the overpass maneuvering their Javelins into position to shoot at the Iraqi armor. Everyone understood now that there was more than one T-72 out there. These tanks did not operate alone.

The Americans were setting up their Javelins when a fire truck appeared out of nowhere and drove at them. An Iraqi in the truck was pitching grenades at American positions along the road. Every American gun opened up on him. Bullets peppered the sides and the windshield of the fire engine. Corporal Alfonso Saenz saw two men in the cab of the truck." One of them rolled out and did the quickest combat roll I've ever seen. The second guy was still in the truck. He starts waving his hand out of the bottom of the door. You couldn't see him, just his hand." Saenz and the other Americans yelled at the man to get out of the truck. He tried, but he was badly wounded. His torso hit the ground, and his legs folded over the top of him."His foot was flopping. That guy was fucked up." In the twisted environment of combat, the man's pretzel-like predicament was almost funny to Saenz.

Not long after this, the Javelin team was in place and ready to shoot. The gunner, Private First Class Jefferson Jimenez, locked in on the first T-72 and fired. The Javelin screamed off the overpass and dipped so low that it looked like it might fall on the TOC. "It was coming down like it was going to land on the roof of my truck [Humvee]," Specialist McNamara said. To his enormous relief, the second engine of the missile kicked in and it roared off in search of its target. Seconds later it slammed into the turret of the T-72, "under the bridge," in Jimenez's recollection, triggering a massive explosion. Specialist Beck, recovered now from his close call, relished seeing the Javelin destroy the tank that had nearly killed him and his crew. "The turret pops off, shit blows up and then about two seconds later you could hear another one . . . BOOM!" The turret flew, end over end, some fifty feet into the air. Ammo cooked off. The explosion ignited a fireball that melted the tank's armor, not to mention the crew inside. The fire was so intense that it damaged another T-72 a few feet away. Every American soldier in the area cheered when they saw or heard the Javelin take out the first T-72. The Four Corners area echoed with their excited voices. Before the crew of the second Iraqi tank could react, the Javelin team squeezed off another shot. Their Javelin scored a direct hit on it, sending it up in angry flames. The team then fired a third shot at another tank but barely missed. This T-72 beat a hasty retreat.[9]

THERE WERE MORE ENEMY TANKS, though. A few hundred meters southeast of the TOC, Captain Matthew Paul, the mortar platoon leader, was on the ground with one of his noncommissioned officers, looking for a good firing spot for his mortars. An Abrams from Bravo Tank drove up and the crew asked Captain Paul where the Unit Maintenance Collection Point (UMCP) was. These men had orders to recover a disabled tank. Paul and his NCO, Sergeant Jose Adorno, directed the tankers to Four Corners where the UMCP was setting up. The Abrams crew thanked them and left.

Seconds later, Paul and Adorno heard the telltale rumble of another tank behind them. Figuring that this was another Abrams, they turned around and waved. To their horror, they saw that the rumble wasn't coming from an Abrams. It came from a pair of T-72s rolling down the road, right at them. Adorno distinctly saw crewmen from one of the T-72s wave back at him. They looked just as stunned to see him as he was to see them. The moment was almost surreal.

"T-72!!" the captain shrieked. He and Adorno scattered to either side of the road. Adorno sprinted right and the captain sprinted left. Sergeant Adorno made it safely back to the mortar platoon in a couple minutes. Captain Paul was not so fortunate. The tanks began chasing him and shooting at him. Running for his life, Paul ducked in among the palm trees and took cover behind a berm and some tall grass. The two enemy tanks stopped about forty meters away from him and began shooting their machine guns into the berm. Paul had never been so frightened in his life. He pressed his face into the mud and lay still. The tanks kept shooting on and off. Bullets ripped through the berm and zinged around Paul. "Oh God, I am about to die," he thought.

Paul managed to key his radio mike and call Sergeant First Class Robert Broadwater, his platoon sergeant. "Move the platoon. There are tanks a hundred meters away," Captain Paul ordered. Instead of leaving, Sergeant Broadwater mounted a rescue effort. He planned to use the platoon's AT-4s to kill the tanks. He himself drove his Humvee into a field in full view of the enemy tanks and waved his arms to draw their attention away from Captain Paul. As the other mortar platoon vehicles set off on their mission, they encountered the Abrams crew that Paul had earlier directed to the UMCP. The tank crew had heard the report of T-72s and was looking for them, even though they were towing a disabled Abrams. The crew of this impromptu tow truck had been searching for the T-72s for several minutes now (at various times they asked Specialist Beck of Bravo Company and Lieutenant Jim Horn of Rage Company for directions). The mortarmen were only too happy to point out Captain Paul's location. The Bravo Tank Abrams got there, sighted the T-72s, and prepared to fire.

Behind his shrinking berm, Captain Paul heard the T-72 crews frantically screaming in Arabic as they spotted the bizarre-looking Abrams. Basically, these Iraqis knew they were about to die. They understood that their tank was no match for an M1 Abrams even when the American tank had another tank riding piggyback on it. The Abrams fired two quick shots. The T-72s exploded. Their turrets spun crazily in the air. Fire and debris flew everywhere. Captain Paul hugged the ground and hoped that nothing would fall on him. The detritus fell harmlessly around him. The hulks of the T-72s burned fiercely. No Iraqis survived. These Republican Guard crewmen were incinerated or melted into a stinking mush. The sickly sweet stench of their burning hair and skin hung in the still, humid air. Paul leaped up, saw one of his mortar tracks, and hopped aboard. He was deafened by the explosions, but he was damned glad to be alive.[10]

THE MAIN THREAT TO THE Americans now was enemy infantrymen, and there were lots of them. All around the Four Corners area, Republican Guard soldiers attacked. The place was crawling with them. Bullets and RPGs were flying everywhere. The popping and crackling sounds of gunfire echoed up and down the walls of the compound. The Americans were shooting back with everything they had, but still the enemy kept coming. The mortars and artillery fired a few fire missions (and they were quite effective), but this was mainly an infantry fight at close quarters. The temperature hovered somewhere around one hundred degrees. Inside the Bradleys it was easily twenty degrees hotter than that. Everyone was sweaty, filthy, and scared.

Engineers were dealing with the walls that bordered the Republican Guard complex. Under fire, bulldozers punched holes in the wall. In some cases, the holes revealed attacking enemy soldiers who wildly fired at the bulldozers or at the Bradleys that were acting as their bodyguards. American return fire shredded many of these brave Iraqis. Others surrendered or took off.

At one section of the wall, not far from the aid station and the mortars, two squads of engineers under Sergeant First Class Paul Smith were building a makeshift prisoner-of-war compound. These engineers were attached to Rage Company. Smith, their platoon sergeant, was a Floridian and Gulf War veteran who tolerated no mistakes from his men. He was a martinet who knew that miscues could and did get men killed in combat. A bulldozer punched a hole in the wall. The compound inside, consisting of a little courtyard, was perfect for POWs. It even had a tower overlooking the courtyard. Several of Smith's men strung concertina wire while others stood guard.

At the far side of the courtyard, one of the guards, Private Thomas Ketchum, peered through an aluminum gate and saw a group of men milling around a bus stop. "Hey, I think I see something," he said.

Sergeant Joshua Henry came up, looked through the power scope on Ketchum's rifle, and saw that these men were Iraqi soldiers. Henry yelled for Sergeant Smith. The sergeant jogged over, took a look for himself, and saw that the enemy group was growing by the moment. He saw at least fifty enemy, toting RPGs, AK-47s, and mortars. The Iraqis were moving left across his field of vision, in the direction of the tower and a couple of buildings that were situated on the other side of the wall from his courtyard. As Smith watched, more enemy troops came into view. Now there had to be at least one hundred of them. "We're in a world of hurt," he muttered. He turned to Ketchum and told him to go get a Bradley. Then Smith positioned machine-gun teams at the gate.

Fifteen tense minutes later, the Bradley arrived. The Bradley, under the command of Staff Sergeant Michael Wilkins, smashed right through the aluminum gate, took up position, and opened fire at the Iraqis. Many of them took cover in ditches and shot back. Smith and three of his men came along, using the Bradley as cover. The sergeant raised his rifle, aimed, and fired twice. Two enemy soldiers fell. Smith put an AT-4 to his shoulder, pointed, and shot. The warhead exploded among the Iraqis in the ditches, roughly one hundred yards away.

To his left, Sergeant Smith saw movement. Iraqi soldiers were climbing into the tower he had planned to use to guard the POWs. The Iraqis fired down into the courtyard, right on top of Smith's men. The GIs hugged the wall of the courtyard, pointed their weapons upward, and shot back. Smith's personal M113 rolled into the courtyard and hosed down the tower with .50-caliber bullets. Private Ketchum was near the hole that the bulldozer had made. He was so scared he could hardly breathe. He saw an Iraqi trying to scale the tower and shot him. The man fell off the wall. An RPG, probably fired by someone in the tower, streaked past and hit the M113 in the side, blowing up Sergeant Smith's rucksack but otherwise doing no damage. Mortars were exploding in the courtyard. Bullets were chipping the walls. A mortar round wounded several Americans. They got hit mostly by flying debris such as pebbles and shards. Many of them were bleeding, wondering if they were hit bad. There were medics on the other side of the courtyard outside the wall, along the road. Someone got the wounded men there.

The mortar platoon and some Rage Company men were also out there, doing whatever they could to suppress the tower and the Iraqis who were on the other side of the wall from Sergeant Smith's courtyard. Sergeant Newcom's fire team was shooting at whatever targets they could see around the tower, but it was tough because the team was dismounted and the wall was about eight or ten feet high. An engineer beside Newcom kept shooting M203 rounds over the wall. The damned thing was loud and it made Newcom's ears ring. He saw his company first sergeant, Benjamin Moore, run between two vehicles and up to the wall. "Cover me!" he yelled at Newcom's team. Moore pitched grenades over the wall. Their explosions were lost in the cacophony of the battle. Undeterred, the first sergeant darted back to another track to get more grenades.

Sergeant Adorno, the mortarman, was close by, shooting fire missions aimed at the Iraqi infantry in the ditches. He stood atop his M577, a small-armored vehicle that housed mortar teams, "banging and shooting and banging." A nearby 240 machine gunner fired at a tree, tearing apart an Iraqi sniper. "You see this guy's body parts just going left and right and everywhere." As Adorno's mortar spat out shells, he saw First Sergeant Moore run up to the wall with a couple of grenades.

"All right, you sonofabitches, wanna play?!" the first sergeant roared, and tossed the grenades over the wall.

Moore's antics struck Adorno and the men around him as humorous, and they broke out laughing. "It was like a comedy show. We was laughing at him 'cos . . . every time he'd throw 'em we'd give him hell."

But RPGs were streaking everywhere and that was not funny at all. The Bradley had been hit several times, as had Smith's M113. As Adorno was concentrating on his fire mission, one of his buddies told him to look out. Adorno turned to the right and, as he did, an RPG scored a direct hit on him. The warhead glanced off his Kevlar, turned downward, split open his flak vest, and slashed open his right side. Either it did not explode or it did so at a safe distance, because Adorno did not remember any effect from a detonation. "I hit the back of my track—my head hit—I dropped down." Adorno's buddy screamed for a medic and helped Adorno get to the aid station, all under fire. His face was badly bruised, and he was bleeding from his side. He had to be medevaced, but he was lucky he was not killed.

Sergeant First Class Terry Mulligan, Lieutenant Gleason's platoon sergeant, was near the aid station, outside of his Humvee. He saw the medics working on Adorno and several other wounded men from Smith's firefight. As he watched, Mulligan grew determined to help Smith and the others. Mulligan grabbed a machine gun, collared his driver, Private Robert Conrad, as an ammo bearer, and took off. When they were within sight of the tower, they set up the machine gun and opened fire. The machine-gun bullets bounced up and off the stone tower, but many whizzed through the aperture. Mulligan was sure he hit several enemy soldiers. He kept firing until his ammo ran out. Then he and Conrad ran back to their Humvee. Mulligan was so hot and tired that he almost passed out.

Just beyond Smith's courtyard, the Bradley suddenly started backing up. "Why is he leaving us like this?" Sergeant Kevin Yetter, one of Smith's men, wondered. All of the other engineers were thinking the same thing. They did not know that the Bradley was low on ammo. It backed around the 113 and all the way out of the courtyard. Sergeant Wilkins knew that in order to reload he had to take his Bradley temporarily out of commission, and he did not want to do that while facing the enemy. Besides, things seemed to have calmed down here. "It seemed like a good time to leave. I figured I would stay as long as I saw the enemy. But at this time the situation was calm."

To the other Americans in the courtyard, the situation did not seem calm, but the vantage point of Wilkins and his crew was different. In combat, two people, even though they are separated by only a few yards, can have a totally different perspective. This was one of those instances.

The exit of Wilkins's Bradley meant that the 113 was very vulnerable. With no Bradley in this fight, the firepower advantage of the Americans was greatly diminished. Sergeant Smith found a driver for the 113—the crew had been wounded by a mortar shell—and supervised as he backed it into the courtyard. Smith hopped on top of the 113 and into the gunner's hatch. Retreat was not an option to Smith. He was dead set on staying here and continuing this fight. From this position he could cover the tower and the remnants of the aluminum gate. If he and his men got pushed out of this courtyard, the Iraqis might very well overrun the mortars, the aid station, and even the TOC a couple hundred yards up the road.

Smith soon saw that there were still plenty of Iraqis in and around the tower. They popped up and shot at his men in the courtyard. In response, the sergeant blasted away with the .50-caliber gun. "Keep me loaded!" he shouted at Private Michael Seaman, his driver. Seaman passed up box after box of ammo, each one consisting of one hundred rounds. Sergeant Smith turned his gun left and right, firing mainly at the apertures of the tower. "He was firing, firing, firing—reloading—firing, firing, firing," Sergeant Robert Nowack recalled.

The noise of Smith's machine gun was deafening, almost like a jackhammer. Spent casings were clinking and dribbling everywhere. First Sergeant Tim Campbell, Smith's superior, and three other GIs were directly benefiting from his suppressive fire. They crept up to the wall at the base of the tower. Campbell looked up and saw the Iraqis shooting from inside the tower. They were dressed in black and were wearing black berets. Campbell and the others pointed their weapons through the aperture and opened fire. Their bullets struck home. The enemy soldiers were shredded. Their blood splattered all over the place. "It was everywhere," Campbell recalled. The Iraqi fire began to peter out.

At the 113, Sergeant Smith's machine gun had gone silent. Private Seaman wondered why. He had just given the sergeant a fresh box, so he had plenty of ammo. All at once, Smith's knees buckled and he slid down inside the vehicle. Private Seaman saw a mess of blood staining Smith's flak jacket. A bullet had hit him in the head and appeared to have exited from his throat. Smith was unconscious. Seaman burst out crying. "Sergeant, we need to leave," he howled. He threw the 113 into reverse.

Nearby, Private Gary Evans also saw that Sergeant Smith had been hit badly. Evans jumped onto the 113 and tried to talk to Smith as the APC backed out of the courtyard: "You're going to be all right. You'll be okay." Smith did not respond. He was barely alive. Just outside the courtyard, on the road, the 113 stalled. Several American soldiers removed Sergeant Smith, put him on a stretcher, and carried him to the aid station about seventy yards away.

There were so many wounded and dying men at the aid station by now that the place stank like rotten meat. Most of the casualties were Iraqis. None of the Americans had life-threatening wounds except, of course, Smith. The medics stuck a tube down his throat and performed CPR. At times his pulse grew stronger, but he died within twenty or thirty minutes. The medic who was holding Smith's IV bag set it down, walked away and lit a cigarette. Another medic started crying and threw up.

The sergeant's actions had resulted in the deaths of many enemy soldiers and, arguably had held the southern flank of 2-7 in place. Lieutenant Colonel Rutter was so impressed with Smith's actions at Four Corners that he put him in for the Medal of Honor and he eventually did receive it.[11]

NORTH OF FOUR CORNERS, BRAVO Company cleared much of the Republican Guard compound. Basically, they were somewhere behind the backs of the Iraqis who had fought Smith's small group near Four Corners. Bravo Company's actions, in addition to those of Sergeant Smith's men, eliminated most Iraqi resistance in that area.

To the southeast, Rutter, Captain Smith, and much of Rage Company were attacking another part of the Republican Guard complex. The Americans went straight in, right through the walls. "We busted through the wall," Sergeant Ziegelmann, Smith's gunner, remembered, "and . . . a couple tracks went to the right and all the RPG's were just flying with rounds going everywhere."

Rutter and Smith decided to back off and pound the place with supporting fire. The vehicles backed out of the complex and rolled to a safe distance while forward observers called in mortar fire (from Paul's platoon), artillery fire, and close air support. The results were devastating. The mortars and artillery collapsed roofs on top of the stalwart Republican

Guard RPG teams. The air strikes reduced the buildings to absolute rubble. The concussion waves were awesome, almost like an earthquake. When the infantry went back in, many of the Iraqis were dead, buried in the rubble. Most of the survivors wanted only to surrender. One building was mostly unscathed, so Smith's FSO called in additional mortar fire. The shells hit the roof, causing the whole thing to collapse. Once again, dismounts went in and secured the remains of the building.

There was almost no resistance from the Iraqi survivors in the rubble. The grunts took some POWs and cleared out the remnants of the building. In the next instant, they heard the high-pitched whine of a T-72 main gun round that whistled in among them. Sergeant Charles Johnson's whole squad was knocked to the ground. "It hit the pavement, came up and hit [a] tree, right where we were at." Luckily, no one was hurt. The Javelin team was feverishly trying to get a shot at the tank, but there was a fence in front of them and they had no clear lane of fire. The combat vehicles were searching for the T-72.

As it turned out, it wasn't very far away. Johnson's squad leader, Staff Sergeant Ray Robinson, saw the enemy tank through a hunting scope that he had taped onto his rifle. The turret of the T-72 was traversing and seemed to be pointed at Captain Smith's Bradley. Robinson could see the Iraqi commander standing in his turret. The squad leader drew a bead on him and fired. The tank commander's head whipped around and he dropped, like a stone, into the turret. As this happened, a Bradley from the 1st Platoon fired two TOW at the enemy tank. The first one missed, but the second one scored a direct hit, turning the T-72 into a funeral pyre .The tank had been the most formidable enemy resistance in this sector. With it gone, the ferocity of enemy opposition began to wane. Captain Smith's men continued hunting small groups of Iraqi infantrymen. They killed or captured several enemy soldiers.[12]

As the fighting raged around Four Corners throughout the morning on April 4, First Sergeant Wilson was trying to rejoin Bravo Company. He and his men had spent a tense night with their stranded 113. Two Bradleys from Bravo Company, under the command, respectively, of sergeants named Miller and Maccabee, guarded his vulnerable track. In the morning, shortly after sunrise, they succeeded in extracting the M113. At this point, Wilson and the two Bradleys linked up with a support column of wheeled vehicles under the command of Captain Knight, the battalion S-4.

They were rolling along, going about 10 miles per hour on a paved road, probably five or six miles away from the airport. The two Bradleys were in the lead, followed by Wilson's vehicles, a medical track, and 120 trucks and Humvees. Everything was peaceful, yet Wilson had a bad feeling. The streets were deserted. Somehow that did not seem right. First Sergeant Wilson keyed his mike and called one of the Bradleys. "Hey, something don't feel right. It's too easy. There's nobody around. There's no people. We're about to enter this highway and there's no American forces around."

The other sergeant had the same feeling. "I know what you mean, Black Seven. Something's wrong."

Within five seconds, they were ambushed. In defending Baghdad, the enemy generally chose to fight along major roads, particularly at overpasses. From here they could harass convoys and hinder the movement of American vehicles. All over the southern margins of the city, thousands of enemy fighters—hailing from all over the Middle East—were in place, waiting to fight the powerful American armored strike forces. Wilson's little collection of vehicles was not so powerful, but it was a target nonetheless.

Wilson heard gunfire from both sides of the road. "All hell breaks loose. About forty dismounted soldiers on both sides. They're launching RPG's at us, small arms fire, machine gun fire . . . and direct laid ADA guns at us. Just incredible." An RPG bounced off the front of the lead Bradley. Another one whizzed past the second Bradley. The Americans returned fire with their 25's, coaxes, and .50-caliber guns. Wilson fired his .50-cal at a dizzying array of targets. He was quite exposed, since his torso and his head were poking out of the turret. Enemy soldiers were in hasty fighting positions—small holes really—on either side of the road. Wilson's fire and the 25mm high-explosive shells of the Bradleys turned many of them into mincemeat. Even as he was shooting, Wilson was talking to Captain Knight, consulting on what to do. Doctrine said to turn into the point of the ambush and destroy it, but doctrine was designed for a much stronger force than this one. Knight and Wilson decided to keep moving.

Sergeant Maccabee, returning fire with everything at his disposal, was shaking his head in wonderment at the temerity of the enemy fighters. "I'll never forget the feeling I had. I was incredulous that they would shoot at us. Those fools."

The ambush lasted a couple minutes at the most. The column kept going. Before they knew it, they hit another ambush. This enemy group was set up at an overpass. They had machine guns and ADA guns and they were significantly better positioned than the group that had sprung the first ambush. The first shots came from the left side, drawing the attention and the fire of the Bradleys, but the major enemy firepower was on the right side where several enemy were ensconced behind a wall. First Sergeant Wilson saw them and realized what was going on. "The ambush is on the right-hand side," he told the Bradley commanders. "The decoy's on the left-hand side."

He heard no response. "I need you to switch your fire over to the right-hand side! You've got enemy on the right-hand side!"

Sergeant Maccabee, whose track had been hit by multiple RPGs, responded in a voice that was unbelievably calm, "Ah, Black Seven, I'm a little busy right now."

Wilson marveled at the composure of the man. As the Bradleys were finishing off the remaining opposition on the left, Wilson swung his .50-cal to the right. "All of a sudden I catch out of the corner of my eye this very large, black object floating at me." It looked like a football and it was heading straight for his head. In that instant the nature of the threat clicked. RPG! "More out of instinct than anything else I threw my body back. It flew inches away from my head. I snapped my body back up. I'll tell you what. You wanna talk about upset." First Sergeant Wilson was enraged, infuriated. The soldier who had fired the RPG had deliberately tried to kill him. Wilson thought, "The nerve of this man. I didn't do anything to him." In the context of combat, this thought might not have been rational, but it was powerful. The angry first sergeant blazed away at the RPG man, killing him at the close range of about one hundred meters. "I really almost emptied every single one of my rounds on that one soldier." Only later, when the shooting died down and they left the ambush site behind, did Wilson allow himself to think about how close he had just come to death.

His column had only a few miles left to link up with the battalion at the airport. Along the way, they were hit with two more ambushes. They fought these off in the same manner, with all the firepower at their disposal. Amazingly, in all of this combat, only one man in the convoy was wounded and no vehicles were destroyed. The two Bradleys and Wilson's M113 did a fine job of eliminating most of the resistance, in effect protecting the wheeled vehicles. Indeed, many of the support platoon men who were at the rear of the column did not even know that they had just weathered four perilous ambushes.

By the time Wilson linked up with the rest of Bravo Company in the afternoon, the fighting around the airport had died down. The soldiers of Charlie 2-7 and some from 3-7 were still clearing the runways and hangars but with very little opposition. Around Four Corners there were still snipers, the area was under intermittent mortar fire, and the dismounts were in the process of securing several buildings, but the Republican Guard had been broken.

After his harrowing experience, Wilson was dying for a cup of coffee. He crouched inside his track and began brewing his coffee. He was looking forward to telling Captain Szymanksi and his NCOs about the four ambushes. Sergeant McNish rolled up in his track and greeted Wilson. "You won't believe what happened to me," Wilson said. He ascended into his cupola and told McNish about the ambushes.

McNish listened patiently and said, "Oh, that's nothing. Sergeant Root's track got hit by a T-72 ..."

Wilson knew his story had been bested and his face showed it. McNish chuckled at the first sergeant's disappointment. The chagrined Wilson was thinking, "You know, I really had a great story before this guy told me this." He slurped his coffee and brooded. A mortar shell whistled in and exploded about twenty feet behind him. Dirt and debris rained down on him and splashed into his coffee, but he was unhurt. "These assholes! If they would just let me drink my coffee! This is all I wanna do," he thought.

A moment later the captain called and asked Wilson if he was OK. The captain wondered if the first sergeant thought they should move the company to avoid any more mortar fire. First Sergeant Wilson was too tired and ticked off to deal with moving the company. His coffee had flecks of dirt floating in it, but—damn it—it was his and he wanted to sit here peacefully and drink it. He keyed his mike. "Black Six, this is Black Seven. That appears to be just a random mortar shot. I suggest we hold the company in place. Out." Then he put his handset down, picked up his coffee, and took a sip. He sure hoped he was right about the random mortar round. Luckily, he was.[13]

WITH THE AIRPORT UNDER CONTROL, the Americans now began their final assault on Baghdad. Brigade-sized elements of the 3rd Division engaged in what were called "Thunder Runs" through the city. The Thunder Runs consisted of mobile armored columns that penetrated deep into the city, even downtown to the palace and building complexes that were the geographic heart of the Hussein regime. These Thunder Runs dealt with fanatical resistance and killed hundreds of suicide fighters. In the main, the Cottonbalers were not part of the Thunder Runs but were affected by them.

On April 6, the 2nd Brigade launched a Thunder Run that was designed to take, in the boldest fashion, the downtown palaces and official government buildings. The day before, the brigade had experienced an intense fight on the highways of southern and western Baghdad. On April 6 the greatest worry for the brigade commander, Colonel Perkins, was his main supply route on Highway 8. As his strike columns penetrated into Baghdad, they fought hit-and-run battles with the usual groups of rabid fighters at overpasses or interchanges. Perkins's tanks and Bradleys needed softer-skinned vehicles to resupply them with ammo, water, food, and maintenance parts. Perkins made sure to guard his supply lifeline and support vehicles with various combat elements from his brigade, mainly at three intersections known as Objectives Moe, Larry, and Curly. Enemy resistance at these intersections was intense—machine guns, AKs, RPGs, mortars, and even some ADA guns. Throughout the morning on April 6 as the lead units of the 2nd Brigade pushed into downtown Baghdad, the intensity of the fighting steadily grew. Perkins needed to reinforce his troops downtown, but much of his brigade was still tied up at Moe, Larry, and Curly. He realized that he needed help from the 1st Brigade. General Blount had designated Rutter's 2-7 as a backup force in case the 2nd Brigade needed help. Blount and Perkins decided to send 2-7 to relieve 3-15 Infantry, the unit that was holding Curly. The plan was for 2-7 to relieve 3-15, after which the latter unit would roll a couple miles north to Moe, so as to make sure the supply line to the 2nd Brigade in Baghdad was secure.

At the airport, the call for help came at 1030. The Cottonbalers had spent the last twenty-four hours in a fairly restful mode. There had been a few firefights and some patrolling, but the airport was pretty quiet. The men had gotten a chance to sleep, throw footballs, and take off their MOPP suits. Some raided Saddam's VIP terminal and one of his palaces for goodies. Others got a chance to go swimming in a pond. Now it was back to business, though.

It took 2-7 only forty-five minutes to get everyone loaded up and on the move. The scouts and Rage were in the lead, followed by Bravo and the tank company. They drove down the same three-lane highway from which they had come more than two days earlier. Storefronts with brightly colored doors lined the route. As they approached the interchange where Highway I met Highway 8 they began to see some evidence of war-blackened cars, ruined buildings, fires, and the like. The day was hot and humid. Inside the Bradleys it was easily 110 degrees, maybe even hotter. The dismounts, as usual, had it the worst, cooped up as they were in the stuffy rear compartment of each Bradley.

At Highway 8, they turned left and proceeded north in the direction of Curly. At the head of the column, Lieutenant Gleason noticed tan Italian-made land mines blanketing one side of the road. The enemy had dumped a shovelful of dirt on each mine in a crude effort to conceal them. "It was comical," Gleason commented. Actually, the enemy probably knew the Americans would see the mines. Most likely, they wished to slow down the GIs rather than deceive them. Engineers from the 2nd Brigade, during the night, had worked to clear many of the mines, literally under the noses of the enemy. There were still enough mines to cause some disquiet for the Cottonbalers, though. Gleason's Humvee was about three feet away from the nearest mine. Ever so carefully, Gleason got his scout sections out of the way so that Rage Company and the other heavier elements could now lead the way. Gleason's scouts had done their job. They had guided the task force to Curly.

In one of the lead Bradleys, Major Coffey was focused on the considerable problem of effecting this relief in place with 3-15. He knew they were under fire at Objective Curly. He also knew that this handover would be tricky. After all, 3-15 was in the middle of a fight. It would be tough to coordinate exactly when and how 2-7 would take control of Curly and 3-15 would vacate. There was the issue of friendly fire to consider. Even in his technologically advanced era, with FBCB2s in many Bradleys, it was risky for two American combat units to approach each other in the middle of a battle.

Major Coffey decided to press ahead himself, find the 3-15 TOC, and coordinate this relief face-to-face with the commanders of that unit: "I conferred with the colonel [Rutter]. We . . . agreed that the bulk of the battalion would remain behind until we could figure out exactly where we needed to go in." He found out where the 3-15 TOC was—right at Curl as it turned out—and drove up to them. Coffey heard some shooting, but it did not seem particularly intense to him. He noticed that the 3-15 vehicles were in the middle of the road and he considered that to be a mistake. In 2-7 the soldiers had been taught when holding a position to push off on either side of the road. "You prevent the enemy from even being able to approach you or establish an ambush position."

Major Coffey hopped off his Bradley and went into the M577 that served as 3-15's TOC. Inside the 577 he spoke with Major Denton Knapp, 3-15's executive officer. The two majors agreed to make an incremental boundary change. One company from 3-15 would leave just as a company from 2-7 arrived to take its place, and so on. Coffey left the 577 and began walking back to his Bradley. As he did so, he noticed that the volume of enemy fire had increased. But the 3-15 soldiers were simply huddling under cover behind their vehicles, not returning fire, and this annoyed him. "Move forward and engage the enemy!" he snarled at them.

He glanced at the interchange and noticed that many of 3-15's combat vehicles were loading up, getting ready to move north: "I began to realize that this wasn't gonna be a . . . one-for-one relief in place. We were just gonna need to rush up there . . . take their sector so they could keep moving north."

He decided to go back to the 3-15 TOC and speak with Major Knapp again. The fire was even more intense now. Bullets were skipping along the road and knocking off chips of concrete from the overpass. Coffey needed cover if he was going to make it to the 3-15 TOC. The major skittered along the road and began climbing through the front seat of a

Humvee that had accompanied him. He had made it as far as the driver's seat when he saw an RPG flash somewhere to his left and heard an explosion as the RPG hit the Humvee. "The bottom of my left leg went numb." Shrapnel and rocks from the RPG explosion tore through his lower leg, breaking his fibula. Another RPG explosion soon followed and now the Humvee was on fire.

As fast as he could, Coffey climbed through the cab of the Humvee and onto the pavement. "I'm not dead yet," he thought. He could see Knapp's vehicle just ahead. Coffey limped on his bloody leg and kept thinking, "I'm not looking down at my leg yet." He heard the dreadful whooshing sound of yet another RPG. This one streaked behind him and smashed into the side of his Bradley. It blew up several rucksacks but did not penetrate the Bradley's armor. Coffey hobbled over to Knapp's 577. The two men had a brief conversation that basically confirmed Coffey's suspicion that there would be no orderly relief in place. The soldiers of 3-15 were pulling out and going north as quickly as they could because they were under intense pressure from brigade to do so. Coffey and Knapp decided to bring up Rage, the lead company of 2-7, as soon as possible. This relief would be done on the fly.

Bleeding and a bit angry, Major Coffey limped away from the TOC. His leg was throbbing now. Rounds were pinging all over the place—off Bradleys, off the pavement, off nearby embankments and guardrails. The Humvee was still burning. The two soldiers who had been riding in it were nowhere in sight. Upon reaching his Bradley, Coffey saw that his driver, Specialist Duran, was not in his slot. Unbeknownst to Coffey, his gunner, Sergeant Stephens, had ordered everyone to evacuate the Bradley when they got hit by the RPG.

"Duran!" Coffey shouted.

The driver materialized from behind a concrete abutment and Coffey told him to get back into his hatch. Coffey assembled the rest of the crew and began climbing into his commander's spot. Sergeant Stephens was on the battalion net, relaying the situation to Rutter, calling for Rage to get moving. Stephens and the other men insisted that they look at Coffey's wounds before they would allow him to get back into the turret. One of his dismounts, Specialist Nicholas Cochrane, put a pressure bandage on Coffey's leg and stopped the bleeding. "My guys were being very kind and loyal and acting worried and not wanting to let me back in the turret." They kept urging him to go back to the aid station, but Coffey would have none of this. "I could tell by that point I wasn't about to die or lose my leg or anything. I . . . got back in the turret."

He told his two dismounts to get out and lay down suppressive fire. Duran pulled the Bradley into a good firing position and Stephens began hosing down a building, to the north, where they saw numerous muzzle flashes.

Several hundred meters to the south, the lead Bradleys of Rage Company were on the move. From their vantage point, they were taking fire. They shot back with their 25mm guns. Without knowing it, they were shooting at 3-15. A Special Forces pickup truck exploded. Other vehicles got hit but did not explode. Rage Company's rounds smashed into the overpass, sending big shards of concrete falling downward. The soldiers of 3-15 screamed over their radios, waved bright orange recognition panels, and flapped their arms wildly. At last the Rage gunners saw them and ceased firing. Miraculously, no one was hurt.

Chastened, Rage Company rolled right through 3-15's position and took up positions just beyond Objective Curly. "We pushed through 'em and got on the far side of the bridge," Captain Smith said. "We set up on the far side and we started suppressing a major apartment complex or it could have been an office complex. It was about an eight-story . . . building."

Just north of the bridge, Major Coffey directed them into place and saw them roll by, but he and his crew were still dealing with a steady volume of enemy fire. Not far away, Rutter's Bradley destroyed a white suicide truck. The enemy concentrated a volley of RPG fire on several support trucks parked across the highway from Coffey, just under the bridge. They scored a direct hit on an ammo truck, igniting it in a deafening explosion. Coffey felt the concussion waves ripple over him. The ammo inside the truck started cooking off, sending bullets and fragments zinging through the air. Two more ammo trucks and a fueler exploded, adding to the maelstrom. The noise was deafening.

Coffey's Bradley was firing at the same building where he had seen muzzle flashes. The major was still peeved at the low level of suppressive fire coming from the Americans around him. Many of the GIs who crewed the support vehicles were in no mood to climb into them and be incinerated by the next explosion. Most were hunkered under cover. "Lay down some damned fire!" he kept shouting at them. A Special Forces soldier bolted from cover, jumped onto his pickup truck, and began spraying the enemy positions with .50-caliber fire. Together Major Coffey's Bradley and the Special Forces pickup truck poured forth a steady base of fire.

Coffey was amazed at the chaos around him. Hot metal was flying everywhere. He kept wondering, "Why am I not getting hit? These guys are really bad shots or something." A few moments later, the throbbing in his leg reminded him that he was anything but unscathed: "Wait a minute, Rod; you were hit!"

Several meters away, Specialist Cochrane was on the ground, covering the rear of the Bradley. He saw three enemy fighters about 150 meters away, attempting to approach the Bradley from behind. Cochrane drew careful aim, fired, and dropped all three of them in a row. Major Coffey thought of this as a classic example of the qualitative difference between American soldiers and their adversaries. "AK-47 spray versus a trained American infantryman who, with a few rounds from an M16, can actually hit what he's shooting at."

Most of the 3-15 vehicles were gone now. They had rolled north in pursuit of their new mission. Captain Smith and three Bradleys from Rage Company were still being shot at by fighters holed up in the eight-story building. The captain decided that this was a job for close air support. He pulled his Bradleys back and called for an air strike. In a matter of minutes, the Air Force dropped two JDAM (Joint Direct Attack Munition) precision-guided bombs. The bombs scored a direct hit on the building, sending a fireball shooting into the air. The blast of the bombs shook the building and shot gray dust everywhere. A score of Bradleys and tanks descended on an adjacent industrial complex from which several holdouts had been shooting. The Americans blasted everything in sight, chewing up the complex. One enemy soldier tried to escape. A Bradley shot him in the chest and he fell into a bloody heap.

Blackened cars and overturned telephone poles were everywhere. Dust and smoke wafted from the rubble of what had, several minutes earlier, been perfectly good buildings. Millions of flies were swarming all over the place. They were attracted by the stinking remains of human feces and rotting garbage that coated the whole area. The nauseating stench of all this refuse mixed with the sulphuric, rotten-egg smell of cordite and gunpowder.

At last, the enemy attack died down and 2-7 secured the area. The battalion had accomplished the challenging, dangerous mission of relieving another unit under fire and guaranteeing the security of an important supply route. The Americans were close to taking Baghdad and toppling Saddam's government. The Cottonbalers were helping make that happen.

THE SPECIAL FORCES SOLDIER WHO had manned his pickup truck's .50-caliber gun approached Sergeant Stephens. "Hey, man, what unit are you with?"

Stephens's face was a grimy, sweaty mess. He had a cigarette dangling from his lips. "I'm with 2-7 Infantry, from 1st Brigade Combat Team," he replied proudly. The Green Beret thanked him for his help. Without it, everyone at the 3-15 TOC could have been killed, he claimed. Coffey now had time to seek some medical attention. He went to the aid station and saw the battalion surgeon. The doctor examined his leg,glanced at him, and said, "You're gonna want to stay, aren't you?"

"Yes," Coffey replied. There was no way he was going to leave his battalion. He was a dedicated, brave officer. He knew the men of 2-7 needed him. He was not going to let himself get evacuated into the netherworld of the "medevac conveyor belt" in the rear. If that happened, who knew when he could get back to the battalion? Coffey had no clue that his leg was broken. He only knew that it hurt, but he could get around on it.

"Well, if you can walk on it," the doctor declared, "I'll know it's not broken, so lemme see you walk on it."

Coffey got up and started walking around. The leg hurt like hell, but he pretended that it did not. Satisfied, the doctor let him stay. Only a week later did Coffey get X-rayed and find out that he had been walking around on a broken leg.[14]

As 2-7 eliminated enemy resistance around Objective Curly, Captain Carter's Attack 3-7 was helping secure the southern approaches to Baghdad. The day before, on April 5, they had cleaned out a deserted Republican Guard complex and had lost one man wounded to an RPG ambush. Now on April 6, the company was engaged in a reconnaissance mission about five miles south of Baghdad. They had no tank support because every available Abrams had been used on the previous day's Thunder Run and now needed maintenance. Thus Carter's company consisted of ten lonely Bradleys with a couple of 113s. They were driving in a column down a narrow two-lane road. The road was bordered by small houses, foliage, irrigation canals, and sunken, muddy fields. Carter did not feel good about this. He and his men were trained to travel in a wedge formation where they could efficiently deploy their firepower, not a column formation where they were like ducks in a row. The confining terrain around the road only made this even worse.

There were dozens of people walking along the road. Obviously they were fleeing something or someone. Several of the wanderers looked like military-age men. Carter's unit had picked up an interpreter back at Hindiyah. He spoke to several people. They told him that there were suicide fighters up ahead, in a little village. They also reported the presence of Saddam Hussein's personal helicopter. Carter moved his 3rd Platoon into the lead and resumed the patrol.

They rolled through a little cluster of buildings that comprised the village. In the lead Bradley, Staff Sergeant Slago, the colorful Californian, saw two flashes emerge from a nearby tree line. Multiple RPGs slammed into his Bradley. Shards flew everywhere. The Bradley filled with acrid smoke. "There was a big boom and a white flash that didn't go away," Specialist Kenneth Clark, a soldier in Slago's vehicle, recalled. "I felt heat and stinging all around my neck." Shrapnel peppered the driver Specialist Sciria's back. Slago's crew and the dismounts bailed out. The enemy expected them to do so and opened up with withering AK-47 fire. Somehow the Americans made it to the cover of a mud wall with no one getting hit. The Bradleys began laying down suppressive fire. First Sergeant Burns and the medical track came up and evacuated the wounded. Most had minor wounds, although Sciria did need to be evacuated.

Carter and Lieutenant Nadig, the 3rd Platoon leader, decided to go forward and eliminate the enemy ambushers. People were streaming out of the area, trying to get away from the shooting. But Lieutenant Hooper and his gunner, Specialist Gary Bipat, saw one man going in the opposite direction. He was in his forties, "kind of balding, a mustache . . . wearing regular clothes . . . the long flowing gown." The man was walking toward the road, straight at the Americans. He could be hiding anything under that long gown, or he could be innocent. Hooper and Bipat were not sure.

"Do you see this guy?" Bipat asked.

"Yeah, I see him," the executive officer replied.

"Can I shoot him?"

Hooper shook his head. "Keep the gun on him. If you see anything that looks the least bit aggressive . . . smoke him."

The words had hardly left Hooper's mouth when the man whipped out an RPG and shot at one of the Bradleys. "We immediately smoke him at that point—coax and twenty-five on him. He didn't live to see the day. Then we turn on the house that he's from and they're shooting from the top. We just dropped twenty-five along the house."

There were two dead enemy now, but several more were shooting back and taking cover "using a complex of canals, irrigation ditches and levees for cover," one witness remembered. These adversaries were fanatics, clad in civilian clothing—one even had an American basketball jersey on with scarves and headbands that trumpeted jihadist slogans. The coax and 25mm fire of the Bradleys was dangerous to the enemy but not immediately fatal. They were too close and a bit too elusive in the maze of ditches alongside the road.

Lieutenant Nadig called Carter: "Hey, sir, we just gotta get on the ground and kill these guys."

Carter agreed. "Let's just go kill 'em."

In one of Nadig's Bradleys, Sergeant Ingram was sitting in the back, right by the ramp, waiting for the order to dismount. For the first several minutes of this firefight, this Bradley, commanded by Sergeant Jason Vandegrift, had lagged behind with maintenance problems. "V's idiot driver, a guy called McGaughy . . . was, like, a complete klutz. There was nothing you could do with this boy. He had thrown the track off the Bradley." They had had to dismount under fire and fix the track. Now they were back in business.

Ingram could almost feel the adrenaline coursing through his veins. He felt a nervous lump in the pit of his stomach. It was always this way in the last moments before dismounting. Actually, it was rather like riding on a roller coaster that was ascending to its apex before the big plunge.

The ramp lowered and he heard the dismount order over his radio. He and his squad spent a minute or two orienting themselves to the situation.

The enemy was somewhere among the irrigation canals. The Bradleys were spaced out along the road. Many were firing short machine-gun bursts into the canals, hoping to kill or suppress the enemy they knew were out there. Sergeant Ingram's nervousness dissipated. Now that he was on the ground, this was just like training. "There was the odd bit of fire, but it was hard to pinpoint." Ingram and the other dismounts took cover behind a berm. The sergeant saw some coax fire tearing into one levee in particular, and at that point he knew the enemy was in there.

One of Ingram's fire teams took cover behind a berm and laid down some fire on this levee while he, Sergeant Shaun Urwiler, and the latter's fire team plunged into the fields and maneuvered forward. These were classic fire and movement tactics. One group laid down fire while another closed with the enemy. Coax fire from the Bradleys added to the protective blanket of bullets as Ingram's team moved. They were running along a ditch line in the middle of some raised irrigation canals. Their weapons were oriented forward, ready to shoot. The day was hot and humid. The soil smelled dank, almost moldy. The enemy may or may not have been shooting at them. With all the noise from the Bradleys and the excitement of the moment, it was hard to be sure.

Panting and sweating, they flopped behind a berm, not far from where the enemy was hiding. Ingram and Urwiler pitched grenades behind the enemy-controlled levee. The grenades exploded, sending plumes of water into the air but otherwise doing no damage. Seeing this, Ingram knew he had to get even closer to the enemy. "These guys not only have cover, but they've got water they can get underneath to negate any effect of a hand grenade," he thought. As the rest of the team covered them, Ingram and Urwiler slithered forward by themselves, right up to the levee. They were going to assault the enemy position on their own. This was contrary to doctrine—the team leader was supposed to assault with one of his guys, not the squad leader—but doctrine was out the window now. Ingram and Urwiler both knew that this was a life-and-death moment that required action from small-unit leaders.

One of them pulled the pin from a grenade and rolled it over the levee and into the ditch where the jihadists were taking cover. The two

Americans were on their knees, ready to spring. The grenade exploded, and like cats they leaped over the levee and into the ditch, firing all the way. Ten feet away, Ingram saw a man with an RPG on his shoulder. The man had lost his balance and was falling away, but he squeezed the trigger of the RPG. At that same moment, Sergeant Urwiler shot him and the man fell heavily into the water. Meanwhile, the RPG swished just past Ingram's right shoulder.

"They just shot an RPG!" Ingram heard his platoon sergeant holler over the radio.

"No shit they fired an RPG," Ingram thought sarcastically. He was lucky he still had thoughts. The RPG missed taking off his head by only a few feet—at the most. All of this had taken one or two seconds. Slightly to the left, Ingram saw the RPG man's buddy in the ditch, so close he could reach out and touch him. The young sergeant opened fire with single semiautomatic shots. "I didn't even aim. I just kinda brought my muzzle up and, in the water, I . . . walked the rounds into his chest. The first round missed him, just from bringing my weapon up and firing 'cos I was already firing when I hit the ditch. I could see the round hit the water, and then the next round hit the water and then the next round hit his chest. Then the rounds started going into his chest. He kind of writhed in the water a little bit as I was shooting him."

In seconds both enemy fighters were dead. Seeing the example of Ingram and Urwiler, the fire team leaped from cover and came forward. They cleared the ditch, killing another enemy fighter and destroying the enemy weapons. Then they made their way back into their Bradley. Ingram needed several minutes to collect himself from this deadly encounter. He had just killed another human being, close-up, face-to-face. "You kind of feel a sense of invincibility 'cos you've just done the ultimate. You've just defeated other people. It's not like . . . a game of soccer . . . and there's next time. There's no next time and you just kicked their ass." Ingram was eventually awarded a Bronze Star for his actions in this fight.

There were still a few enemy left. When Ingram's squad was remounting, Specialist Choice Kinchen pulled security for them and spotted an enemy fighter trying to sneak up on them. He shot at him and either killed him or drove him away. Not long after this, Captain Carter, who was a few vehicles away, spotted at least two jihadists trying to sneak up on his Bradley from a nearby culvert. They were swimming under the green-colored water, trying to use it as cover. The captain told his driver to pull forward a bit. Carter started pitching grenades at the culvert. They exploded, sending water splashing everywhere. The enemy kept ducking under the culvert and then emerging to pop off a few shots.

Now, as Carter reached into his turret and grabbed his shotgun, he saw one of the men emerge, not more than five yards away, and point an assault rifle at him. The captain leveled his shotgun and fired. The shells tore into the man's chest, killing him instantly: "He was definitely a fanatic and not a soldier. That was the first time I had personally shot someone." The ordeal wasn't over. Another fanatic stood up and started coming at Carter's Bradley. He had an RPG on his shoulder.

Carter's eyes widened. "Kif! Kif! Kif!" he screamed. The captain was armed with a captured AK-47 now, since his shotgun was out of shells. He pointed the rifle at the man and screamed at him some more. Still he would not stop. He was only a few yards away. Carter aimed between his eyes and fired. The bullet hit him dead-on, tearing out the back of his head and dropping him to the ground like a sack of tomatoes.

"That's what you get for trying to be a hero!" Carter bellowed. He hated the idea of having to kill this guy and was angry at him for it. "That stupid little fucker. He wouldn't give up," he muttered. "I think every infantry officer has a desire deep in his heart to prove himself as a combat leader. After a while, I guess you learn it's not really something you should hope for."

With Carter's terrifying showdown, the battle ended. Attack Company searched the dead enemy fighters and found that they had been carrying loads of ammo, several RPG launchers, and rifles. They had been in their early twenties. Many of them were wearing red headbands that said "Allah Akbar" (God is Great), the telltale insignia of suicide fighters.

Attack Company mounted up and returned to its assembly area just outside of Baghdad.[15]

IN THE DAYS THAT FOLLOWED, Attack Company and other Cottonbalers moved into Baghdad and helped take the capital against diminishing resistance. Attack Company occupied one of Saddam's palaces and did experience several firefights, including an intense one near the Tigris River bridges. Rutter's 2-7 encountered some opposition in western Baghdad but spent much of its time dealing with civilians or destroying abandoned Iraqi vehicles. For the Cottonbalers, the fighting was winding down.

Saddam's regime was finished and the Iraqi people knew it. For decades they had been oppressed by a tyrant whose cruelty compared with that of the worst butchers of history. Sensing he was gone, his people took to the streets in celebration, but more than that, they looted everything they could get their hands on. Thousands of people roamed Baghdad, taking mattresses, furniture, food, clothing, vehicles, and practically anything else of value. American soldiers had not been prepared, in their intelligence briefings or their training, to deal with this kind of looting. They did the best they could to make sure that the people did not loot weapons, but this was a difficult task. The environment was chaotic and difficult to control.

The looting ran its course in a matter of several days, and the Cottonbalers now made the transition from conventional combat operations to stability and support operations. This was a great challenge. They were being asked to go from being killers to nation-building peacekeepers in the blink of an eye. But that was the point of the war, even though there had been precious little planning for it. The Americans wished not only to depose Saddam; they also wanted to transform Iraq from a totalitarian Crock-Pot of hatred, torture, and terrorism to a democratic, prosperous ally. The Bush administration hoped that Iraq would be the beginning of a democratic revolution in the repressive Middle East. Only then, in the view of Bush's key policy makers, could Islamic terrorism be destroyed at its roots. Basically, they hoped that the spread of democracy in the Middle East would eliminate terrorism because they believed that free countries with representative governments would not breed terrorists.

From the middle of April onward, the soldiers of both 2-7 and 3-7 settled into assigned sectors in Baghdad. They had hoped to go home after winning the conventional war, but that was not to be. They were needed for the massive and ultimately more challenging job ahead—the job of "winning the peace." They lived amid a variety of conditions. Some lived in the remnants of Saddam's palaces. Others lived in shabby office buildings or apartments, with no running water and no air-conditioning.

They spent their days engaged in a dizzying array of tasks. They patrolled, night and day, as part of convoys or dismounted platoons. They confiscated weapons and traded shots with Saddam's die-hards and local street gangs. They apprehended criminals. They rebuilt infrastructure, dispensed medical care to the locals, and gathered intelligence on who was a Baath Party loyalist and who wasn't. They reopened schools, worked on restoring power to city blocks, fed people, clothed people, established relationships with local leaders, played soccer with children, and, at night, hunted for terrorists. They sent out ordnance teams to find and destroy mines, rifles, machine guns, bullets, and other munitions. They policed up and buried bodies left over from bombing raids or firefights. They cleaned up rubble, rebuilt neighborhoods and roads, and reopened hospitals that were staffed by skeleton crews of local doctors and nurses. They digested thousands of tips from Iraqis as to the whereabouts of Saddam and searched for the deposed tyrant. They found out who the troublemakers were on any given block and incarcerated them.

Days turned into weeks and weeks turned into months. The majority of the Iraqis around the Cottonbalers were friendly and grateful that Saddam was gone. The Americans earned their respect, and likewise. But, to be sure, there was tension and even some bloodshed. The Cottonbalers were not yet cognizant of the kind of organized insurgency that would eventually plague the occupation, but they did encounter some opposition from guerrilla-style fighters. One day a man snuck up on a Cottonbaler who was guarding a crowded bridge and shot him in the head. The sentry, Private First Class Marlin Rockhold, was mortally wounded. There were mines, improvised explosive devices (IEDs), and the occasional firefight. Lieutenant Gleason lost a soldier to a mine. Lieutenant Gendron of 2-7 and his driver were badly wounded one day when their Humvee struck a command-detonated mine. The driver lost both legs below the knees. Lieutenant Gendron went through nearly a year of painful rehabilitation for shattered bones in his lower legs. Sergeant Ingram and several members of his squad were decorated for killing several Iraqi fighters in a nighttime firefight in July. The Iraqis had opened fire on Attack Company Bradleys and had tried to detonate an IED.

Mostly, though, the problems consisted of everyday concerns. The Baghdad Iraqis wondered when their lives would get back to normal—when would they have power again, running water, and so many other necessities of urban life? They could not understand why the powerful Americans could not make all of this happen in an instant. Some of them believed that the Americans wore X-ray sunglasses that allowed them to see beneath the robes of local women. Others believed that the Americans possessed mystical powers of healing. For instance, one woman with a gravely wounded child believed that the child could be healed if only an American medic would lay his hands on her. The Cottonbalers tried to disabuse her of this notion, but she would not listen. Finally, they relented and did what she wanted. The woman seemed happy, but the Americans were sure the child would not live.

Overall, relations were good. In the 7th Infantry there were no recorded instances of rape, murder, torture, or other maltreatment of Iraqis, whether civilians or captives. Almost to a man, the soldiers believed that they were helping the Iraqis and doing some real good. Of course, they also understood that this job would take many years, not many months. First Sergeant Wilson believed that it would take generations. He told one Iraqi man that his grandchildren would enjoy freedom, but in the meantime, things would be tough, a daily struggle for existence: "Every day it got better. When you saw the people and the way they lived and you really dealt with the people, you really wanted to stay there for the people. You really wanted to stay there to give them a place to live. This is a messed-up place. We need to try to help 'em out."

Some soldiers shared Wilson's resolve and wished to stay in Iraq for altruistic reasons. But by late summer, most wanted little more than to go home. They knew they were doing some good, but they had had enough of Iraq. They had been away from their loved ones for nearly nine months. They had fought a bold campaign, taken control of a country, deposed an evil dictator, and done their best to transform a country. Now they were ready for someone else to take over for them.

In August 2003 the soldiers of the 7th Infantry came home. Ebullient family members and friends greeted them at Fort Stewart, in homecoming scenes that were a carbon copy of what returning Cottonbalers had experienced after the Gulf War in 1991. The soldiers went on block leave during their first month back home. Many struggled with the memory of their wartime experiences or had difficulty relating to civilians, even their own families. Some left the Army and went back to school or got civilian jobs. Many stayed on and even reenlisted. They hoped their war was over, but as the insurgency grew in 2003 and fighting continued into 2004, it became clear that the 7th would someday return to Iraq. In early 2005 they did return for another tour of duty. Some served north of Baghdad, in Tikrit, others in the capital itself. Their main job was to train soldiers for the new Iraqi Army and provide security for the population, while seeking out and destroying insurgents.

The Iraq War, then, did not have the closure of previous wars. Major combat operations may have ceased in May 2003, but the struggle continued. The conventional war of the spring of 2003 turned into a guerrilla war, a protracted fight against an elusive and wily enemy. By 2008, even with Saddam gone (and the Cottonbalers in the midst of yet another tour of duty in Iraq), the violence and bloodshed persisted. The longer it continued, the more controversial the war became in American culture and politics. When the soldiers were unable to find Saddam's WMD, some Americans argued that Bush had lied or misled the country into war. Others believed that Iraq was a distraction from the real war on terror and not a necessary fight at all.

The Cottonbalers who fought in Iraq largely disagreed. To them, the war was an important component of the fight against terrorism and a war that, in the end, rid the world of a despot, Saddam Hussein. First Sergeant Wilson, who fought in both wars involving Iraq, summed up the typical sentiment that prevailed among the soldiers of the 7th Infantry: "This one was much more gratifying. We got on the ground and actually got results from people, got to talk to people, listen to the torture that they went through, see some of the places. We didn't care about any WMDs. All we cared about was that there were a whole bunch of people . . . that really needed our help."

Without a doubt, the war brought tremendous terror, bloodshed, and destruction to Iraq. It led to the deaths of several thousand American soldiers. Like any war, it was a tragedy of monumental proportions. But the prevailing sentiment among the Cottonbalers was that the war was an important step toward the greater good of American security, stability in the Middle East, and the destruction of terrorism. They may have been right or wrong about that. One thing is certain, though. In the Iraq War the soldiers of the 7th Infantry fought with great skill, courage, ingenuity, and even decency. The noncommissioned officers, in particular, were nothing short of outstanding. Their performance, and that of everyone else, was yet another example of the triumph of professionalism and the high quality of the American infantry soldier in the modern era.[16]

Afterword

AND SO THE STORY CONTINUES with no real ending. In the context of American history, the 7th Infantry is timeless. The unit has existed for most of America's history, and as long as there is a U.S. Army, the 7th Infantry will probably continue its service. The Cottonbalers have always been at the center of the action. As long as the unit exists, this will never change. Their calling is eternal vigilance. Their challenge is personal sacrifice. Their arena is the ugly beast of combat. In a dangerous, deeply flawed world it has always been this way. Nor will this ever change, unless human beings start to listen to the better angels of their nature, relinquishing war, thus opening up a new and better road to peace.

VOLENS ET POTENS!

Notes

INTRODUCTION

1. 1st Brigade Combat Team, 3rd Infantry Division, After Action Critique, pp. 13–17; Bravo 3-7 Infantry, Group Combat After Action Interview, March 11, 2004; Raul "Rudy" Belloc, Steven Collier, Robert Gasman questionnaires; Silver Star Citation, Sergeant Rudy Belloc; author conversation with Belloc. See Daniel Bolger, *Death Ground: Today's American Infantry in Battle* (Novato, Calif.: Presidio Press, 1999), pp. 123–130, for an excellent description of the inside of a Bradley Fighting Vehicle and the modern role of dismounted infantry.

CHAPTER 1. HOT AND COLD WAR: KOREA

1. John A. Heintges, oral history transcript, United States Army Military History Institute, Carlisle, Pa.; hereafter referred to as USAMHI.

2. Fred Long, *The Cottonbaler*, Summer 1996, p. 14. This is the regimental association newsletter.

3. Fred Long, *The Cottonbaler*, Fall 1996, p. 7.

4. National Archives, College Park, Md., Record Group 407, "Command Report, 7th Infantry, December 1950" (copy in author's possession). In this report, the regimental executive officer scathingly criticized the Koreans, claiming they were susceptible to a "dangerous mob instinct."

5. National Archives, Record Group 338, Box 66, Folder 4, Organizational History Files, "A Description of Combat Rifle Squads"; Morris MacGregor, Jr., *Integration of the Armed Forces*, 1940–1965 (Washington, D.C.: Center of Military History, United States Army, 1981); William Bowers, William Hammond, George MacGarrigle, *Black Soldier, White Army: The 24th Infantry in Korea* (Washington, D.C.: Center of Military History, United States Army, 1996).

6. Paul Mentis, interview with the author, May 5, 2001.

7. Terry Tennant, *The Cottonbaler*, Fall 1997, pp. 13, 18.

8. Rudy Tomedi, *No Bugles, No Drums: An Oral History of the Korean War* (New York: John Wiley & Sons, 1993), pp. 97–100.

9. National Archives, Record Group 407, "Command Report, 7th Infantry, November 1950" (copy in author's possession).

10. Tomedi, *No Bugles, No Drums*, p. 100.

11. General Orders, Number 29, Silver Star Citation for Private First Class Oliver Green (copy provided to me by Mr. Oliver Green); *The Huntsville Times*, January 7, 1951, p. 3.

12. Tennant, *The Cottonbaler*, Fall 1997, pp. 21–22.

13. Tomedi, *No Bugles, No Drums*, p. 101.

14. National Archives, Record Group 407, "Command Report, December 1950"; Max Dolcater, *Third Infantry Division in Korea* (Paducah, Ky.: Turner Publishing, 1998), pp. 88–90.

15. Sam Kail to Clay Blair, December 9, 1984, Clay and Joan Blair Papers, USAMHI.

16. Biography of Ricardo (Rick) Cardenas, pp. 1–3, and Rick Cardenas to Bill Strobridge, September 9, 2001 (copies of the biography and the letter provided to me by the late Colonel Strobridge).

17. Tennant, *The Cottonbaler*, Fall 1997, p. 22.

18. Ed Bruger, *The Cottonbaler*, April 1992, p. 2.

19. Kail is quoted in Fred Long, *The Cottonbaler*, Winter 1997, p. 5.

20. Tennant, *The Cottonbaler*, Fall 1997, p. 22–23.

21. National Archives, Record Group 407, "Command Report, December 1950"; Dolcater, *Third Infantry Division in Korea*, p. 90.

22. Clay Blair, *The Forgotten War: America in Korea, 1950–1953* (New York: Times Books, 1987), p. 460.

23. Harry Cooke, Korean War Veterans Questionnaire, USAMHI.

24. Ben Winser, transcript of phone conversation with Bill Strobridge, circa 2001. My thanks to Colonel Strobridge for providing me with a copy of this transcript.

25. Tomedi, *No Bugles, No Drums*, p. 98. Chosin is rather similar to Belleau Wood in that the Marines and the Army fought side by side, but the Marines got most of the laurels for the campaign. A residue of hard feelings and recriminations spread through veterans of Chosin. The Marines were quick to criticize the fighting quality of the army soldiers, particularly those who served with the 7th Division. The soldiers accused the Marines of being glory hounds. In the final analysis, the Marines fought superbly at Chosin but could *not* have escaped without vital help from army soldiers, the clear majority of whom fought well (the Cottonbalers being a prime example). For an interesting point-counterpoint on this issue, see Martin Russ, *Breakout: The Chosin Reservoir Campaign, Korea 1950* (New York: Fromm International, 1999). Russ, who served with the Marines later in the war, dismissed the army role at Chosin and portrayed the soldiers as dishonorable incompetents. Colonel George O. Taylor, a rifle company commander in the 3rd Battalion, 7th Infantry, wrote a blistering but thorough rebuttal to Russ in *The Cottonbaler*, Winter 2001, pp. 6–7, 10–12, 21–23.

26. David Cliffton, Korean War Veterans Questionnaire, USAMHI.

27. Tennant, *The Cottonbaler*, Fall 1997, p. 23.

28. *The Cottonbaler*, Spring 1993, p. 8.

29. Tennant, *The Cottonbaler*, Fall 1997, p. 23.

30. Cliffton Questionnaire, USAMHI; Long, *The Cottonbaler*, Winter 1997, p. 6.

31. Winser transcript.

32. Blair, *Forgotten War*, pp. 543–545; Dolcater, Third Infantry Division in Korea, p. 105.

33. Tomedi, *No Bugle, No Drums*, pp. 101–102; National Archives, Record Group 407, "Command Report, 7th Infantry, January 1951" (copy in author's possession).

34. Donald Knox and Alfred Coppel, *The Korean War: Uncertain Victory* (San Diego: Harcourt Brace Jovanovich, 1988), pp. 47–48.

35. Dolcater, *Third Infantry Division in Korea*, pp. 133, 143–144.

36. Knox and Coppel, *Korean War*, pp. 59–61.

37. Dolcater, *Third Infantry Division in Korea*, pp. 147–148; Bill Strobridge, interview with the author, May 5, 2001, "Cold Korean Hills," unpublished manuscript, and "A Squad on Perimeter in Korea," unpublished manuscript, pp. 1–7 (copies provided to the author by Colonel Strobridge). On another occasion previous to February 14, Strobridge's squad cornered an entire Chinese platoon during a reconnaissance mission and shot the enemy unit to pieces. "The Chinese did not truly understand the danger of American firepower," he said.

38. "Letters from Elmer Eugene Owen During Korean Conflict, 1950–1951," unpublished manuscript of letters, pp. 8–9. The manuscript is included with Owen's response to a Korean War Veterans Questionnaire at US.AMHI.

39. Edward Murphy, *Korean War Heroes* (Novato, Calif: Presidio Press, 1992), pp. 151–152.

40. "Letters from Elmer Eugene Owen," pp. 12–13.

41. Blair, *Forgotten War*, pp. 607–608; author interview with anonymous headquarters soldier, May 5, 2001.

42.James Boswell, transcript of interview with Clay Blair, p. 86, Clay and Joan Blair Collection, USAMHI.

43. Strobridge, "Cold Korean Hills."

44. "Letters from Elmer Eugene Owen," pp. 21–22; National Archives, Record Group 407, Box 2950, Folder 2, "Command Report, 7th Infantry, March, 1951"; "Command Report, 7th Infantry, April 1951" (copy in author's possession); Dolcater, *Third Division in Korea*, pp. 164–169.

45. Long, *The Cottonbaler*, Winter 1997, p. 7; Blair, *Forgotten War*, p. 677. Interestingly enough, Bill Strobridge told me in an interview that he was, at first, not terribly impressed with the 7th because the unit was always retreating. But that was at Chosin, when all UN forces were retreating, and he came to realize that. By early 1951 he felt that the 7th was the best unit in which he had served, and over a long military career his opinion did not change.

46. Fred Long, *The Cottonbaler*, Spring 1997, pp. 4–5; John Middlemas, *The Cottonbaler*, February 1990, p. 1; "Command Report, April 1951"; Dolcater, Third Infantry Division in Korea, pp. 196–197; For a good account of an armored commander's

experiences in this action, see George O. Taylor, Jr., "Fighting Retreat from the Imjin River," *Military History Quarterly*, Spring 2004, pp. 56–63. Taylor commanded a platoon of tanks that was attached to the 7th Infantry.

47. Citation, "William Strobridge, Recommendation for Award-Heroism," Don Grant to Bill Strobridge, November 9, 1988; and operations log for I & R Platoon (copies provided to the author by Colonel Strobridge).

48. Middlemas, *The Cottonbaler*, February 1990, pp. 1–2.

49. Edward Bunn, *The Cottonbaler*, April 1992, p. 7.

50. Dolcater, *Third Infantry Division in Korea*. p. 197. Bill Strobridge told me that Gaybrant originally joined his I & R Platoon as a replacement and immediately announced to Strobridge that he was in Korea to "win the Medal of Honor." Perhaps that revelation sheds some light on his motivation for performing such a dangerous mission that night in support of that machine gun. Colonel Bill Strobridge to author, May 19, 2001.

51. "Command Report, April 1951"; Eric Bartelt, "Secret Hero Recounts Unforgettable War," *American Forces Press Service*, April 2001; Edward Hymoff, "Personality: Hiroshi Miyamura's Medal of Honor Was a Tightly Guarded Secret," Military History, April 1996; Hiroshi Miyamura, *The Cottonbaler*, Winter 1998, p. 20; Murphy, *Korean War Heroes*, pp. 165–169; Hiroshi Miyamura, interview with the author, May 5, 2001.

52. Knox and Coppel, *Korean War*, pp. 172–173.

53. Murphy, *Korean War Heroes*, pp. 164–165; Martin O'Brien, *Above and Beyond the Call of Duty: The Corporal Clair Goodblood Story* (Augusta, Maine: HR Applications, 2000), pp. 35–40, 52–55, 69–81. Two other Cottonbalers earned the Medal of Honor for their valor that night: Private First Class Charles Gilliland of I Company and Corporal John Essebagger of A Company.

54. Dolcater, *Third Infantry Division in Korea*, pp. 202–203; Long, *The Cottonbaler*; Spring 1997, pp. 5–6; Russell Gugeler, *Combat Actions in Korea* (Washington, DC: Center of Military History, United States Army, 1987), pp. 144–153.

55. Knox, *Korean War*; pp. 189–190.

56. "Command Report, April 1951"; Long, *The Cottonbaler*, Spring 1997, pp. 5–6.

57. National Archives, Record Group 407, Box 2951, Folder 3, "Command Report, May 1951"; Long, *The Cottonbaler*, Spring 1997, pp. 6–7; Strobridge, "Cold Korean Hills."

58. "Letters from Elmer Eugene Owen," p. 27.

59. Strobridge, "Cold Korean Hills."

60. "Letters from Elmer Eugene Owen," pp. 28–29. From late May onward, the topic of rotation dominated Owen's letters. In a conversation with me in 2006, he expressed substantial guilt over his obsession with rotating home.

61. Jack Sebzda, *The Cottonbaler*, Spring 1999, p. 15.

62. Dolcater, *Third Infantry Division in Korea*, pp. 266–267; National Archives, Record Group 407, Box 2951, Folder 1, "Command Report, 7th Infantry; June 1951."

63. "Letters from Elmer Eugene Owen," pp. 30–32.

64. Dolcater, *Third Infantry Division in Korea*, pp. 241–244; "Command Report, June 1951"; National Archives, Record Group 407, Box 2952, Folder 1, "Command Report, 7th Infantry, July 1951," and Record Group 338, Box 277, Folder 8, "Unit Histories: Distinguished Unit Citation, 3rd Battalion, 7th Infantry"; Long, *The Cottonbaler*, Spring 1997, pp. 7, 11; Frederick Weyand, *The Cottonbaler*, Summer 1997, p. 11; Mentis interview.

65. "Letters from Elmer Eugene Owen," pp. 35–38.

66. Mentis interview. Mentis came home, went back to school, and became a high school football coach in Ohio.

67. National Archives, Record Group 407, Box 2953, Folder 1, "Command Report, 7th Infantry, September 1951"; Dolcater, *Third Infantry Division in Korea*, pp. 245–248; Murphy; *Korean War Heroes*, pp. 195–197; Owen Questionnaire, USAMHI; "Letters from Elmer Eugene Owen," pp. 39–40.

68. Robert Jensen, *The Cottonbaler*, Summer 1997, pp. 6–8; Jensen, "Bloody Snow: A Doctor's Memoir of the Korean War" (Carmel, Ind.: Cork Hill Press, 2005), pp. 370–375. I thank Dr. Jensen for speaking with me on May 5, 2001, as well as on several other dates, and relating some of the details of this story.

69. Strobridge interview.

70. Dolcater, *Third Infantry Division in Korea*, pp. 289–290, 300; Robert Crepeau, *The Cottonbaler*, 1991, p. 10; *The Cottonbaler*, December 1990, p. 10.

71. Dolcater, *Third Infantry Division in Korea*, pp. 294, 300–301.

72. Leroy Keeney; unpublished memoir, pp. 1–7, included with Keeney Korean War Veterans Questionnaire, USAMHI.

73. Dolcater, *Third Infantry Division in Korea*, p. 294; National Archives, Record Group 407, Box 2954, Folder 1, "Command Report, 7th Infantry; November 1951"; "Action Around Hill 355, November 1951," copy located in library of USAMHI-II.

74. Bob Barfield, *Watch on the Rhine*, April 1999, p. 17. This is the newsletter of the 3rd Infantry Division Association.

75. Ernest Clifford, *Watch on the Rhine*, March 1999, p. 19.

76. Stanley Cahill to author, July 18 and September 6, 2001, and unpublished manuscript, p. 3 (copy provided to author by Cahill).

77. I have relied on many accounts for this description of the Boomerang battle: Fred Brown, "Just Call It the Saving of Lt. Hotelling," *Knoxville News Sentinel*, September 3, 1998; Barfield, *Watch on the Rhine*, April 1999, p. 17; Lewis Hotelling, Rene Silva, and Thomas Innocenti, personal, notarized statements (copies provided to author by Bob Barfield); Pat Rampino, unpublished manuscript, pp. 1–2 (copy provided to author by Rampino); phone conversations with Barfield, July 24, 2001, and February 17, 2007, and Rampino, July 2001. The commander of F Company was none other than Rick Cardenas, who accepted a battlefield commission and rejoined the 7th Infantry as a company commander on his second tour in 1953. He, Hotelling, and several others have launched a crusade to get Barfield the Medal of Honor. In spite of losing his foot and part of his leg, Hotelling stayed in the Army until 1968. Barfield went on to serve in the paratroopers and even the

Navy, in addition to pursuing a professional boxing career. Cardenas retired from the Army in 1972.

78. National Archives, Record Group 407, Box 3072, Folder 2, "Command Report, 7th Infantry, June 1953."

CHAPTER 2. BECOMING GRUNTS: VIETNAM

1. National Archives, Record Group 472, Box 1, Folder 3, "3rd Battalion, 7th Infantry, Organizational History, Vietnam." For a look at this picture, see the photographic insert of this book.

2. Ronald Spector, *After Tet: The Bloodiest Year in Vietnam* (New York: Vintage Books, 1993), pp. 26–38. To call this book excellent would be an understatement. It is outstanding, extremely well researched and documented.

3. Frederick Weyand interview, "Troops to Equal Any," *Vietnam*, August 1998. Happily enough, recent decades have seen the publication of many revealing, factual studies about the true origin and nature of American soldiers in Vietnam. They include Spector, *After Tet*, pp. 26–70; Christian Appy, *Working Class War: American Combat Soldiers and Vietnam* (Chapel Hill: University of North Carolina Press, 1993); Eric Bergerud, *Red Thunder, Tropic Lightning: The World of a Combat Division in Vietnam* (New York: Penguin Books, 1993); and James Ebert, *A Life in a Year: The American Infantryman in Vietnam, 1965–1972* (Novato, Calif: Presidio Press, 1993).

4. Gary Masuda, interview with the author, June 18, 2001.

5. Roland Merson, interview with the author, May 5, 2001.

6. National Archives, Record Group 472, Box 1, Folder 1, "Organizational History."

7. Mike Braun, interview with the author, July 13, 2001. Note: In the twentieth century, the companies were sometimes referred to by nicknames rather than their letters, i.e., Able (A), Baker (B), Charlie (C), etc. However, the nicknames varied widely until the Vietnam era, when they became pretty much standard: Alpha, Bravo, Charlie, Delta, and Echo. For that reason, I have chosen to refer to the companies by letter until the Vietnam era.

8. National Archives, Record Group 472, Box 1, Folder 1, "Organizational History."

9. Braun interview.

10. For more on the opposing side in the Vietnam War, see Michael Lee Lanning and Dan Cragg, *Inside the VC and NVA: The Real Story of North Vietnam's Armed Forces* (New York: Ivy Books, 1992).

11. National Archives, Record Group 472, Box 1, Folder 1, "Organizational History."

12. Braun interview.

13. Andy Krasnican, interview with the author, June 20, 2001.

14. Paul Hindelang to Judy Hindelang, March 2, 1967, "Timeline of Letters: Paul Hindelang to Judy Hindelang, Dec. 23, 1966–Dec. 18, 1967" (copy of "Timeline" given to the author by Paul Hindelang).

15. Braun interview.

16. Paul Hindelang to Judy Hindelang, March 5, 1967, "Timeline."

17. Braun and Krasnican interviews; Paul Hindelang to Judy Hindelang, March 10, 1967, "Timeline."

18. Braun interview; Paul Hindelang to Judy Hindelang, March 19, April 12, 13, 17, 22, 28, 1967, "Timeline."

19. For an excellent discussion of understrength rifle platoons in Vietnam, see Spector, *After Tet*, pp. 59–70, and Ebert, *Life in a Year*.

20. Paul Hindelang to Judy Hindelang, May 6, 16, 1967, "Timeline."

21. National Archives, Record Group 472, Box 1, Folder 4, "Annual Historical Summary, 3d Battalion, 7th Infantry, 1967"; Krasnican interview:

22. Paul Hindelang to Judy Hindelang, May 21, 1967, "Timeline."

23. Braun interview.

24. Paul Hindelang to Judy Hindelang, June 20, 22, 25, 1967, "Timeline"; Krasnican interview.

25. Braun interview; Paul Hindelang to Judy Hindelang, July 19, 1967, "Timeline." In the process of speaking and corresponding with many unit veterans who served with the 7th over its four years of deployment to Vietnam, I found that not one of them ever claimed to have seen or heard of an instance in which innocent Vietnamese were intentionally killed. Nor do the official unit records in the National Archives mention any such instance. This is not to say that it did not happen, just that such atrocities were, most likely, every bit as unusual as in previous Cottonbaler wars.

26. Braun interview; Paul Hindelang to Judy Hindelang, July 19, 1967, "Timeline." Braun came home, went back to school, eventually married, and enjoyed a successful construction contracting and real estate career.

27. Weyand, "Troops Equal to Any"; Keith William Nolan, *The Battle for Saigon, Tet 1968* (New York: Pocket Books, 1996), pp. 141–144.

28. National Archives, Record Group 472, Box 1, Folder 2, "199th LIB, After Action Report, 5 February 1968."

29. National Archives, Record Group 472, Box 1, Folder 1, "Organizational History; Antonio Smaldone: Infantryman 'Thrives' on War," and Box 4, Folder 1, "3rd Battalion, 7th Infantry; Intelligence Summaries," January 28–31, 1968; Nolan, *Battle for Saigon*, pp. 145–146; David T. Zabecki, "Battle for Saigon," *Vietnam* magazine, February 2001; author conversations with Dan Shaw, July 15–17, 2004. In September 1968, Shaw was badly wounded by a mine and an errant ARVN bullet that split his ribs and necessitated the removal of his spleen and part of a lung. He was evacuated to Japan and sent home. He became a truck driver in Ohio.

30. National Archives, Record Group 472, Box 1, Folders 1 and 2, "After Action Reports" and "Annual Update Summary 1968, Unit History"; Zabecki, "Battle for Saigon"; Shelby Stanton, *The Rise and Fall of an American Army: US. Ground Forces in Vietnam, 1965–1973* (New York: Dell, 1985), p. 215; author conversation with Shaw, July 2004.

31. Weyand, "Troops Equal to Any."

32. Spector, *After Tet*, p. 55.

33. *The Redcatcher*, May 5–June 17, 1968; *199th Light Infantry Brigade, Redcatcher Yearbook*, 1970; National Archives, Record Group 472, Box 1, Folder 2, "Annual Update Summary; 1968." I have deliberately omitted casualty numbers, both enemy and American, because they are so notoriously unreliable for the Vietnam War, even in the official records. The American "body count" mania routinely inflated enemy

losses. Plus, the controversial nature of the war sometimes caused American commanders to "deflate" their own casualty statistics.

34. *Redcatcher Yearbook.*

35. National Archives, Record Group 472, Box 4, Folder 3, "3rd Battalion, 7th Infantry; Intelligence Summaries, June 24–November 23, 1968"; Jerry Lyons, unpublished memoir, pp. 1–4, "Vietnam Scrapbook"; American Radio Works Web site; conversation with the author, July 2004.

36. Center of Military History; Washington D.C., "Combat After Action Interview, 3d Battalion, 7th Infantry, 199th Infantry Brigade . . . 27–29 January 1969."

37. Jim Norris, interview with the author. June 20, 2001.

38. John Parker, unpublished memoir, pp. 1, 6–8, (copy provided to author by Roland Merson).

39. National Archives, Record Group 472, Box 4, Folder 4, "3rd Battalion, 7th Infantry, Intelligence Summaries," and Box 1, Folder 3, "Organizational Histories, 7th Infantry, 1969"; *The Redcatcher*, September 15, 1969; Larry Compton, personal Web site, "Images from Vietnam." I thank Mr. Compton for giving me permission to quote from his site.

40. Roland Merson, biographical sketch, "The Making of a Cottonbaler"; Roland Merson to author, June 8, 2001; Roland Merson interview with the author, June 11, 2001, and numerous subsequent conversations.

41. Norris interview.

42. National Archives, Record Group 472, Box 4, Folder 5, "3rd Battalion, 7th Infantry, Intelligence Summaries"; George Sheehan, interview with the author, June 29, 2001, and author conversation with Sheehan, July 17, 2004. Author conversations with Dave McClure, Al Watson, and several other Alpha Company men, July 2004. McClure and Watson were junior officers in Alpha Company. Sheehan returned to the unit six weeks later, made it through the rest of his tour unscathed, and became a dentist after the war.

43. National Archives, Record Group 472, Box 1, Folder 3, "Organizational Histories, 7th Infantry, 1969"; Masuda interview.

44. National Archives, Record Group 472, Box 4, Folder 5, "3rd Battalion, 7th Infantry, Intelligence Summaries"; Roland Merson, "Monkey Business," unpublished article in author's possession; Merson to author, June 8, 2001; Merson interview; June 11, 2001; Masuda interview.

45. Roger Soiset, *The Two Dollar Bill: One Man's Year in Vietnam* (Columbia, S.C.: Palmetto Bookworks, 1993), pp. 41–45, 102–111. In all likelihood, Charlie Company sprang the most successful ambush of any outfit in the 7th Infantry that fall. Operating with a local Ruff Puff unit (a more frequent occurrence at this time because of Vietnamization), the men of Charlie Company destroyed an entire enemy platoon on the evening of November 8–9, resulting in the deaths of nineteen enemy soldiers, against only one American lightly wounded. Only a staid, brief description of that battle survives in the National Archives, Record Group 472, Box 8, Folder 3, "S-3 Command Report Files, After Action Report, 8 November 1969, 3rd Battalion, 7th Infantry," and in Box 1, Folder 3, "Organizational Histories, 7th Infantry, 1969."

46. Merson interview, June 11, 2001.

47. The combined operations with Ruff Puff units are discussed in many 7th Infantry official documents in the National Archives, Record Group 472, Box 8, Folders 1, 2, and 3, "S-3 Command Report Files," "After Action Reports."

48. Stanton, *Rise and Fall*; Spector, *After Tet*.

49. Norris interview.

50. Masuda interview.

51. Merson interview, May 5, 2001; James Edwards, interview with the author, July 10, 2001.

52. Merson interviews, May 5 and June 11, 2001; Merson to Captain Dave Gardner, July 2, 2001, author copied; Merson to author, June 8, 2001; Merson, "Making of a Cottonbaler," plus numerous subsequent conversations.

53. Masuda and Edwards interviews and interviews with various Alpha Company veterans who did not wish to be quoted individually on the topic of Captain Iszqveirdo.

54. Phil Salois, interview with the author, July 2, 2001; Philip G. Salois, "The Turning Point," *Vietnam*, October 1994, pp. 26–29; Philip Salois, *The Cottonbaler*, Spring 1997, p. 8; National Archives, Record Group 472, Box 152, Folder 1, 3rd Battalion, 7th Infantry, 53 Journal, March 1, 1970.

55. Norris and Masuda interviews.

56. Salois, Masuda, and Norris interviews; Salois, "Turning Point," pp. 30–32, and *Cottonbaler*, Spring 1997, p. 9. For years, Salois felt guilty about Klug's death. Salois felt responsible because he had come up with the idea of rescuing the point element. He decided to contact Klug's parents in Dayton. "I told them I was guilty for coming up with the plan that ultimately took their son's life. Herb's mother took me by the hand and reassured me that I did what I had to do. Now, I'm their adopted son." In the summer of 2000, Alpha Company veterans held a reunion and memorial service for Klug and his family in Dayton. In 2002 they did the same for Bowell's family in his hometown of Denver, Colorado.

57. *The Redcatcher*, April 8, 1970.

58. Edwards interview.

59. Masuda, Norris, and Edwards interviews.

60. Salois interview.

CHAPTER 3. THE TRIUMPH OF PROFESSIONALISM: THE PERSIAN GULF WAR

1. Al Santoli, *Leading the Way: How Vietnam Veterans Rebuilt the US. Military; An Oral History* (New York: Ballantine Books, 1993), pp. 73–189; Robert Scales, *Certain Victory: The US. Army in the Gulf War* (Washington, D.C.: Brassey's, 1994), pp. 6–7; Thomas Houlahan, *Gulf War: The Complete History* (New London, N.H.: Shrenker Military Publishing, 1999), pp. 133–134.

2. Scales, *Certain Victory*, pp. 12–23; Daniel Bolger, *Dragons at War: Land Battle in the Desert; An Inside Look at the National Training Center* (New York: Ivy Books, 1986); Rick Averna, interview with the author, June 25, 2001; Alan Huffines, interview with the author, June 12, 2001.

3. William Hartzog, *American Military Heritage* (Washington, D.C.: Center of Military History; 2001), pp. 220–224.

4. Kirk Allen, interview with the author, August 17, 2001.

5. Scales, *Certain Victory*, pp. 22–25, 36; Houlahan, *Gulf War*, pp. 133–134. Houlahan's discussion is mostly accurate, but it is marred with inappropriate comparisons to the U.S. Army in World War II. For instance, Houlahan repeats, as fact, the oft-stated and grossly inaccurate World War II "research findings" of S.L.A. Marshall that only 15 percent of American combat soldiers ever fired their weapons. Houlahan also rehashes the outdated contentions of such historians as Trevor DuPuy that the German Army was vastly superior soldier for soldier to the U.S. Army. DuPuy and his adherents asserted that the U.S. Army only won in Europe because it enjoyed superior numbers and logistics. This contention has not held up to prolonged scrutiny. More recent work by many authors, including Michael Doubler, Peter Mansoor, Stephen Ambrose, Robert Sterling Rush, and Keith Bonn, and my own *Deadly Brotherhood* have demonstrated, beyond much doubt, the proficiency and combat power of American soldiers at the individual level in World War II.

6. Scales, *Certain Victory*, pp. 42–86. This book is an excellent official history of the war from an army perspective. Even better for a larger-picture view of the war is Rick Atkinson, *Crusade: The Untold Story of the Gulf War* (Boston: Houghton Mifflin, 1993). Houlahan's *Gulf War* is a thoughtful, well-written operational history with a heavy emphasis on the ground war.

7. Huffines interview, June 12, 2001; Alan C. Huffines, "Hawgs of War," unpublished memoir, diary; and letters of his experiences in the Gulf War, p. 4 (copy given to author by Lieutenant Colonel Huffines). I am very grateful to Alan for providing me with a copy of this valuable document and for being so generous with his time in discussing nearly every aspect of his wartime service with me.

8. Huffines, "Hawgs of War," pp. 5–7.

9. Jason Kamiya, *The Victory Book: A Desert Storm Chronicle* (self-published yearbook of the 24th Infantry Division Mechanized, 1991), pp. 128–130.

10. Alan Huffines, interview with the author, July 8, 2001. Huffines wrote an excellent, well-received history of the Alamo called *Blood of Noble Men: The Alamo Siege and Battle*. He has also published a novel called *A Pilgrim Shadow*.

11. Charlie Company, 2-7 training schedule, October 8–November 11, 1990, and Elaine to Rick Averna, September 4 and 30, 1990 (copies of schedule and letters provided to author by Lieutenant Colonel Rick Averna); Averna interview. I would like to thank Rick for providing me with copies of many of the letters he and Elaine wrote back and forth during his time in the Gulf, as well as detailed after action reports and photographs from his experiences in combat.

12. Huffines, "Hawgs of War," pp. 20–21; Huffines interviews.

13. Averna interview.

14. Rick to Elaine Averna, November 14 and 16, 1990; Averna interview.

15. Bryan Crochet, interview with the author, July 2, 2001.

16. Ron Martz, "Troops Show the Thanksgiving Spirit with 'Cottonbalers' Parade," reprinted in *The Cottonbaler*, 1991, pp. 2–3; Huffines, "Hawgs of War," pp. 50–51.

17. Lieutenant Colonel Stephen S. Smith, "The 1st Battalion, 7th Infantry in the Gulf War," United States Army War College Paper, USAMHI, p. 2.

18. Steve Vogel, "Killer Brigade: 3d Infantry Division 'Phantoms' Hunt the Enemy," *Army Times*, November n, 1991, pp. 14–15.

19. Jamie Narramore, interview with the author, August 15, 2001; Smith, "1st Battalion, 7th Infantry in the Gulf War," p. 10.

20. Narramore interview.

21. Smith, "1st Battalion, 7th Infantry in the Gulf War," pp. 13–14.

22. Craig McClure, interview with the author, June 21, 2001.

23. Smith, "1st Battalion, 7th Infantry in the Gulf War," pp. 15–16.

24. Huffines, "Hawgs of War," pp. 79–81.

25. Averna interview.

26. Atkinson, *Crusade*, pp. 105–139; Scales, *Certain Victory*, pp. 106–207; Houlahan, *Gulf War*, pp. 107–136.

27. Michael St. Peter to Harry Cooke, February 18, 1991, reprinted in *The Cottonbaler*, 1991, p. 6.

28. McClure interview.

29. Kurt Dabb, interview with the author, June 13, 2001. In addition to Dabb's account, I consulted David Pierson, *Tuskers: An Armor Battalion in the Gulf War* (Darlington, Md.: Darlington Productions, 1997), to get a sense of what Alpha Company 2-7 experienced in the war. Dabb's company was cross-attached to 4-64 Armor, a unit nicknamed the Tuskers and the subject of Pierson's fine book.

30. Vogel, "Killer Brigade," p. 15.

31. Smith, "1st Battalion, 7th Infantry in the Gulf War," pp. 22–23.

32. Vogel, "Killer Brigade," p. 15; Smith, "1st Battalion, 7th Infantry in the Gulf War," p. 23; Tom Clancy and Fred Franks, *Into the Storm: A Study in Command* (New York: Putnam's, 1997), pp. 13–14 (in this book, Franks gives his account of this incident by way of Tom Clancy's writing); Narramore interview. There is a postscript to this story. After the war, when the Raiders were about to board a plane taking them back to Germany, they met up with Franks again. He spoke with them and told them that they had made "the biggest impact of the war on him," Jamie Narramore related. "We all took pictures and ... he said, 'You guys have what it takes.'" The general later sent a personal, handwritten letter to Narramore telling him about the picture on his office wall.

33. Averna interview. None of the 2-7 soldiers interviewed for this book or who contributed memoirs expressed positive feelings about Lieutenant Colonel Ware's leadership.

34. Major Kim Stenson, "Cottonbalers, by God: The Persian Gulf Campaign," unpublished paper, pp. 1–4 (copy provided to the author by Lieutenant Colonel Rick Averna); Allen interview, "Scouts Hostile Fire Record, 2nd Battalion, 7th Infantry; 24th Infantry Division," pp. 1–2. This document is a synopsis of the combat activities of the scout platoon. I thank Kirk for providing me with a copy.

35. Huffines, "Hawgs of War," p. 98; Huffines interview, July 8, 2001.

36. Bryan Crochet, interview with the author, July 9, 2001.

37. Averna interview; Stenson, "Cottonbalers, by God," p. 5.

38. Mike Tschanz, "My Combat Experience," unpublished memoir, pp. 1–2; Robert Jones, "A Platoon Perspective," unpublished memoir, pp. 1–2; Leon Grube, "A Narrative of the Gulf War," p. 2 (copies of each of these memoirs were provided to the author by Lieutenant Colonel Rick Averna). The details about the transient experience of the first couple days of the war come from various interviews, including those with Crochet, Dabb, and Averna, and the details about the problem of the Bradley exhaust are from the Narramore interview.

39. Narramore interview.

40. Tom Carhart, *Iron Soldiers: How Americas 1st Armored Division Crushed Iraqi's Elite Republican Guard* (New York: Pocket Books, 1994), pp. 210–212.

41. Narramore and McClure interviews; Smith, "1st Battalion, 7th Infantry in the Gulf War," pp. 24–25; Vogel, "Killer Brigade," p. 15.

42. Smith, "1st Battalion, 7th Infantry in the Gulf War," p. 26.

43. Narramore interview. Desegregation in the twentieth-century Army worked so well that by the 1990s Cottonbalers seldom gave a second thought to the racial or ethnic origins of their comrades. To be sure, blacks, whites, and Hispanics sometimes had differences with one another, but rarely anything serious. This statement is corroborated by every interview I conducted and every firsthand account dealing with the unit in the post-Vietnam era.

44. Narramore interview; Smith, "1st Battalion, 7th Infantry in the Gulf War," p. 27.

45. Allen interview; "Scouts Hostile Fire Record," p. 2.

46. Stenson, "Cottonbalers, by God," pp. 7–8.

47. Huffines, "Hawgs of War," p. 100.

48. Allen interview.

49. Averna interview.

50. Jones, "A Platoon Perspective," p. 2.

51. Averna interview.

52. Grube, "A Narrative of the Gulf War," p. 2; James Howell, "2nd Platoon in Iraq," unpublished memoir, p. 2 (copy of Howell's memoir provided to the author by Lieutenant Colonel Rick Averna).

53. Huffines, "Hawgs of War," p. 100.

54. Crochet interview, July 9, 2001.

55. Dabb interview.

56. Huffines, "Hawgs of War," pp. 100–106; Huffines interview, July 8, 2001.

57. Stephen A. Bourque, "Desert Saber: The VII Corps in the Gulf War," Ph.D. dissertation, Georgia State University, 1996, pp. 469–473; "After Action Report: Briefing Slides, 1st Armored Division, Desert Storm," GWC, 370.2, Gulf War Collection, U.S. Army Center of Military History, Washington, D.C. Note: There are three spellings of Medina commonly in use: "Madinah," "Medinah," and "Medina." I have simply chosen to employ the latter because it seems to be the most correct.

58. Smith, "1st Battalion, 7th Infantry in the Gulf War," p. 29.

59. McClure interview.

60. Smith, "1st Battalion, 7th Infantry in the Gulf War," pp. 29–31.

61. McClure interview.

62. Vogel, "Killer Brigade," p. 69.

63. Crochet interview, July 9, 2001; Narramore interview.

64. Huffines, "Hawgs of War," pp. 108–109.

65. Dabb interview; Kurt Dabb, "The Tomatoes," *The Cottonbaler*, Winter 1999, p. 9.

66. General Schwarzkopf discussed the cease-fire terms, along with the equipment question, in his autobiography: H. Norman Schwarzkopf with Peter Petre, *It Doesn't Take a Hero* (New York: Bantam Books, 1992), pp. 468–480.

67. Averna interview.

68. Allen interview; "Scouts Hostile Fire Record"; Stenson, "Cottonbalers, by God," pp. 13–14.

69. Dabb interview. Interestingly enough, Dabb described the experience of seeing all this carnage as "like being in a movie, almost surreal. You thought that only Hollywood could create something like this." In this comparison he was not alone. From World War II through the present, American soldiers have been almost unanimous in this comparison when trying to describe combat. They will often use the phrase "It was like a movie." In addition, they have sometimes sought in combat to re-create famous scenes or phrases from films. For instance, Alan Huffines remembered hearing his battalion commander announce, before an attack: "I feel the need ... the need for speed!" The commander then, over the radio, blasted the song "Danger Zone" by Kenny Loggins, the one made so famous in the film *Top Gun*, from which the "need for speed" line came. Perhaps these pervasive references to film by American soldiers stem from the video/entertainment-obsessed nature of American culture.

70. This account is the product of several sources: Atkinson, *Crusade*, pp. 481–484; Houlahan, *Gulf War*, pp. 270–272; Pierson, *Tuskers*, pp. 185–209; Averna and Allen interviews; Stenson, "Cottonbalers, by God," pp. 14–16; Tschanz, "My Combat Experience," pp. 4–5; Jones, "A Platoon Perspective," p. 3; Grube, "A Narrative of the Gulf War," p. 3; "Ch/2-7 Infantry Sequence of Events (Combat Action 02 March 1991, AR Rumaylah," Gulf War Collection, Group Swain Papers, U.S. Army Combined Arms Center, Fort Leavenworth, Kansas (thanks to Dr. Lewis Bernstein for passing this document along to me); Rick Averna, "Small Unit Action in the Battle of Al Rumaylah," unpublished article, sworn statement on the Battle of Rumaylah, August 23, 1991; and Briefing Slides, "Action of Charlie Company, 2d Battalion, 7th U.S. Infantry 0530 to 1000 Hours on 2 March 1991 Vicinity Rumallya Oil Fields Iraq"; Kim Stenson, "Recommendation Statement" and "Memorandum for Record." I thank Rick Averna for providing me with copies of his article, briefing slides, sworn statement, and Major Stenson's statements as well.

71. Seymour Hersh, "Overwhelming Force," *The New Yorker*, May 22, 2000, pp. 49–82. Averna and Allen interviews; Stenson, "Cottonbalers by God," pp. 15–16, and "Recommendation Statement" and "Memorandum"; Averna, sworn statement; "Scouts Hostile Fire Record"; Atkinson, Crusade, pp. 481–484; Schwarzkopf, *It Doesn't Take a Hero*, pp. 478–479; Scales, Certain Victory, pp. 310–314. Scales incorrectly states in his account that the Iraqis first opened fire on the scouts at Rumaylah. Houlahan also made the same error in his Gulf War, p. 270.

72. Averna interview; Averna, "Small Unit Action in the Battle of Al Rumaylah."

73. Crochet interview, July 9, 2001.

74. Huffines interviews, June I2 and July 8, 2001; Huffines, "Hawgs of War," pp. 114–115.

75. Averna interview.

76. Crochet interview, July 9, 2001.

77. Smith, "1st Battalion, 7th Infantry in the Gulf War," p. 37.

78. Narramore, McClure, Dabb, Crochet, Allen, Huffines, and Averna interviews.

CHAPTER 4. THE POST-9/11 WAR ON TERROR: KOSAVO AND THE BEGINNING OF THE IRAQ WAR

1. At times the United States did respond militarily to specific terrorist provocations, such as the attempted rescue of American hostages in Iran in 1980 and the bombing of the enclave of Libyan leader Mu'ammar Gadhafi in 1986. But these were atypical events subsumed by a larger policy of legalistic opposition to terrorism.

2. Captain Dave Gardner to author, July 24, August 5, 26, 2001; "KFOR Online," news, announcements of NATO Web site.

3. Source for testing statistics: U.S. Army. Harry Levins, "All Volunteer Army Is 30, and Looking Good," St. Louis Post-Dispatch, no date; Carl Nolte, "A Day in the Life of the 'Boys in the Bradley,' " San Francisco Chronicle, April 9, 2003; Paul Ingram, interview with the author, July 1, 2004; Eric Hooper, interview with the author, June 29, 2004; Steve Gleason, interview with the author, January 19, 2004; Rod Coffey, interview with the author, November 14, 2003; Raul "Rudy" Belloc questionnaire.

4. Chris Carter, personal correspondence and interview with the author, May 18, 2004; Ingram and Hooper interviews.

5. For the material about the way most soldiers found out about the deployment, I have relied on conversations with dozens of Cottonbalers. The information about the departure from Hunter Army Airfield is from "Operation Iraqi Freedom," Task Force 2-7 After Action Report (hereafter referred to as 2-7 AAR), p. 2, and Mark Schenck questionnaire.

6. *The Cottonbaler*, Spring 2003, pp. 8–9; Lieutenant Colonel Scott Rutter to Colonel Richard Rhoades, February 10, 2003, an e-mail communication from Lieutenant Colonel Rutter, commander of 2-7, to Rhoades, the president of the 7th Infantry Regiment Association, I was copied on the e-mail; Gleason interview; Bravo 2-7 Group Combat After Action Interview, March 10, 2004; Bravo 3-7 Group Combat After Action Interview, March 11, 2004.

7. Alpha 2-7 Group Combat After Action Interview, March 12, 2004; conversations with various Cottonbalers.

8. 2-7 AAR, pp. 3–4; *The Cottonbaler*, Spring 2003, p. 9; Bravo 2-7 Group Interview.

9. 2-7 AAR, p. 3; Gleason interview; Bravo 2-7 Group Interview; Robert Wilson, interview with the author, February 3, 2004.

10. Charlie 2-7 Group Combat After Action Interview, March 11, 2004.

11. 2-7 AAR, p. 5; Sergeant Miguel Lugo questionnaire.

12. Carl Nolte, "Pep Talk for Ready, Waiting Troops," San Francisco Chronicle, March 17, 2003.

13. Carl Nolte, "President 'Sounded like John Wayne,' Army Medic Says," *San Francisco Chronicle*, March 18, 2003; Gleason and Ingram interviews; Charlie 2-7 Group Interview; Alpha 2-7 Group Interview; Bravo 3-7 Group Interview; Cottonbaler conversations.

14. 2-7 AAR, pp. 5–7; Michael Corkery, "Staging on the Border Music to Soldiers' Ears," *Providence Journal*, March 20, 2003.

15. Gleason interview. All throughout training at Fort Stewart, the scouts had been equipped with uparmored Humvees. However, when they got to Kuwait, the brigade reconnaissance team promptly confiscated the Humvees for their own use. This was devastating to the morale of the scouts, but by the time of the war, Lieutenant Gleason and his NCOs had succeeded in appropriating five uparmored Humvees. The fact that Gleason chose a thin-skinned Humvee for himself was a good indication of his courage and dedicated leadership.

16. Carl Nolte, "Some U.S. Troops Learn of Attack from BBC," *San Francisco Chronicle*, March 20, 2003, and "Anxious Troops Play Cards, Read and Gripe About Chow," March 21, 2003; Will Neubauer, interview with the author, June 30, 2004; Carter, Hooper, and Ingram interviews. To Ingram's dismay, one of the augmentees was a sergeant of equal rank who was supposed to join his squad. However, the man never rode with Ingram's squad or presented any sort of threat to Ingram's authority.

17. 2-7 AAR, pp. 8–9; Wilson interview; Alpha 2-7 Group Interview; Nicholas Driggers questionnaire.

18. 2-7 Powerpoint Presentation; Kevin Peraino, "The View from the Front," *Newsweek*, March 31, 2003; Todd Kelly, interview with the author, March 12, 2004; Charlie 2-7 Group Interview; Curtis Kelly questionnaire. The U.S. Army's field manual on building clearing expressly forbids the use of small arms to open locks or doors.

19. 2-7 Powerpoint Presentation; 2-7 AAR, pp. 8–9; Michael Corkery, "Bravo Pushes Across the Line," *Providence Journal*, March 21, 2003; Bravo 2-7 Group Interview; Wilson interview. The helicopter report was erroneous. The helicopter had crashed; it was not downed by enemy fire.

20. Carter interview.

21. 2-7 AAR, p. 9; Michael Corkery, "An Overwhelming Force Encounters No Resistance," *Providence Journal*, March 22, 2003; Coffey interview.

22. 2-7 AAR, pp. 9–10; Alpha 2-7 Group Interview; Carter and Coffey interviews.

23. 2-7 AAR, pp. 9–rn; Coffey interview; Kevin Cooney, interview with the author, March 10, 2004.

24. Carter interview; Bravo 2-7 Group Interview; Bravo 3-7 Group Interview; Alpha 2-7 Group Interview; Steven Collier questionnaire.

25. Alpha 2-7 Group Interview; Bravo 2-7 Group Interview; Bravo 3-7 Group Interview.

26. 2-7 AAR, pp. 12–14; 1st Brigade Combat Team (BCT), Escarpment After Action Critique (AAC), pp. 8–9 (copy of this and all subsequent after action critiques furnished to me by Jim Lacey, who has written a history of the 3rd Division in the Iraq War); Michael Corkery, "We Had Let Our Guard Down," *Providence Journal*, March 23, 2003; Gleason and Coffey interviews; Alpha 2-7 Group Interview; HHC

2-7 Group Combat After Action Interview, March 12, 2004; Ed Cuevas, interview with the author, December 30, 2003; Rob Smith, interview with the author, March 12, 2004. The crashed SUV belonged to a renegade TV crew that was not embedded with any military unit. The Iraqis had ambushed the crew, wounding at least one man. Rage Company gave the reporters first aid and protection for the next couple of days.

27. 2-7 AAR, pp. 13–14; Coffey and Gleason interviews; R. Lee Simmons, interview with the author, November 24, 2003. Thanks to laser technology, sophisticated computers, and excellent ordnance, U.S. artillery in this day and age has the capability to put shells within one or two meters of a target.

28. 2-7 AAR, pp. 14–16; 1st BCT Escarpment AAC, pp. 9–10; Michael Corkery, "Iraqi Tactics Blur Rules of Engagement," *Providence Journal*, March 25, 2003; Simmons, Coffey, and Gleason, interviews; HHC 2-7 Group Interview; Jimmy Lee to author, November 12, 2003.

29. 2-7 AAR, p. 13; Smith and Cuevas interviews; Alpha 2-7 Group Interview.

30. 2-7 AAR, p. 16; 2-7 Powerpoint Presentation; Kelly interview; Rick Atkinson, *In the Company of Soldiers: A Chronicle of Combat* (New York: Henry Holt, 2004), pp. 193–194. Sadly, Najaf and the burial ground around Ali's tomb has repeatedly become a battlefield. U.S. Marines and soldiers fought insurgent rebels loyal to Muqtada al-Sadr, an anti-American Shiite cleric under indictment for killing a fellow religious leader. For many months fighting flared and waned in Najaf, as al-Sadr continued to be a problem for the Americans and the new, post-Saddam Iraqi government.

31. Kevin Peraino and Evan Thomas, "The Grunt's War," *Newsweek*, April 9, 2003; Craig Zentkovich, "3rd Infantry Division Raiders Advance Far into Iraq," www.silverstatenews.com; Kelly interview; Charlie 2-7 Group Interview; Curtis Kelly questionnaire.

32. 2-7 AAR, pp. 16–17; 1st BCT Escarpment AAC, pp. 9–12; Bravo 2-7 Group Interview; Bravo 3-7 Group Interview; HHC 2-7 Group Interview; Wilson and Coffey interviews.

33. 2-7 AAR, p. 18; Task Force 3-7 After Action Report, p. 2 (hereafter referred to as 3-7 AAR); Coffey, Smith, and Cooney interviews; Cottonbaler conversations.

34. 2-7 AAR, pp. 18–19; 1st BCT Al Kifl AAC, pp. 15–17; Michael Corkery, "Sniper Delivers a Chilling Wake-up Call," *Providence Journal*, March 28, 2003; Gleason and Simmons interviews; HHC 2-7 Group Interview; Alpha 2-7 Group Interview.

35. Michael Corkery, "Sand Stalls Army's High-tech Units," and "Army Teams Look for 'Smoking Gun,'" *Providence Journal*, March 27, 2003; Ingram, Carter, and Gleason, interviews; Alpha 2-7 Group Interview; Bravo 2-7 Group Interview. Many American soldiers with whom I spoke used the Mars analogy to describe the storm.

36. 3-7 AAR, pp. 2–3; 1st BCT Escarpment AAC, pp. 4-7; Carl Nolte, "The Troops: From Inside the Horse, It's Cavalry Hunting Down the Enemy;" *San Francisco Chronicle*, March 30, 2003; Arian Campo-Flores, "Tougher Tactics," *Newsweek*, March 25, 2003; Scott Rutter, interview with the author, February 10, 2008; Neubauer interview. The captain kept his promise. All of his soldiers survived the war. The

assessments of the leadership of Kammerer and Rutter come from conversations with many Cottonbalers, most of whom chose to remain anonymous for obvious reasons. First Sergeant Wilson, for the record, did register criticism of Rutter. Wilson felt that Rutter was a good man and courageous but sorely lacking in tactical proficiency. Kammerer did not respond to my repeated interview requests.

37. Bravo 3-7 Group Interview; 1st BCT Al Kifl AAC, pp. 6–14; Belloc, Shawn Swears, and Collier questionnaires.

38. 2-7 AAR, p. 19; Michael Corkery, "1 Soldier Dead, 6 Hurt After Bradley Plunges into Hole," *Providence Journal*, March 28, 2003; Alpha 2-7 Group Interview; Smith, Cuevas, and Gleason interviews. Lieutenant Gruber recovered physically but, according to Gleason, still blamed himself for what happened. The Cottonbalers of both 2-7 and 3-7 were blessed with outstanding mechanics. These unsung, resourceful men dug down to the buried Bradley, stripped it of everything that could be salvaged, and used these parts to keep other Bradleys in service. The mechanics of 3-7 had recently won the Phoenix Award, the top maintenance honor in all branches of the service.

39. 2-7 AAR, pp. 19–20; 1st BCT Al Kifl AAC, pp. 15–20; Michael Corkery; "We Have No Problem Shooting a Person with a Helmet," *Providence Journal*, March 30, 2003, and "Car Bombing Blurs the Lines Between Friendly, Hostile Iraqis," March 31, 2003; Scott Rutter, "Terrorism Up Front and Personal" www.campbell.edu news, www.sptimes.com, Gleason, Simmons, Cuevas, Smith, and Coffey interviews; Alpha 2-7 Group Interview; HHC 2-7 Group Interview; Bravo 2-7 Group Interview.

CHAPTER 5. THE IRAQ WAR: ON TO BAGHDAD AND BEYOND

1. 2nd Brigade Combat Team (BCT), An Hindiyah After Action Critique (AAC), pp. 1–12; Chris Tomlinson, "GIs Rescue Elderly Woman amid Battle for Bridge," *St. Louis Post-Dispatch*, April 1, 2003, and personal notes; "News from Iraq," *The Cottonbaler*, Summer 2003, pp. 7–8, 16; Chris Carter, interview with the author, May 18, 2004; Eric Hooper, interview with the author, June 29, 2004; Paul Ingram, interview with the author, July 1, 2004. Many of the Cottonbalers believed that the Fedayeen were using the woman on the bridge as a human shield and had shot her when she tried to escape. CNN visited the Carter home in Watkinsville after the story broke, and that is when Chris's mother found out that her prayer had come true. 2-7 AAR, pp. 21–22; Michael Corkery, "His Mission: Seek and Destroy Saddam's Guard," *Providence Journal*, March 30, 2003; Kevin Peraino and Evan Thomas, "The Grunt's War," *Newsweek*, April 9, 2003; Rod Coffey, interview with the author, November 14, 2003; Todd Kelly, interview with the author, March 12, 2004; Robert Wilson, interview with the author, February 3, 2004; Charlie 2-7 Group Combat After Action Interview, March 12, 2004; Alpha 2-7 Group Combat After Action Interview, March 12, 2004; Bravo 2-7 Group Combat After Action Interview, March 10, 2004.

3. 1st BCT, Objective Peach AAC, pp. 1–13; Peraino and Thomas, "Grunt's War"; Kelly interview; Charlie 2-7 Group Interview; Bravo 3-7 Group Combat After Action Interview, March 11, 2004; Robert Gasman questionnaire; Shawn Swears questionnaire.

4. 1st BCT, Objective Peach AAC, pp. 13–17; Bravo 3-7 Group Interview; Raul "Rudy" Belloc, Steven Collier, and Gasman questionnaires; Narrative, Silver Star Citation, Sergeant Rudy Belloc. In a paper for the Strategic Studies Institute titled "Why They Fight: Combat Motivation in the Iraq War," authors Leonard Wong, Thomas Kolditz, Raymond Millen, and Terrence Porter demonstrated that comradeship was the primary combat motivation for American soldiers in that war. I also found this to be true among the Cottonbalers. Almost everyone said they fought primarily for their buddies. Sergeant Belloc won acclaim for more than his actions on April 3, 2003. During his tour of duty in Iraq, he served as a sniper/bodyguard on several occasions and was credited with killing forty-two armed enemy fighters. He even guarded Secretary of Defense Donald Rumsfeld during one of his visits to Iraq. My account of Belloc's actions east of Objective Peach is derived from interviewing him and the men of his company. These men demonstrated universal respect and admiration for him. There is one other relevant point: At first Belloc was reluctant to tell me of his exploits. He had to be prodded by his buddies to do so. He told me later, in private, that he did not wish to seem like he was bragging in front of the other guys.

5. 2-7 AAR, pp. 22–23; 1st BCT, Objective Peach AAC, pp. 23–27; Michael Corkery, "Iraqi Guerrillas Are No Match for U.S. Soldiers," *Providence Journal*, April 4, 2003; Coffey interview; Ed Cuevas, interview with the author, December 30, 2003; Rob Smith, interview with the author, March 12, 2004; Alpha 2-7 Group Interview.

6. 1st BCT, Baghdad International Airport AAC, pp. 20–24; Peraino and Thomas, "Grunt's War"; Kelly interview; Charlie 2-7 Group Interview.

7. 2-7 AAR, pp. 24–25; Michael Corkery, "U.S. Forces Push to Edge of Baghdad," Providence Journal, April 4, 2003; Cuevas, Coffey, and Wilson interviews; Robert Wilson questionnaire; Scott Rutter interview with the author, February 10, 2008; Bravo 2-7 Group Interview.

8. 2-7 AAR, p. 26; Cuevas and Coffey interviews; Rutter interview; Kevin Cooney, interview with the author, March 10, 2004; Alpha 2-7 Group Interview; HHC 2-7 Group Combat After Action Interview, March 12, 2004. Cooney told me jokingly, "There were two things I really didn't want to be known for—Cooney's Carnival and my exploits as Mother Nature called."

9. 2-7 AAR, pp. 26–27; 1st BCT, Objective Lions AAC, pp. 3–4; Michael Corkery, "U.S. Troops Repel Iraqi Ambush at Airport," *Providence Journal*, April 4, 2003; Rutter interview; Bravo 2-7 Group Interview; HHC 2-7 Group Interview. Private First Class Davis was the other Javelin shooter. I could not ascertain his first name. There were three PFCs named Davis in 2-7. Phillip, Warren, and Wesley—so it was certainly one of them.

10. 2-7 AAR, p. 27; "Baghdad Battles: A Frontline Report"; Cuevas and Coffey interviews; Rutter interview; Alpha 2-7 Group Interview; HHC 2-7 Group Interview; Bravo 2-7 Group Interview; Matthew Paul, "Getting Heavy Mortars into the Fight" and "TF Mortars in a 360-Degree Battlefield: Lessons Learned from Operation Iraqi Freedom," *Infantry*, January–February 2004. Paul had been promoted to captain during the months leading up to the war, but Lieutenant Colonel Rutter decided to leave him in place even though he technically had too much rank to be a platoon leader.

11. 2-7 AAR, pp. 27–28; Alex Leary, "The Last Full Measure of Devotion," *St. Petersburg Times*, January 25, 2004; Michael Corkery, "When Engineers Crashed Gate, Iraqi troops Charged," *Providence Journal*, April 7, 2003; Coffey interview; Rutter interview; Steve Gleason, interview with the author, January 19, 2004; Alpha 2-7 Group Interview; HHC 2-7 Group Interview.

12. 2-7 AAR, pp. 29–30; Cuevas and Smith interviews; Rutter interview; Alpha 2-7 Group Interview.

13. 2-7 AAR, p. 30; 1st BCT, Objective Lions AAC, pp. 1–3; Rutter interview; Bravo 2-7 Group Interview; Wilson interview and questionnaire.

14. 2-7 AAR, pp. 31–33; Michael Corkery, "Infantry Battalion Takes Fight into Capital," *Providence Journal*, April 8, 2003, and "These Are the Guys Who Hate Americans," April 9, 2003; David Zucchino, *Thunder Run: The Armored Strikes to Capture Baghdad* (New York: Atlantic Monthly Press, 2004), pp. 217–220, 222–223, 227–228, 312–313; Cooney, Cuevas, Coffey, Gleason, and Smith interviews; Alpha 2-7 Group Interview; HHC 2-7 Group Interview. Rutter's men experienced more combat around Objective Curly in the next twenty-four to forty-eight hours. None of it was as intense as the relief of 3-15, but 2-7 lost two men killed—Staff Sergeant Lincoln Hollin said, who was Sergeant First Class Smith's successor as Rage's engineer platoon sergeant, and Specialist Jason Myers, who was killed by friendly fire.

15. Chris Tomlinson, "US. Troops Encounter Suicide Paramilitary in Fire Fight South of Baghdad," *Associated Press*, April 6, 2003; *The Cottonbaler*, Summer 2003, p. 16; Zucchino, *Thunder Run*, pp. 314–315; Hooper, Carter, and Ingram interviews; "Narrative for Bronze Star 'V' for SGT Paul Ingram" (copy in author's possession). Kinchen was the same soldier who had accompanied Captain Carter onto the bridge at Hindiyah. While Carter's reaction to killing two men at close range was circumspect, his driver's reaction was less mature but typically American. According to Carter, "[He] loved it. He said it was like a video game ... where you have a pistol or something and the guy's popping up and ... you shoot him."

16. My account of stability and support operations and the general attitude of the soldiers is based on a wide array of sources: 2-7 AAR, pp. 35–37; 3-7 AAR, pp. 3–4; Michael Corkery, "It's Still Tough to Distinguish Friend from Foe," *Providence Journal*, April 11, 2003, and "Death and Danger Mixed with the Ordinary," April 20, 2003; "Coalition's Departure Said to Be in the Hands of Iraqis," Associated Press, July 15, 2003; Carter, Ingram (Ingram left the Army and is in college studying to be a physicist), Hooper, Wilson, Gleason, and Coffey interviews; R. Lee Simmons, interview with the author, November 24, 2003; Smith and Kelly interviews; Alpha 2-7 Group Interview; Bravo 2-7 Group Interview; Charlie 2-7 Group Interview; HHC 2-7 Group Interview; Bravo 3-7 Group Interview; soldier questionnaires; author conversations with numerous Cottonbalers; plus a new set of group combat after action interviews with 2-7 and 3-7 Cottonbalers who served in the regiment's second tour in Iraq. The units were there from January 2005 to January 2006.

Select Bibliography

Archives and Manuscript Collections

Carlisle, Pa. United States Army Military History Institute.

College Park, Md. National Archives and Records Administration (II).

Knoxville, Tenn. University of Tennessee Special Collections Library (repository of the Center for the Study of War and Society).

Leavenworth, Kan. Combat Studies Institute.

Washington, D.C. U.S. Army Center of Military History.

Dissertations and Theses

Bourque, Stephen A. "Desert Saber: The VII Corps in the Gulf War." Ph.D. dissertation, Georgia State University, 1996.

Journals, Magazines, Newspapers, Pamphlets

Army History.

Army Times.

The Cottonbaler Newsletter: The 7th Infantry Regiment Association.

Headquarters: 7th US. Infantry Association.

Infantry Journal.

Journal of Military History.

Knoxville News Sentinel.

Military Affairs.

Military History.

Military History Quarterly.

Newsweek.

The New Yorker.

Providence Journal.

The Redcatcher.

San Francisco Chronicle.

St. Louis Post-Dispatch.

St. Petersburg Times.
Vietnam.
Watch on the Rhine.

Books

Appy, Christian. *Working Class War: American Combat Soldiers and Vietnam.* Chapel Hill: University of North Carolina Press, 1993.

Atkinson, Rick. *Crusade: The Untold Story of the Gulf War.* Boston: Houghton Mifflin, 1993.

———. *In the Company of Soldiers: A Chronicle of Combat.* New York: Henry Holt, 2004.

Bergerud, Eric. *Red Thunder, Tropic Lightning: The World of a Combat Division in Vietnam.* New York: Penguin Books, 1993.

Blair, Clay. *The Forgotten War: America in Korea, 1950-1953.* New York: Times Books, 1987.

Bolger, Daniel P. *Dragons at War: Land Battle in the Desert; An Inside Look at the National Training Center.* New York: Ivy Books, 1986.

———. *Death Ground: Today's American Infantry in Battle.* Novato, Calif: Presidio Press, 1999.

Bowers, William, William Hammond, and George MacGarrigle. *Black Soldier, White Army: The 24th Infantry in Korea.* Washington, D.C.: Center of Military History, United States Army, 1996.

Carhart, Tom. *Iron Soldiers: How America's 1st Armored Division Crushed Iraq's Elite Republican Guard.* New York: Pocket Books, 1994.

Chambers, John Whiteclay, editor. *The Oxford Companion to American Military History.* New York: Oxford University Press, 1999.

Clancy, Tom, and Fred Franks. *Into the Storm: A Study in Command.* New York: G.P. Putnam's Sons, 1997.

Dolcater, Max. *Third Infantry Division in Korea.* Paducah, Ky.: Turner Publishing Company, 1998.

Ebert, James. *A Life in a Year: The American Infantryman in Vietnam, 1965-1972.* Novato, Calif: Presidio Press, 1993.

Fontenot, Gregory, E. J. Degen, and David Tohn. *On Point: The United States Army in Operation Iraqi Freedom.* Annapolis, Md.: Naval Institute Press, 2005.

Gouge, Robert J. "'These Are My Credentials': The 199th Light Infantry Brigade in the Republic of Vietnam, 1966-1970." Bloomington, Ind.: Author House, 2004.

Gugeler, Russell. *Combat Actions in Korea.* Washington, D.C.: Center of Military History, United States Army, 1987.

Hartzog, William. *American Military Heritage.* Washington, D. C.: Center of Military History, United States Army 2001.

Houlahan, Thomas. *Gulf War: The Complete History.* New London, N.H.: Schrenker Military Publishing, 1999.

Jensen, Robert Travis. *Bloody Snow: A Doctor's Memoir of the Korean War.* Carmel, Ind.: Cork Hill Press, 2005.

Kamiya, Jason. *The Victory Book: A Desert Storm Chronicle*. Self- published, 1991.

Knox, Donald, and Alfred Coppel. *The Korean War: Uncertain Victory*. San Diego: Harcourt Brace Jovanovich, 1988.

Lacey Jim. *Takedown: The 3rd Infantry Division's Twenty-one Day Assault on Baghdad.* Annapolis, Md.: Naval Institute Press, 2007.

Lanning, Michael Lee, and Dan Cragg. *Inside the VC and NVA: The Real Story of North Vietnam's Armed Forces*. New York: Ivy Books, 1992.

MacGregor, Jr., Morris. *Integration of the Armed Forces, 1940-1965.* Washington, D.C.: Center of Military History, United States Army 1981.

Mahon, John K. *History of the Second Seminole War, 1835-1842.* Gainesville: University of Florida Press, 1967.

Murphy, Edward. *Korean War Heroes*. Novato, Calif: Presidio Press, 1992.

Nolan, Keith William. *The Battle for Saigon, Tet 1968*. New York: Pocket Books, 1996.

O'Brien, Martin. *Above and Beyond the Call of Duty: The Corporal Clair Goodblood Story.* Augusta, Maine: HR Applications, 2000.

Pierson, David. *Tuskers: An Armor Battalion in the Gulf War.* Darlington, Md.: Darlington Productions, 1997.

Pratt, Sherman. *Autobahn to Berchtesgaden: A View of World War II from the Bottom Up by an Infantry Sergeant*. Baltimore, Md.: Gateway Press, 1992.

Russ, Martin. *Breakout: The Chasin Reservoir Campaign, Korea 1950.* New York: Fromm International, 1999.

Santoli, Al. *Leading the Way: How Vietnam Veterans Rebuilt the US. Military; An Oral History*. New York: Ballantine Books, 1993.

Scales, Robert. *Certain Victory: The US. Army in the Gulf War*. Washington, D.C.: Brassey's, 1994.

Schwarzkopf, H. Norman, and Peter Petre. *It Doesn't Take a Hero*. New York: Bantam Books, 1992.

Soiset, Roger. *The Two Dollar Bill: One Man's Year in Vietnam*. Columbia, S.C.: Palmetto Bookworks, 1993.

Spector, Ronald. *After Tet: The Bloodiest Year in Vietnam*. New York: Vintage Books, 1993.

Stanton, Shelby. *The Rise and Fall of an American Army: US. Ground Forces in Vietnam, 1965-1973*. New York: Dell 1985.

Tomedi, Rudy. *No Bugles, No Drums: An Oral History of the Korean War*. New York: John Wiley, 1993.

Vernon, Alex. *The Eyes of Orion: Five Tank Lieutenants in the Persian Gulf War*. Kent: Kent State University Press, 1999.

White, Nathan W. *From Fedala to Berchtesgaden: A History of the 7th United States Infantry in World War II*. Brockton, Mass.: Keystone Print, 1947.

Zucchino, David. *Thunder Run: The Armored Strike to Capture Baghdad.* New York: Atlantic Monthly Press, 2004.

Index of Subjects and Persons

Note: For military units, see the Index of Military Units

Index of Military Units

Military groups are American unless otherwise noted.